Praise for *China Goes Global*

"David Shambaugh is one of the world's leading experts on China. Based on first-hand experience and good social science, he presents a compelling picture of China as a partial power. The analysis of China's efforts to increase its soft power is one of the real highlights. This is a must read for anyone who wants to understand China's global role."—**Joseph S. Nye, Harvard University Distinguished Service Professor, and author of** *The Future of Power*

"Relying on prodigious research and his own deep understanding, David Shambaugh has written an impressively thorough and fascinating book about China's quest to find new respect and status in the world. But what distinguishes *China Goes Global* is Shambaugh's argument that China actually possesses far less real power and influence than many imagine, and thus poses far less of a challenge than often feared."—**Orville Schell, Arthur Ross Director of the Center on U.S.-China Relations at The Asia Society**

"Here's a book that has its title right—a statement worth making because so many stretch or bend them for marketing purposes. And that's only the beginning of the elegant distillation George Washington University political scientist David Shambaugh provides in this useful volume, which offers a detailed yet concise portrait of a nation widely perceived as on the cusp of what the Chinese government often ascribes to its American rival: hegemony."—*History News Network*

"[T]imely and highly readable . . . With copious data and not a few anecdotes of his own experience, Shambaugh lays out systematically the case that China's reach, while undeniably global, is almost universally shallow."—*Global Policy Journal*

"The meticulous exploration of the multiple ways in which China does not live up to its current reputation brings a breath of fresh and cooling air to an overheated topic. It's about time."—*The Christian Science Monitor*

"This is a book those who take a close interest in China have been waiting for: an assessment of the global impact of Beijing's increasing power and influence by a leading expert on the country."—*YaleGlobal Online*

"This is a must read for those interested in China's foreign affairs particularly and international relations generally."—*Library Journal*

"[A] lucid, highly readable overview of China's government policy-making apparatus, media, military ambitions and capabilities, trade and investment patterns, and strained relations with almost every region of the world . . . Drawing on interviews with Chinese policymakers and his own perceptive observations of their conflicting impulses, Shambaugh pointedly corrects the usual hysterical exaggerations of Chinese power. His is an illuminating profile of a colossus that does not-yet-bestride the world."—*Publishers Weekly*

Previous Books by David Shambaugh

China's Communist Party: Atrophy and Adaptation (2008)
The Odyssey of China's Imperial Art Treasures (2005, with Jeannette Shambaugh Elliott)
Modernizing China's Military: Progress, Problems, and Prospects (2002)
China and Europe: 1949–1995 (1996)
Beautiful Imperialist: China Perceives America, 1972–1990 (1991)
The Making of a Premier: Zhao Ziyang's Provincial Career (1984)

Selected Edited Volumes

Tangled Titans: The United States and China (2012)
Charting China's Future: Domestic and International Challenges (2011)
American and European Relations with China (2008, with Gudrun Wacker)
China-Europe Relations: Perceptions, Policies, and Prospects (2008, with Eberhard Sandschneider and Zhou Hong)
International Relations of Asia (2008, with Michael Yahuda)
China Watching: Perspectives from Europe, Japan, and the United States (2007, with Robert Ash and Seiichiro Takagi)
Power Shift: China and Asia's New Dynamics (2005)
Making China Policy: Lessons from the Bush and Clinton Administrations (2001, with Ramon H. Myers and Michel C. Oksenberg)
The Modern Chinese State (2000)
Is China Unstable: Assessing the Factors (2000)
China's Military Faces the Future (1999, with James R. Lilley)
The China Reader: The Reform Era (1999, with Orville Schell)
China's Military in Transition (1997)
Deng Xiaoping: Portrait of a Chinese Statesman (1995)
Chinese Foreign Policy: Theory & Practice (1994, with Thomas W. Robinson)
American Studies of Contemporary China (1993)

CHINA
GOES
GLOBAL

THE PARTIAL POWER

DAVID SHAMBAUGH

OXFORD
UNIVERSITY PRESS

OXFORD

UNIVERSITY PRESS

Oxford University Press is a department of the University of Oxford.
It furthers the University's objective of excellence in research, scholarship,
and education by publishing worldwide.

Oxford   New York
Auckland   Cape Town   Dar es Salaam   Hong Kong   Karachi
Kuala Lumpur   Madrid   Melbourne   Mexico City   Nairobi
New Delhi   Shanghai   Taipei   Toronto

With offices in
Argentina   Austria   Brazil   Chile   Czech Republic   France   Greece
Guatemala   Hungary   Italy   Japan   Poland   Portugal   Singapore
South Korea   Switzerland   Thailand   Turkey   Ukraine   Vietnam

Oxford is a registered trade mark of Oxford University Press
in the UK and certain other countries.

Published in the United States of America by
Oxford University Press
198 Madison Avenue, New York, NY 10016

Library of Congress Cataloging-in-Publication Data
Shambaugh, David L.
China goes global: the partial power / David Shambaugh.
p. cm.
Includes bibliographical references and index.
ISBN 978–0–19–986014–2 (hardback); 978–0–19–936103–8 (paperback)
1. China—Foreign economic relations.   2. China—Economic
policy—2000–   3. Globalization—China.   I. Title.
HF1604.S48 2013
303.48'251—dc23
2012028861

1 3 5 7 9 8 6 4 2

Printed in the United States of America
on acid-free paper

To Ingrid, Chris, and Alex

CONTENTS

Preface and Acknowledgments   ix

1. Understanding China's Global Impact   1

2. China's Global Identities   13

3. China's Global Diplomatic Presence   45

4. China and Global Governance   121

5. China's Global Economic Presence   156

6. China's Global Cultural Presence   207

7. China's Global Security Presence   269

8. Coping with a Globalized China   307

Notes   319
Index   383

PREFACE AND ACKNOWLEDGMENTS

———⊶⊷———

AS A SCHOLAR, PROFESSOR, AND public educator, I try to understand, research, write about, and explain China to multiple audiences around the world. I decided to investigate this subject because I thought, as a specialist on both China and international relations, I might be able to shed some light on the nexus of these two phenomena—China and the world—and thereby could contribute to global public understanding of one of the key issues of our era.

There was a second reason I took on this project: because I am deeply concerned by the academic profession's tendency to "know more and more about less and less" and its increasing inability to generalize about China's development (in all aspects).[1] That is, for the past three decades, the academic China community has produced studies of progressively more micro-level phenomena. Although this has perhaps allowed us to know more about the "trees," it has not necessarily led to a better understanding of the "forest." The excessive disaggregation has not led to better aggregate understanding of China writ large. The rise of China is *the big story* of our era, and I believe it is incumbent upon scholars to be able to explain China to nonspecialist audiences worldwide. I further feel that scholars' increasing obsession with social science theories and methodologies have created further impediments to understanding—more often blurring than clarifying the object of

ix

study. Unfortunately, testing of theories and application of methodologies is becoming an end, rather than a means, to furthering knowledge and understanding. As a result, scholars in the China field are becoming more and more divorced from their professional mission and responsibility: to illuminate and educate. More and better knowledge of China now seems to reside in the professions of business, banking, consulting, law, diplomacy, intelligence, journalism, think tanks, and NGOs than in the scholarly community. China scholars are no longer the "go to" repository of knowledge on China that they once were. This may be natural, but it is regrettable.

Thus, in part, this study grows out of my frustration with the academic China field. It also grows out of the pressing need to understand China's global emergence in its *totality*. As Napoleon prophetically predicted, China's awakening is now shaking the world. But how and in what ways? Do we really understand the various dimensions, complexities, and implications of China's "going global"? Conventional wisdom now holds that China's rise is the most important phenomenon in contemporary world affairs. But a skeptic may challenge this conventional wisdom and ask, *Is* China really shaking the world? Has it really become a global power? If so, exactly in what ways? Or is China's assumed international influence hollow hype?

This study wrestles with these big questions, and it provides a straightforward answer captured in the book's subtitle: China is *The Partial Power*. The elements of China's global power are actually surprisingly weak and very uneven. China is not as important, and it is certainly not as influential, as conventional wisdom holds. The following eight chapters elaborate this theme and offer a wide range of supporting data in as intelligible a fashion for readers as possible.

China Goes Global has been five years in preparation. I began work on it in 2007, just after completing my previous book *China's Communist Party: Atrophy and Adaptation*. Having delved into China's internal political scene in that volume, I decided to devote this volume to assessing China's external behavior. Even though I have been interested in Chinese foreign policy throughout my career, and have published a fair amount on diverse aspects of the subject, it seemed to me that China's emergence on the global stage today consisted of far more than diplomacy. Thus, what I felt was needed was a study that examined various aspects of the totality of China's emergence and impact on the world. This is not a book so much about China's *rise* as its *spread*. At first I contemplated organizing the study geographically, examining China's multifarious interactions with different countries and regions—but, on further reflection, I decided a better (albeit more difficult) way to approach the subject was functionally. That is, through individual chapters that examined a number of dimensions of China's global "footprints": Chinese perceptions of their global roles, Chinese diplomacy, China's role in global governance, China's global economic presence, China's global cultural impact, and China's global security presence. This approach allows readers to view China's impact in a truly global—rather than regional—perspective. It also allows a more nuanced understanding of China's strengths and weaknesses.

* * *

Any study of this magnitude requires many things. First, on the part of the author, it requires tenacity and patience. There were many days and many points when I lamented the complexities of several chapters and thought it would never end. There was also a constant tension between going into depth, but not too much depth. As a result, a great deal of data and many pages of writing wound up on the "cutting room floor." I also had to constantly remind myself to follow my own admonition above to write "accessibly" and to try and illuminate the "Big Picture" for general readers.

Second, it requires the patience, understanding, and support of family members. My wife of thirty years, Ingrid Larsen, and our two wonderful sons, Christopher and Alexander, offered steadfast support, patience, and curiosity throughout the protracted five-year process, and I therefore wish to gratefully dedicate the book to them. Special mention should also be made of our golden retriever, Ollie, who lay at my feet and stayed by my side throughout—providing adoring canine company in what is an inevitably lonely writing process.

Third, writers need conducive writing spaces. I am most fortunate to have had that at our home in Arlington, Virginia—but also our apartment in Beijing, and at our family cabins in the forest of northern

Michigan. The latter have been a godsend where I have retreated and written for more than thirty years while gazing out over Grand Traverse Bay.

Fourth, like all professors, I had to juggle writing with the demands of undergraduate and graduate teaching, doctoral student supervision, program administration, university service, much public lecturing, conference participation, consulting, a lot of national and international travel, and writing articles and editing books unrelated to this one—all while doing my best to be a husband and parent. I even survived one computer crash in which, for a while, I thought I had lost the entire manuscript!

This study has also benefited from important financial and institutional support. Financially, I was the fortunate recipient of a number of travel grants from the Sigur Center for Asian Studies in the Elliott School of International Affairs at George Washington University (my institutional home). The China Policy Program in the Elliott School also provided supplementary funding, and I am particularly grateful to Elliott School International Council Advisory Board member and GWU alumnus Christopher J. Fussner for his long-standing financial support of the program. These grants helped to facilitate fieldwork throughout Asia, Europe, Latin America, Oceania, Russia, and Central Asia. Without them, I would not have been able to gain a firsthand sense of China's activities, and how it is being perceived, in these countries and regions. Unfortunately, I was unable to travel to Africa or the Middle East for research but was fortunate to visit every other continent in the world for interviews and data collection. I also wish to acknowledge a grant from the Ford Foundation to the China Policy Program for the 2011–12 project "Integrating China Globally: Bilateral and Regional Dialogues," and a grant from the German Marshall Fund for the 2004–2007 "European-American Dialogues on China." Although these were not research grants specifically for it, this book nonetheless benefited from the conferences and discussions they facilitated. I am also grateful to the Fulbright Commission of the U.S. Department of State for a yearlong grant as a Senior Fulbright Research Scholar. I spent the 2009–10 year based in Beijing as a senior visiting scholar (高级访问学者) at the Chinese Academy of Social Sciences' Institute of World Economics and Politics. Though I had to arrange much of my research on my own, I am very grateful to CASS and the institute for its hospitality during that year. I traveled extensively throughout China during the year, lecturing at many universities and research institutes, and familiarizing myself with China's international relations community.[2]

I am also extremely grateful for arrangements made to facilitate my research by the Ministry of Foreign Affairs, the International Department of the Central Committee, the State Council Information Office, the Foreign Affairs Office of the Ministry of Defense, the Central Party School, the China Institutes of Contemporary International Relations, the China Institute of International Studies, the Shanghai Institutes of International Studies, the Shanghai Academy of Social Sciences, Chinese People's Institute of Foreign Affairs, and China Foreign Affairs University.

Conducting research in China still presents formidable obstacles for foreigners, so I am most grateful to these institutions for facilitating it. As a result, as the text and footnotes of the book reveal, I was able to interview more than a hundred individuals (mainly in Beijing). In this book I have decided to break with the past convention of not naming names of Chinese interviewees. For many years foreign scholars protected their sources from possible political persecution by granting them anonymity in interviews; I believe that those days are now past, and Chinese intellectuals and officials (like those abroad) must be responsible for what they say (they are definitely responsible for what they commit to print). To be sure, there are individual cases where anonymity needs to be protected. But, unless they specifically asked to speak off the record (which I honor), I have quoted my interview subjects by name. Finally, I also benefited a great deal from interactions with various foreign embassies in Beijing (too numerous to list) and wish to acknowledge their willingness to meet with me and respond to my questions. I believe that foreign embassies and consulates in China are an important potential source for scholars on both Chinese domestic and foreign affairs.

In other parts of the world, I would particularly like to acknowledge the hospitality and research facilitation offered by the Instituto Brasileiro de Estudos da China e Asia e Pacifico (IBECAP) in Brazil; the College of Asia and the Pacific and Department of International

Relations at the Australian National University; the S. Rajaratnam
School of International Studies at Nanyang Technological University
in Singapore; the East Asia Institute and the Institute of Southeast Asian
Studies of the National University of Singapore; the Contemporary
China Research Center at Victoria University in New Zealand; the
Institute of the Far East of the Russian Academy of Sciences; the Center
for Area Studies at Keio University in Japan; the Institute of Chinese
Studies of the Jawaharlal Nehru University in India; the Chile-Pacific
Foundation; the Contemporary China Studies Department of the
University of Salvador in Argentina; the Ministry of Foreign Affairs in
Germany; the Ministry of Foreign Affairs in Sweden; the Ministry of
Foreign Affairs in Brazil; the Ministry of Foreign Affairs in Chile; the
Department of Foreign Affairs and Trade in Australia; the China Unit
of the European Commission; the British Foreign and Commonwealth
Office; and the Brazil-China Business Council. Many other individu-
als in these and other locales went out of their way to make and arrange
contacts with a wide variety of governments, nongovernmental organizations, corporations and banks, foundations, research institutes,
journalists, and other organizations.

This book has also benefited enormously from a number of valued
colleagues, who have taken their valuable time to either read draft
chapters or discuss aspects of the subject with me. The following individuals (listed in alphabetical order) were kind enough to read, com-
ment on, and offer important corrections and suggestions on portions
of the manuscript: Philip Andrews-Speed, Robert Ash, Dennis Blasko,
Pieter Bottelier, Anne-Marie Brady, Gregory Chin, Paul Clifford,
Erica Downs, Edward Elmendorf, Paul Evans, Martha Finnemore,
Rosemary Foot, Chas W. Freeman, Jr., Michael Fullilove, Bates Gill,
Charles Grant, Thilo Hanemann, Lonnie Henley, Ingrid d'Hooghe,
Alastair Iain Johnston, David M. Lampton, Nicholas Lardy, Jim
Laurie, Kristin Lord, Mary Kay Magistad, James Miles, Katherine
Morton, Henry Nau, Peter Nolan, Joseph Nye, John Pomfret, Daniel
Rosen, Derek Scissors, George E. Shambaugh IV, Ren Xiao, Hongying
Wang, and Zhu Liqun. Each of these individuals contributed signifi-
cantly in improving the manuscript and saving me from embarrassing
errors. In addition to these individuals, I have benefited enormously
from conversations with, and presentations from, a number of others

on aspects of this study. I would like to single out (alphabetically) the contributions to my research and thinking made by Shaun Breslin, Richard Bush, Jean-Pierre Cabestan, Tom Christensen, Cui Liru, Cui Tiankai, Elizabeth Economy, Peter Ferdinand, Aaron Friedberg, John Frisbie, Fu Ying, John Garver, Bonnie Glaser, Francois Godement, Avery Goldstein, Michael Green, Harry Harding, Paul Heer, Huang Renwei, Jon Huntsman, John Ikenberry, Karl Inderfurth, Martin Jacques, Jiang Shixue, Willem van Kemenade, William Kirby, Charles Kupchan, James Kynge, Terry Lautz, Ken Lieberthal, Börje Ljunggren, Jorge Melena, Dawn Murphy, Douglas Paal, Qin Yaqing, Qu Xing, Stapleton Roy, Ruan Zongze, Eberhard Sandschneider, Michael Schaefer, Shen Dingli, David Shinn, Susan Shirk, Yoshi Soeya, Song Xinning, Volker Stanzel, Robert Sutter, Michael Swaine, Ashley Tellis, Ezra Vogel, Alan Wachman, Wang Gungwu, Wang Jisi, Wang Yizhou, Hugh White, Peter Wilson, Sebastian Wood, Wu Xinbo, Joerg Wuttke, Michael Yahuda, Yan Xuetong, Zha Daojiong, Zhou Hong, Zhu Feng, and David Zweig. This is not simply a list of important China watchers and valued colleagues (which they all are); each has specifically influenced my thinking on various aspects of this book. To all, I owe a deep debt.

I also benefited a great deal from the research assistance of several of my B.A., M.A., and Ph.D. students at George Washington University: Lance Noble, Dawn Murphy, Chen Chunhua, Robert O'Brien, and Chelsea Peoples. Chelsea's extraordinary computer skills are also responsible for producing all the graphics in the book. Although not my student, Henry Hoyle voluntarily offered his excellent Chinese skills and research assistance in Beijing. Several students at China Foreign Affairs University also assisted in going through and summarizing a large volume of Chinese publications. I am indebted to all for their invaluable research assistance.

I am also extremely grateful to my editor at Oxford University Press (OUP), David McBride, for seeing the value in this study and being patient when I exceeded the deadline for delivery. It has not been an easy undertaking, but David's support throughout has been exceedingly important. Moreover, the careful editorial eye, critical questions, and sharp editorial knife of David and assistant editor Alexandra Dauler helped to improve the manuscript immeasurably in its penultimate stage. Following final submission, the book has benefited more from the efforts of my excellent copy editor, Tom Finnegan, and production editor, Jashnie Jabson. All in all, I am very pleased to be publishing this volume with OUP—as I wanted a truly global publisher to publish *China Goes Global*.

FINALLY, I BEAR full responsibility for the contents of this book. There are, no doubt, errors of fact and issues of interpretation with which others will disagree. It would be unusual for a study of this size and complexity not to contain some, and thus I bear full responsibility for any remaining errors.

David Shambaugh
Old Mission, Michigan
July 2012

CHINA
GOES
GLOBAL

———◦◦◦◦◦———

THE PARTIAL POWER

I

Understanding China's Global Impact

It is China's intention to be the greatest power in the world.
—LEE KUAN YEW, 2011[1]

China does not see itself as a rising, but a returning power...It does not view the prospect of a strong China exercising influence in economic, cultural, political, and military affairs as an unnatural challenge to world order—but rather as a return to a normal state of affairs.
—HENRY KISSINGER, 2012[2]

China's peaceful development has broken away from the traditional pattern where a rising power was bound to seek hegemony.
—China's White Paper on Peaceful Development, 2011[3]

The United States welcomes China's rise as a strong, prosperous and successful member of the community of nations.
—PRESIDENT BARACK OBAMA, 2011[4]

SITTING IN THE REVIEWING stand on the north end of Tiananmen Square on the occasion of China's national day and the sixtieth anniversary of the People's Republic of China on October 1, 2009, under the watchful eye of Mao's giant portrait on Tiananmen Gate, I had an uneasy feeling. There, before my eyes, were the stark contradictions of China's rise.

As I watched the columns of ten thousand goose-stepping soldiers marching past in tight formation, touting automatic weapons with heads cocked toward the official reviewing stand, followed by massive trucks ferrying huge intercontinental ballistic missiles and stealthy cruise missiles, modern tanks, rocket launchers, artillery, armored personnel carriers, with jet fighters and bombers cruising overhead, I did some live commentary by cell phone for CNN (which was beaming the images worldwide). The anchorwoman in Hong Kong asked for my impressions. I observed that the orchestrated military display—an eerie flashback to similar Soviet and North Korean martial displays—was a perfect metaphor for the contradictions that China's rise engendered. On the one hand, the parade was primarily intended for domestic consumption—for the 1.4 billion Chinese who had been told for sixty years that their nation must stand tall in the world. Carefully choreographed and practiced with meticulous precision over the previous year, for the Chinese audience it was meant to assuage the national craving for international respect and demonstrate that China now stood tall and had retaken its rightful place as one of the world's powers. On the other hand, the military hardware was meant to impress the world with China's new hard power—offering a complete contradiction to the government's repetitive mantra about its "peaceful rise" and benign intentions.

The hour's display of military might was presaged by China's President Hu Jintao cruising the Avenue of Heavenly Peace in an open-top Red Flag limousine reviewing the troops and barking out words of encouragement: *Tongzhimen hao! Nimen xinku le!* (Greetings, comrades! You're suffering!). Hu's steely demeanor fit the seriousness of the moment. After the weaponry rolled past, we witnessed a second hour of flowered floats of propaganda slogans, singing children, dancers, colorful ethnic minorities, and other displays of China's softer side. This contradictory collage of images was jarring and made me wonder what messages the Politburo and czars in the Propaganda Department of the Chinese Communist Party (CCP) wished to convey to the world.

I also reflected on the extraordinarily intense security dragnet that had blanketed Beijing over the previous month. Police and special forces were deployed and patrolled neighborhoods, roads into the capital were blocked; migrants and dissidents were rounded up; foreigners' IDs were checked and double-checked; manhole covers throughout the city were taped shut so no terrorists could hide inside and spring forth to launch a surprise attack; and checkpoints were set up throughout the city. Along the parade route, all offices were closed for a week before and several days afterward while residents in flats facing onto Chang'an Avenue (where I lived) were told to stay away from their windows on the day of the parade. On October 1, the whole city went into lockdown— scores of police and threatening-looking commando squads dressed in black were posted at intersections, streets were blocked to traffic, and people were not permitted to go within a one-kilometer perimeter of the parade route. Those fortunate enough to have an invitation to the event were ferried to Tiananmen Square by special buses from a staging area at the Workers Stadium.

The only time I had experienced such intensive security in Beijing was in the aftermath of the June 4 "massacre" in 1989, and I could not help but think there was a connection between the two; the 2009 parade (and the 2008 Olympics the year before) afforded China's security services with opportunities to sharpen their regimens so there would never be a repeat of 1989. But, more deeply, I wondered: If the Communist Party is so proud of its achievements and sixty years in power, what is it so afraid of? Why the need for such intensive security? The answer is that the authorities genuinely feared sabotage of the military equipment or disruption of the festivities by "ethnic separatists" or domestic terrorists; either would have left a very dark stain on the government's image and would expose the undercurrent of bubbling discontent that ripples throughout Chinese society. But it belied a deeper insecurity on the part of the regime.[5] The juxtaposition of pride and patriotism, on the one hand, mixed together with the Party's deep insecurities and the obsession with control, on the other, spoke volumes to me about China's current conflicted (and insecure) condition.

Following the two-hour spectacle and after comparing impressions with American Ambassador Jon Huntsman and German Ambassador Michael Schaeffer back at the Workers Stadium staging area, I mounted my trusty bicycle and navigated the Beijing neighborhoods and circumvented roadblocks back to our apartment (where I was spending the year on sabbatical). As I pedaled through Chaoyang District I could not help but compare that exhibition with another spectacle I had witnessed just fourteen months before in Beijing: the closing ceremony of the 2008 XXIX Olympiad. Sitting with my son Alex that warm summer evening in the "Bird's Nest" Olympic Stadium, we were treated to a demonstration of China's "soft power": several hours of creative choreography, breathtaking theatrics, colored floodlighting, as the athletes of 204 nations and territories swayed on the stadium infield to the Chinese theme of "One World, One Dream." It was an impressive display (as were the opening ceremonies). It left me hoping that, having had its moment in the international spotlight during the impressive and successfully managed Olympic Games, China might be able to shed its sixty-year national identity of victimization by foreigners and move forward in the world with a new confidence.[6]

One year later, having just experienced the martial display of China's "hard power," as I bicycled home through Beijing's neighborhoods I reflected on these twin events—the first of which reassured the world, the second of which frightened the world. The juxtaposition left me wondering which of these two Chinese "faces" would the new China project on the world stage. The answer came quickly. Over the course of the next year (2010), which has become known as China's "year of assertiveness," the Chinese government took a number of disconcerting diplomatic actions toward its Asian neighbors, the United States, Australia, and the European Union. Collectively, as I opined in a newspaper op-ed at the time, the "Chinese tiger was showing its claws."[7] In the wake of these actions, during 2011–12, China recoiled and recalibrated its diplomacy somewhat. It undertook a campaign of diplomatic reassurance toward these countries and launched a multifaceted soft-power and public-diplomacy drive aimed at improving China's image worldwide. Yet, embedded in these events and personal vignettes lie the complexities of China's "rise."

Grasping China's Global Impact

China is the world's most important rising power. In two decades, China has moved from the periphery to the center of the international system. Every day and everywhere, China figures prominently in global attention. Wherever one turns, China is in the news—gobbling up resources, soaking up investment, expanding its overseas footprint, asserting itself in its Asian neighborhood, being the sought-after suitor in global governance diplomacy, sailing its navy into new waters, broadening its global media exposure and cultural presence, and managing a mega-economy that is the engine of global growth. China's global impact is increasingly felt on every continent, in most international institutions, and on many global issues. By many measures, China is now clearly the world's second leading power, after the United States, and its aggregate economy is due to surpass that of the United States sometime around 2025.

For the past three decades, observers have watched how the world has impacted China; now the tables are turning and it is necessary to understand how China is impacting the world. China's emergence on the world stage is accelerating dramatically in pace and scope—and it is important to understand the different manifestations of its "going global."

China's global expansion did not occur by happenstance. It grew directly out of Communist Party and government policies launched at the famous Third Plenary Session of the Eleventh Central Committee in December 1978 to engage in "reform and opening" (改革与开放). Throughout the 1980s, China "invited the world in" (引进来) and began its hesitant baby steps on the world stage—particularly in overseas educational and science and technology exchanges. By the early 1990s, there was a conscious government policy launched to encourage Chinese commercial firms to "go out" (走出去) and for Chinese localities and organizations to more generally "go global" (走向世界). The encouragement to Chinese companies did not really begin to materialize fully until the mid-2000s, while considerable international initiatives were being launched by a wide variety of Chinese organizations, localities, and individuals. In 2008, China launched its global cultural blitz, attempting to improve its international image and build its soft power. Militarily, during the same decade the People's Liberation Army (PLA) stepped up its international foreign exchanges, amounting to more than four hundred annual exchanges. Thus, the origins of China's "going global" date back several decades, even if the manifestations of it are more recent.

Over a longer period of time, a distinguishing feature of China's modernization mission has been the national pursuit of "comprehensive power" (综合国力). The Chinese have wisely learned one key lesson from studying the experiences of other previous powers: genuine global powers possess multidimensional strength. Chinese strategists have observed the failings of other powers that possessed strength in only a single dimension or a few, and they have thus concluded that it is important to build and cultivate power comprehensively across a variety of spheres: the economy, science, technology, education, culture, values, military, governance, diplomacy, and other sectors. The Chinese grasp the idea that power is comprehensive and integrative, not atomistic. Nor is power today the same as in the nineteenth or twentieth century, when industrial and military power prevailed; today it must reflect a strong cultural and normative dimension (soft power) as well. Thus, China's contemporary effort to regain its status as a global power has consciously included multiple dimensions.

But *how* is China's newfound comprehensive power manifest globally today, and *how* will China influence global affairs in the future? These are *the* grand strategic questions of our era, and the subject of this book.

This book joins an expansive existing literature on China's rise published over the past two decades. There are many excellent studies.[8] What makes this study different is its comprehensiveness and its argument. In individual chapters, this study comprehensively covers six distinct dimensions of China's global emergence (perceptual, diplomatic, global governance, economic, cultural, and security) and multiple manifestations of each. In this way, this study differs from most other "China rise" books that examine only one or two of these dimensions (usually economic or military) and largely describe the country's ascent in a "vertical" fashion—its asymmetrical encounter with the world's leading power (the United States) and the historical propensity for conflict to result between the principal established power and the challenging rising power.[9] Some hype the "China threat."[10] This book takes more of a "horizontal" approach to China's "spread" rather than its vertical rise, examining how its impact is expanding across the globe in these six specific spheres.

Some observers have already triumphantly proclaimed that China will "rule the world."[11] This perspective is profoundly overstated and incorrect, in my view. I argue in this book that China has a very long way to go before it becomes—if it *ever* becomes—a true global power. And it will never "rule the world." The evidence presented in this book reveals that China has an increasingly broad "footprint" across the globe, but it is not particularly deep. Even its presence varies substantially by sector and region. China's appeal as a "model" to others is weak to non-existent, I argue. Moreover, China's global posture is beset by multiple weaknesses—not the least of which are domestic—and that the nation's strengths are not as strong as they seem on face value.

I further argue that China remains a lonely power, lacking close friends and possessing no allies. Even in China's closest relationships—with Russia, Pakistan, and North Korea—strong elements of distrust percolate beneath the surface of seemingly harmonious state-to-state relations. In other words, China is *in* the community of nations but is in many ways not really *part* of the community; it is formally involved, but it is not normatively integrated. It is a member of most international organizations, but is not very active in many (aside from when it seeks to assiduously protect its narrow national interests). I also judge its diplomacy to be hesitant, risk-averse, and narrowly self-interested. China often makes known what it is *against*, but rarely what it is *for*. It often stands aside or remains passive in addressing international security challenges or global governance issues. The common denominator to most of China's global activities and foreign policy is China's *own economic development*, which leads to a mercantilist trade and investment posture. I also find that China possesses little soft power, if any, and is not a model for other nations to emulate. For these and other reasons, elaborated in subsequent chapters, I have subtitled the book *the partial power*.

But perceptions sometimes belie reality. Whether China will become a global power or not, or is already one, it is already *perceived* as such by many around the world. Global publics already view China as a global power and *expect* China to overtake the United States as the world's leading power sometime in the next quarter century. The 2011 Pew Research Center Global Attitudes Project polled publics in twenty-two nations and found that in fifteen countries the balance of opinion was that China will—or *already has*—replaced the United States as the world's leading power.[12] China certainly already possesses many of the trappings of a global power: the world's largest population, a large continental landmass, a manned space program, an aircraft carrier, the world's largest museum, the world's largest hydroelectric dam, the world's second-largest economy, the world's second-largest military budget, the world's annualized highest growth rate over the past three decades, the world's largest exporter, the world's largest foreign exchange reserves, the world's second-largest recipient of foreign direct investment, the world's largest number of millionaires and billionaires, and the world's largest producer of many goods.

Despite these attributes, this book argues and demonstrates that China lacks real global power. I argue that China is a global *actor* without (yet) being a true global *power*—the distinction being that true powers *influence* other nations and events. Merely having a global presence does not equal having global power unless a nation influences events in a particular region or realm. Shaping the desired outcome of a situation is the essence of influence and exercise of power.

In these regards, I follow Harvard Professor Joseph Nye's definitions in his recent book *The Future of Power*.[13] Nye's definition of power is similar to the often cited one offered by Robert Dahl: that power is the ability of A to make B do what it would otherwise not do.[14] Professor Nye also argues that, by themselves, resources do not constitute power unless they are used to try to influence the outcome of a situation.[15] In other words: wealth ≠ power ≠ influence. The essence of power, Nye argues, lies in the *conversion* of resources into influence, which is the exercise of power.

Adopting these definitions of power offered by Professor Nye, this study shows that *only in some sectors* does China actually exercise global influence: global trade patterns, global energy and commodity markets, the global tourism industry, global sales of luxury goods, global real estate purchases, and cyber hacking. In these areas, China is markedly influencing global trends. Other than in these limited areas, though, this study finds that China does not really influence global events.

This is a somewhat surprising conclusion for me to come to, as I had expected when embarking on this research project in 2007 to find China exerting power and influence in many areas on a global basis. Instead, I found that China is *present* and *active* in various parts of the globe and in various functional spheres—but is not (yet) *influencing* or shaping actors or events in various parts of the world. Sometimes, ironically, it influences events through *non*action, negative action, and diplomatic passivity, such as on North Korea, Iran, Syria, or climate change. Moreover, in my view one does not see Beijing proactively and positively trying to resolve *any* global problem. Sometimes it perpetuates problems through exercising vetoes in the United Nations Security Council or propping up dictatorial regimes against Western will—teaming up with Russia and other authoritarian regimes in what might be described as "coalitions of the unwilling."

Generally speaking, Chinese diplomacy remains remarkably risk-averse and guided by narrow national interests. Chinese diplomacy takes a kind of lowest-common-denominator approach, usually adopting the safest and least controversial position, and usually waits to see the positions of other governments before revealing their own. The notable exception to this rule concerns China's own narrow self-interests: Taiwan, Tibet, Xinjiang, human rights, and its maritime territorial claims; on these issues Beijing is hypervigilant and diplomatically active. Other than protecting these narrow national interests, though, Chinese diplomacy remains extremely passive for a state of its size and importance. Perhaps this relative passivity reflects Beijing's conscious strategy of "maintaining a low profile" (韬光养晦), as directed by Deng Xiaoping more than two decades ago. Perhaps it reflects Beijing's long-standing discomfort with, and opposition to, what it describes as "power politics" (强国政治) and the "Cold War mentality" (冷战思维). Perhaps it just reflects uncertainty and inexperience with its newfound role of being a global power. Whichever is the case, China demonstrates a conscious decision or distinct inability to shape world events. For years, many scholars and diplomats have praised China's ability to compensate for its strategic weaknesses over time, allowing the People's Republic to "punch above its weight" in world affairs. On the contrary, I argue in this volume that Beijing punches well below its weight. The world should expect much more from Beijing.

When examining other dimensions of China's global posture, one finds a similar pattern of breadth but not depth, presence but not influence. Militarily, China is not able to project power outside of its Asian neighborhood (other than ballistic missiles, space program, and cyber warfare capacities), and even within Asia its military power projection capacities remain limited (although growing). Culturally, despite the enormous efforts and resources being poured by the Chinese government into trying to build its soft power and improve its international image since 2008, China continues to have a mixed-to-negative global reputation (as shown below), while its cultural products—art, film, literature, scholarship, music, etc.—are not setting global trends and are little known outside of China. Even economically—the one area where one would expect China to be a global trendsetter—we find in Chapter 5 that China's impact is much more shallow than anticipated. Its products have poor international brand recognition; only a handful of its multinational corporations are operating successfully abroad; its overseas direct investment (ODI) ranked only fifth in the world in 2010 with five times *less* ODI than the United States; and (despite being the world's second-largest economy) China's overseas aid is a fragment of that of the United States, European Union, Japan, Scandinavian countries, or the World Bank.

Other measures also do not give China very positive rankings. For example, in 2009 Freedom House ranked China 181 out of 195 countries for freedom of the press.[16] Since 2005 the World Bank's global governance indicators have consistently ranked China in the 60th percentile for government effectiveness and 40th percentile for rule of law.[17] The World Economic Forum ranked China only twenty-sixth globally on its composite Global Competitiveness Index in 2011, forty-eighth for corruption, fifty-seventh for business ethics, and sixty-sixth for corporate accountability.[18] Transparency International ranks China even lower (seventy-eighth) in its 2011 international corruption index.[19]

By these and other measures, it is clear that China's global presence and reputation is mixed. It remains a long way from becoming a global superpower like the United States (which has comprehensive power and global influence across economic, cultural, diplomatic, security, governance, and other realms). Over time it may gain these attributes, but for the time being China remains very much a *partial power*.

The World Views China

China's global reputation has fluctuated over the past decade and has in fact declined globally in recent years. During 2000–2007, China enjoyed a generally positive international image in most countries and Beijing was credited as being on a "charm offensive."[20] But since 2008 China's global reputation has generally declined worldwide, except in Africa and some countries in Asia. For their part, many Chinese remain indignant about how their country is perceived abroad, claiming that Western media bias distorts the "real China." As State Council Information Office Vice Director Wang Guoqing told the World Economic Forum in 2010, "What is on our top agenda is to find a way accepted by other nations to tell China's story and help the international community understand China."[21]

Perhaps this is true to some extent, but various factors influence and complicate China's global persona. It is not merely a matter of the inept messages Beijing seeks to project, but also a result of negative Chinese behavior and policies at home and abroad. China's huge trade surpluses have contributed directly and indirectly to job losses around the world (this has particularly been a factor in China's declining image in Europe and Latin America). China's military modernization and regional muscle flexing in Asia has tarnished its reputation there. Its domestic human rights situation has been a long-standing concern to Western countries. China's political system is not admired abroad, although its economic growth is. China's environmental record and contributions to global warming are similarly criticized abroad.

As a result, China's rise in world affairs has been disconcerting for many, with China often seen as enigmatic, nontransparent, truculent, propagandistic, and dismissive of foreign concerns. China is also seen by many as not comfortably fitting into the existing international liberal order and having a hidden "revisionist" agenda to overturn that order. For those in the "Global South" (Africa, Asia, and Latin America) there is thus some sympathy with China on this score, but much greater angst exists in the West. Simplistic foreign stereotypes and biases also preclude many from seeing an increasingly complex and nuanced China at home and abroad.

Although there are no regular public opinion polls taken concerning global public opinion of China, since 2005 a number of significant ones have been undertaken. Of these, the most systematic and comprehensive data come from the Pew Global Attitudes Poll, which provides fairly consistent polling of more than twenty countries since 2005. What we see in the Pew polls is, first, a *globally mixed perception* of China, combining favorable and unfavorable views.[22] Indonesia, Kenya, Pakistan, and Russia have held consistently positive views of China. Conversely, Germany, Japan, Mexico, Spain, and Turkey have held consistently negative views over time. Every other country shows mixed results, straddling the favorable-unfavorable divide. Second, with a few exceptions the Pew polls also clearly indicate a significant decline in China's global image from 2006 to 2008, but a general rise in the favorability rating from 2009 to 2011 (Mexico and Turkey excepted, which continued to hold overwhelmingly negative views of China).

The British Broadcasting Service (BBC) conducts annual global surveys as well. Their country sample is similar, but slightly different from the Pew dataset—adding Canada, Peru, Chile, Portugal, Italy, Nigeria, Ghana, South Africa, China, Philippines, Australia, and South Korea. They poll 27 countries, providing a richer sense of how Africans, Asians, Europeans, and Latin Americans view China. The survey for 2011 shows generally positive views of China in Asia (with four exceptions: Australia, South Korea, India, and Japan), Africa, and Latin America (with the exception of Mexico)—but predominantly negative views across Europe and in North America.[23]

In some ways, the BBC polling reaffirms the findings of the Pew survey for 2011. Overall, as with Pew, the BBC findings also showed an overall rise in positive global views of China from 2010 to 2011, with the notable exceptions of Canada, India, Japan, Mexico, and the United States (where they all declined from 2010 to 2011). Taken together, the Pew and BBC data provide an interesting window into how China is presently perceived in the world. China continues to enjoy "pockets of favorability" in Africa, Latin America, and parts of Asia. But it also suffers from persistent "pockets of negativity" across Europe and parts of Asia. North Americans seem more ambivalent. The most important conclusion is that China's global image remains mixed and the majority of the world is very ambivalent about China's rise.

How does China see its own rise and role in world affairs? We turn to this in the next chapter.

2

China's Global Identities*

China is not prepared for world leadership. When the world asks China: what do you want to be? It doesn't know, and that's the problem.
—PROFESSOR YAN XUETONG, Tsinghua University, 2012[1]

Internationally, our country's goal should change from saying what we don't want to [saying] what we do want.
—PROFESSOR WANG JISI, Peking University, 2011[2]

China remains an inward-looking country. It is essentially not interested in the outside world, except to make money. So the West should not expect too much from China in global affairs.
—PROFESSOR JIN CANRONG, Renmin University, 2010[3]

China is a Big Power; we can handle any country one-on-one. No one should try to lead us; no one should tell us what to do.
—PROFESSOR SHEN DINGLI, Fudan University, 2010[4]

ALTHOUGH THE FUTURE OF China's impact on the world will depend on a wide variety of domestic and international determinants,[5] one key variable of importance is how the Chinese perceive their nation's international position and roles. The quotations from four of China's leading professors of international relations are indicative of the diversity of opinion among the expert community in China.[6] At present, China is experiencing something of an international identity crisis; it possesses a number of competing international identities and cultivates a number of international constituencies. This is summed up in the phrase "The major powers are the key, surrounding areas are the first priority,

13

developing countries are the foundation, and multilateral forums are the important stage" (大国是关键,周边是首要,发展中国家是基础,多边是重要舞台).

As a consequence of its competing international identities, China's foreign policy exhibits diverse—sometimes conflicting, sometimes complementary—emphases and orientation. Sometimes the world witnesses China's leaders sitting at the "high table" of intergovernmental gatherings, acting as global power brokers and playing the pragmatic role of an engaged and responsible power. Other times the world hears belligerent rhetoric from official government spokesmen or from cyber hypernationalists. Sometimes China bullies its neighbors over conflicting territorial claims, or acts in neo-imperialist fashion by exploiting faraway nations for their natural resources. Elsewhere China is busy pragmatically striking trade deals or signing exchange agreements to broaden its global network of partners. This contradictory behavior from Beijing is indicative of conflicted internal debates and different directions China is pulled internationally.

Few nations have had such extensive, animated, and diverse domestic discourse about its roles as a major power as has China over the past decade. Official, semiofficial, and unofficial circles in China all actively debate the roles, opportunities, dangers, risks, and responsibilities of being a major power (大国). Understanding these competing perceptions is crucial to anticipating Beijing's increasingly multidimensional behavior on the world stage in the years to come.[7] As China continues its rise in world affairs, and its impact becomes more consequential, it will concomitantly become more important for foreign analysts to dig deep inside of and understand China's international relations (IR) discourse (as well as mass opinion) in order to ascertain China's possible directions and actions. As discussed in Chapter 3, the foreign policy-making milieu itself has become increasingly pluralized with a range of voices and actors interacting in an unprecedentedly complex policy process.[8] In addition to the perceptions of China's IR experts who are based in research institutes and universities, as well as foreign policy officials, the Chinese internet, blogosphere, and newspapers are rife with opinions concerning world affairs (much of it hypernationalist).[9]

Open Discourse in a Constrained Environment

The Chinese international relations discourse is very diverse and remarkably open.[10] The relative freedom would surprise many who consider China to have a censored environment. To be sure, censorship certainly exists and it has in fact gotten tighter in recent years; yet the totality and diversity of what is permitted to be discussed online and in print would surprise many foreign pundits. Previous conceptual constraints—ideological and political—have been eased and Chinese scholars of international relations are exploring an unprecedented range of new topics (both theoretical and policy-related). To be sure, there still remain "no go zones"—such as critically analyzing China's own foreign policy, human rights, or humanitarian interventions—but Chinese scholars are otherwise embracing a much broader menu of research subjects.

Though active and diverse, China's international identity discourse nonetheless still takes place in a constrained political environment—which has an impact on the parameters, terminology, content, and conclusions of discourse. Moreover, Chinese academic political culture does not have a tradition of scholars directly criticizing each other, and thus it is difficult to ascertain who specifically advocates what. Professor Shi Yinhong of Renmin University, a leading historian of international relations, put it succinctly: "We don't criticize others by name in our articles, but we openly attack other's ideas."[11] Unlike the public policy political culture in the West, Chinese scholars rarely advocate publicly that their government should do this or that, and they certainly do not explicitly criticize specific policies (to do so would be seditious). Policy recommendations are more obliquely or privately offered.

IR debates in China thus have an opaque quality to them. Those writings that are theoretical have an even more abstract quality to them. Moreover, viewpoints on international affairs are not easily demarcated by institution. Distinct viewpoints are much more associated with individuals than with institutions, thus crosscutting the system. Cohorts of those who share similar views certainly exist, but they tend to transcend organizations and localities. These academic views do not exist in a vacuum: various mechanisms exist to transmit unofficial views to officials. For this reason, it is important to understand the nongovernmental discourse—as these views and debates often mirror (and sometimes influence) government policy. Although scholarly debate is increasingly broad gauged and animated, government officials tend to maintain tight Leninist discipline. Officials rarely express their personal views in print until they retire (if then), and they are remarkably scripted when speaking with foreigners; one never senses that they are expressing an individual opinion as distinct from official policy (the presence of note takers and other officials in the room ensures this conformity, as any variance would be reported to more senior authorities). All official speeches are carefully vetted by government agencies and propaganda authorities. Leaks of official policy deliberations to the media generally do not occur. For these reasons, the IR discourse in China offers a "window" into official policy thinking, even if it is difficult to decipher (requiring the venerable Sinological tradition of "tea leaf reading").

Importantly, it must also be remembered that Chinese debates over international relations and China's role in the world are inextricably linked to Chinese domestic politics. Wang Jisi of Peking University, probably China's most well-known IR scholar who regularly briefs top leaders and officials, notes, "Our leaders are constantly concerned with the potential domestic costs and impact of a given foreign policy or action."[12] The broad conservative-reformist cleavage that has prevailed in domestic politics for thirty years (with various permutations) has direct foreign policy linkages. For example, the domestic reformers (generally speaking) are linked to the "cooperative internationalist" component of China's IR community, while the hard international realists are more closely aligned with the domestic conservatives. Since 2009 there has been a shift from the former to the latter. As one prominent IR scholar described it, "There is a combination of insecurity and arrogance in China's behavior at present—insecure at home and arrogant abroad. The government is insecure about a lot of things, so there is an increase in domestic controls. Externally, there is a kind of overconfidence of China's position in the world and a strong reluctance to get involved in foreign entanglements."[13]

Despite the constrained political environment that still exists for Chinese intellectuals, the diversity and growing openness of policy-relevant discourse offers important prisms into Chinese thinking about other nations, regions, and international issues. It also permits insights into Chinese thinking about the nation's own evolving role as an emerging major power in world affairs. To be sure, there is still a segment of official opinion that *denies* China is a major power—arguing instead that China remains a developing (socialist) country. Another significant segment of opinion denies that China is a global power, arguing it is a regional power at best. Another tenacious self-identity, still deeply rooted in the Chinese mind-set and frequently articulated in media and specialist publications, is that of historical victimization and humiliation at the hands of other major powers. This traditional *weltanschauung* has fueled modern Chinese nationalism and carries two distinct aspects. First, China is an aggrieved nation that has endured a "century of shame and humiliation" and various indignities at the hands of the West and Japan; and second, China has been a great power historically and deserves to return to that status. Deeply held and long-standing aspirations for restored pride and dignity, wealth and power, animate both beliefs and are deeply embedded in China's national psychology.

These traditional identities reflect existing insecurities about China's potential as a global power. These traditional identities continue to be articulated in official government speeches and documents, but over the past decade the preponderance of domestic discourse recognizes that China *is* a major world power—or at least is well on the way to becoming one. As a result, the discourse in recent years has shifted to discussing *what kind of major power* China should be. This chapter specifically examines the domestic Chinese discourse on this question.

Even though such discussions take place primarily in the semiofficial policy and academic communities, they also extend to society at large. For example, on November 13–24, 2006, China Central Television (CCTV) aired a twelve-part documentary entitled "Rising Powers" (大国崛起). This popular series was watched by hundreds of millions of Chinese and was rebroadcast several times. It portrayed the conditions that gave rise to other modern great powers in history (Portugal, Spain, Holland, France, Great Britain, Germany, Russia/

USSR, Japan, and the United States), so that China's own rise could be contextualized and informed by these historical experiences over five hundred years. Seven separate CCTV production teams fanned out around the world to film the series.

The CCTV series coincided with a series of lectures on the subject given by academics to the Chinese Communist Party Politburo. On November 24, 2003, party leader Hu Jintao presided over the "ninth collective study session," entitled "An Historical Investigation of the Development of the World's Main Powers Since the Fifteenth Century." This was one of the new monthly Politburo "study sessions" convened since the end of 2002, to brief Politburo members on a variety of policy issues.[14]

The impetus for both the elite gatherings and the popular television series was the same: to learn the lessons of other rising (and falling) powers, so that China could anticipate problems typically experienced by previous powers and manage them effectively. Of special Chinese concern was how to avoid the historical repetitive "asymmetry trap" between a major established power and the primary rising power, in which the latter challenged the former's hegemonic position in the international system—thus causing tensions, competition, clashes, even wars. Another concern was to understand patterns of the decline of great powers, so as to anticipate America's future.

Contentious Issues

Several specific issues animate recent debates about China's international posture. Some have come to closure, while others are ongoing. Let us examine a sample of these contentious issues.

The Debate Over "Biding Time, Hiding Brightness, Not Taking the Lead, But Doing Some Things"

One of the longest running debates is linked to the late Deng Xiaoping, the leader of China who in 1978 catalyzed China's policies of "reform and opening" (改革, 开放). On September 4, 1989, in the wake of China's June 4 "massacre" of protesting students in Tiananmen Square and the collapse of East European communist party-states, Deng argued that China should "observe clearly, secure our position, and cope with affairs calmly" (冷静观察, 稳住阵脚, 沉着应付).[15] Many foreign scholars attribute Deng's famous aphorism "bide its time, hide its brightness, not seek leadership, but do some things" (*taoguang yanghui, bu dang tou, yousuo zuowei*—韬光养晦,不当头,有所作为) to this 1989 speech, but there is no evidence Deng actually said it. It is not to be found either in this speech or in Deng's *Selected Works*.[16] The only time Deng appears to have used part of this phrase was in 1992 during his famous "Southern Sojourn" (南巡), when he said, "We will only become a big political power if we keep a low profile (韬光养晦) and work hard for some years, and then we will have more weight in international affairs."[17] It fell to Deng's successor Jiang Zemin in 1998 to actually first use the terminology usually attributed to Deng.[18] Regardless, the phrases collectively became the "guiding terminology" (指导提法) internally and attracted much attention externally as a blueprint for stealth development of Chinese power, although they should be interpreted as calling for China to adopt a grand strategy of maintaining a low profile in world affairs.

In the same full statement of twenty-eight characters, it was argued that China "should not take the lead" but could still "do some things," which has been interpreted as counseling China to selectively engage in world affairs. Taken together, these phrases have caused intense debate in recent years, as Chinese scholars and officials wrestle with exactly *how low a profile* to keep and *how much* China should do on the world stage.[19] Jin Canrong, a noteworthy America specialist at Renmin University in Beijing, observed: "At the strategic level, everyone agrees we should continue to follow Deng's *taoguang yanghui* concept, but tactically there are many different views. Some think China is too reactive, while others think China should be more proactive."[20]

Some Chinese scholars have challenged this dictum of Deng's, however, arguing that it is out of date and inappropriate to China's newfound international status. It is time for China to stand tall and be more assertive and protective of its interests, they say. The majority argue that China should "do *more* things" (更有作为), while a few say China should "do nothing" (无所作为) and stay out of international entanglements. Professor Yan Xuetong of Tsinghua University, a well-known advocate of a more assertive Chinese foreign policy, argues that "China should take charge as a great, responsible power instead of maintaining a low profile. Deng Xiaoping's 'keeping a low profile' policy of the early 1990s was right for China at the time, given the international environment and China's former status, but now China's international status has undergone a fundamental change. Continuing low-profile type policies will bring more harm than benefit to China."[21] Other scholars, such as Ye Zicheng of Peking University, argued in the early 2000s that *taoguang yanghui* was too vague to serve as a master (or grand) strategy for China since it suggested to many abroad a sinister intention of stealth diplomacy, and that China should improve its transparency rather than conceal its capabilities. Others countered by arguing that ambiguity was *precisely* a good strategy for China at this stage of development. Yet the mainstream consensus holds that *taoguang yanghui, yousuo zuowei* remains an appropriate guiding principle for Chinese diplomacy, given the nation's developmental status and limited power.

At the 2010 annual meeting of China's Association of International Relations in Lanzhou, participants from all over China heatedly debated the continuing efficacy of the *taoguang yanghui* paradigm and concluded that it was still a good guide for China's diplomacy. As a result of this macro conclusion, the participants came to nine other principal policy recommendations:

- Do not confront the United States;
- Do not challenge the international system in general;
- Do not use ideology to guide foreign policy;
- Do not be the chief of the "anti-Western camp";
- Do not conflict with the majority of countries, even when we are right;
- Learn to make compromises and concessions, and learn the game of reciprocal interests;
- Do not compromise China's core interests concerning unification of the country;
- Provide public goods in needed areas of international affairs;
- Change China's international image by taking advantage of important global events.[22]

The Debate over "Peaceful Rise"

The preoccupation with rising powers generated the theory of China's "peaceful rise" (和平崛起), a theory most forcefully articulated by leading Chinese Communist Party theoretician Zheng Bijian.[23] Before retirement in 2009 Zheng enjoyed a distinguished career at the upper echelons of party officialdom. Zheng served as a junior aide to the late President Liu Shaoqi, was vice president of the Chinese Academy of Social Sciences during the height of its involvement in reforms, and served as vice minister of the CCP Propaganda Department, vice president of the Central Party School, speechwriter for Deng Xiaoping and Jiang Zemin, and founding director of the China Reform Forum.

Following a visit to the United States in 2006, Zheng became alarmed at the growing predisposition against China and the rising "China threat theory." Thus he began to elaborate his own retort: the concept of China's "peaceful rise." Zheng and other scholars did much to popularize the concept, but it eventually fell into disfavor with the Chinese government.[24] The term *rise* was thought to be too threatening to some abroad, while others favored "revival" (*fuxing*). Instead a compromise solution was reached: the official terminology of "peaceful development" was authorized, which was consistent with Deng Xiaoping's dictum of "peace *and* development."

Debating the Structure of the International Order

Chinese IR scholars actively discuss and debate the structure and nature of the international structure (国际格局), international system (国际体系), or international order (国际秩序).[25] Most Chinese IR scholars are in the realist tradition (which emphasizes states, insecurity, and the search for power). They are somewhat like geometrists, constantly looking for structures, pivots, nodes, triangles, etc. More than anything, they are wed to the concept of "poles" (极) in international relations, either individual powers or collections of them. Both official policy and Chinese scholars have long posited that the international order is inexorably moving toward multipolarity (多极化) over time.[26] But they debate whether all regional powers in the world constitute a "pole" in the international system—e.g., Japan, India, Iran, Brazil, and possibly Nigeria and South Africa—or just the United States, Russia, and China. What about collectivities of states such as the Association of Southeast Asian Nations (ASEAN), the European Union (EU), the Shanghai Cooperation Organization (SCO), and the group of Brazil, Russia, India, China, South Africa (BRICS)?

Closely related in this discourse has been the discussion concerning the role and dominance of the United States and unipolarity (一极化). Chinese scholars ask, Why has American "hegemony" and unipolarity not collapsed? If the United States is in decline, is it absolute or relative? What is the pace of America's decline? Can it be reversed? Can it be hastened? How severely wounded was the United States from the 2008–2010 global financial crisis?

These questions animate such discussions. Over the years it should be noted that Chinese IR analysts have several times (e.g., late 1970s, mid-1980s, 2001–2005) pronounced and predicted America's decline in world affairs—only to be proven wrong by America's resilience and staying power. "We consistently underestimated the United States," said Guo Zhenyuan of the China Institute of International Studies, one of China's leading analysts of international strategic relations.[27] Another leading realist scholar, Zhang Ruizhuang of Nankai University, argued: "There is a strange euphoria about the U.S. decline and China's rise. Some [Chinese] analysts have been smoking opium and believe Chinese power is much greater than it is."[28] Some key analysts, such as Yang Jiemian, president of the Shanghai Institutes of International Studies, argue that "While in relative decline, in 20–30 years the United States will *still* be the world's only superpower."[29]

Differing views exist, but a consensus emerged among most analysts in the late 1990s that still prevails today: the global structure is *simultaneously* unipolar and multipolar (一超多强). Yet another group argued *just the opposite* during the first year of the Obama administration—that the potential for U.S.-China global cooperation meant that a pseudo G-2 world order could emerge—although this minority viewpoint soon disappeared. One variant was the view of "two superpowers, many powers" (两超多强), with the United States and China acting globally with other powers acting regionally. A smaller segment of opinion argues that the international system is in *transition* from unipolarity to multipolarity.[30] The transition from the Bush to the Obama administrations seemed to convince many Chinese analysts that indeed the U.S. decline had finally begun to emerge and the pace of multipolarization was picking up.[31] As one analyst succinctly put it: "The United States has been falling from the apex of its power since the Bush administration. A mood of 'new declinism' has emerged in the United States.... The peak of American hegemony is over."[32] The 2008–2010 global financial crisis convinced many Chinese that America's decline has truly and finally come. The simultaneous rise of the BRICS (Brazil, Russia, India, China, South Africa) and emergence of the G-20 further fueled this perception,[33] with some analysts arguing that these "intermediate forces" were becoming the dominant actors in world politics.[34]

Debating Global Governance, Multilateralism, and the "Responsible Power" Theory

One of the most animated and active discourses in China today concerns the issue of China's contributions to international global governance, its role in intergovernmental multilateralism, and what it means to be a "responsible power" (负责任的大国). The discussion has been going on since former U.S. Deputy Secretary of State Robert Zoellick's 2005 call on China to become a "responsible international stakeholder" (负责任的利益相关者) in the international system.

Chinese analysts ask: What are the roles of intergovernmental and regional institutions in the new world order? How should China think about the concept of global governance, and how much should China contribute? They also debate the concept of "global responsibility,"[35] the responsibilities of major powers,[36] and specifically China's responsibilities.[37]

A broad range of opinion has emerged.[38] A substantial segment are very leery of global governance and believe that the whole concept is a Western/U.S. "trap" that tries to undermine China's sovereignty, lure it into a variety of foreign entanglements where China does not belong, and retard China's growth. As one senior official suspiciously put it, "First you [the United States] tried to subvert our political system in the 1980s, then you tried to contain us in the 1990s, now you are trying to bleed us through international entanglements in the 2000s."[39] This perspective was echoed in the pages of the Xinhua News Agency's

International Herald Leader: with the rise and global influence of China, "'China's international responsibility theory' has become a new weapon and a new means for the West to suppress China."[40] Others argue that China is not ready and does not possess the capabilities to become fully engaged in global governance. Another group believes that China *should* do more in contributing to global governance, commensurate with its newfound position and power. Yet others believe China should do more, but do so selectively. Still others argue that China should do more in tandem with the United States (G-2). So diversity of opinion prevails.

Closely connected to global governance is multilateralism, over which a related but somewhat separate discussion emerged.[41] Chinese scholars use the term *multilateralism* (多边主义) but have a very different concept of it than is commonly used in the West. As Professor Song Xinning of Renmin University observed: "For Chinese, multilateralism is a *tool* and a *tactic*, not an intergovernmental mechanism or institutional arrangement. China also worries that multilateralism is a tool for others to contain China. Since the 1990s, China has used multilateralism to solve bilateral issues—to this end, multilateral meetings are a useful platform (舞台) to negotiate bilaterally. But we are still uncomfortable with multilateralism, and prefer bilateralism and multipolarity."[42] Another scholar similarly observed: "Many scholars think the Western effort to integrate China into the global system is a trap to tie China down."[43]

Chinese analysts also debate the relationship between multipolarism and multilateralism. How does the former phenomenon among individual sovereign nation-states relate to the latter phenomenon of collectivities of sovereign states? There is evidence of two competing camps of theorists in China on this question (the former rooted in realism and the latter influenced by European liberal institutionalism and Asian constructivism), with the former recently gaining the upper hand in debates. The former argue that the actions of individual powers largely determine world affairs, while the latter argue that it is the interplay of poles that is determining.

Concerning international institutions, Chinese scholars have debated the role of the United Nations and other global institutions, as well as a variety of regional blocs and organizations. Interestingly, the Chinese government and scholars have become some of the world's strongest advocates of the United Nations. Regionally, China has also pushed forward what it describes as a "new type" of regional organization, based on the model of the Shanghai Cooperation Organization (SCO): based on "comprehensive, cooperative security" rather than alliances, respect for sovereignty and territorial integrity, and confidence-building measures.

The Concept of "Harmonious World"

Another key concept in recent years is that of the "harmonious world" (和谐世界), although a discourse per se has not emerged.[44] This is because the concept is so closely identified with former President Hu Jintao that no one would dare to criticize it. As one scholar put it: "Of course there are those who don't like the idea (of harmonious world), but nobody can openly criticize it. So the way that some oppose the concept is *not* to talk about it!"[45] Nonetheless, the concept permeates recent articles on Chinese foreign policy in academic journals.

According to Hu Jintao, a "harmonious world" should have four principal attributes: (1) effective multilateralism with a strong role for the United Nations, (2) development of a collective security mechanism, (3) prosperity for all through mutually beneficial cooperation, and (4) tolerance and enhancement of dialogue among diverse civilizations.[46] Like "peaceful rise," "harmonious world" posits that China's rise will not be a threat or disrupt the existing global order. The Chinese government has invested enormous resources and effort in trying to popularize this theory in recent years—but with little effect abroad. A multinational survey of Asian nations by the Chicago Council on Global Affairs found that the concept hardly registered, with an affirmative response from less than 1 percent of those polled.[47]

The Newest Debate: Soft Power

One of the newest and most active areas of discussion in China's international relations community concerns the issue of "soft power" (软实力) in major power diplomacy—its content, strategy, tactics, and instruments. As is discussed at length in Chapter 6, China has seemingly become obsessed with soft power. What is it? Does China have it? If not, why not? Where can China find it? Can it be bought? What should China do with it? Chinese scholars and officials working in the media and propaganda system work overtime on the subject. None other than Hu Jintao himself first drew attention to the importance of building China's global cultural soft power in his official report to the Seventeenth Congress of the Chinese Communist Party in 2007. Since then, China has grown increasingly sensitive to its (relatively poor) image abroad and launched what some describe as a "charm offensive" in its public diplomacy.

The Hearty Perennial: Hegemony

Finally, the concept of "hegemony" (霸权主义), in which one nation dominates all others, remains central to the major power discourse in China, although its usage has dropped off in recent years and it is not debated per se. But anti-hegemony (反霸) remains the *sine qua non* of the Chinese worldview and foreign policy. Though the term is not used as frequently as before, it remains an intellectual pillar of China's thinking about other powers—particularly the United States—as well as itself. Beijing steadfastly continues to remind the world that it will "never seek hegemony" once it emerges as a major international power. Even if China eschews hegemony, some scholars do discuss the possibility of taking a "leadership" role in world affairs. Observed one scholar: "China doesn't have the desire or history to be a hegemon. But we do want to be a leader!"[48]

The Spectrum of Discourse on China's International Identity

Thus the discourse inside China about what it means to be a major power has been both intensive and extensive, revolving around these key issues in recent years. The following section elucidates further the finer distinctions within the Chinese discourse and places these issues in the context of contending schools of thought.

These concepts all compete within the marketplace of ideas in China's domestic discourse about its identity and role as a major power, different "schools" or "tendencies" of thought and analysis are evident[49]; these are captured in Figure 2.1. Though intellectually

Spectrum of Chinese Global Identities

FIGURE 2.1 Spectrum of Chinese Global Identities

distinct, it would be incorrect to see these schools as mutually exclusive. Even if sometimes contradictory, they can also be complementary. Research and interviews reveal that individual IR scholars and officials in China (indeed elsewhere!) are *eclectic* thinkers—strongly rooted in one school of thought, but often voicing views associated with other schools of thought. Cognitive complexity prevails. I also find, as noted above, that intellectual schools of thought do *not* correlate with institutions. Although it would be nice to be able to label one institution as "realist" or another as "multilateralist," it is not so simple. Cohorts of thinkers crosscut institutions.

The Nativists

At one end of the spectrum are the "Nativists." This cohort is a collectivity of populists, nationalists, and Marxists. They distrust the outside world, seek international autonomy, and view international multilateral involvement as "traps" (laid by the West) to ensnare and embroil China in costly commitments overseas. They are vociferous critics of the West; some in this cohort bear a strong traditional Marxist orientation. This group is the twin of the "new left" (新左派) in domestic policy debates, as they believe the "reform and opening" policy of the past thirty years has cost China its socialist integrity, corroded its culture with negative foreign influences, and has compromised China's sovereignty and autonomy in world affairs. Earlier examples of this thinking emerged during the 1990s with the lightning-rod book *China Can Say No!* (中国可以说不!) and a series of revisionist "10,000 character essays" penned by Marxist ideologue Deng Liqun and his intellectual coterie. More recent manifestations have been the popular books *China Is Unhappy; Why Is China Unhappy?; Who in China Is Unhappy?;* and *China Doesn't Express Its Dissatisfaction.*[50]

China Is Unhappy is the most well known of this genre of "China Is Dissatisfied" literature. A collection of firebrand essays written by five authors (Song Xiaojun, Wang Xiaodong, Song Qiang, Huang Jisu, and Liu Yang), the book quickly became a best seller across China in 2009–10.[51] The authors come from eclectic backgrounds. Wang Xiaodong is a mathematician-turned-writer. Song Xiaojun, previously a naval officer specializing in radar and sonar, became a popular media commentator and military magazine contributor. Song Qiang was a middle school teacher who went into advertising before becoming a contributor to television programs and a freelance media personality. Huang Jisu was a playwright and is a Western-trained sociologist. Liu Yan is a venture capitalist investor with an economics and history background. Two (Wang and Huang) have studied abroad (in Japan and the United States, respectively). According to the Chinese Encyclopedia website (www.hudong.com), Wang Xiaodong is the "flag bearer of Chinese nationalism."

China Is Unhappy is more of a chest-thumping, coarse, conversational-style, nationalistic rant than a serious policy analysis. Some of the contributing authors earned earlier fame during the 1990s with the diatribe *China Can Say No!*[52] Both books are rabid anti-Western and anti-American diatribes. All the contributing authors to *China Is Unhappy* adopt a position of open enmity against the United States and Europe, even if it would mean military conflict. They call for a "qualified break" (条件地决裂) with the West, a concept implying a xenophobic campaign to purge China of foreign influences and ideas. The book particularly rails against those Chinese (elites) who worship the West and accept China as weak or backward: "Our elites have been frightened into complacency by Westerners," lead author Song Xiaojun asserts.[53] But the other lead co-author, the well-known nationalist rabble-rouser Wang Xiaodong, argues that standing up to the West is not enough. China must "punish" the West, Wang asserts: "If someone harms you and you are too weak to respond, you need to build up your strength and then, when you are strong enough, you need to respond with force and severely punish them!"[54] In addition to rejecting and standing up to the West, *China Is Unhappy* contributor Wang Xiaodong calls for China to "lead the world."[55] Wang's notion of "leadership" is more than a little fuzzy, but essentially he seems to argue for China's "management" of global resources, "guiding" international politics,[56] and ridding the world of "international bullies."[57] More radically, he also calls for China to form an "American-style Blackwater company" that can go out into the world and protect China's economic interests overseas. Perhaps most provocatively, he argues that "China must conduct business with a sword in its hand" (持剑经商), i.e., that China's international commerce must be backed up with a strong military that the government is ready and willing to use (note that this view is not too different from that of the realist scholar Yan Xuetong, below).[58]

All in all, *China Is Unhappy* is quite representative of nativist/hypernationalist discourse in China today. Though it is clearly intended as a moneymaker by its publisher, because of its intrinsic mass popular appeal it should not be dismissed as a frivolous commercial publication. Even if not that representative within the elite spectrum of foreign policy opinion discussed in this chapter, it is quite indicative of a significant segment of mass sentiment in China.

The contributors to *China Is Unhappy* and other "nativists" are a loose coalition spread across a number of institutions, and indeed many of this school's leading advocates are pundits who operate independently. A number of them have become popular social media commentators. To the extent that they have an institutional home, it is in research institutes under the Central Committee of the Chinese Communist Party that are involved in Communist Party history and Marxist ideology. The Marxism Academy of the China Academy of Social Sciences (CASS) is one bastion of such Nativist-Marxist thought. Another home for the Nativists has been the Contemporary China Institute of the CASS, particularly when it was under the active influence of Marxist theoretician Deng Liqun (Deng has been the intellectual "godfather" of the Nativist school).

Since 1989, this group has argued that reform inevitably led to China's restoration of capitalism, and that its "opening-up" (开放) policy was destroying socialism. For them, therefore, "peaceful evolution" (和平演变)—a policy whereby the West attempts to peacefully evolve China away from Chinese Communist Party rule—became the "main contradiction" (主要矛盾) for China, and thus they argue the main policy priority should be to counter peaceful evolution by closing

China's doors. For this group, every reform measure had to be evaluated as to whether it was intrinsically socialist or capitalist in nature.

Against this backdrop, Deng Xiaoping's "southern tour" in 1992 decidedly changed the trend. Deng was aging and ailing, but frustrated with the post-1989 political climate in China; he elected to make one last bold foray into the political arena by touring Guangdong province and giving several hard-hitting interviews and speeches. In them he attacked "leftism" as the main danger to China at the time. Although they came under attack by Deng, the Nativists survived in different forms. Their arguments continued to be couched in terms of national development under a "socialist-market economy," arguing that the main struggle was between the "two roads" of being autonomous or dependent, having a planned economy or an unregulated one, favoring state-owned and collective enterprises or the private sector. With respect to international affairs, in an unjust and unreasonable international system, the Nativists argue that developing countries cannot eradicate poverty just through hard work; there needs to be a fundamental change in the global order so as to force redistribution of income from North to South. They argue that "globalization" is in fact a process of the globalization of capital, similar to Lenin's description of imperialism.[59]

The onset of the 2009 global financial crisis further emboldened this line of thinking, as many argued that "state monopoly capitalism" (国家垄断资本主义) had brought the world economy to the brink of disaster (just as Lenin had predicted). Fang Ning, director of the CASS Institute of Political Science, argues this phenomenon dates to the 2002 Iraq War, which marked the arrival of an era of "new imperialism." For Fang and others, Deng Xiaoping's era of "peace and development" was over. Earlier in 1999, the outbreak of the Kosovo War already prompted Fang and others to conclude that the new imperialism had three major policies: economic takeover, political patronage, and military control.[60]

Indeed, the foreign policy of the George W. Bush administration gave rise to a revival of Marxist—to be more accurate, neo-Leninist—studies of international relations. A number of articles and books on "new imperialism" appeared.[61] Whereas they regurgitated much earlier analysis from the 1980s, the new scholarship went much further in dissecting both the new developments in "state-monopoly capitalism" and the international order. With respect to the former, these analyses had premonitions of the coming global financial crisis of 2008–2010. With respect to the latter, they also challenged the long-prevailing Chinese prediction concerning the emergence of a multipolar world—arguing that (American) unipolarity was showing surprising tenaciousness.[62] These authors also accused China's U.S. policy of being far too "soft" and that a Sino-U.S. "strategic partnership" was an illusion. This school of thought often contains nationalistic and anti-American elements (although not as vituperative as found on the Chinese internet). The "color revolutions" in Central Asia and Arab Spring created greater cause for concern among this cohort and in the Chinese government.

Although the Nativists are the most extreme example of isolationist thinking in China, a broader insularity and distrust of the international system is evident across the spectrum (except among the Globalists). The Nativist School of thought contains extremely conservative, predominantly Marxist, hypernationalistic, and anti-American elements. These views are reinforced by similar voices in Chinese cyberspace. Throughout the Nativist discourse is a strong sense of aggrievement and entitlement. That is, Nativists regularly harp on the nationalist theme of the "century of shame and humiliation" and argue that China is entitled to global respect (particularly from those powers that previously humiliated China).

The Realists

A second group is the "Realists." Like the Nativists, they are staunch nationalists—but of a more pragmatic and less xenophobic variety. They may also be considered dogmatic "China Firsters," caring little about the interests of other countries or constituencies in world affairs (unlike the subsequent schools considered below). This school is, in fact, the *dominant* one in Chinese IR discourse today (if not forever). Realism has deep roots in China's intellectual worldview, dating to the "Self-Strengthening Movement" of the late Qing dynasty—or even further back, to the Three Kingdoms era (220–280 A.D.). Even during the more ideological periods of the People's Republic, realist calls to strengthen China were prevalent.

Chinese realists take the nation-state as their core unit of analysis. They uphold the principle of state sovereignty above all else, rejecting arguments that transnational issues penetrate across borders. Like realists elsewhere, they tend to see the international environment as anarchic and unpredictable—thus placing a premium on building up a strong state that can navigate its own way in the world and resist outside pressures. For example, some go so far as to proclaim that "the world is a place where there are many wolves and tigers. Only when you are armed well and possess power can you possibly have a civilization. After all, wolves and sheep cannot dance together."[63]

The realists may be subdivided into "offensive" and "defensive" realists, as well as "hard" and "soft" realists. For each group, the state has to build its own strength, but what distinguishes them are the purposes to which state power is put. Hard-power realists argue for the strengthening of comprehensive national power (综合国力), but particularly the military and economic dimensions, while the soft-power realists emphasize diplomacy and cultural (soft) power. The offensive realists argue that China should *use* its newly built military strength, economic might, and diplomatic influence to essentially coerce others toward ends China desires. They believe that power is worth little if it is not used. They argue, for example, that China should leverage its holding of U.S. treasury bonds to get Washington to stop selling arms to Taiwan, or penalize large U.S. corporations for selling weapons. They argue that China should establish a much broader military (particularly naval) presence in the western Pacific in order to deter the United States from operating close to China's coastline. Defensive realists agree that China should possess strong military might but feel it should "keep its powder dry" and use it essentially to deter aggression and Taiwanese independence. They advocate problem solving through diplomacy and enhancing China's soft power.

Realists are also pessimists about China's external environment, and particularly the United States. That is, they find the world a dangerous place and are particularly distrustful of the United States. Like many realists in the United States, they see an intrinsic competitive—even adversarial—dynamic at work in U.S.-China relations. As such, they counsel that China should prepare for long-term competition, and even conflict, with the United States.

Discussions with realists also reveal a certain frustration. They *want* China to *use* its newfound power, but they feel constrained in doing so. Ding Kuisong, secretary general of the China Reform Forum, observed, "As China's posture abroad grows, our investments and interests abroad are growing. We need to think about how to protect our nationals, investments, and interests. One way is to behave as an imperialist country with gunboat policies—but given our past history this is not feasible."[64] Tsinghua University's Yan Xuetong argues that "military, economy, and culture are all resources of power. Without being used they have no political influence on others. This means a military that is not used is no military. This is similar to the role money plays in life—if it is not spent it means nothing."[65]

Discussions with realists also reveal a certain sense of vindictiveness and retribution. That is, many harbor a strong sense of aggrievement from China's long period of weakness, and they believe that once China is strong it should retaliate against those countries that have done China wrong in the past. Shen Dingli, dean of the School of International Studies at Shanghai's Fudan University and a leading security expert, observed: "In ten to twenty years China will be a major exporter of high-technology—it may impose restrictive sanctions on those that previously imposed them on us!"[66]

There is also a strong sense of triumphalism among the Realists in the wake of the 2008–2010 global financial crisis. They feel the Chinese development model of mixed state capitalism and socialism has been vindicated, while the Western *laissez-faire* system has been vanquished. This has contributed to an upsurge in writings about the China Model.

Professors Yan Xuetong of Tsinghua University and Zhang Ruizhuang of Nankai University are both staunch and well-known realists. Over the years, Yan has held a hawkish position on a variety of issues. For him, "peaceful rise" is a dangerous theory because it gives potential adversaries (including Taiwan) a message that China will not act forcefully to protect its national sovereignty and interests. Yan has argued that China should resort to use of force when necessary and without hesitation to counteract Taiwan's move toward legal independence.[67] Yan's 1997 book *China's Rise* was a manifesto for building *and using* China's comprehensive and hard power.[68] But Yan Xuetong also recognizes the role of soft power in China's foreign policy,[69] and both Yan and Zhang argue for increased Chinese activism on global issues.

For Zhang Ruizhuang, the official "peaceful development" view taken together with the "multipolar world" and "U.S.-China strategic partnership" theses represent mistaken ideas that misjudge the international situation and can lead to policy errors for China. Zhang argues for a much more assertive policy toward the United States: "The United States has been damaging China's interests for a long time. China *should* be *dis*satisfied, not satisfied, with the state of U.S.-China relations. It is not a relationship in good condition. If China does not oppose the United States, the U.S. will abuse China's interests and China will become America's puppet."[70] Zhang also thinks multipolarism is an overly optimistic view of the post–Cold War order, underestimating the daunting challenges China faces and undermining China's vigilance toward American hegemony.[71]

In these respects, the "realists" are "pessimists" about China's external environment, cross-strait relations, and the United States. Above all, the Realist School takes a narrow and self-interested definition of China's national interests. They reject concepts and policies of globalization, transnational challenges, and global governance. They argue (like the Nativists) that Western attempts to enlist greater Chinese involvement in global governance are a dangerous trap aimed at tying China down, burning up its resources, and retarding its growth. The Realists are not isolationists, however. They just argue for a very hardheaded definition and defense of China's narrow national interests.

The Major Powers School

Another group, which I identify as the "Major Powers School," argues that China should concentrate its diplomacy on managing its relations with the world's major powers and blocs—the United States, Russia, perhaps the European Union—while paying relatively less attention to the developing world or multilateralism. *Daguo shi shouyao* (major powers are of primary importance) are their watchwords. Not surprisingly, scholars in this school are almost entirely regional specialists on the United States, Russia, and the EU. The vast majority of Chinese IR writings still remain concerned with the United States.

This group of analysts stress the crucial importance of relations with other great powers in China's foreign affairs, arguing that if China's ties with the major powers are not right, then this will be detrimental to a range of Chinese interests and will complicate China's other regional relationships. A major power orientation is demanded by China's modernization drive: the Western powers are the major source of advanced technology as well as of capital and investment. Analysts in this group often see the Sino-U.S. relationship as the "key of the keys," thus arguing that maintaining harmonious ties with Washington should be the number one priority in Chinese diplomacy. This group was dominant during Jiang Zemin's tenure as president and remained influential under Hu Jintao. Over the past decade, however, as Chinese power rises and frictions with Washington occur more frequently, Chinese intellectuals and the informed public increasingly advocate a tougher posture toward the United States.

Not all in this school are fixated on maintaining good ties with the United States. For Pan Wei of Peking University, working with the United States is a dead end and it is wishful thinking to seek a "Sino-U.S. strategic partnership," which has more disadvantages than advantages.[72] Pan and like-minded thinkers argue that China's foreign policy should be adjusted and geared toward a closer relationship with Russia. Russia is seen as a significant supplier of energy resources and military equipment, important to China's national security, and philosophically aligned in worldviews. Feng Yujun, a senior Russia expert at the China Institutes of Contemporary International Relations, argues that "Russia is *the most important* country for China on all four dimensions of importance in China's diplomacy: neighboring countries, major powers, developing countries, and multilateral relations. Although Russia's power is weakening, we still think Russia is a major power with global influence and we have much in common."[73] Many Chinese critics call for a "tougher" policy toward the United States. The holders of these views are actually skeptical of the line of thinking Deng Xiaoping adopted for the last thirty years, i.e., putting emphasis on opening up to the developed powers in the West. Instead, the proponents advocate "new foreign policy thinking" and a "strong and independent socialist China."[74] Some are academic Russia specialists, some are Marxists, and some in official foreign policy circles believe that Beijing and Moscow share intrinsic worldviews concerning sovereignty, the use of force, the United States, and the future of the international system. As such, they argue that it is Moscow—not Washington—that is China's real "strategic partner." The influence of this cohort should not be exaggerated, however, as many in China recognize that Russia is a *declining power* that actually has very little to offer China.

A third subgroup of the Major Powers School advocated, until a few years ago, that China should emphasize the European Union in its diplomacy, as the EU was a key pillar in the emerging multipolar world and had much to offer China in terms of trade, investment, and technology transfer. Not surprisingly, many of these voices were Europeanists (based primarily in the China Academy of Social Sciences' Institute of European Studies and China Institutes of Contemporary International Relations). But their voices began to dissipate in 2006–07 as various frictions emerged in Sino-European relations, and they have almost completely disappeared since 2008 given the disorganization in Brussels and the impotence of EU foreign and security policy. Chinese analysts have become very disillusioned and dismissive of the EU, after having hoped for a long time that the EU would become a "new emerging power" (新兴大国) in world affairs.

Despite the critics, a majority of senior leaders and working-level foreign affairs officials still endorse a major power orientation. Their logic is that it would just be too costly for China to have strained ties with any of the three major powers noted above. Despite this recognition, it is apparent that there was a reorientation away from an "exclusive" focus on major powers (as was practiced during the Jiang Zemin period) toward a more balanced and omnidirectional and global policy under Hu Jintao.[75]

Asia First

Another group in the middle of the spectrum argues for concentrating China's diplomacy on its immediate periphery and Asian neighborhood (put Asia first). They argue that if China's neighborhood is not stable this will be a major impediment to development and national security. Thus, priority should be placed on building ties and a stable environment all around China's periphery. As Zhu Feng of Peking University put it, "Every power must protect its own yard."[76] Another Chinese analyst notes, "If Southeast Asia is our front yard, then Central Asia is our back yard."[77] As China sits at the heart of Asia, bordering fourteen countries by land and many more by sea, it is hard to overestimate the importance of the Asian neighborhood for China. Unsurprisingly, those in the Foreign Ministry responsible for Asia prioritize the region in China's overall foreign policy.

In this context, Chinese scholars discuss a variety of regional trends, including the evolving regional institutional architecture; the roles of the United States, India, and ASEAN; the North Korean issue; nontraditional security issues; and other matters. These discussions are more of a discourse, without significant cleavages and lines of debates.

This "Asia First" contingent found expression in China's foreign policy in the late 1990s. During that time, following the 1997 Asian financial crisis and the "peace and development debate" of the same year, China began to emphasize much more its neighborhood diplomacy (周边外交).[78] The result of this debate was that China decided to become far more proactive on its periphery to shape a peaceful environment. It embarked on a sustained period of cooperative regional diplomacy under the rubric of "establish good neighborliness, make neighbors prosperous, and make them feel secure." This policy bore much fruit, as China managed to dramatically improve and stabilize relations all around its periphery. Certain tensions remained in Beijing's ties with Japan, Vietnam, and India, but even in these cases bilateral ties were stable overall. Still, much of the progress made during the decade from 1998 to 2008 unraveled almost overnight during 2009–10 with a sudden spike in Chinese nationalism and assertiveness in the region (see Chapter 3).

One important subgroup of this cohort are those who advocate "multilateral regionalism" and East Asian community building, as distinct from a more state-based strategy. Professors Qin Yaqing of China Foreign Affairs University and Zhang Yunling of the China Academy of Social Sciences have been at the forefront of this movement, each contributing significantly to building regional institutionalism in Asia and increasing China's involvement in such institutions.

Those who emphasize China's ties within Asia do not do so to the exclusion of relations with other regions or nations; rather, they argue in favor of not neglecting Asia relative to the major powers or China's relations with the developing world. But the Asia Firsters do believe in giving Asia relatively greater emphasis over relations with the United States, Russia, Europe, or the developing world.

The Global South School

Another group I identify as the "Global South" School. They argue that given China's historical experience with colonialism and imperialism, and as a developing country, its main international identity and responsibility lies with the developing world. They argue for at least a more balanced foreign policy that takes account of China's longtime partners and client states in developing countries, and that should advocate their interests. This reasoning finds expression, for example, in China's strong support for the UN Millennium Development Goals, a doctrine of nonintervention, "no strings attached" aid programs and debt relief, and placing the climate change burden on developed countries. The Global South School's identity has much to do with China's long-standing self-identification as a developing country.

Within China's IR community, there has always been tension between those whose work focuses on the West (North) and those who work on the South. For the latter group, since the 1990s, Chinese analysts have increasingly taken notice of the differentiation and fragmentation occurring in the developing world. Proponents in this group have realized that there are various kinds of developing countries and it is not appropriate to simply lump them together. Cooperation between China and those countries has been growing, but new frictions are also proliferating. For example, Shanghai scholar Yu Xintian argues that developing countries need to be divided into three groups economically. The first is newly industrializing economies, such as South Korea, Taiwan, Brazil, Mexico, Turkey, and South Africa; the second group is average developing countries, with per capita GDP varying from $800 to $7,000; and the third group is the least-developed countries. Since they are considerably differentiated, Yu and others argue, the developing countries should not be seen as a whole, and more concrete policies need to be formulated to replace a general approach.[79] However, the strategic goal of development that China has set, to become a medium-level developed country by the mid-twenty-first century, means China's eventual departure from developing country status.

Nevertheless, for proponents of this school of thought, China should continue to see itself as a developing country for a long time to come, and it is still obliged to work with developing countries for common development even though it has already risen to global power status.[80] From this perspective, continuing to self-identify as a developing country is required by Beijing's need for diplomatic support from the developing world to fend off the West on issues such as Tibet, human rights, Taiwan, climate change, etc.

Not surprisingly, many analysts in this camp advocate a fundamental restructuring of the global system so as to redistribute financial resources, institutional influence, and power from North to South.[81] They perceive the *existing* international institutional order to be unjust and weighted in favor of developed countries. In this regard, China is a *revisionist* and dissatisfied power, not a status quo and satisfied one. Not surprisingly, this school is a staunch advocate of the BRICS group (Brazil, Russia, India, China, South Africa),[82] and they also strongly support the G-20, as an effort to both build global multipolarity and increase South-South solidarity. Indeed, China is active in promoting any number of measures for redefining and redistributing power from North to South in global institutions.

Selective Multilateralists

Moving along the spectrum to the right, another group are the "selective multilateralists," who believe that China should expand its global involvements gradually, but only on issues where China's national (security) interests are directly involved. The Selective Multilateralists generally eschew increasing China's global involvements, but they realize that China must be seen to be contributing to global governance. For them, contributing to global governance is a *tactic*, not a *philosophy*. They are *not* Liberal Institutionalists, but more an internationalist version of realists. The Selective Multilateralists are wary of foreign entanglements, but they recognize that China must "do some things" (as Deng Xiaoping suggested) in the international arena so as not to be perceived as a self-interested free rider in international affairs. There are several variations and splinter factions of this group: one argues China should engage only in UN-mandated activities, another argues that China should become involved only on its periphery and not far away, while another believes it should not so constrain itself from getting involved in multinational (as distinct from multilateral) actions together with other major powers.

The Selective Multilateralists have advocated raising China's participation in UN peacekeeping operations, disaster relief, fighting international piracy in the Gulf of Aden, and diplomatic involvement in the North Korean and Iranian nuclear issues; but they eschew deeper involvement in sensitive and risky areas such as Iraq, Libya, Syria, or Afghanistan. They essentially reject the entire transnational nontraditional security agenda. There remains a strong reluctance to engage in international security operations for "humanitarian" reasons.

One member of this school, Chang Gong, authored the book *China Is Not Disruptive*, which is essentially a call for modest global governance engagement. Chang is quite explicit that it is important that China "display the *image* as a responsible power" (发现负责任大国形象), but in other parts of his book he persistently claims that the West's call for China to play a greater role in global governance is an attempt to fool or deceive (忽悠) China by saddling it with responsibilities and ultimately costs it cannot and ought not bear.[83] Tsinghua University's Yan Xuetong is direct on this point: "This is a trap to exhaust our limited resources!"[84] As noted earlier and discussed further in Chapter 4, Yan is not alone in his suspicions. Not only do many see global governance as a trap for China, they also question the concept of "responsible power." "Responsible to whom? To whose standards? The United States? Never!" shouted one scholar.[85]

Actually, the selective multilateralists are not in favor of multilateralism per se (in the sense of international institutions). They are perhaps more accurately described as "selective multi*nationalists*." That is, they are more comfortable working within small ad hoc groups of nations than institutions per se, reflecting China's general discomfort with global regimes. The Six Party Talks on North Korea (China, Japan, United States, South Korea, North Korea, Russia) and the Sextet on Iran (United States, Russia, China, France, Germany, UK) are prime examples.

The Globalists

At the far end of the spectrum are those "Globalists" who believe that China must shoulder an ever-greater responsibility for addressing a wide range of global governance issues commensurate with its size, power, and influence. They are the equivalent of "liberal institutionalists" in the West. They are also more philosophically disposed to humanitarianism, embrace globalization analytically, and believe that transnational challenges require transnational partnerships. They are more supportive and trusting of multilateral institutions than the Selective Multilateralists, and they believe China should become much more fully engaged in global governance around the globe. They are interested in soft, not hard, power, and they put their faith in diplomacy and pan-regional partnerships. The Globalists are of the view that it is incumbent upon China, given its global rise, to contribute much more to global governance and to act as a "responsible power" in the international arena. As Renmin University professor Jin Canrong has observed, "China should learn to be a real leader in the international community and should learn to make a real contribution to public goods. But China hasn't decided this yet."[86]

The Globalists are "interdependence institutionalists" in essence, and their analytical starting point is globalization. As with their counterparts in the West, they recognize that in the era of globalization sovereignty has its limits as various "nontraditional" challenges regularly cross sovereign borders and must be dealt with multilaterally. Much of their analytical focus therefore is on nontraditional security, e.g., human security, economic security, counterterrorism, public health, organized crime, smuggling, cyber hacking, piracy, etc.

The Globalists are strong advocates of the United Nations and China's activism in the Security Council. They are also strong proponents of

China's participation in regional diplomatic groupings all over the world (especially in East Asia but also in Central Asia, the Middle East, Africa, and Latin America) where it has been centrally involved in forming new dialogue groupings as well as becoming observers or full members of existing ones.

Articles in China's IR journals evince a growing interest in globalist and transnational issues and concepts associated with liberal international relations discourse: globalization, global governance, international cooperation, interdependence, multilateralism, and international organizations.[87] Leading officials sometimes evince a strong commitment to global governance. The official view, from Foreign Minister Yang Jiechi, is that:

> A more developed China will undertake more international responsibilities and will never pursue interests at the expense of others. We know full well that in this interdependent world, China's future is closely linked to that of the world. Our own interests and those of others are best served when we work together to expand common interests, share responsibilities, and seek win-win outcomes. This is why while focusing on its own development, China is undertaking more and more international responsibilities commensurate with its strength and status.[88]

The Globalists are not the only ones who support China's growing global involvement. There seems to be a general consensus across the spectrum from the realists to the globalists on the necessity for China *to be involved* in international institutions—although there is disagreement among these groups over *how* and *where* it should participate. Only the Nativists reject international cooperation. Some scholars believe that China should still essentially benefit from and "free-ride" on international institutions (keeping a low profile, as Deng Xiaoping suggested). This cohort asks, "What can international institutions do for China?" The "Globalists" instead ask, "What can China do for international institutions?" In between, there are those who believe that international institutions and international commitments require selective involvement.

Finally, the Globalists also show a predilection for soft power. They argue that China has much to contribute to international norms from its traditional culture and philosophy. Men Honghua of the Central Party School, the "dean" of soft power studies in China, argues that four key Confucian and Mencian values are particularly pertinent: 和 (peace and harmony), 德 (morality), 礼 (ritual of proper conduct), and 仁 (benevolence).[89] This is discussed at length in Chapter 6.

Perspectives on China's Conflicted International Identities

This is the spectrum of opinion in China today regarding China's international identity and global roles. The fact that it has such a broad spectrum of opinion says much about the identities that are competing with each other in IR discourse. On this basis, I argue that China possesses *multiple* international identities and is a conflicted country in its international persona.

When the spectrum of opinion described in this chapter is considered in its totality, it is clear that China's international identity is not fixed. It remains contentious and under debate, and it is fluid rather than static. Recognizing this, I see that the center of gravity on the spectrum does not lie in the middle or toward the Globalist end of the spectrum; rather, it resides down toward the left end, anchored on the Realists but with a strong pull from the Nativists and weaker influence from the Major Powers and Global South schools. The People's Liberation Army is a core constituency of the Realist School. Government officials in the Foreign Ministry and Central Committee Foreign Affairs Office are pragmatically centered between these two schools (Major Powers and Global South), but they must respond to Nativist and Realist voices in society, the military, and the Communist Party. The assertive behavior the world saw from China during 2009–10—when Beijing irritated almost all of its neighbors, the United States, and the European Union—is evidence of an increasingly tough but narrowly self-interested nation seeking to maximize its own comprehensive power and throw its weight around. This behavior owes itself in part to the prevalence of these institutional actors and the dominance of the Realist school.

China's intense discourse on the nation's international roles will continue to evolve. As it does so, it is likely to become more diverse and also possibly more polarized, as views may harden. Certainly, an incident or crisis could also shape the debate—if a Chinese embassy is seized, Chinese workers abroad are killed in large numbers, or a Chinese naval vessel is attacked. But for the foreseeable future we anticipate a multiplicity of voices and policy advocates—which will sustain China's multidimensional and omnidirectional foreign policy.

3

China's Global Diplomatic Presence

China is a civilization pretending to be a state.

—LUCIAN PYE, 1990[1]

A prosperous and stable China will not be a threat to any country. It will only be a positive force for world peace.

—VICE PRESIDENT XI JINPING, 2012[2]

China's diplomacy cannot be labeled simply as "soft" or "hard line".... We Chinese believe in combining firmness and flexibility.... This means we must know when to fight, when to cooperate, and when to avoid direct confrontation.

—ASSISTANT FOREIGN MINISTER LE YUCHENG, 2011[3]

CHINA'S DIPLOMACY HAS TRULY gone global. Over the past forty years China has traveled a path from a nation isolated from the international community to one integrated into it. Today the People's Republic enjoys diplomatic relations with 175 countries, is a member of more than 150 international organizations, and is party to more than 300 multilateral treaties.

Despite integration into the international community, the diplomatic sphere is another realm where China's position as a *partial power* is apparent. On the one hand, it enjoys the trappings of being a major world power: being a permanent member of the UN Security Council, a member of the G-20, a participant in all major international summits, etc. On the other hand, with the possible exception of its central role in the Six Party Talks process on North Korea, Chinese officials remain remarkably reactive and passive in these venues. China does not lead.

It is not actively involved in trying to solve *any* major global problem. It does not shape international diplomacy, drive other nations' policies, forge global consensus, or solve problems.

Thus, China is not really *influencing* world affairs—the measure of a true global power. Real superpowers shape events and produce outcomes. By contrast, China repeatedly takes a low-key, backseat approach in its diplomacy. It meticulously negotiates international documents, but usually to strip out clauses it disagrees with philosophically and to protect its own narrow national interests on issues like Taiwan, Tibet, and human rights. In many of its official statements on international issues, Beijing adopts anodyne language that lacks substantive meaning and credibility. Even in the Six Party Talks, Beijing has been quite passive in its role—facilitating but not leading—and it has not produced a positive outcome. Quite the contrary: North Korea has *grown* its nuclear arsenal and engaged in *more* threatening and provocative behavior precisely during the period when China was supposed to be playing the central role to bring about resolution of the issue. When one examines a number of other recent international challenges or crises—Sudan, Iran, Iraq, Syria, Libya, Afghanistan, Somalia—an aloof and unhelpful China is also evident. On such issues that concern the international community and require multilateral action, China prefers to remain on the sidelines. Two exceptions to this rule are China's contributions to UN peacekeeping operations and the antipiracy naval operations in the Gulf of Aden. We will examine China's multilateral diplomacy on "global governance" issues more carefully in the next chapter.

On the other hand, China's bilateral diplomacy is extremely active. As such, I find China to be an international *actor*, but not an international diplomatic *power*. There is a curious incongruity in China's diplomacy: it seems much more interested in protecting its own narrow national interests than in bringing other nations along to a common position. As is discussed below, Beijing also places priority on the *form* rather than the *substance* of diplomacy. Another anomaly is that Beijing likes to argue that its foreign policy has always been both principled and consistent, but in fact it has been very fluid and often fluctuant.

Before we survey the current state of China's diplomacy, it is useful to briefly review this checkered history. Following that survey, the remainder of the chapter is divided into two broad sections, the inputs into and the outputs from China's diplomacy.

Strategic Maneuvering

Over the past six decades the diplomacy of the People's Republic of China has passed through roughly ten distinct phases. The only pattern that was constant during most of this history was Beijing's consistent maneuvering to offset its perceived threats and enhance national strength.

From 1949 to 1957 China was largely isolated, caught in the tight embrace of the former Soviet Union and the polarizing grip of the Cold War world. Only eighteen nations had diplomatically recognized the new regime by the end of 1950. It was soon embroiled in a costly hot war in Korea against the United States and UN forces. Following the armistice in 1953, Beijing sought to gain some diplomatic breathing room during its "Bandung phase" (1954–1957), when it tried to cultivate what Mao termed the "intermediate zone" in the developing world ("intermediate" between the two superpowers). The period was also punctuated by a tense crisis in the Taiwan Strait.

This gave way during 1958–1965 to increased tensions with the Soviet Union and China's belligerence elsewhere. Simmering problems between Moscow and Beijing ruptured openly in 1959–60, and a full split between the communist giants ensued in 1962. At the same time, China launched a punitive border war against India, confronted the United States in Vietnam, and intimidated Taiwan (causing a second Taiwan Straits crisis). Meanwhile, in 1964 Mao's defense minister, Lin Biao, published *Long Live the Victory of People's War!*, a manifesto advocating global revolution and Chinese support for "liberation movements" worldwide. As a revolutionary power, during this period Beijing ramped up its supplies of arms and training for insurgencies around the globe. Given that China now confronted both superpowers as dual adversaries, it prepared for nuclear attack from one or the other (or both) by initiating a "Third Front" strategy to move the nation's industrial base deep into the interior of the country.

From 1966 to 1970, China recoiled again, entering an isolationist phase as the nation erupted in the xenophobic and radical Cultural

Revolution. This phase was nicely captured in Richard Nixon's 1967 depiction of "Communist China" as "living in angry isolation." All ambassadors except one (Huang Hua in Egypt) were recalled from abroad. The Foreign Ministry itself was occupied by Red Guards, which also laid siege to foreign embassies in Beijing. While suspending normal diplomatic relations with other states, Beijing stepped up its material and rhetorical support for communist insurgent movements across the developing world. Sino-Soviet animosities deepened and tensions flared, erupting into a brief border conflict in March 1969. We now know that Soviet leaders were seriously planning a "surgical" strike on Chinese nuclear facilities at the time. The direct threat from Moscow, coupled with the Soviet invasion of Czechoslovakia and proclamation of the "Brezhnev Doctrine" in 1968 (justifying intervention into socialist countries), made even Mao realize the severity and danger of China's international isolation and escalating Sino-Soviet tensions.

This led Mao to begin winding down the Cultural Revolution domestically while contemplating strategic initiatives to improve China's security externally. From 1971 to 1978, a fourth phase evolved in Chinese diplomacy. This period was characterized by a strategic opening to the United States, coupled with the PRC's admission to the United Nations and normalization of diplomatic relations with a number of Western and Asian countries. Thus commenced China's formal integration into the international system and community of nations, from which it had been estranged over the previous two decades. These diplomatic openings not only offered China the fruit of normal commercial and cultural ties with other countries, but the strategic tilt to the West bolstered Beijing's confidence and security in the face of continuing hostilities with the Soviet Union.

From Beijing's perspective, these hostilities intensified in 1978 with the Soviet invasion of Afghanistan, Vietnam's invasion of Cambodia, and the signing of a mutual security pact between Moscow and Hanoi. The noose of Moscow's encirclement of China was tightening. Drastic action was needed. So, from 1979 to 1982, Deng Xiaoping and the reformist group that succeeded Mao and ousted his radical disciples (the Gang of Four) upped the counterpressure on Moscow. First, Deng consummated full normalization of diplomatic relations and engineered a tight alignment with the United States. He launched a punitive attack on Vietnam in February 1979 (with American foreknowledge). He then strengthened ties with Thailand and support for the Khmer Rouge in Cambodia. He also improved relations with other Southeast Asian states. And he stepped up Chinese aid to rebel groups in Africa to counter those supported by the Soviet Union and Cuba. All these moves were part of a global strategic effort to put Moscow on the defensive.[4]

By 1982, though, it was time for another tilt (which would last until 1989). At the Twelfth Congress of the Chinese Communist Party, it was announced that China would now pursue an "independent foreign policy" (独立外交). This was code for gaining greater equidistance between the two superpowers—which, in turn, required drawing relatively away from Washington while beginning some modicum of ties with Moscow (which had been completely frozen for twenty years). Many in the Chinese leadership were then of the view that Deng had drawn China too close to the United States and this was compromising China's cherished autonomy. Deng also deemed that Moscow was now so strategically overstretched internationally and economically stressed domestically that the imminent Soviet grab for "global hegemony" and "inevitability of world war" had diminished. The following year, when I was a student at Peking University, I witnessed the first signs of a new thaw with the Soviet Union: Russian students returned for the first time since 1960, and the head of the Soviet aid mission to China during the 1950s (Vice Premier Ivan Arkipov) became the highest-ranking Soviet official to visit China since 1959.

Thus Beijing was recalibrating its foreign policy again—but it was a relative recalibration. Strategic ties with the United States remained strong but were now supplemented by bilateral exchanges in many fields (many of which had awaited full establishment of diplomatic relations in 1979). The real shift, though, came in Beijing's ties with Moscow. Beginning in 1982, Deng initiated a seven-year, step-by-step process of *rapprochement,* culminating in Mikhail Gorbachev's visit to Beijing in May 1989 in the midst of the unprecedented demonstrations in Tiananmen Square.

Having adjusted relations with the two superpowers, Chinese diplomacy during this period was driven by the necessities of economic reform. Relations with foreign countries were evaluated almost entirely on their potential contribution to China's modernization. Hence, developed countries in Western Europe, North America, and Asia became priorities, as they provided foreign direct investment (FDI), access to international financial institutions (IFIs) and loans, scientific knowledge and technology transfer, technical expertise and management know-how, educational training, and trade.

Thus, for the first time since its establishment forty years earlier, the People's Republic enjoyed normal and peaceful relations with all major powers and blocs in the world, had a secure periphery and beneficial relations with its neighbors, and reaped the benefits of membership in international institutions. It was no accident that these external factors contributed to an unprecedented boom in China's domestic development.

But this unprecedented positive situation unraveled literally overnight—the night of June 3–4, 1989, to be precise. The Chinese regime's military crackdown on students, demonstrators, and citizens in Beijing triggered the seventh period in Chinese diplomacy, which lasted from mid-1989 through 1997. This period was marked by two principal defining factors. The first was the fallout from the "June 4th Incident," and the second was the collapse of European communist party-states and the Soviet Union. The June 4 crackdown resulted in the worst crisis in Chinese diplomacy since the Cultural Revolution; China was again totally isolated from the West. But not all other nations reacted as severely. In fact, Asian countries (led by Singapore's Prime Minister Lee Kuan Yew) made a point of *not* isolating Beijing, instead reaching out in an effort to reintegrate China into the regional order. China's neighbors had previously had the experience of an isolated China being a disruptive China, so they threw Beijing a diplomatic lifeline. By the mid-1990s, the European Union had come to the same conclusion and renormalized its ties. By the second Clinton administration (1997–2001), the United States too had concluded that isolation of China was unsustainable and unproductive. Thus, China's international isolation and stigmatization was gradually lifted. Yet, in the midst of this process, the worst occurred: most of the communist world came crashing down before Beijing's eyes. But Beijing didn't blink diplomatically. As traumatized and concerned as it was over the implosion of the East European, Mongolian, and Soviet regimes, China did not miss a beat in diplomatically recognizing the new successor states. As I have written elsewhere, the Chinese regime also undertook a prolonged postmortem assessment of the causes of their collapse, with an eye to learning lessons to avoid a similar fate.[5] One lesson (re)learned was the importance of economic growth. After three years of stagnation following June 4, 1989, elder leader Deng Xiaoping reignited economic reforms with his famous "Southern Sojourn" of 1992. Thereafter, to this day, China's economy has been on a tear.

From 1998 to 2008, China practiced omnidirectional diplomacy. During this decade, under the successive leaderships of Jiang Zemin and then Hu Jintao, China's diplomacy branched out and truly went global. Beijing maintained stable relations with the two major powers, Russia and the United States. After a heated internal debate in 1997 over foreign policy priorities,[6] it prioritized strengthening relations with its Asian neighbors and engineered a ten-year run of ever-improving ties all around its periphery.[7] Europe, Africa, Central Asia, and Latin America similarly enjoyed new diplomatic attention from Beijing. Ties across the Taiwan Strait also improved markedly. This was an excellent and effective period in Chinese diplomacy. But (just as with the positive period during the 1980s) it was not to last.

Beginning in mid-2009 and lasting through the end of 2010, Beijing returned to a more combative stance on the regional and world stage. This manifested itself in sharp rhetoric, policy disagreements, and confrontations bilaterally and multilaterally. Viewed from inside China, where I lived during this period, the catalysts seemed to be a combination of acerbic Chinese nationalism, hubris over the Western financial crisis and its own economic success, the domestic politics of an insecure regime facing rising domestic social unrest, and territorial disputes with its neighbors. In relatively short order China managed to pick fights and irritate its relations with South Korea, Japan, Vietnam, India, ASEAN, the EU, and the United States. Even ties with some African and Latin countries began to reveal new tensions. In multilateral meetings such as the Copenhagen Climate Change Conference, Beijing dug in its heels and thwarted a global agreement on capping greenhouse gas emissions. It was not as if the Chinese government systematically set out to strain its relations with so many countries, as each instance had its own catalyst (or set of them). But there was a cumulative (negative) effect on China's global diplomatic image. As a result, these were the worst years in Chinese diplomacy since 1989–1992.[8]

Yet, as in the past, China showed a capacity for diplomatic recalibration. The years 2011–12 mark the beginning of the tenth period in PRC diplomacy to date. During this period, we witnessed China attempting to mend frayed ties with all of these states. However, the attempt did not produce the intended result for three reasons. First, each of those countries viewed China with a new wariness as a result of its 2009–10 assertiveness and arrogance combined with their historical fears of a regionally dominant China. Second, in 2011–12 China continued to press its maritime claims in the East and South China Seas, thus exacerbating already acute diplomatic sensitivities with its neighbors. Relations with the United States also revealed new frictions and growing strategic distrust. China-Europe ties stabilized somewhat, but underlying discord remains. China's energy-driven diplomacy in the Middle East, Africa, and Latin America began to produce further strains in Chinese diplomacy. Thus, although Beijing sought to return its diplomatic relations to a modicum of normalcy after 2009–10, not far beneath the surface China's global diplomacy reveals many stresses and strains.

This abbreviated periodization of China's diplomacy over the past six-plus decades reveals several patterns and practices that should be borne in mind as we examine in more detail the current state and future of China's global diplomacy. First, China has had an enduring sense of insecurity and periodic isolation. This resulted in repeated tactical alignments and diplomatic adjustments to try to bolster national security. This insecurity was particularly acute with adjacent countries, given China's traditional sensitivities about its borderlands and territorial integrity. Second, domestic politics frequently affected foreign affairs (particularly under Mao), but after Mao the foreign policy process became much more institutionalized. Third, it took China a long time to become accepted by the international community and integrated into the international system, although it continues to exhibit discomfort with it (see Chapter 4). Fourth, China's relations with many of its neighbors and major powers have endured cycles of estrangement, antagonism, ambivalence, and normalcy—with the cycle often repeating itself. Fifth, Chinese perceptions of the world order have been very fluid and contentious (see Chapter 2). Finally, consistency of policy has *not* been a characteristic of Chinese foreign policy, rhetorically or behaviorally. The only thing that has remained constant over time is a professed adherence to the "Five Principles of Peaceful Coexistence." Taken together, these factors and this past inconsistency in Chinese foreign policy should be kept in mind when considering the present and future.

The Inputs to China's Diplomacy

In order to understand China's foreign policy today, one must begin by examining drivers that collectively contribute to shaping China's diplomacy. One cannot understand the output of China's foreign relations, discussed in the subsequent section of this chapter, without an appreciation of the shaping forces. Every analyst has his or her own sense of such factors, but I find four to be particularly pertinent.

The Imperatives of History

A separate book could be (and has been) written about the subcategory of historical imperatives alone. All nations are shaped by their history, but few more so than China. As British scholar William F. Jenner noted, China lives under a "tyranny of history."[9] Thus, there is no shortage of attempts to draw on China's past for explaining and predicting its future foreign relations. Each has its own emphasis, although many concur. Earlier scholars such as Mark Mancall, John King Fairbank, Morris Rossabi, and Warren Cohen did much to try to link Chinese historical to contemporary "foreign relations."[10] More recently, David Kang has sought to portray the future Asian order as a repeat of the past: anchored on a resurgent Sinocentric system.[11] There exist many more scholarly efforts to explore imperial China's foreign relations.[12] One interesting recent effort is a compendium by a group of scholars who attempt to explore the tendency toward asymmetrical hierarchies in traditional China's regional relationships and how this legacy of China's inability to deal with others as equals has an impact on the present.[13] In my view, a number of traditions are notable.

Historically, China has been acutely sensitive to its border security (particularly from the northern land and eastern maritime regions); thus the imperative of maintaining *territorial* integrity.

China has long possessed a sense of cultural centrality, greatness, and superiority ("Sinocentrism"), and thus the imperative of maintaining its *cultural* integrity. As a result, it is hypersensitive to linkage of internal disorder inviting (it is believed) external pressure (内乱外患). Externally, China's preference has always been for a regional hierarchy of asymmetrical interstate relations centered on itself, and the practices of the "Sinicization" of neighbors to cooperate with the "tribute system" of relations. China has traditionally had difficult relationships with most of its neighbors—but particularly with Russia, Japan, and Vietnam. With regard to the West, China has long demonstrated an ambivalence about, but essential willingness for, borrowing ideas and technologies—symbolized by the classic dictum "Chinese learning for essence, Western learning for application" (中学为体, 西学为用). Chinese traditions of statecraft include constantly shifting tactical alignments, balance of power, avoidance of dependency and manipulation while maintaining autonomy and maneuverability, personalization of external relationships, a propensity toward militarily punitive actions against neighbors and escalating patterns of conflict (mis)management, and use of propaganda and myths to legitimize Chinese identity. Over time, there has been an obsession with maintaining China's status, ritualistic practices, and saving "face" (面子) in dealing with foreigners—so as to legitimate Chinese leaders in the eyes of their own people. Finally, intense nationalism—often negative, xenophobic, and directed against the foreign "other"—frequently characterized modern China's interactions with the world.

All of these traditional features of China's external interactions continue to resonate today. They may not be readily apparent at all times, but they certainly exist in Chinese minds, experience, and practices.

Diplomacy in Service of Economic Development

Ever since the late Qing dynasty's Self-Strengthening Movement (自强运动) of 1861–1895, there has been a tradition that Chinese diplomacy should serve the overriding goal of economic and national development. This was less the case during the republican period (1911–1949), but very much so during the People's Republic. Mao's tilt toward the Soviet Union in the 1950s was highly motivated by the need for Soviet economic assistance. Then Mao sent the nation through a decade of convulsive campaigns, many of which were aimed at economic transformation and modernization, but after the proclamation of the "Four Modernizations" program in 1973 and particularly following the "reform and opening" policies announced in 1978–79 economic development became the paramount national goal. Although Mao's opening to the United States, Japan, and Western Europe at that time was immediately motivated by national security concerns (vis-à-vis the Soviet Union), gaining access to Western technology and economic assistance was an important secondary goal.

Once Deng Xiaoping took command in 1978 and reoriented the national policy agenda singularly toward economic development, all spheres of state power were directed toward serving this end. Diplomacy and foreign policy were primary among them. Overriding emphasis was placed on those nations that could provide China with advanced technology, FDI, expertise, and export markets. This meant a two-decade orientation toward the West and the advanced economies of Asia. But as China's industrial growth boomed in the late 1990s and 2000s, its appetite for energy and raw materials grew accordingly and exponentially. This produced a shift in foreign policy toward natural resource supplier states in Central Asia, the Middle East, Africa, and Latin America. More recently (as is discussed at length in Chapter 5), these regions grew increasingly important to China's own outbound investment and as export markets. China's diplomacy went global because China's commerce had gone global. China's diplomacy in these regions is quite transparent in these respects: Chinese officials visit, contracts are signed, trade and investments follow.

Economic motivations are thus a distinguishing feature of Chinese foreign policy. China is not unique in this regard, but it is perhaps so in terms of the overriding priority attached to facilitating commercial opportunities. Other powers, such as the United States and Europe, do not devote diplomatic resources in pursuit of economic ends anywhere near the extent that China does, and they better balance national security and normative interests with the commercial dimension. For China, all instruments of the state are to serve the overriding goal of strengthening China's national economic power.

Diplomacy in Service of Politics

Another driver of Chinese diplomacy is to support the Chinese Communist Party (CCP) and keep the regime in power. Diplomacy is supposed to enhance the domestic political legitimacy of the party-state and the head of state.

The Party came to power by staking its legitimacy on overturning the old order in which Western imperialists and Japanese "devils" plundered, killed, exploited, humiliated, and carved up the Chinese nation. This period is described in Chinese Communist lore as the "century of shame and humiliation" (百年国耻). The CCP anchored its legitimacy on restoring the nation's territorial integrity and sovereignty, and its (inter)national dignity. This means that its relationships with Japan and the West are particularly sensitive, because they are so inextricably tied to the CCP's own identity and political legitimacy, and it means that China has a low tolerance for criticism from these countries. This is a kind of *defensive nationalism* in that China is defensive in the face of foreign demands. Sometimes it involves a kind of *retributive nationalism* where, implicitly or explicitly, China seeks retribution and compensation from foreigners for perceived past wrongs. The CCP's claim to political legitimacy also directly involves China's long-running feud with its rival regime on Taiwan; thus Beijing's global diplomacy is premised on a zero-sum, zero-tolerance policy of "one China." According to stock CCP propaganda, "no Chinese Communist Party, no New China" (没有中国共产党, 没有新中国). It is the CCP, according to this national mythology, that has delivered China out of its plundered and divided past and into its prosperous present and bright future.

Because of the claim to political legitimacy based on restoring China's dignity, Chinese diplomats and media go to extraordinary lengths to stage-manage its leaders' and officials' foreign interactions. They make great efforts to try to maximize the formality and grandeur in which China's leaders are received abroad and minimize (to zero) the possibility of their being embarrassed by public protests in their presence or openly aired disputes with foreign leaders. Why? Because the controlled visual images are broadcast back into China by state media and are intended for one purpose only: to give the impression that Chinese leaders are being received with respect and deference. Similarly, when foreign dignitaries come calling to Beijing, the reception—whether at the airport, Tiananmen Square, Great Hall of the People, Diaoyutai State Guest House, or Zhongnanhai leadership compound next to the Forbidden City—are all carefully scripted to show the foreigner following time-honored solicitous practices. For example, photographs of President Hu Jintao are always staged to show him standing in a statesmanlike welcoming pose to the foreign leader's left, right hand and arm outstretched, while the foreigner is forced into a less comfortable stance with the right hand awkwardly crossing the body to shake Hu's hand. As a result, the Chinese leader always appears relaxed and confident, whereas the foreigner often seems physically uncomfortable. When receiving a foreign leader, the Chinese official always waits behind closed doors until they are opened and the foreigner is ushered in and walks up to the stationary, standing Chinese official—a practice reminiscent of approaching the emperor's throne. Another ritual is sitting in a semicircle of large, overstuffed chairs in the Great Hall of the People, where the Chinese official commands a presence.

These traditional theatrical practices are what the American scholar Peter Hays Gries perceptively describes as "face diplomacy" (面子外交), i.e., China's obsession to maintain "face."[14] This is all about seeking status and confirming legitimacy through manipulation of symbols. Thus Chinese diplomacy is carefully orchestrated to show China's leaders in the best possible light, so that these images can be transmitted to the Chinese public and bolster their domestic image and legitimacy. Another form is "smile diplomacy" (微笑外交), a term used to describe China's more recent "charm offensive" to improve its international image and build soft power.

Face diplomacy is but one form of what can be described as *affirmative nationalism*. It seeks to affirm China's status as a respected nation state. This is very much at the heart of the national narrative and diplomacy that emphasizes China's five thousand years of civilization. This was on display at the 2008 Olympic Games and is at the heart of China's current push for soft power. It is a rather positive form of Chinese nationalism. On occasion, however, the world witnesses more negative manifestations of Chinese political culture and nationalism. Sometimes there are targeted outbursts of *populist nationalism*, venting public rage at certain foreign countries (usually Japan or the United States). Sometimes this is coupled with *assertive nationalism*, whereby China issues demands against foreign governments or threatens coercive action (again, Japan and the United States are examples, but also some European states). This usually also involves demonization of the foreign party by the Chinese media. Then there is what can be described as *defensive nationalism* and *retributive nationalism* (described above), whereby China displays a certain sense of entitlement growing out of its historical identity of victimization.

All of these types of nationalism are on display in current Chinese diplomacy. But, as was described in the previous chapter, it is primarily the more assertive, populist, and retributive forms that emerge out of the current domestic discourse on China's global identities. This means that however moderate or pragmatic the government seeks to be in its diplomacy, there are powerful domestic forces and voices that call for a more muscular foreign policy. Chinese Foreign Ministry officials now frequently claim that they are under significant pressure from the public, and it is true. Some Foreign Ministry officials have reported receiving packages of calcium tablets from the public—meant to strengthen their spine against foreign pressures.

Chinese diplomacy also seeks to short-circuit any foreign actions that touch raw domestic political nerves—particularly concerning Tibet, Taiwan, religion, and political dissent. The spiritual Falun Gong movement is another example. Chinese diplomats are neuralgic about these issues and go to extraordinary lengths to suppress *any* actions by foreign governments (and nongovernmental actors) that support the Dalai Lama or criticize China's suppression of Tibetans, Taiwanese independence, Christian proselytizers, Falun Gong practitioners, or domestic dissidents and critics of the CCP. This might be described as "preemptive diplomacy." The neuralgia over these issues all arises out of the regime's own *insecurities* about its legitimacy and grip on power.

In these three ways, domestic Chinese politics and political culture shape external diplomacy. They produce an odd paradox: on one hand, China is extraordinarily proud and secure in its historical identity, but on the other hand it is extraordinarily thin-skinned and insecure toward certain foreigners because of its historical experiences. This is the *yin* and *yang* of Chinese diplomacy: extreme confidence and extreme insecurity.

Diplomacy in Service of Security

Every nation's diplomacy is meant to enhance its security. China may be no different, but because of its history (described above) it may be more sensitive to perceived security threats than most major powers. Moreover, China conceives of its security in more comprehensive terms than most nations. The very term for security, *anquan* (安全), translates as "complete tranquility"—a concept that says more about China's internal order than about external threats to security. In 2012, for example, the Chinese government's budget for internal security exceeded that of the military for external security ($111 billion vs. $107 billion).[15] For the Chinese, internal stability has always been *the* essence of security. This very much involves what they describe as cultural security (文化安全)—preserving Chinese cultural traditions from external contamination. It also involves social stability and maintaining public order. To suppress domestic insurrections has long been viewed as a legitimate act of statecraft throughout Chinese history (霸道), if they threatened dynastic rule; but the best way to maintain order has always been benevolent rule (王道). Proper leadership will ensure loyal followership. It has also long been thought in China that a strong state and cohesive leadership will help ensure (but not guarantee) domestic and external security.

Conversely, when leadership divisions become evident and the state is shown to be weak, this is seen as an open invitation for internal and external forces to try to take advantage of the situation for their own gain and usurp central rule. Thus, China is also acutely sensitive to what may be described as "political security" (政治安全). This was true in the late imperial period as eunuchs conspired within the court and rebels revolted outside the court. The republican period (1911–1949) was never politically stable, with perhaps the exception of the decade 1927–1937 following the Northern Expedition that suppressed and co-opted the warlords. Nor has the period of the People's Republic (since 1949) been particularly stable politically. The past twenty years since the tumult and open factionalism of 1989 have been the most stable of the six decades, but even this recent period was punctuated by elite maneuvering, occasional purges, and public dissent. The Chinese Communist Party has also had a longtime fear of political subversion from the West, which is termed "peaceful evolution" (和平演变)—the process of peacefully evolving the CCP-led political system into a Western-style state. For all these reasons—cultural, social, political, even economic—*internal* security has always figured foremost. As leading China scholar Susan Shirk astutely observed in her book *China: Fragile Superpower*, "Paranoia is the occupational disease of all authoritarian leaders no matter how serious the internal threats they actually face. The Chinese suffer from a particularly acute form of this disease because of their Tiananmen trauma, the other regimes they have watched collapse, and the dramatic changes in Chinese society that surround them.... Paradoxically, the fears of Communist autocrats make them hypersensitive to public attitudes."[16]

Given China's geographic location—it shares land borders with fourteen nations and (disputed) maritime boundaries with six others—and history of encroachment from the northern steppes and along the eastern maritime seaboard, external security has also long been a concern. As discussed earlier, China has a particular sensitivity about its border security and territorial integrity—and for good reason. Thus, external security for China begins right on its doorstep. More broadly, though, the People's Republic of China (PRC) was subject to geostrategic encirclement during the Cold War by both the United States and the Soviet Union. During the first three decades of the PRC, China fought more border wars and skirmishes than *any* country on earth. Although the past three decades have been more peaceful, and all but one land border (that with India) have been mutually demarcated,[17] volatile maritime disputes still exist in the East China Sea and South China Sea. As we saw in Chapter 2, this has led to a school of thought in China arguing that Chinese diplomacy should prioritize its periphery (周边外交) through "good neighbor diplomacy" (睦邻外交). We will see below how China undertook eleven years of substantial efforts (1997–2008) in regional Asian diplomacy aimed at pacifying the periphery and improving regional relationships—only to undo much of the hard work during a brief bout of verbal and behavioral diplomatic assertiveness during 2009–10.

As a result of these persistent internal and external security concerns over time, Chinese diplomacy has had the dual purpose of countering foreign threats to internal and external security. This is done bilaterally through a blizzard of diplomatic interactions with various states. No nation in the world receives as many visiting heads of state every year as does China, while the president, the premier, and the twenty-four politburo members regularly travel the globe. Multilaterally, China has sought to enhance security through institutions such as the Shanghai Cooperation Organization (SCO) and the ASEAN Regional Forum (ARF). China eschews entering into alliances with other nations, but it does enter into "strategic partnerships" that are meant to enhance mutual security and relations with other states.

The Foreign Policy Decision-Making Milieu

The institutional actors and process of foreign policy making in China have long been a puzzle for outside analysts. The proverbial "black box" of decision making in China is indeed opaque. Nonetheless, international scholars (and intelligence agencies) have learned a great deal about the system over the years. We now have full and fairly accurate knowledge of all the institutional *actors* in the system, though we still have only a sketchy sense of the *process* of decision making within or among institutions. Unfortunately, the Chinese system does not permit declassification of recent documents,[18] former officials do not write memoirs after retiring, and those still in office maintain tight discipline and secrecy. This makes it very difficult to pin down the actual process by which decisions are made and implemented in the foreign affairs system (外事系统). Things are even murkier in the national security (国家安全), intelligence (情报), and military (军事) systems. One recent Chinese study argues that the institutional dimension is only one of five principal influences on the Chinese foreign policy process, the other four being the international environment, China's constitution and law, ideology, and mass media and public opinion.[19] To be sure, these and other factors all impinge on the policy process—but, for our purposes, we are most interested in the bureaucratic actors.

Many detailed analyses have been published,[20] but here I summarize the essentials of the process as I understand it. My own sense of these actors has benefited to no small degree from interviews with key officials in the Chinese system.

One way to conceptualize the actors in the foreign policy process in China is in five concentric circles. The innermost circle includes the highest-level decision-making authorities. The second circle includes ministries (primarily the Ministry of Foreign Affairs, but others as well) and Central Committee departments that both make and implement decisions. The third ring includes intelligence agencies, research institutes (think tanks), policy advisory bodies, and universities. The fourth ring comprises provinces and municipalities, corporations, and other institutional actors outside of the central government bureaucracy. The outer ring is society, which expresses its views via the internet, blogs, newspapers, television, and other media. The five concentric circles are depicted in Figure 3.1.

Of these five concentric circles, foreign policy *decisions* are made by actors only in the two inner circles, whereas the outer three ones all try to *influence* these decisions. The exception to this rule is that corporations make commercial decisions that result in actions overseas, which have consequences for foreign policy, but they are not foreign policy decisions per se. Let us briefly discuss each.

FIGURE 3.1 Actors in the Foreign Policy Process in China.

The first sphere includes China's top leaders and the institutions in which they interact. This means the CCP Politburo and its Standing Committee, the Central Military Commission, the Foreign Affairs Leading Small Group, the National Security Leading Small Group, the External Propaganda Leading Small Group, the Taiwan Affairs Leading Small Group, other leading groups (e.g., Energy, Outbound Investment, Finance and Trade, Climate Change), the Secretariat of the Central Committee, the General Office of the Central Committee, the Policy Research Office of the Central Committee, the Foreign Affairs Office of the Central Committee, and the State Council Information Office.

In this top-level "inner sanctum," foreign policy and national security issues must compete with all other pressing affairs of state for the time and attention of the top leaders. One senior CCP Central Committee member privately opined that only 10–15 percent of Politburo leaders' time is spent on international affairs, and only some of them have responsibility for foreign policy matters.[21] The Politburo itself (currently 24 members) is reported to meet once per month on average, although its Standing Committee (政治局常委) of nine members usually meets weekly.[22] When either body considers or makes a foreign policy decision, it is usually at a general rather than specific level.[23] Once a decision (in any policy sphere) is made, it is transmitted down to the bureaucracy, usually via the Central Committee's General Office (中央办公厅) and occasionally by its Secretariat (秘书处) for implementation.

When the Politburo or its Standing Committee considers a foreign policy issue, it has usually been previously deliberated in the Foreign Affairs Leading Small Group (中央外事工作领导小组 or FALSG) or sometimes by the Policy Research Office of the Central Committee (中央政策研究室), which prepares briefings and policy option documents for the top leaders' consideration. Although the vast majority of its responsibility concerns domestic issues, the Policy Research Office does have some responsibility for international affairs,[24] and its director from 2002 to 2012 (Wang Huning) regularly traveled abroad as part of President Hu Jintao's entourage. But the FALSG is the primary nerve center of foreign policy making. It was established on June 10, 1958, directly under the Politburo and Secretariat. It ceased to function

(停止) during the Cultural Revolution but was revived (恢复) in 1981. Since 1993 it has been chaired by the Party leader (Jiang Zemin, Hu Jintao, and Xi Jinping) and is composed of the state councilor in charge of foreign affairs, minister and executive vice minister (Party secretary) of foreign affairs, minister of state security, minister of commerce, minister of defense, minister of the Central Committee International Department, and other ministerial level officials as necessary (e.g., minister of culture, minister of science and technology, minister of commerce, director of Xinhua News Agency, State Council Information Office). Chinese sources are contradictory about the exact role of the FALSG; according to one study it is the "highest level foreign policy decision making body" in China,[25] although another study contradictorily claims it is "not a decision making entity."[26]

In 2000 a National Security Leading Small Group (国家安全领导 小组 or NSLSG) was established. It is said to have exactly the same membership as (or slightly larger than) the FALSG,[27] which is an example of what the Chinese call "one organ with two signboards" (一个机构,两快牌子). But the NSLSG has a broader mandate to consider internal and external security; thus the Politburo member in charge of security issues and the minister of public security and minister of culture also participate.[28]

The FALSG and NSLSG are two of more than twenty such leading groups under the CCP Central Committee, while a greater number exist under the State Council (China's government apparatus),[29] each one of which sits atop a national bureaucracy organized around a single functional issue area. On occasion, temporary leading groups are established to deal with a crisis or short-term issue, such as the evacuation of thirty-six thousand Chinese nationals from Libya in 2011.[30] Leading groups are known in Chinese as "openings," or the "mouth" (口), between the bureaucracy and top leadership. Although very important bodies for deliberating and deciding policies, these leading groups follow their own meeting schedules. The chairman of the FALSG, State Councilor Dai Bingguo, used the term "irregular" (没有固定) when asked by the author to describe the frequency of its meetings.[31]

On a day-to-day basis (日常工作), it is the Foreign Affairs Office (FAO) of the Central Committee (中央外事办公厅) that oversees China's foreign policy for the national leadership. Not much is known publicly about this organ, but some Chinese publications and the author's interviews with FAO deputy directors shed some light on its operations.[32]

The FAO was originally established at the same time as the FALSG in 1958 but was dissolved by "executive order" in 1970, before being resurrected in 1982. After its reinstatement, the FAO was administratively switched under the State Council, until it reverted to the Central Committee in 1998. One study notes six functions of the FAO: to carry out investigations and research, and raise (foreign) policy suggestions; to make and revise documents and laws related to foreign affairs work on the national, provincial, and municipal levels; to be responsible for overseeing organizations involved in foreign propaganda work (对外宣传工作)[33]; to organize meetings and prepare documents for the FALSG, and ensure implementation of decisions made at the meetings; to issue instructions to central Party, State Council, provincial, autonomous region, and municipal-level organs concerning foreign affairs; and to arrange the (foreign) travel and activities of Central Committee and State Council leaders.[34] Today, the FAO has a small staff of only about thirty people, most seconded from other ministries and the People's Liberation Army, and is the staff office for *both* the FALSG and the NSLSG. According to Deputy Director Qiu Yuanping, in 2008 the staff was divided into four sections: comprehensive (综合), strategic (战略), contingency planning (天占星), and macro management (宏观管理) work. Previous publications indicate it has four sections: secretarial (秘书组), comprehensive (综合组), regional (地区组), and external propaganda (对外宣传组). The FAO's duties were described by deputy directors Qiu Yuanping and Du Qiwen as "inter-agency consultation, coordination, and macro management." Deputy Director Du claimed, "Most of our work is at the macro level and we deal with overarching and strategic issues. Day-to-day decision making is *not* our job—we seldom get involved in this. We are an executive body (办事机构) with no decision making responsibility—which is vested in the CCP central leadership."[35] One way the FAO performs a coordination function is the reported weekly meeting that Dai Bingguo and the FAO convene with "representatives of all ministries" involved in foreign policy (e.g., those actors in the second sphere), usually at the vice ministerial level but sometimes with ministers, to share information on their current and future foreign exchanges.[36]

The second sphere includes the International Department of the Central Committee, the Ministry of Foreign Affairs, Ministry of Commerce, Ministry of Culture, Ministry of Science and Technology, Ministry of State Security, Ministry of Defense, Ministry of Finance, National Development and Reform Commission (NDRC), State Council Information Office, Xinhua News Agency, and People's Bank of China.

Of these ministries and ministerial-level agencies, clearly the most important is the Ministry of Foreign Affairs (MFA). Despite its authority being diminished and diluted over the past decade, the MFA still remains *the principal* organ for both formulating and implementing China's foreign policy. This being the case, the MFA must now contend with, attempt to coordinate, and manage multifarious institutions and societal forces—to say nothing of foreign governments, international institutions, media, and other actors outside China. As Vice Foreign Minister Cui Tiankai observed in an interview with the author:

> Diplomacy is no longer the business of a few elite people. It is increasingly embedded in the public and public opinion. Even within the government, there are so many voices—the PLA, companies, ministries, scholars. This makes the process of decision making extremely complicated. This is very new and very challenging for the Foreign Ministry. China is now just like the U.S. in terms of the numbers of players in the process. This is an irreversible process. We cannot stop it. We must manage it.[37]

It is, however, important not to overstate the MFA's relative declining role. It remains the main interlocutor for all foreign governments and embassies in Beijing, and its own embassies around the world are still the principal conduit for official communications, meetings, exchanges, diplomacy, and oversight of all aspects of bilateral relations with foreign countries. The MFA goes on managing day-to-day relations with all foreign countries and *formulates* policy, as well as implementing it. The MFA's professional foreign service of approximately 4000 officers, posted at home and abroad,[38] exhibits commendable professionalism and sophistication and has earned the respect of diplomats around the world. It is not uncommon that Chinese ambassadors and senior embassy staff are fluent in the languages of the nations where they serve, and increasingly they demonstrate this skill in public interactions. Most MFA personnel have received some form of training in foreign universities (some in degree courses, some as visiting scholars), while those trained in China are graduates of the elite international affairs programs (China Foreign Affairs University, University of International Relations, Peking University, Renmin University, Tsinghua University, Nankai University, Fudan University, Beijing Foreign Studies University, and Shanghai Foreign Studies University). Interestingly, many in the top echelon of the MFA studied at the London School of Economics and Political Science during the mid-1970s, notably Minister Yang Jiechi, Vice Minister Zhang Zhijun, Ambassador to the United States and former Ambassador to the United Nations Zhang Yesui, former Ambassador to the United States Zhou Wenzhong, and former Ambassador to the United Nations and currently Director of the State Council Hong Kong and Macao Affairs Office Wang Guangya.[39] After the normalization of U.S.-China relations in 1979, four of America's leading international affairs programs (Johns Hopkins University School of Advanced International Studies, Georgetown's Walsh School of Foreign Service, George Washington's Elliott School of International Affairs, and the Fletcher School of Law and Diplomacy at Tufts) all established regular training programs for MFA personnel. The Asia Foundation, Ford Foundation, and many other foreign foundations and governments have financially supported the training of Chinese diplomats and intelligence analysts abroad—although the Chinese government itself now covers most of these costs. Organizationally, the MFA currently has thirty departments,[40] responsible for carrying out nineteen core missions.[41] Although it must now grapple with an unprecedented number of domestic pressures as well as international issues and actors, while straining to keep pace with these challenges, it must also be credited with serving the nation with professionalism and advancing China's bilateral and multilateral relations abroad.

The other key actors in this second sphere all manage foreign exchanges within their functional areas. But the fact that all are now deeply engaged in foreign exchanges is testimony to China's embrace of globalization and integration into the international order.

The dramatically increased role of the Ministry of Culture and State Council Information Office is also testimony to China's new soft power push abroad (see Chapter 6).

Also of note is the important role played by the International Department of the CCP.[42] This Party organ has existed since before 1949 and was formerly charged with maintaining China's fraternal ties with other communist and socialist parties around the world, but in the wake of the Cold War the CCP/ID drastically broadened its mandate to interact with virtually all political parties abroad (except fascist and racist parties). Today it claims to maintain ties with more than 400 political parties in 140 countries, receives about 200 delegations, and dispatches about 100 abroad every year.[43] CCP/ID exchanges are an important prism through which the CCP and other organizations in China monitor the outside world and absorb lessons for China's own modernization. This kind of information gathering goes well beyond traditional intelligence collection (although, to be sure, the ID also engages in this activity). Through its interactions with political parties all over the world, the CCP/ID serves an important function as a kind of "early warning indicator" for identifying up-and-coming foreign politicians, before they attain national prominence and office. Having identified such rising stars, the CCP/ID brings them to China on all-expenses-paid visits—usually offering them their first exposure to China and trying to make the best possible impression on them. Another key dimension of this function has been to expose CCP leaders at the provincial and subprovincial levels to the outside world, again often for the first time. Many provincial Party secretaries, governors, mayors, and other leading local cadres are taken abroad on ID delegations every year. The CCP/ID has also played a key diplomatic role in certain instances, such as providing a liaison dialogue channel between the United States and North Korea.

The third ring includes the China Institutes of Contemporary International Relations (CICIR), China Institute of International Studies (CIIS), China Institute for International Strategic Studies (CIISS), China Foundation for International Strategic Studies (CFISS), Shanghai Institutes of International Studies (SIIS), PLA Academy of Military Sciences, National Defense University Institute of Strategic Studies, Chinese Academy of Social Sciences, Chinese Academy of

International Trade and Economic Cooperation, Central Party School Institute of Strategic Studies, China Reform Forum, China Center for International Economic Exchanges, other more minor research institutes (think tanks), and key universities (Peking University, Renmin University, Tsinghua University, China Foreign Affairs University, Beijing Foreign Studies University, University of International Relations, Fudan University, Shanghai International Studies University, East China Normal University, and others).[44]

All of these institutions contribute information, intelligence, and advice to the ministerial-level organizations in the second ring.[45] They do not make policy decisions, but rather advise decision makers. Some are directly attached to individual ministries (the CICIR to the Ministry of State Security, the China Institute of International Studies to the Ministry of Foreign Affairs, China Center for International Economic Exchanges to the State Council's National Development Reform Commission, China Academy of International Trade and Economic Cooperation to the Ministry of Commerce, the Academy of Military Sciences to the Central Military Commission, etc.), which affords direct access to the parent line ministries, but their analytical products also circulate throughout the central government to other ministries and organs outside their vertical "system" (系统). In addition, individuals in many of these institutions have their own personal connections (关系) to officials in the second ring (very rarely the first). This is particularly the case with university scholars, who have very episodic contact with policy makers. The Central Committee FAO and Ministry of Foreign Affairs Policy Planning Department are the organs most regularly engaged in tapping academic expertise.

The fourth concentric circle includes mainly those of China's large state-owned enterprises (SOEs) that operate abroad. Many of these are discussed in Chapter 5. They make their own investment decisions with foreign entities and send Chinese personnel abroad, usually without considering the foreign policy implications of their actions; nor do they consult with the Foreign Ministry or embassies. As Assistant Foreign Minister Ye Lucheng succinctly put it: "Sometimes we find companies doing things inconsistent with China's policies and interests. We tell them to stop, but they don't stop."[46] This sphere also involves provincial and municipal governments, which make autonomous decisions, sign agreements, and enter into a wide variety of exchanges with international entities. In this regard, it may be useful to distinguish between "foreign policy" (外交政策) and "foreign affairs" (外事). The former involves the central government and declaratory national policy (circles one and two), whereas the latter involves an incredibly broad range of interactions between Chinese citizens and entities with their foreign counterparts.

The outermost zone includes individuals in society. They make their voices and views on foreign policy issues known through various media. Experts from think tanks and universities (third circle) frequently voice their views on television, in newspaper articles, and on the internet and are quoted by journalists. Individual bloggers constantly vent on micro media (*weibo*) and the internet. All of these add to the cacophony of voices and actors trying to influence Chinese foreign policy.[47]

What these domestic actors add up to is an unprecedentedly complex foreign policy process. As Assistant Foreign Minister Ye Lucheng observed:

> Compared with the past, when foreign policy was made in a small circle in the *Zhongnanhai* [central headquarters of the Chinese Communist Party], now it is much more open and pluralized. Our authoritarian system is now democratic. We try to drive the car forward, but sometimes do not know the directions. Sometimes there are too many backseat drivers in the car, arguing over the map. All the actors are trying to influence policy making—provincial leaders, interest groups, oil companies, and others. This is a big challenge for the MFA. We try to listen to these segments of opinion, including cyber citizens (网民). This all makes our decision making process very complicated. The time pressures of external events add to these domestic pressures. Many of us feel very over-worked, and some are in the hospital.[48]

Yang Jiemian, president of the Shanghai Institutes of International Studies and the younger brother of the foreign minister, agrees with Ye: "We used to have a monolithic singular voice and system, but after 1996 our foreign policy discourse has become more diversified and assertive. There has been an eruption of views—as every ministry and locality wants to have its voice heard—and there has been a proliferation of actors."[49]

Many foreign scholars believe the Chinese foreign policy process and decision-making system to have a contradictory dual character: on the one hand, it is excessively stovepiped and vertically hierarchical, slow and inefficient, without integrating horizontal mechanisms, and on the other hand it is increasingly pluralized and chaotic. Linda Jakobson and Dean Knox describe this as "fractured authority."[50] In a study of the system in 2001, China scholar David M. Lampton posited that four features were changing the policy process: professionalization, pluralization, decentralization, and globalization.[51] The lack of a specified legal or regulatory basis for the policy-making process is a further factor (and handicap). As Brookings Institution visiting scholar Yun Sun observed in a 2012 study, "China has almost no legislation that governs the national security decision making process.... The complete lack of such legislation leaves the entire process unclear, uninstitutionalized, and unregulated."[52] Many foreign specialists argue that China needs a U.S. National Security Council type of system, in order to better centralize and coordinate the disparate actors. But Chinese officials disagree. The FAO's Du Qiwen disagrees: "China's foreign policy decision making process and mechanisms function well. It is an effective process that can provide in-time responses to pressing issues."[53] Vice Foreign Minister Cui Tiankai similarly argues:

> The foreign policy decision making system has evolved a lot. Institutionally it looks the same, but it has evolved and the procedures have changed. The very top leaders are very much in control of foreign policy, and they are very well informed. On the whole, the system is still working well. But the biggest challenge is for the Foreign Ministry. Previously the MFA would just give instructions and others would follow—this is no longer the case. Critics of the Foreign Ministry do not realize how much Chinese diplomacy has progressed over the past thirty years.[54]

One thing is certain: as China goes global, the pressures on the foreign policy system are only going to continue to increase. The system is likely to continue to strain to keep pace and manage these complexities. Leninist systems are inherently good at managing policy in a hierarchical vertical fashion, but foreign policy challenges and actors are requiring bureaucracies to cooperate horizontally. Somehow the Chinese policy process and decision-making system must adapt to better integrate the horizontal with the vertical.

The Outputs of China's Diplomacy

In recent years China's international diplomacy displayed various characteristics that parallel the seven schools of thought described in Chapter 2. On some occasions, it has been accommodating, pragmatic, confident, cooperative, constructive, decisive, friendly, proactive, and globally oriented. On others it has been assertive, truculent, difficult, combative, hypernationalistic, narrowly self-interested, uncooperative, reactive, and occasionally aggressive. Other times, Chinese diplomacy seems confused, contested, uncertain, passive, and risk-averse. Writing in 2003, the noted Chinese foreign policy scholar Alastair Iain Johnston of Harvard University argued that China has been a "status quo" rather than "revisionist" power; that is, it sought to integrate itself into the existing international system, to take advantage of the system but not overturn it.[55] Although this did seem to be the case at the time, subsequently Beijing has shown itself to be ever more discontent with the international system, and since 2009 it has sought to revise elements of that system. It is also more assertive in pressing other governments (and private-sector actors) to comply with its wishes. On occasion, Beijing bullies other countries and suspends exchanges (usually over the issues of Tibet, the Xinjiang Autonomous Region, human rights, or maritime disputes). Thus, there has been a kind of schizophrenic quality to Chinese diplomacy in recent years. Let us examine how this contradictory diplomacy has been manifest with a number of nations and regions.

As a major power itself, China places priority on managing its relations with other major powers: the United States, Russian Federation, and European Union. In each case, the relationship is exceedingly complex, and there exist many fine studies of all three. My intent is to present readers with a summary of the state of the recent relationships, their current condition, and the deeper dynamics that shape them.

China's Relations with the United States

The relationship between the United States and the PRC has rightly been described by officials on both sides as the most important bilateral relationship in the world. It is also the most complex one. These two powers are interconnected in innumerable ways: strategically, diplomatically, economically, socially, culturally, environmentally, regionally, internationally, educationally, and in many other domains.[56] By many measures, they are the world's two most important powers. The United States and China today have the world's two largest economies, in aggregate the two largest military budgets and navies, are the two largest consumers of energy and importers of oil in the world, are the two largest national emitters of greenhouse gasses and contributors to climate change, contribute the two largest numbers of Ph.D.s and patent applications in the world, and are the only two true global actors on the world stage today. They are one another's second-largest trading partners, the growth of American exports to China is the highest in the world (growing an impressive 542 percent from 2000 to 2011), the United States is the third largest source of foreign direct investment in China, and China is the largest foreign creditor of the United States. Every day about nine thousand people travel between the two countries, with tourism and business booming. During the 2011–12 academic year nearly 160,000 Chinese students studied in American universities, with about 20,000 Americans studying in China. There are 38 sister-province/state and 169 sister-city relationships binding localities together and offering opportunities for exchanges. There are three hundred million Chinese learning English and approximately two hundred thousand Americans learning Chinese. By these and other measures, the United States and China are inextricably tied together and exert the greatest impact on world affairs of any two nations today.

Despite the interdependencies, relations between Beijing and Washington have not been easy, and have grown more difficult in recent years. Competition is rising, cooperation is declining, and strategic mistrust is pervasive. Despite the many linkages between the two countries, many observers share the view that the U.S.-China relationship has increasingly tended toward competition in recent years. The two nations coexist, but in an uneasy and competitive manner—a condition I term *competitive coexistence*.[57] This is plainly evident in the economic, ideological, normative, security, and geopolitical realms. *Divergence* rather than *convergence* of interests, approaches, and policies seems to characterize the relationship. As Kenneth Lieberthal, Wang Jisi, and many other officials and informed observers have noted, there exists a significant deficit of strategic trust.[58]

On the other hand, there are attempts by both governments to cooperate and coordinate policies bilaterally through mechanisms such as the Strategic and Economic Dialogue (SAED) and multilaterally via various international institutions. But it must be said that these efforts are increasingly ephemeral and episodic, while the deeper competitive forces threaten to overwhelm the efforts for cooperation. Indeed, the bilateral mechanisms themselves seem to have changed from their original purpose of *forging cooperation* to forums for discussing differences and *managing competition*. In virtually every subject area of the two governments' sixty-plus dialogues, substantive differences and frictions are evident. What these dialogues amount to, more than ever, is *consultation*, where each side informs the other of its (differing) preferences and policies, rather than forging real cooperation or coordination. In international institutions, Washington and Beijing continue to find themselves on different sides of various global issues.

It seems that both sides are attempting to present a façade of cooperation and harmony in official exchanges, but under the surface of these dialogues—indeed, through the entire relationship—there exists deepening distrust. Sometimes the differences bubble to the surface and transcend the protocol of diplomacy, as occurred in Vice President Joe Biden's welcome of Vice President Xi Jinping in February 2012.[59] The two governments simply do not agree on how to approach many international problems, and powerful domestic interests in both countries limit the ability of both to manage bilateral problems. They sometimes seem subliminally locked in a titanic struggle over competing visions of world order: the United States seeks to expand the liberal order and the number of democratic states, whereas China is highly ambivalent about and often opposed to the liberal order and seeks to protect authoritarian regimes. Some observers, notably Princeton Professor G. John Ikenberry, argue that China has no real option other than to accept and accommodate itself to the global liberal order,[60] but as we see in the next chapter, China is evincing increasing discomfort with and opposition to the Western liberal order.

All of this is not good news for the future of U.S.-China relations, or the world. But it is the reality at present and likely into the near-to-medium-term future. The sphere of cooperation seems to be shrinking while the zone of competition is expanding. The two great nations are still some way from becoming adversaries, and it is difficult to conceive of how two societies and economies that are so interconnected could become adversarial. To some extent, the interconnectedness serves as a buffer against conflict, but the trend lines have definitely moved from the cooperative to the competitive direction. Some observers attribute this to China's growing self-confidence and hubris in the wake of the post-2008 global financial crisis, which coincided with rising American self-doubt and uncertainty about its economic health and global role, as it withdraws from wars in Iraq and Afghanistan. Others believe that China has simply been "lying low," practicing the *taoguang yanghui* strategy and are now convinced that the United States is inexorably declining and it is time for China to assert itself more forcefully on the world stage. Yet other knowledgeable observers argue that the two governments and leaderships simply do not trust each other's motives and believe the other side is out to undermine it—producing not only a deficit of strategic trust but a negative action-reaction dynamic where each side overinterprets and overreacts to the other's words and actions.[61]

Diplomatically, Washington and Beijing constantly confront a dizzying array of bilateral, regional, and global issues. The relationship has always operated at the first two of these levels, but what is *new* is the globalization of the relationship. As China goes global, so too does the Sino-American relationship.[62] China's growing presence on every continent in a variety of spheres is contributing to a redefinition of the U.S.-China relationship. The United States and China are bumping up against each other in parts of the planet (as well as space and cyberspace) where they never have before. Yet, to date, the two countries are really acting in *parallel* with each other around the world. That is, they pursue their interests and policies in an autonomous—rather than interactive—fashion with each other. To be sure, U.S. officials and intelligence agencies are keeping an eye on China's activities in the Western Hemisphere, and to a lesser extent in Africa and the Middle East, but Washington is not yet setting its priorities or policies in *reaction* to China. For its part, China is very conscious of America's strategic sensitivities; Beijing has gone out of its way not to irritate Washington or put itself in America's strategic headlights in Latin America or the Middle East (China's ties with Iran are perhaps the exception to this rule). Thus, a global Sino-American relationship now truly exists for the first time, but it is not (yet) an intrinsically strategically competitive relationship—as was the case during the Cold War between the United States and former Soviet Union. This may change over time as China's global footprint deepens, if it begins to build close ties to "rogue" regimes that are hostile to the United States, directly challenges long-standing U.S. alliances or partnerships, begins to establish a naval presence in or near the Persian Gulf, works to undermine U.S. regional security arrangements, or undercuts U.S. economic or energy interests.

Although not competing, neither are the two nations acting *in tandem* or working in a truly coordinated fashion with each other on global governance issues, or in any region of the world—thus dispelling any operative notion of a "G-2."[63] They issue high-sounding communiqués following summit meetings, proclaiming their cooperation on various global issues, but these quickly bog down after the summits adjourn and are not fully (or even partially) implemented.[64] When sensitive global issues arise, more and more the two governments find themselves on opposite sides or straining to find some middle ground that preserves the façade of cooperation. Libya, Syria, North Korea, and Iran are all recent cases in point. Not so long ago, Sudan and Myanmar offered additional examples. In each case, China demonstrated a profound allergy to the use of coercive measures to bring about a regime's compliance with international demands. When one examines a series of functional issues, one finds the same thing: with climate change, military transparency, reform of international institutions, intellectual property rights, human rights, anti-dumping measures, and even some aspects of counterterrorism.

When the U.S.-China relationship is viewed in the Asian regional context, one sees further evidence of geopolitical maneuvering and nascent rivalry. This has been particularly evident since China's 2009–10 regional "assertiveness"—during which China picked fights and irritated ties with Australia, ASEAN, India, Japan, the Philippines, South Korea, and Vietnam. Even China's ties with Myanmar and Mongolia began to exhibit frictions. In the wake of these negative experiences, all of these nations turned to Washington in a worried fashion. This resulted in the famous 2011 U.S. "pivot" to Asia, a major strategic reorientation by the United States that prioritized the Asia-Pacific in American global foreign, economic, and security policies. Beijing read this reorientation as confirmation of what it had long suspected U.S. policy to be: "containment." I use quotation marks because that is *not* American policy; nor could the United States "contain" China if it wanted to do so. China is not the Soviet Union, the international system is far more integrated and globalized than during the Cold War, and China is thoroughly integrated into that system. A country already integrated cannot be contained. Yet this is what Chinese officials, international relations experts, and netizens nearly unanimously believe American strategy and policy to be. The strengthening of U.S. alliances with its five Asian allies (Australia, Japan, South Korea, the Philippines, and Thailand) and strengthened defense and intelligence ties with several other Chinese neighbors (India, Indonesia, Malaysia, Mongolia, Singapore, Vietnam) further fuel Chinese strategic anxieties. The Chinese side also continues to be agitated by ongoing American arms sales to Taiwan, as well as intelligence surveillance along China's coastline within China's two-hundred-mile Exclusive Economic Zone. China also (rightfully) points out the limits placed on military-military exchanges by U.S. congressional legislation. China also remains strongly dissatisfied with the European Union's continuing arms embargo, which Beijing blames Washington for in part. For all these reasons, the strategic/security component of the relationship is more strained than ever.

Examining the bilateral economic dimension of U.S.-China relations, one finds evidence of both interdependence and sharp irritants. Bilateral trade in goods topped $503 billion in 2011, with the United States running a deficit of $295.4 billion.[65] Beneath these impressive numbers, however, lie a number of frictions. The United States is concerned over Chinese manipulation of their currency (RMB); Chinese intellectual property rights (IPR) theft; Chinese investments in sensitive national security sectors; Chinese industrial espionage and cyber hacking of American companies; Chinese "indigenous innovation" and industrial policies, government procurement, and export subsidies; and Chinese barriers to foreign investment, domestic distribution, and technical standards. For their part, China is concerned about U.S. restrictions on export of high-technology items; U.S. restrictions on Chinese investments in the United States; continuing U.S. national security and economic sanctions dating to 1989; and U.S. debt and fiscal policy, and the security of its federal bond holdings.

In all of these economic/commercial areas, the two sides find themselves at loggerheads. The longer the frictions persist and the deeper they go, the greater the corrosive impact on the overall Sino-American relationship. Taken together with the aforementioned strains in the diplomatic and security realms, Sino-American relations have taken a turn for the worse in recent years. To some extent, the interdependencies that the two nations share offset the growing fissures in the relationship; but the balance between cooperation and competition seems to have tipped in the direction of the latter. Behind the frictions lie large bureaucratic interests and enormous financial resources that are being invested in countering the other, which makes it increasingly difficult to rebalance the relationship to establish equilibrium and renewed cooperation. Nonetheless, despite this recent trajectory in the relationship, longtime observers of Sino-Americans know that there is constant ebb-and-flow, frequent frictions, and a kind of love-hate repetitive cycle in mutual images. Those who have followed the relationship for many years know that it is never as bad as it seems, or as good as it seems.

China's Relations with Russia

China-Russia relations have a long history. Although it is not necessary here to recapitulate, it is important for readers and analysts alike to keep it in mind when considering the recent past, present, and future relations between these two giant neighbors and Eurasian powers.

This historical experience was mixed, and not necessarily positive. In pre-modern times, both experienced invasions from the Central Asian steppes and Mongolia, and both peered across the Eurasian landmass at one another with strategic suspicion and no small degree of racism. In the modern era, direct contact dissipated the intrinsic suspicion to some extent. Both republican and then communist China sought to emulate and learn from the Soviet Union. However, Stalin's hands-off approach to the Chinese communist revolution and continual efforts to force the CCP into a united front government with the Nationalists produced suspicions on all sides. The strains this produced in CCP-Soviet relations continued to be evident as Stalin humiliated Mao during his February 1950 visit to Moscow, only to rescue the relationship with an eleventh-hour treaty and alliance. Immediately thereafter, things went from bad to worse as event after event—beginning with the Korean War and ending with the Great Leap Forward—contributed to the unraveling of the Sino-Soviet relationship. The subsequent estrangement lasted from 1960 to 1983, after which the six-year process of *rapprochement* culminated in Gorbachev's historic visit to Beijing in the midst of the 1989 Tiananmen demonstrations. Although Deng Xiaoping and the Chinese leadership were prepared to go ahead with normalizing ties for their own strategic reasons, they had already begun to look upon Gorbachev with great suspicion because of his internal *perestroika* and *glasnost*. Chinese suspicions were only fueled when Gorbachev refused to keep the communist dominoes from tumbling across Eastern Europe during the summer and autumn of 1989. The overthrow of these regimes came on the heels of the CCP's own near-death experience on June 4, 1989. Then, for the Chinese Communist Party, the unthinkable occurred in 1991: Gorbachev and the Soviet Communist Party (CPSU) were overthrown and the Soviet Union was dissolved.

This tectonic geopolitical shift had two ironic effects on China. The first, as I detailed in my book *China's Communist Party: Atrophy and Adaptation*, was to initiate an in-depth examination of the causes of the collapse of the Soviet Union and CPSU (and other collapsed communist party-states).[66] The Soviet Union's collapse was a deeply disturbing experience for the Chinese communists, but they tried to pragmatically draw lessons that would affect their own fate. The intensive and protracted postmortem lasted thirteen years, until 2004, when its conclusions and principal "lessons" were unveiled at the Fourth Plenary Session of the CCP's Seventeenth Central Committee.[67] The lessons drawn stimulated a series of measures—some reformist, some retrenching—that the CCP undertook thereafter as a means to sustaining its own longevity. The second effect was that, despite the CCP's traumatized state, Beijing pragmatically moved with dispatch to recognize the new Russian Federation government and all of the successor governments in the newly independent Eurasian republics. Of course, Russian President Boris Yeltsin, Ukraine's Leonid Kravchuk, Kazakhstan's Nursultin Nazarbayev, and other post-Soviet rulers were well known to the Chinese from their Soviet pasts.

After a hiatus and brief unease in Sino-Russian relations during 1991–92, as the dust was settling and the new Russian government was taking shape, Moscow and Beijing pragmatically decided to resume relations.[68] The Chinese invitation for Yeltsin's state visit to Beijing in December 1992 was a key step (ostensibly reciprocating Jiang Zemin's Moscow visit in May 1991 prior to the Soviet *denouement*). Yeltsin's visit was reciprocated by another Jiang Zemin presidential visit to Moscow in September 1994, which triggered subsequent annual summits between either premiers or presidents.

Throughout these 1990s exchanges,[69] the two sides signed a series of important bilateral agreements. The more important included a military cooperation pact (1993, renewed in 1998 and 2003); a "constructive partnership" agreement (1994), which morphed into China's first "comprehensive strategic partnership" (1996); an Agreement on Mutual Non-Aggression (1994); an agreement on mutual nuclear de-targeting and "no first use" (1994); agreements on a "zone of stability" together with three Central Asian states (this became the basis of the "Shanghai Five," which later morphed into the SCO); and a series of agreements on trade, energy development, culture, and scientific cooperation (1997). All of these agreements did much to institutionalize the new Sino-Russian relationship. The capstone of this process came in 2001 with the signing of a Treaty of Neighborliness and Friendly Cooperation. Although not an alliance (and both sides were quick to point out that it was not one), the treaty did contain two clauses typically associated with alliances.[70] Article 8 specifies that "The contracting parties shall not enter into any alliance or be a party to any bloc nor shall they embark on any such action, including the conclusion of such treaty with a third country which compromises the sovereignty, security and territorial integrity of the other contracting party." Article 9 pledges that "When a situation arises in which one of the contracting parties deems that peace is being threatened and undermined or its security interests are involved or when it is confronted with the threat of aggression, the contracting parties shall immediately hold contacts and consultations in order to eliminate such threats." The remainder of the 25-article treaty covers a wide range of political, societal, scientific, regional, border, and other elements. The treaty was an impressive document and set of bilateral commitments.

If there had been doubt about whether postcommunist Russia and still-communist China could work together, the treaty and more than fifty other bilateral agreements signed since 1991 put these doubts to rest. Only one important outstanding issue remained: the long-disputed border. After intensive negotiations, in June 2005 and July 2008 the two sides concluded twin agreements formally demarcating the 4300-kilometer border. Under the agreements, Russia returned to China 174 square kilometers of territory seized in a 1929 border skirmish.

Over this period Beijing and Moscow built a sound and strong relationship on many levels.[71] In 2009, on a visit to the Shanghai Expo, Russian President Dmitry Medvedev effused that Sino-Russian ties had reached their "highest point in history."[72]

Trade has grown from a negligible $5 billion during most of the 1990s to $83.5 billion in 2011. That year China surpassed Germany as Russia's largest trading partner. During President Vladimir Putin's June 2012 state visit to Beijing (his first after returning to the Russian presidency), the two sides set the goal of attaining $100 billion in bilateral trade by 2015 and $200 billion by 2020. As part of the expanding trade and economic cooperation, the two sides have particularly focused on building linkages between the Russian Far East (East Siberian) and China's northeast (东北) regions. A master plan for 205 "major cooperation projects" was concluded in 2010.[73] Energy cooperation also proceeds apace, especially following the 2009 completion of a thousand-kilometer oil pipeline linking the two. The pipeline was not without its problems during protracted negotiations, but its opening is a significant step forward in bilateral energy cooperation. The pipeline is part of a broader bilateral loan-for-oil deal consummated in February 2009 whereby Russia supplies China with 300 million tons of oil between 2011 and 2030 in exchange for a $25 billion loan from China.[74]

Military ties and defense cooperation have also been key components of the relationship.[75] After China found itself with no other sources of foreign arms and defense technology supplies in the wake of the 1989 U.S. sanctions and European arms embargoes, Russia came to Beijing's rescue. To be sure, Russia had its own interests in mind as it needed to keep its own arms industries on life support following the demise of the Soviet Union. Throughout the 1990s and 2000s, Moscow supplied China a wide variety of advanced arms and military technologies (these are detailed in Chapter 7) and assistance to China's space program. At its height, arms transfers to China accounted for 40 percent of Russia's worldwide sales, amounting to approximately $3 billion annually and $16 billion in total from 1991 to 2005. But after 2006, the sales and assistance began to drop off considerably, ranging between $700 million and $1 billion per annum (one-tenth of Russia's $10 billion in global sales in 2010). One Russian expert identified seven principal reasons for the precipitous decline.[76] First, many of the contracts and production cycles reached their planned conclusion, and follow-on agreements were not signed. Second, China's own defense industries had made significant progress—in no small part owing to Russian assistance—and could produce new model platforms and systems. Third, China's pirating of Russian defense technologies irritated Moscow. Fourth, Moscow's unwillingness to supply China with the latest equipment angered China (particularly as Russia continued to supply this equipment to India). Fifth, China is discontent with Moscow's unwillingness to transfer the means of production for weapons, instead relying on end-use items that make the Chinese military dependent on Russia for spare parts. Sixth, a significant body of opinion in Russia's military and strategic community was questioning whether it was in Russia's national interests to be arming China. These sentiments had long existed in Moscow, but following the collapse of the Soviet Union Russia's defense industries needed the market. Seventh, and finally, in the 2000s new export markets opened up for Russian arms, and

Moscow was no longer as dependent on the China market to keep its defense industrial sector afloat. Despite these constraints, in November 2010 the two announced a new, more limited, defense cooperation pact at the Fifth Strategic Security Dialogue.[77]

China and Russia also see eye-to-eye on a series of regional and global issues, and they have forged a geostrategic axis and voting bloc in the UN Security Council. The heart of this axis is anti-Americanism and anti-interventionism. Beijing and Moscow jointly vetoed Security Council resolutions on Syria in 2012 and regularly water down numerous U.S. diplomatic initiatives and sanctions on Iraq, North Korea, Sudan, and other sensitive international issues. What the two sides term "strategic coordination" has become a diplomatic headache for Washington. It runs deeper than tactical opposition to the United States and their mutual strategic desire to reduce America's preeminent role in world affairs; it is also philosophical. Both share strong opposition to coercion and the use of force in international affairs, and both cherish state sovereignty as the most basic principle of diplomacy.

Looking to the future of Sino-Russian relations, we can see different views emerging in both countries. Some Chinese are skeptical of Russia's importance for China. Says Professor Song Xinning of Renmin University, "Russia is a neighbor China has to deal with—not a global partner to rely on."[78] But most Chinese are bullish on Russia. Feng Yujun, one of the leading Russia analysts at CICIR, is of the view that "Russia is *the most important* country for China on all four dimensions of importance in China's diplomacy: neighboring countries, major powers, developing countries, and multilateral relations. Although Russia's power is weakening, we still think Russia is a major power with global influence and we have much in common."[79] Shi Zhe, a longtime Russia hand in the Chinese Foreign Ministry, is similarly optimistic. When I met Shi for lunch at the Chinese embassy in Moscow in 2010 (where I got food poisoning and fell ill), he observed that "Since the 1990s our relations have become more practical (事习的). We have institutionalized coordination mechanisms for a broad range of shared bilateral, regional, and global interests. We both think that we should maintain our independence, but at the same time coordinate internationally. We enjoy a good consensus and trust in our relationship."[80]

There is a more mixed assessment from Russians. Officials are predictably upbeat about the relationship. For example, Konstantin Vnoukov, the director of the Foreign Ministry's First Department (Asia), observed in an interview with the author:

> We see no elements of Chinese foreign policy as threatening to Russia's interests. We have no serious differences with China on the international scene and see China as playing a very positive and constructive role on international problems. For Russia, in some markets China is becoming a competitor, but we have a high level of cooperation. We do our best to pre-empt potential "fires" in our relations. There are more than fifty working groups to do this bilaterally, and the SCO is an excellent mechanism multilaterally.[81]

Russian China expert Vladimir (Sasha) Lukin also notes a number of commonalities that Russia and China share: "a common vision of the international structure and preference for a multipolar world; support for international law; sensitivity about interference in internal affairs; mutual support for the battle against separatism; cooperation on regional issues; a need for economic cooperation; a desire to change the existing international financial system; and the need for a stable common border."[82]

Academician Mikhail Titarenko, director of the Institute of the Far East in the Russian Academy of Sciences and Russia's leading Sinologist, is similarly optimistic. In a discussion we had in his office (decorated with many gifts from Asian institutions and awards received during the Soviet era), Dr. Titarenko praised numerous aspects of China's reforms, its role in the world, and the good state of Sino-Russian relations. But even he acknowledged that doubts about China remain in the Russian Duma and society: "Despite great progress in our relations, there still remains some distrust from the past in our society. Some Russians are not sure about China and whether they really seek a long-term partnership with us—or if it is just expedient and tactical."[83] Other Russian experts are more candid and skeptical. Vassily Mikheev, deputy director of the Institute of World Economics and Politics (IMEMO), observed:

> Anti-Chinese feelings are very strong [in Russia] and changing. There is a feeling that China wants to conquer the Russian Far East. In the past five to six years, these primitive anti-China sentiments are

being joined by new anti-China feelings based on a fear of economic threat. This new viewpoint joins with the racially biased anti-China feelings. There is also a growing sense that the SCO isn't good for Russia—this is Russia's "near abroad" and we need to check China in Central Asia. All told, China is turning into a competitor and is becoming a big headache.[84]

The flood of Chinese immigrants into the Russian Far East, but also increasingly into Russia's heartland, is a particularly sensitive issue for many Russians, triggering historic fears of the "yellow peril." But Konstantin Vnoukov of the Russian Foreign Ministry argues that since 2008 new controls have been put in place to stem the tide of immigration. When I met him in his cavernous ministry office in one of Stalin's neo-gothic "seven sisters" skyscrapers in Moscow, Vnoukov somewhat jokingly observed: "Russia is performing the role of blocking Chinese immigration into Europe. Russia blocked Genghis Khan and the Mongols from invading Europe—now we are doing the same with China."[85]

Professor Alexey Voskresensky, a leading China specialist and dean of the Moscow State Institute of International Affairs, noted when I met him in Moscow in 2009 that there was a "sophisticated, but underground, struggle and debate within Russian decision-making circles. There are those who see China as a rival and say we should be alert to the China threat. Others see China as an economic model."[86] Voskresensky's colleague Professor Dmitri Streltsov was more blunt: "Most Moscow policymakers think in the back of their minds of China as a potential threat. China is trying to manipulate us."[87] Deputy Dean Mikhail Troitskiy elaborated:

We see China pushing Russia to the forefront of opposition to the United States in the world and trying to use Russia for its anti-Americanism, while still trying to be the leader of the developing world. Beijing tells us: you have to stand up to the U.S.! We are also suspicious of China's actions in Central Asia and Africa. The debate that is beginning to go on here [in Moscow] is about how China is trying to subjugate Russia. Many see China as a rival and we should be alert to the potential China threat—especially in the Far East, where there are deep fears of falling into China's orbit.[88]

Sergey Rogov, director of the Institute of the USA and Canada in Moscow, agreed: "Everywhere we see China much more assertive internationally, and it may not coincide with our interests."[89]

Clearly, despite the rosy official relationship on the surface, there is a subterranean debate under way in Moscow concerning Russia's relations with China.[90] It is a useful reminder that these two great powers and large neighbors have a long history filled with suspicions and latent animosity. As Bobo Lo, a scholar of Russia-China relations, aptly describes it:

> The Russia-China relationship is neither an authoritarian alliance nor a genuine strategic partnership. It is a limited partnership sustained by the perception of mutual if asymmetrical gains, and the wisdom to underplay significant differences where they occur.... The question is how long this accommodation can last. The combination of tactical convenience, prophylaxis, thin substance and willful self-deception is hardly the stuff of long-term relationships. The time will come when the differences between Russia and China cannot be so easily fudged.[91]

Even though the generally good health of the China-Russia relationship today should be seen as positive and conducive to regional stability and security, historical memories and contemporary fears still cast a long shadow.

China's Relations with the European Union

Since the end of the Cold War, the China-Europe relationship has grown to be both intensive and extensive. It is anchored in commerce. Trade and investment have grown more than sixtyfold since 1978 to the astonishing point of Europe being China's number one global trading partner, although China ranks second for Europe. Total two-way trade reached €464.8 billion in 2011, with a rapidly growing trade surplus of €152 billion in China's favor.[92] Europe has also become the largest source of technology and equipment transfer to China, transferring a total of 22,855 "technological items" to China by June 2006.[93] This amounts to about half the total technology

China imports from abroad every year. Extensive scientific collaboration also takes place, including energy and space cooperation.[94]

In the field of education, there are now more Chinese students (more than 150,000 in 2011) studying in European institutions of higher education. Academics enjoy a range of interaction through various means, such as the China-EU Think Tank Roundtable Mechanism. Exchanges between a broad range of European political parties and the CCP's International Department take place regularly.[95] Altogether, more than three million Chinese visit Europe for tourism, business, or study every year.

From minimal official interaction, the diplomatic relationship is now extensive. This entails annual summits with the EU presidency, EU troika foreign ministers, and individually with the main member states. Thirty-two sectoral dialogues take place between the European Commission officials and Chinese ministries annually to discuss detailed areas of collaboration, while candidly discussing differences in areas such as human rights.[96] Similar interactions occur bilaterally between China and EU member states. The two sides also collaborate extensively on a range of international issues in the United Nations and other contexts. In 2003 the EU and China proclaimed a "comprehensive strategic partnership." In a May 2004 speech in Brussels, Chinese Premier Wen Jiabao defined the meaning of this partnership:

> It is a shared view of the two sides to work for a comprehensive strategic partnership. By "comprehensive," it means that the cooperation should be all-dimensional, wide-ranging and multi-layered. It covers economic, scientific, technological, political and cultural fields, contains both bilateral and multilateral levels, and is conducted by both governments and non-governmental groups. By "strategic," it means that the cooperation should be long-term and stable, bearing on the larger picture of China-EU relations. It transcends the differences in ideology and social systems, and is not subjected to the impact of individual events that occur from time to time. By "partnership," it means that the cooperation should be on equal footing, mutually beneficial and win-win.[97]

Beijing has also agreed to individual "strategic partnerships" with ten European states.

China has been a recipient as well of European Union overseas "cooperation assistance" (external aid), with the EU spending €250 million on such cooperation projects during the four-year period 2002–2006,[98] but there was a decline during 2007–2011 as a combination of factors impinged: Chinese government restrictions on funding for many NGO, media, civil society, and rule-of-law projects; the European sovereign debt crisis; and individual European states (notably Germany) deciding to zero out development assistance to China on the conclusion that it was no longer a needy "developing country." In January 2007, when European Commissioner for External Relations Benita Ferrero-Waldner visited Beijing to launch negotiations on a new comprehensive China-EU Partnership and Cooperation Agreement (PCA),[99] some further agreements were reached totaling €62.6 million in support of a Europe-China School of Law at Tsinghua University, the EU-China Project on the Protection of Intellectual Property, and the Europe-China Business Management Training Project. European foreign direct investment into China has also been substantial and has supplemented cooperation assistance—while (as is described at greater length in Chapter 5) Chinese investment has been flooding Europe since 2009.

The relationship has developed dramatically since establishment of formal relations in 1975, but the breadth and depth of relations today is even more astonishing and impressive when one considers that it is only since 1995 that it has really blossomed. Prior to that time the relationship was beholden to broader international forces—particularly the Cold War and Sino-Soviet antagonism. China-Europe relations were predominantly derivative from these broader factors. This all began to change, though, around 1995, when two events occurred: the EU dropped all sanctions (except military arms sales and defense technology transfers) dating from the June 4, 1989, incident in Beijing, and the European Commission unveiled the first of its several subsequent strategy documents and policy papers (known in Eurospeak as "Communications") on China.[100] The China strategy mapped out by the European Commission in the official documents between 1995 and 2006 offered a benign view of China's rise and identified a range of areas for collaboration. More broadly, a number of other factors contributed to the post-1995 surge in the relationship. The limiting effects of the

Cold War passed and the relationship could finally begin to develop on its own, free of the shadow and influence of the U.S.-Soviet rivalry. Importantly, there is hardly any Taiwan lobby in Europe (as there is in the United States) to influence the public and politicians, and there is no "Taiwan issue" between European governments and China, as all faithfully subscribe to the "One China Principle." Moreover, Europe has no military presence and few security interests in East Asia (unlike the United States), thus not causing security tensions with China. There exist great complementarities of commercial and economic interests. Taken together, these factors collectively influenced the Sino-European relationship beginning in the mid-1990s and contributed to its dramatic growth over the past decade.[101]

However, after a decade of rosy rhetoric and steadily improving ties, beginning around 2007 China-Europe relations entered a more complicated and difficult period. During this time, the relationship passed from the "honeymoon" into its "marriage" phase. Some disputes erupted, and both sides began to realize the complexities of the relationship, the fact that they do not see identically on many issues, and that outside factors and actors exerted an impact. Both the atmosphere and the substance of the relationship turned sour during 2007–2010, but both sides took steps to stabilize ties in 2011.

The arrival in office of German Chancellor Angela Merkel, French President Nicolas Sarkozy, and British Prime Minister David Cameron contributed to the changed atmosphere; they were all more skeptical of China than their predecessors. Thus, the change of governments among Europe's "Big Three" and admission of the "New Twelve" former communist Central European states into the EU was another factor in the hardening of Europe's China policy. The European public mood has also been affected by publicized incidents of Chinese industrial espionage and attempted hacking into the computer networks of the German Chancellor's Office and the British Foreign Office, as well as concerns over human rights in China (particularly Tibet). The awarding of the 2010 Nobel Peace Prize to the imprisoned dissident Liu Xiaobo symbolized Europe's sentiments about China's human rights situation. Criticism of China's government and human rights record has always been harsher among many of the new EU member states in Central Europe—particularly the Czech Republic, Poland, and

Baltic states—as they tend to view Beijing through the prism of their communist past and are also more sympathetic to secessionist forces in Taiwan, Tibet, and Xinjiang. China's behavior on global governance issues—notably climate change—did not live up to European hopes and expectations.[102] European corporations are also voicing their frustrations with China. A variety of discriminatory trade and investment practices plague European (and other) businesses in China, particularly the continuing widespread theft and pirating of intellectual property, as well as numerous market access barriers to China's financial services industries, distribution networks, and protected "strategic industries." China's reluctance to contribute to stabilizing the European sovereign debt crisis irritated some European leaders. Finally, for its part Beijing remains distressed by the EU's continuing arms embargo and failure to grant China Market Economy Status.

There were a variety of reasons for the bloom to have gone off the rose in the relationship and for the honeymoon to have been short-lived. This is reflected at the government and society levels. Public opinion polls regularly reveal China's reputation in Europe to be the lowest of anywhere in the world (see Chapter 1). There is a consensus across Europe today that the relationship with China is neither "strategic" nor a "partnership." In Beijing, there is a pervasive view that the EU remains disorganized in its foreign relations (even after the Lisbon Treaty) and is not a reliable partner in world affairs. With this perspective, Beijing has been ignoring Brussels to deal with individual member states, particularly the UK and Germany. The German-China commercial relationship has expanded dramatically in recent years, and Berlin is Beijing's partner of choice in Europe.[103] At the time of this writing (2012), German Chancellor Angela Merkel had made six official visits to China during her term in office.

The release in October 2006 of the European Commission's official Communication on China, and the accompanying policy paper on EU-China trade and investment, made explicit many of the concerns about China that had been bubbling beneath the surface in Europe.[104] In the Communication, for the first time in such a policy document, the European Commission made a number of requests of China: "open its markets and ensure fair market competition"; "reduce and eliminate trade and non-tariff barriers"; "level the [commercial] playing field"; "fully implement WTO obligations"; "better protect intellectual property rights"; "end forced technology transfers"; "stop granting prohibited subsidies"; "work on clean energy technologies"; "be a more active and responsible energy partner"; "ensure balance in science and technology cooperation"; "[recognize] the international responsibilities commensurate to its economic importance and role as a permanent member of the UN Security Council"; "better protect human rights"; "[ensure] more accountable government"; be more "results oriented with higher quality exchanges and concrete results" in the human rights dialogue; ratify the UN Covenant on Civil and Political Rights; enter into formal dialogue with the EU and "improve transparency" concerning aid policies in Africa; "maintain peace and stability in the Taiwan Strait"; improve "transparency on military expenditures and objectives"; "comply with all non-proliferation and disarmament treaties"; and "strengthen export controls of WMD-related materials."[105] This laundry list of requests gave the 2006 Communication a harder edge than any of its predecessors, but it also reflected the new sobriety in Europe concerning certain aspects of China's policies and behavior. The European Council ratified the Communication at its meeting on December 11, 2006, and produced its own 23-point list of observations and concerns about the relationship.[106]

The publication of these documents took China's government and Europe watchers by surprise. On the day the new Communication was released, I was in Brussels participating in a conference on China-Europe relations at the European Commission. I witnessed the look of shock on the faces of the Chinese participants as they read the newly minted document; their discomfort was palpable. Both the tone and the substance of the documents reflected a departure from the effusive rhetoric and lofty goals set forth in previous communications. China's Europe watchers were blindsided by the shift in European policy and tone; they had not seen it coming and no doubt feared the criticisms they would hear from government officials back in Beijing for not warning the government of the shift in EU policy. This led some notable Europe specialists in Beijing to accuse Brussels of adopting confrontational or "containment" policies similar to what they sometimes perceive from the United States. Privately, Chinese Foreign

Ministry officials apparently assured their official European counterparts that they "understood" European concerns and were not overly alarmed by the tone or the substance of the Communication. The Chinese decision to move ahead with negotiations on a new EU-China Partnership and Cooperation Agreement was perhaps indicative of the more pragmatic official reaction. Nonetheless, the EU documents did reflect a change in tone, substance, and approach to China from past precedent.

The official documents coincided with a spate of more critical assessments published by European think tanks; one, by the European Council on Foreign Relations, was particularly critical and attracted a good deal of attention in Europe and in China.[107] Premier Wen Jiabao personally denounced the report in an official meeting with high-level EU officials.

Subsequent to the changed tone and substance of the relations emanating from Brussels in late 2006, 2007–08 brought more difficulties. The most noteworthy was the ballooning EU trade deficit with China, which reached €169.6 billion in 2008—growing at the alarming rate of €15 million per hour (according to Peter Mandelson, who was the EU trade commissioner at the time). Then, in September 2007, just after she returned from a state visit to China, Angela Merkel became the first German chancellor to receive the Dalai Lama in an official capacity in an official residence (the Chancellor's Office). This enraged Beijing (and drew public criticism from her predecessor, Gerhard Schroeder), which suspended a series of governmental exchanges with Berlin until a private exchange of letters smoothed out the tensions. Merkel, herself a product of the former communist German Democratic Republic (GDR), adopted a much stronger stand on human rights with Beijing than did Schroeder. She subsequently indicated that she would not attend the opening ceremony of the Olympic Games, to protest China's March 2008 crackdown on the uprising in Tibet.

The Tibet issue resonates deeply among European publics. Well before the March 2008 uprising and subsequent crackdown by Chinese security forces, Europeans supported the Dalai Lama and the cause of Tibetan independence (although the Dalai Lama himself does not). The Tibet issue immediately became fused with the

Olympic Games—and the running of the Olympic torch through Athens, London, and Paris. In all three cities, the ceremonies were disrupted by pro-Tibetan and anti-Chinese demonstrators. Various European parliaments passed motions condemning China, and a series of European leaders (notably former Czech President Vaclav Havel) criticized Beijing publicly. Havel, Merkel, and Sarkozy all boycotted the opening ceremony of the Olympics, although British prime minister Gordon Brown was present for the closing ceremonies (as London was to be the next host city). For its part, Chinese national pride was injured by these incidents (particularly in Paris), resulting in an upsurge of internet nationalism and public protests. The French retail chain Carrefour was boycotted by Chinese citizens for several months. The decision by French President Sarkozy to meet the Dalai Lama in the fall of 2008 added to Sino-European strains and resulted in China's decision to "punish" him and France for the action. As part of the "punishment" China announced cancellation of the China-EU Summit due to be held in Lyon in December 2008 (the capstone to the rotating French presidency). When Wen Jiabao toured several European countries in early 2009, in an effort to stabilize deteriorating ties, his itinerary purposefully circumnavigated France. Subsequently the Danish prime minister also met the Dalai Lama, and China reacted similarly by suspending all exchanges for more than a year. The relationship seemed to be unraveling. As the EU Ambassador to China at the time, Serge Abou, observed in an interview with me in early 2010: "We are not in a comfortable situation with China. There is a deep feeling of mutual frustration between the EU and China. China is not at all helpful or responsive to our concerns. Our dialogues are more like monologues. We need to be strategic, but practical, in pursuing our interests with China."[108]

It took the Chinese side a while to grasp the depth and rapidity with which its image in Europe had deteriorated. Indeed, Chinese officials tried to put the best face on strained ties. Vice Foreign Minister Fu Ying (who was responsible for European affairs at the time) said: "We do not see Sino-European relations as deteriorating. In fact, in a fast changing world, the areas of our overlapping and common interests are growing. The European relationship with

China has grown into a multifaceted, rich, sophisticated, comprehensive one. The problems that we have are like hiccups—they are not fundamental problems."[109] Executive Vice Foreign Minister Zhang Zhijun has also invested most of his career in European affairs (mainly with the International Department of the CCP). When I interviewed him around the same time as Madame Fu Ying, Zhang admitted to some strains in the China-Europe relationship but pinned most of the blame on the European side:

> European politicians complain that the EU is not treated [by China] on the same level and given the same status as the United States. They also complain about the trade imbalance, political issues like human rights, and dumping [goods]. In the eyes of many Europeans, China is a communist country led by a communist party—a kind of alien. And Europeans are nervous about the implications of China's rise for their futures. European knowledge of China remains quite low. And Europe has occupied the central stage in the world for centuries, but now it is China and Asia. It is difficult for some Europeans to adapt to this new reality.[110]

By 2010 both sides realized that the deterioration needed to be arrested, and efforts were made to stabilize and improve Sino-European relations. A series of bilateral summits with European leaders were scheduled, and Chinese public diplomacy and research institutes organized several symposia with European think tanks. The Chinese People's Institute of Foreign Affairs organized a high-level Forum on the China-EU Strategic Partnership, inviting many key opinion makers in Europe on an all-expense-paid trip to Beijing, where they were very well received at high levels (including a two-hour meeting with Premier Wen Jiabao in the Zhongnanhai leadership compound).[111] The year 2012 was designated the "EU-China Year of Intercultural Dialogue," an umbrella initiative meant to improve China's image in a variety of forums across Europe.[112] Despite the deterioration of relations and emerging strains since 2007, continuing frictions in several policy areas, and a reservoir of suspicion about China among European publics, since 2010 the Sino-European relationship has stabilized somewhat. It remains an important one in world affairs—but for Chinese diplomacy the EU is a declining priority.[113]

China's Relations with Asia

Not surprisingly, of all regions in the world, Asia receives priority attention in China's diplomacy. Geographic proximity dictates this. Its economic interests are anchored in the region, as the lion's share of China's trade and investment flows through the region. Its manufacturing base is inextricably tied to regional production chains. Sharing land borders with fourteen nations and (disputed) maritime boundaries with a number of others, China's national security is also profoundly shaped by proximity; historically, threats have emanated from the northern and eastern periphery. People-to-people interactions have also been most intensive with China's neighbors, with large communities of overseas Chinese (华侨) living in many Asian countries.

Even though China enjoyed a kind of benign hegemony in Asia for more than two thousand years through the eighteenth century, on the basis of what is known as the "tribute system"[114] one concludes that its modern interactions with Asian neighbors have not always been so positive. During the 1950s, the new People's Republic was cut off from the region—the product of its alliance with Moscow, the Cold War, the Korean War, the separation of Taiwan, and deteriorating relations with India. With the exception of the brief "Bandung Interregnum" in 1955–56 following the Afro-Asian Conference in Bandung, Indonesia, China was at odds with most of its neighbors. It did maintain socialist solidarity with North Korea and North Vietnam but otherwise was cut off from its own neighborhood. This situation only hardened in the 1960s following the Sino-Soviet split, escalating war in Vietnam, 1962 border war with India, and the self-imposed isolation of the Cultural Revolution. If anything, during this period China sought to export revolution throughout the region (and world). It was only after Deng Xiaoping returned to power in 1978 and inaugurated a policy of building state-to-state relations instead of undermining regimes through support for insurgencies that ties with China's neighbors began to stabilize. Although more stable, it was not really until the 1990s that ties actually began to improve. This was the result of five events.

The first was Asia's reaction to the June 4, 1989, "massacre" in Beijing. Unlike much of the international community, many Asian countries did not respond to the Chinese military's killing of civilians in Tiananmen Square and Beijing with condemnation, sanctions, or ostracization.[115] Only Japan explicitly condemned the use of force; the South Korean government merely stated that the "incident was regrettable," while Southeast Asian states remained silent or, as in the Thai and Malaysian cases, noted simply that it was an "internal affair."[116] Japan, which had been reticent about imposing sanctions on China, announced at the Group of Seven summit in Houston, Texas, in 1990 that it would no longer participate in the sanctions process.[117] Thereafter, the ASEAN states led a diplomatic campaign to engage rather than isolate China.[118] Although more critical of Beijing's actions than other Southeast Asian states, Singapore and its then prime minister and senior statesman, Lee Kuan Yew, was the principal conceptualizer and mover behind this strategy.[119] ASEAN's desire to engage China at this critical time left a positive impression on the leadership in Beijing. When the West was doing its best to isolate China, ASEAN chose to reach out.

The second turning point was the 1997–98 Asian financial crisis. Deeply shaken by the suddenness and scope of the crisis, the Chinese government feared that the contagion would spread to China and destabilize its vulnerable banking system. China already had currency controls in place that did not exist in ASEAN states, its currency was not convertible on capital accounts, and Beijing possessed a large reservoir of foreign exchange reserves—all of which helped to buffer the Chinese economy. The government nonetheless acted responsibly and in a stabilizing way by not devaluing its currency and by offering aid packages and low-interest loans to several Southeast Asian states. These actions not only were appreciated in the region but also stood in stark contrast to the dictatorial posture taken by the International Monetary Fund and international creditors in response to the crisis. This assistance punctured the prevailing image of China in the region as either aloof or hegemonic and replaced it with an image of a responsible power. To some extent, Beijing's policies also served to arrest the crisis. The success of its actions boosted the confidence of China's leaders in their role as regional actors.[120]

The third catalyst to a new regional policy was more of a gradual process than a single event. Between 1997 and 2001, the Chinese government significantly modified its assessment of regional, and particularly security-related, multilateral organizations.[121] During this period, the perception of such organizations evolved from being suspicious to uncertain, to supportive. Until the mid-1990s, China viewed such organizations with suspicion, as potential tools that the United States would use for containment. After a year or two of sending observers to the meetings of the ASEAN Regional Forum (ARF), the Council on Security Cooperation in the Asia-Pacific (CSCAP), and nongovernmental "Track II" meetings, China's Foreign Ministry became more agnostic and open to learning about them. Analysts there soon discovered that the United States did not control these organizations; to the contrary, it became evident to China (and other Asian participants) that Washington tended to dismiss or ignore them.[122] Delegates to these organizations further discovered that the cooperative security approach adopted by these organizations, as pushed by the ASEAN states and Japan, was compatible with China's "New Security Concept" (NSC), which officials began to discuss in the late 1990s.

The NSC was first proposed by Foreign Minister Qian Qichen at the annual meeting of the ARF in 1996 and was more fully elaborated by President Jiang Zemin at the UN Conference on Disarmament in March 1999.[123] The NSC is not really all that new; it is in essence a warmed-over and repackaged version of the Five Principles of Peaceful Coexistence, first enunciated by Zhou Enlai at the Afro-Asian People's Solidarity Conference in Bandung, Indonesia, in 1955. In addition to the Five Principles (mutual respect for territorial integrity and sovereignty, nonaggression, noninterference in each other's internal affairs, equality and mutual benefit, and peaceful coexistence), the core purpose of the NSC is "to conduct dialogue, consultation, and negotiation on an equal footing.... to solve disputes and safeguard peace. Only by developing a new security concept and establishing a fair and reasonable new international order can world peace and security be fundamentally guaranteed."[124]

By 1999–2000, Beijing's greater receptivity had given way to full-blown participation in a range of regional multilateral organizations (paralleling China's deeper integration into a number of international organizations). Thus in a relatively short period China moved from passivity and suspicion to proactive engagement in regional regimes and institutions. As Cui Tiankai, then director general for Asian affairs in China's Ministry of Foreign Affairs, reflected, "It was a gradual learning process for us, as we needed to become more familiar with how these organizations worked and to learn how to play the game."[125]

A fourth impetus came during a tour through Asia in 1997 by a group of Chinese diplomatic and military officials, who called for abrogation of all international alliances, declaring them to be unnecessary vestiges of the Cold War. It is unclear if the officials were enunciating a new policy position or were trying to probe the strength of U.S. alliances in the region. Regardless, they described China's NSC as an alternative to Cold War–era alliance-based interstate relations. According to their reasoning, alliances that were forged against the Soviet Union during the Cold War were no longer necessary because it had ceased to exist and the Cold War had ended. China's logic was grounded in a zero-sum understanding of alliances (i.e., they are needed as protection against another state) rather than a positive-sum view (i.e., they have utility for maintenance of security and stability). This argument applied not only to bilateral alliances (e.g., those between the United States and Australia, Japan, the Philippines, the Republic of Korea, and Thailand) but also to multilateral alliances such as NATO. It is difficult to know how seriously China took its own official rhetoric, but in any event Beijing's calls fell on deaf ears both regionally and internationally. In fact, a number of Asian governments privately but sternly told Beijing that such calls were unwelcome and that they had no intention of severing their alliances with the United States.[126] The response caught Chinese officials off guard, as they apparently had not expected other countries to defend their security ties with the United States. Within a year Beijing had cooled its public rhetoric on the issue.

The fifth catalyst to China's new proactive Asia policy was, ironically, the mistaken U.S. bombing of the Chinese embassy in Belgrade during the 1999 war in the former Yugoslavia. This understandably prompted an outbreak of anti-U.S. demonstrations in China (including attacks on the U.S. Embassy in Beijing). But it also triggered a heated foreign policy debate in China. Skeptical of U.S. protestations that the bombing was a mistake, international relations experts and government officials began to question whether Deng Xiaoping's 1985 dictum that China's guiding principle, both internationally and domestically, should continue to be "peace and development" (和平与发展). Not only had Deng deemed this to be the trend of the times in international relations, but he had also come to the obvious conclusion that, to pursue economic development, China needed a peaceful environment. In asserting his theory, Deng had rejected previous Chinese assessments of the inevitability of world war and the unstable nature of the international order. A corollary to Deng's thesis was that the leading global hegemon, the United States, had entered a period of gradual decline. Yet by 1999, in the eyes of many Chinese analysts, neither Deng's core thesis nor the corollary appeared to be valid. This realization spurred an intense domestic debate about the validity of the peace-and-development concept. After several months of intensive discussions, a consensus emerged within the Chinese leadership that, despite some notable "global contradictions" (a code word for conflicts) and the fact that the United States did not appear to be in decline (just the opposite), Deng's general thesis was still accurate as an overall assessment of and guide to China's foreign policy.[127] Importantly, however, Chinese international affairs experts concluded that for a peaceful environment conducive to domestic development to emerge, China needed to be less passive and more proactive in shaping its regional milieu.

Taken together, these five factors stimulated a thorough review and reorientation of regional policy toward neighbors. China's new regional posture involved four new initiatives: (1) stepped-up participation in regional organizations, (2) establishment of "strategic partnerships" and deepening of bilateral relations, (3) expansion of regional economic ties, and (4) reduction of distrust and anxiety in the security sphere. Over the course of the next decade, these initiatives bore much fruit, as China managed to allay much residual angst in the region and stabilized relations with all countries except Japan.[128]

What was painstakingly built by Beijing over the decade 1998–2008, however, quickly unraveled in the short span of eighteen months from mid-2009 through 2010. During this brief period, China got into diplomatic scrapes with virtually *every* one of its neighbors, with the net result that the previously positive perception of China in the region plummeted. This has become known as the period of China's "assertiveness."[129] It seems there was no planned or integrated strategy on the part of Beijing to alienate its neighbors; each case had its own catalysts and circumstances. But the net effect was profoundly damaging to China's image and diplomacy in the region. Ties with South Korea, Japan, India, and a number of Southeast Asian countries suffered. It also contributed directly to many nations' approaches to Washington to step up its involvement in Asia to protect them and "balance" against China. The United States responded in 2011–12 with a broad new strategic reorientation to Asia known as the "pivot."

Going forward, China's ties with its neighbors will be a mixture of continuing interdependence, frictions, and suspicions (on the part of Asian nations toward China). *No* Asian nation (save perhaps North Korea and Pakistan) fully trusts China. Yet they all have to live next door and interact with it. This is particularly true in the economic realm, where trade and investment ties are thick. China has become the largest trading and investment partner for most Asian countries. This economic interdependence is not going to change, although growing commercial frictions could further aggravate existing strains in the diplomatic and security spheres.

Small, but fiercely independent, neighbors Mongolia, Myanmar, and Nepal all fear being swallowed by Chinese capital and immigration. Each government has taken steps since 2011 to distance itself from Beijing's growing influence in that country.

South Korea has very ambivalent relations with China. On the one hand, it is anchored in dense trade and investment relations; yet on the other hand, strategic suspicions and China's ties to North Korea cloud their relationship. China is South Korea's largest trading partner and destination for FDI. More than one million South Koreans visit China every year, while more than half a million Chinese visit South Korea. There are currently 64,000 South Korean students studying in Chinese universities and vocational institutions (more than *any* other nation!). Approximately 75,000 South Koreans are long-term residents in China and 10,000 South Korean companies operate in China, with many having representative offices in addition to production facilities in the country. Transport ties are thick; every week 700 flights shuttle back and forth between the two countries, with various civilian and commercial sea links as well. South Korean businessmen regularly fly to China for the day and return by evening.

China's strategy for building ties with South Korea has both an economic motive and a strategic dimension. In the early 1990s, Chinese strategists concluded that China would have little leverage in shaping the eventual outcome of the divided Korean Peninsula if it did not enjoy strong ties with South Korea. Improved ties would also offset any potential threat to China from the U.S.–South Korean alliance and presence of U.S. forces on the peninsula. Further, a more robust Chinese–South Korean relationship would blunt any attempt by Japan to gain a stronger foothold on the peninsula. Beijing's strategy has been a net success for Chinese strategic interests; the bourgeoning relationship has greatly benefited both countries and become a central element in the evolving balance of power in Northeast Asia.

Despite the overall strength of Chinese–South Korean relations, disagreement over a recent historical interpretation of the ancient kingdom of Koguryo (37 B.C. to A.D. 668) has created some tension. Assertions by Chinese historians that the ancient kingdom was part of China deeply anger Koreans (in both the North and the South).[130] A much more significant strain in relations, though, concerns China's unqualified support for North Korea. South Koreans have grown impatient with Pyongyang's armed provocations, and Beijing's unwillingness to publicly condemn them. Moreover, after years of on-again, off-again sessions of the Six Party Talks, which are convened by Beijing, no progress has been made in reversing North Korea's nuclear weapons program. From China's perspective, "stability" on the peninsula takes precedence—and therefore Beijing has been willing to indulge Pyongyang's aggression. Regime implosion in the North is Beijing's worst nightmare, and therefore it works to prop up the Stalinist state.[131] For their part, Chinese officials claim that they try to restrain North Korea from taking provocative actions—but fail. Says Vice Foreign Minister Cui Tiankai: "We have made it absolutely clear to them—we are against any provocation. We have told them in a very direct way, time and again, we are against it. If they refuse to listen to us, we can't force them. They are a sovereign state."[132]

Japan's relationship with China is even more ambivalent. The troubles are rooted, of course, in the negative legacy of World War II. This will never disappear or cease to be an underlying irritant (especially for China). But the "history issue" is far from the only problem. Other factors—maritime disputes in the East China Sea, China's growing military might—further aggravate ties. In the military sphere, a classic "security dilemma" is growing. Japan's strong alliance with the United States, and its potential application in a Taiwan scenario, is a serious source of concern to Beijing. Despite enduring suspicions and frictions arising out of history and security, the two countries are economically both complementary *and* competitive. With more than $300 billion in two-way trade, China is Japan's largest trading partner while Japan is China's fifth-largest partner. China is the number two destination for Japanese FDI ($7.3 billion in 2010). As is the case with South Korea, large numbers of Chinese and Japanese visit, study, and work in one another's country. The relationship has often been described as "hot economics, cold politics"—which remains an apt characterization—but now the security dimension is increasingly frigid as well.

The situation in Southeast Asia is the same as in Northeast Asia: ASEAN countries are bound deeply together with China economically (even ethnically) but worry about China strategically. Although trade ties are booming, historical fears and China's exaggerated claims to the South China Sea are a particular irritant in relations. In the case of Southeast Asia, they also fear living under China's shadow *economically* as well as strategically. Two-way trade topped $362 billion in 2011, with the prospect of it surging to $500 billion by 2015 according to some estimates.[133] The advent of the ASEAN-China Free Trade Area (CAFTA) in 2010 has given a major boost to trade ties. With a combined population of 1.9 billion, CAFTA ranks as the world's third-largest trade zone after the North American FTA and European Union. Yet, Southeast Asian states fear being overwhelmed by Chinese goods, which have served to undermine their own indigenous light industrial and electronics industries. But the main impediment to ties is the disputed South China Sea claims of China, Vietnam, Indonesia, Malaysia, Brunei, and the Philippines. China's expansive claims—in which nine "dotted lines" run virtually down to Indonesia—and Beijing's refusal to negotiate the problem multilaterally or under the UN Law of the Sea Convention (UNCLOS) is a persistent irritant in regional relations.

Australia finds itself in a similar bind. Overly dependent on mineral exports to China and lacking comparative advantage in other traded goods and services, Australia finds itself economically tethered to China ($150 billion in trade in 2011); yet a large majority in society and government see China as a looming strategic and military threat.[134]

The government has been trying to forge a more stable and enduring relationship, in the wake of sharp strains during 2009–2011, but
as one senior official in the Department of Foreign Affairs and Trade
put it to me when I visited Canberra in 2012, "We try to engage them
[China] pragmatically, but all they want to do is beat up on us!"[135]
Despite recent strains in the relationship, there exist extensive interactions between the two countries in a variety of areas: commerce, science
and technology, tourism, education, environment, and a range of bilateral governmental exchanges.[136] For its part, Australia's neighbor New
Zealand has traditionally enjoyed a positive relationship with China,
but since 2010 strains have emerged over Chinese investments in the
country.

In South Asia, China's ties could not be more different with Pakistan
and India. In India, suspicions of China run deep. Although the two rising
powers have established a *modus vivendi* in diplomatic dealings, and trade
and social linkages are deepening, a stable lasting relationship is going
to be hard to achieve between Delhi and Beijing. The lingering border
dispute (4500 kilometers) remains a tenacious problem and impediment
to building better ties. There also exists a competitive dynamic between
Beijing and Delhi as the world's two largest rising powers, a nascent
rivalry that is enhanced by geostrategic competition along the Himalayan
frontier, the Indian Ocean littoral, and in Myanmar. Each nation's military modernization program (particularly naval) drives a classic "security
dilemma" whereby the country invests in its military for what it perceives
to be defensive purposes, but what is interpreted as offensive and threatening by the other country. Both being nuclear powers, and developing
delivery systems aimed at the other, adds a further combustible element
to the strategic relationship. The Tibet issue and the fact that the Dalai
Lama and his government in exile reside in India is a further complicat-
ing factor. Competition for energy security and secure sea lines of communication (SLOCs) is increasingly sensitive.

In sum, a combination of strategic distrust and growing conflicts of
interest will continue to circumscribe Sino-Indian relations.[137] Perhaps
the greatest impediment (from India's perspective) remains China's
"all weather friend" Pakistan. Beijing and Islamabad have maintained
a close alignment (indeed an alliance) since the early 1950s. China has
backed Pakistan on virtually all disputes with India over the decades,

has been the principal supplier of military equipment to Pakistan, and has not been responsive to Delhi's concerns on Kashmir and other sensitive issues. The Sino-Pak axis only contributes to tensions between Delhi and Beijing.

Finally, China has made better headway in Central Asia. Engaging the region both bilaterally and multilaterally via the Shanghai Cooperation Organization, Beijing has been able to offset Moscow's residual influence in the region and build both economic and security ties. Given China's traditional security concerns on its northern flank, Beijing has worked hard to shore up ties with its Central Asian neighbors. From its inception in 2001, the SCO has focused primarily on nontraditional security threats, particularly terrorism. It is also Beijing's example of what a "new type" of post–Cold War "comprehensive security" organization should be—China's answer to the American "collective security" alliance system. The SCO's predecessor (the "Shanghai Five") also did much during the mid-1990s to institute military confidence building and security measures among its member states, such as force reductions and prenotification of exercises, in their border regions.[138] More recently, the SCO has begun to evolve into a broader and more comprehensive organization, reflecting Beijing's goal of building comprehensive strategic partnerships. At its 2003 annual meeting, the SCO expanded the focus to include economic cooperation; Premier Wen Jiabao proposed setting up a free trade zone among member states and reducing nontariff barriers in a variety of areas. At its 2012 summit in Beijing, the SCO adopted a "Strategic Plan for Medium-Term Development" and took initiatives to establish a development bank, a food security mechanism, and other measures to boost trade and investment.[139] The political interaction among SCO members is also intensive. In addition to the annual summit and frequent bilateral state visits, SCO ministerial-level officials meet and consult regularly, and a large number of joint working groups have been established. Although cross-border support for Uighur separatists is a troubling dimension for Beijing, the overall relationship between China and its northwestern neighbors seems sound.[140]

There exist considerably more detail and dimensions of China's interactions with its Asian neighbors, and many of these elements are explored in subsequent chapters.[141] Suffice it to say, however, that two things are not going to change: geography and history. All of these nations live adjacent to China (and vice versa), and memories of China's historical "tribute" relationships still run deep for all parties. These factors will continue to simultaneously bind and divide China and its Asian neighbors.

China's Relations with the Middle East

Other than the historic Silk Road link to Persia and Admiral Zheng He's final voyage, which reached Mecca and modern-day Iran in 1432, China and the Middle East have long been cut off from each other—geographically, culturally, commercially, religiously, politically, and strategically. Unlike India, China was always considered by Arabs as an outsider to the region.[142] This began to change in the 1950s, when several newly independent Arab states (Syria, Egypt, Yemen) diplomatically recognized the People's Republic of China in 1956. Iraq, Morocco, and Algeria followed in 1958. This connection was cemented—particularly with Egypt—during the decade as the post-colonial Nonaligned Movement and Afro-Asian People's Solidarity Organization took shape. But internecine feuds within these movements, fueled by the Sino-Soviet split, led to a drift in Sino-Arab relations. However, the drift soon turned into alienation. China's leftist lurch, beginning in the Great Leap Forward (1958–1960) and continuing through the Cultural Revolution period (late 1960s through early 1970s), led to pursuing a politically radical agenda in the region. Beijing promoted communist insurrections and aided, abetted, and trained radicalized guerrilla groups across the Arabian peninsula, in North Africa, and against Israel. This resulted in deteriorated relations with several governments in the region, notably Egypt, Syria, and Iraq. Iraq had been the second Gulf state after Yemen to recognize the PRC, but Beijing's atheistic pro-communist policy did not go down well in Baghdad or other Arab capitals. The 1967 War coincided with the height of the Cultural Revolution as China stepped up its support for pro-communist groups and nascent insurgencies. This contrasted distinctly with Moscow's state-to-state approach to the region. As a result, Beijing found itself increasingly isolated and unwelcome in the region.

Like much of China's foreign policy, this began to change after Mao's death in 1976; in fact, it had begun slightly changing before then. Discreet diplomatic and commercial contacts began in the early and mid-1970s, as several of the more conservative states became suspicious of the Soviet Union's strategic designs on Persian Gulf oil and states, after Moscow moved to establish a foothold in the Horn of Africa. Kuwait, the Shah's Iran, and Oman all moved to establish diplomatic relations with Beijing (although it took the United Arab Emirates, Qatar, Bahrain, and Saudi Arabia more than another decade to do so). By the time Deng Xiaoping came to power and reoriented foreign policy after 1978, China had, in fact, already laid a better foundation across the Arab world. One hiccup came with the 1979 Islamic revolution in Iran. The Chinese had previously cultivated the Shah's regime, largely on the basis of its anti-Sovietism. So the Shah's overthrow and replacement by the Ayatollah Khomeini and a new Islamic republic concerned Beijing at first; but when the new Iranian regime proved to be just as anti-Soviet as the Shah, the Chinese were relieved. Another challenge for Beijing came with the 1980–1988 Iran-Iraq war. At first, Beijing accused the Soviet Union of instigating and benefiting from the conflict but then became involved itself in arming *both* sides, finally assisting in the UN-brokered cease-fire. But before peace arrived, Beijing profited handsomely from providing weapons to both combatants. China furnished aircraft, artillery, ground-to-ground and surface-to-air missiles, armored vehicles, and a range of other equipment to both sides (but primarily to Iran).[143] Even after the conflict ended, it continued to supply Iran with a range of military equipment and technical support for Tehran's military-industrial complex.

This history is important background in understanding China's continuing relationship with Iran and stance on its nuclear program. China's relations with Iran run long and deep. As John Garver argued in his sentinel study *China and Iran: Ancient Partners in a Post-Imperial World*, there is a long and strong civilizational dimension to the relationship, i.e., deep respect for one another's historical civilizations and efforts to build a world free from Western dominance.[144] But there are more contemporary reasons for the relationship as well. For an isolated, defiant, and threatening Iran, Beijing has been one of the only sources of support. China is Iran's largest trading partner (an estimated $25 billion in 2009) and source of economic support. The two governments and ruling parties enjoy extensive exchanges. From Beijing's perspective, relations with Tehran meet several priorities. First, Iran is seen to be a major—if not *the* major—regional power in the Middle East. This fits into China's desire to build a "multipolar world." Second, Iran is implacably opposed to the United States and keeps Washington preoccupied and away from China. Third, Iran has become China's second-largest regional supplier of oil and the largest supplier of natural gas. Over the past ten years, 13 percent of China's imported oil has come from Iran (roughly one-third of Iran's total oil exports). At the same time, Iran is a sensitive test case in Beijing's credentials as a responsible international actor. To date, Beijing has therefore voted for various UN resolutions (1696, 1737, 1747, 1803, 1929) and (seemingly) has not violated United Nations sanctions against Iran. Thus, the Chinese government is walking a tricky tightrope in managing its relations with Tehran and the West, as its national interests pull in two directions.[145]

China's relations with the region more broadly are driven primarily by two overriding factors: the desire for regional stability, and as a consequence energy supplies continuing to flow to China. A third, more recent, factor is the growing Middle Eastern market for Chinese investment, construction, and products. But energy is the big driver. By 2009, China was importing 70 percent of its oil, 45 percent of which was sourced from the Middle East. Saudi Arabia and Iran provide more than half of this amount, with Oman, Kuwait, the UAE, Yemen, and Iraq all contributing. China's overall trade with the region topped $100 billion in 2010, but three-fourths of this amount was energy-related. The remainder comprises a range of light manufactured goods, machinery equipment, vehicles, foodstuffs, and engineering and labor services. Chinese companies see much potential for investment in the region and are flooding in; more than a hundred now operate in the UAE alone. Chinese state oil companies are now operating all over the region (see Chapter 5).

Diplomatically, Beijing maintains sound bilateral ties with all the nations in the region, including Israel. This is no mean trick. Beijing's "offend no one" and "attach no strings" approach has worked well. Senior leaders regularly visit the region, and a steady stream of Arab officials pass through Beijing. Multilaterally, China has also launched the China-Arab States Cooperation Forum (CASCF) in 2004. It is similar to, and modeled on, the Forum on China-Africa Cooperation (FOCAC), which is discussed below. CASCF is the first such forum the Arab League has participated in with any other nonregional nation or organization. It is a high-level dialogue mechanism emphasizing political and economic cooperation.[146] China's ties with the Arab League were, however, strained in 2012 by Beijing's double veto (with Russia) of UN resolutions on Syria. China's own crackdown on ethnic Uighurs in Xinjiang has further damaged its image in the Arab world, and particularly with Turkey. Finally, in 2002, at the urging of the Arab League, China officially designated a special envoy for Middle East issues. Over the past decade the envoy has put forward various peace proposals, which have been supportive of an independent and sovereign Palestinian state, a return to pre-1967 borders, and the "land for peace" principle.[147]

Despite the strains introduced by the 2012 Syria situation and China's own suppression of Uighurs, Beijing's relations with the Middle East remain stable and sound.[148] China's presence in the region is growing but remains low-key, and this has allowed Beijing to stay out of America's strategic headlights. Iran remains the key test of whether China can continue this balancing act.

China's Relations with Africa

China's ties to Africa are deep and growing deeper. They have both an historical and contemporary character. Historically, interactions date to the Song dynasty (960–1279 A.D.), when there was evidence of trade in ceramics and silk. Then, in the fifteenth century, Admiral Zheng He took at least two of his famous voyages to the east coast of Africa. In the seventeenth century Africa came to China; that is, Holland brought African slaves to its colony on the island of Formosa (Taiwan). Some escaped across the strait to the Chinese mainland and joined the warrior Koxinga in his abortive uprising against the Qing dynasty (which actually led to expulsion of the Dutch from Taiwan). Following the abolition of slavery in the British and French empires in 1833 and 1848, respectively, European colonizers began to import indentured Chinese labor to Africa to work in mines and on construction projects. Such was the pre-1949 history.

After the founding of the PRC, Beijing engaged Africa in six principal ways. First, it fought a diplomatic war with Taiwan for sovereign recognition and admission to the United Nations. Second, it supported African anti-colonial and anti-imperialist "liberation" struggles. Third, it sought to spread communist revolution and Maoist ideology throughout the continent (and across the "third world"). Fourth, Mao saw Africa as part of the "intermediate zone" struggle between the two superpowers. Fifth, after 1960 Beijing competed fiercely with Moscow for followers in Africa as part of the Sino-Soviet global competition. Finally, Africa became a test ground for Beijing's diplomatic and foreign aid principles. For these six reasons, China grew deeply involved on the African continent from the 1950s through the mid-1970s. But with the death of Mao, the overthrow of the Gang of Four, and the reorientation of national strategy to economic growth, in the late 1970s China's attention to Africa waned. The relative decline continued until the mid-1990s.

At that time, a set of three new factors became apparent in China's posture, which continue to this day: very active bilateral and multilateral diplomacy, a heavy commercial presence oriented around the import of raw materials and energy supplies in exchange for exports of a range of manufactured goods and exports, and stepped-up developmental aid assistance. Premier Zhu Rongji and President Jiang Zemin made high-profile trips to Africa in 1995 and 1996, respectively, and set out Beijing's new agenda. Jiang's speech at the African Union headquarters was particularly significant insofar as he proposed establishment of the Forum on China Africa Cooperation (FOCAC), which after six years of preparatory meetings was launched in Beijing in the fall of 2006. I happened to be visiting Beijing at the time, and it was extraordinary to see heads of state and dignitaries from no fewer than fifty-three African countries in attendance. No non-African nation had ever initiated anything like FOCAC. In his welcoming speech, President Jiang Zemin made an extraordinary series of pledges: doubling development assistance, creating a $5 billion development fund to encourage Chinese companies to invest in Africa, building a new African Union headquarters in Ethiopia, canceling all outstanding debts, more than doubling the number of African export items exempt from tariffs in China, establishing three to five "trade and cooperation zones" in Africa, training 15,000 African professionals, doubling scholarships (from 2000–4000) for African students in China, building thirty hospitals and a hundred rural schools, establishing a "Youth Corps" of Chinese volunteers to work in Africa, and launching a series of agricultural and public health initiatives. The scope and substance of China's FOCAC initiatives were simply stunning. FOCAC meets every three years, and Beijing has subsequently set forth similarly impressive initiatives.

Since that time, China-Africa relations have fully blossomed.[149] Trade went from less than $5 billion in 1995 to $127 billion in 2010. The growth in trade is largely the result of Africa's abundant oil and mineral reserves. Oil companies account for *80 percent* of African exports to China (Angola accounts for 37 percent of China's oil imports alone). It is followed by timber, diamonds, copper, and iron ores. In return, China exports machinery and equipment, appliances, apparel, and footwear to Africa.

China has also made good on its aid pledges. I discuss China's aid program at greater length in Chapter 5, but suffice it to note here that nearly half of China's worldwide aid disbursements go to Africa. *The Dragon's Gift*, by scholar Deborah Brautigam, offers an extensive and exhaustive treatment of this subject.[150] Much of this aid is commendable (particularly in the areas of anti-malarial and public health work, tertiary education, and agricultural assistance), but not all of China's aid is without controversy. Although China prides itself on its no-strings-attached aid policy, Beijing has come under sharp international criticism for providing assistance to some of Africa's most repressive and corrupt regimes, and thus undercutting efforts by other international donors to either ostracize such regimes or leverage "tied aid" to implementation of specific domestic governance reforms. Much of China's aid comes in the form of hard infrastructure: roads, rails, buildings, stadiums, etc. Even though these do have a positive impact on the recipient country in the end, they are normally built entirely with imported Chinese labor by Chinese construction companies with contracts from the Chinese government. This, combined with an excessive and obsessive focus on extractive industries and raw materials, has led to charges of "neo-colonialism" (which Beijing is hypersensitive and defensive about). China's relationship with Sudan and its indicted president, Omar al-Bashir, has been another black mark on Beijing's regional (and global) reputation.

On the whole, however, African nations welcome China's engagement, because increased trade, aid, investment, education, vocational training, and debt relief have all benefited these societies. Public opinion polling in Africa shows the most positive perceptions of China *anywhere* in the world. Although China enjoys a privileged reputation in Africa, according to Song Aiguo, the Foreign Ministry's director general for West Asian and African affairs, "China does not seek any kind of sphere of influence in the region."[151]

China's Relations with Latin America

China's expanded relations with Latin America and the Caribbean began in earnest in the late 1990s.[152] Since then, China's inroads into the region have involved all of the dimensions covered in this book: diplomatic, economic, cultural, and military.[153] Its approach has been quite systematic, comprehensive, and rapid. When I visited the Chinese embassy in Brasilia in 2008, I was given an internal (内部) Foreign Ministry document that outlined in considerable detail the elements of China's regional strategy, policies, and programs. It was an unmistakable example of an approach to Latin America orchestrated by the government—which contradicts other observers of China-Latin relations who argue that Beijing's approach is much more ad hoc and uncoordinated. When I asked Wu Baiyi, the deputy director of the Institute of Latin American Studies in the Chinese Academy of Social Sciences, if China had a "strategy" toward Latin America, he replied: "I don't think so. It is *ad hoc*. It is led by social and commercial interests, not long-term geostrategic aims. It is opportunistic. It has been built bottom-up, not top-down. China's overall approach is dictated by immediate needs, particularly resources."[154]

Whether or not China has a Latin America strategy, it is clear that Latin America does *not* have a China strategy. During my visits and extensive interviews in Argentina, Brazil, Chile, and Peru in 2008 and 2010, I repeatedly probed my interlocutors in government, business, and academe about China's rapidly growing presence in the region and

China's rise in world affairs more generally. Of government officials, I often asked, "What is your China strategy?" My question was usually met with bewilderment and awkward silences, as if to say, "Strategy? What strategy?" Indeed, Latin governments, the business communities, academia, and research institutes seem thoroughly unprepared for the complex challenges of coping with China's offensive into the region. Around 2008–09 such an awareness was beginning to take shape in some of the larger Latin countries. As a result, Chinese is being taught in universities, some more Confucius Institutes have opened, and the media is beginning to report on China. Still, knowledge of China and Chinese is sorely lacking throughout the region. When Latin American leaders meet Chinese officials, the Chinese government usually has to provide the interpreters. One finds only a few Latin diplomats based in their embassies in Beijing able to speak and read Chinese, even though China's ambassadors and diplomats in the region are usually fluent in Spanish and Portuguese. In interviews in Rio, and when I visited the Brazilian Foreign Ministry (Itamarichy) in Brasilia in 2008, I was told there was not a *single* fluent Chinese speaker or cohort of China specialists in the entire Brazilian Foreign Service! The ministry did not even have a China desk or department. Nor does the Brazilian intelligence service (ABIN) have any China expertise. The situation in Brazil is mirrored throughout other regional governments.

The lack of translators backfired badly when Chinese President Hu Jintao addressed the Brazilian Parliament in 2004. Given its own lack of interpreters, Itamarichy employed a local Brazilian of Chinese descent—but the person made a major error of interpretation. Hu claimed in his speech that China would like to raise the level of trade with Latin America to $100 billion by 2010 (a target that was easily eclipsed), but the amateur interpreter mistranslated trade (*maoyi*) as *investment* (*touzi*)! This major mistake was caught by the Chinese diplomats present (who were fluent in Portuguese), but it was too late: Brazilian and other Latin journalists immediately filed their stories as "Chinese President Promises $100 billion in Investment into Latin America by 2010"! Needless to say, this caused quite a stir across the continent—and raised false expectations—that were subsequently dashed when the money did not materialize.

The asymmetry of expertise is evident in the research and academic world as well. China has had a Latin American Studies Association for more than fifty years, and the Institute of Latin American Studies of the Chinese Academy of Social Sciences has been operating since 1979. Together they publish the informative Chinese-language journal *Latin American Studies* (拉丁美洲研究). But no similar Chinese studies association, institute, or journal exists in Latin America. There are only a handful of China specialists in each of the major Latin nations, and they tend *not* to speak Chinese. There are only two degree-granting programs in Chinese studies (which include courses on China *other* than the language), in Argentina (Salvador University) and Mexico (National Autonomous University). Small research programs on China have been established at Pontifica Universidad Católica de Chile and Universidad del Desarrollo in Santiago, and the Universidad de Bogotá. Shockingly, there is still no Chinese studies program in all of Brazil. All Latin universities face a Catch-22: How to train students in Chinese studies without professors trained in Chinese studies? Until a cohort of Latin professors are trained—not only in China but also in American or European universities—there is no professorial "supply" to meet the student "demand." This mismatch in Chinese-Latin mutual understanding is likely to redound to China's advantage in the years ahead.

Let us now turn to examine the several components of China's position in the region.

Diplomatically, it must first be noted that Central America, the Caribbean, and Latin America still represent an area of diplomatic competition with Taiwan. Eleven of the twenty-three nation-states in the world that still diplomatically recognize Taiwan lie in the region. Even though Beijing and Taipei have declared an unofficial "truce" in their diplomatic competition over the last few years as relations across the Taiwan Strait have improved, it is still an essential element of Beijing's regional strategy. Another important element to bear in mind is that, like its ties in Africa and the Middle East, the Latin American region represents China's solidarity with developing countries as well as its desire to foster a multipolar world—so both sides tout their so-called South-South cooperation. Brazil is a key actor in both respects for Beijing, and vice versa. There is a real identity of international interests between Brasilia and Beijing. As Ambassador Regina Dunlop, the director for Asian affairs in the Brazilian Foreign Ministry, expressed it when I met her at the ministry in 2008: "We do not see China's rise as a concern. On the contrary, we share a lot of values and common visions of the world. We both favor a multipolar world and multilateral decision-making in international affairs. For many years we have noticed this coincidence of interests, but now we are cooperating more closely. And we share a lot with other emerging economies."[155] This coincidence of views led, of course, to the 2009 formation of the BRICS grouping: Brazil, Russia, India, China, and South Africa. Other notable Brazilian diplomats do not agree with this viewpoint, however. The former Brazilian ambassador to China and the United States, Roberto Abdeneur, counters: "There is an element of illusion in the minds of these people in the Itamarichy. To say that China and Brazil have identical foreign policies and worldviews is an exaggeration. It represents an ideology—not a practical approach."[156] The government of Lula da Silva was more reflective of Ambassador Dunlop's views, although the successor government of Dilma Rousseff is more representative of Ambassador Abdeneur's viewpoint.

China has forged a variety of diplomatic "strategic partnerships" (no fewer than eight types!) with most countries in the region, and this designation provides an overarching framework to develop bilateral ties. Brazil's ties with China are particularly strong—perhaps the strongest of all Latin countries. In 2010, during a state visit by former Brazilian President Luiz Inácio Lula da Silva to Beijing, the two governments signed a Joint Action Plan 2020 to guide their "strategic partnership."[157] Yet China has also managed to build sound relations with most other regional states, notably Argentina, Chile, Cuba, Mexico, Peru, and Venezuela. The rise to power of leftist governments in Argentina, Bolivia, Brazil, Chile, Ecuador, Nicaragua, Paraguay, and Venezuela in recent years also helped cement Beijing's ties to the region. High-level bilateral diplomacy is surprisingly active (if not always reported in the international media). During 1997–2010, more than 110 Latin American heads of state and government leaders visited China, while its president visited the region five times and a steady stream of Politburo-level leaders toured various Latin countries.

Multilaterally, Beijing is also active in a range of organizations in the region. In 2008 China became a full member of the Inter-American

Development Bank, it joined the Caribbean Development Bank in 1997, and it has held permanent observer status in the Organization of American States (OAS) since 2004. China has held numerous rounds of dialogues with the Rio Group since 1990 and established a dialogue mechanism with the MERCOSUR common market group, as well as the Caribbean Community and Latin American Conference. China is a full member of the Asia-Pacific Economic Cooperation organization (APEC), and Beijing has initiated a series of separate forums with the region, including the China–Latin America Forum, the China-Caribbean Economic and Trade Cooperation Forum, the China–Latin America Common Market Dialogue, the China-Andean Community Consultation Forum, and the China–Latin American Business Summit. Through all of these multilateral mechanisms, China is now extensively linked multilaterally to the region. Thus, both bilaterally and multilaterally, China has built strong diplomatic and political ties throughout the Western Hemisphere.

In addition to state-to-state diplomacy, the CCP/International Department is also extremely—albeit quietly—active in exchanges with a range of political parties across the region (even in countries that diplomatically recognize Taiwan). The CCP now has working relations with more than eighty political parties in more than thirty countries in the region. This ties China not only to ruling parties but perhaps more importantly to opposition parties and politicians in waiting, so that when they come to power Beijing is already familiar with them (and vice versa). Party-to-party exchanges also give Beijing a good mechanism for intelligence collection. China engages as well in parliamentary exchanges with a number of Latin countries, although this is not nearly as widespread as party-to-party diplomacy.

China's cultural presence is also rising in the region. Chinese tourists are beginning to arrive in large numbers, a result of Beijing having signed group tourism accords with nineteen countries. China is trying to raise its profile through several media initiatives. For example, the Spanish-language edition of *China Daily* (*China Hoy*) was launched in November 2011. There are also more than a hundred pairs of sister province and city relationships between Chinese and Latin localities. Immigration is also growing. There are now, for example, 30,000 ethnic Chinese living in Argentina, and a large number in Peru.

Another element in China's attempts to increase its cultural exchanges in the region has been the establishment of 24 "Confucius Institutes" across the region (out of 350 worldwide), while the Chinese government provides one thousand university scholarships for Latin students to study in China every year.[158] Numerous government-to-government cultural exchange accords have been agreed, and a variety of universities are beginning to sign their own MOUs as well. Nonetheless, the level of understanding in the academic world and throughout Latin societies remains abysmally low.[159]

China's military-security presence in the Latin American region is not large, but it is growing. Beijing is very aware that there are already concerns in Washington concerning China's growing presence in the region, and the military dimension is particularly sensitive. There are several levels of this military-security presence in the region. The first is professional military exchanges, some of which are very high-level. For example, four members of China's Central Military Commission visited the region between 2008 and 2010—more than any other region of the world—while a steady stream of Latin defense ministers and service chiefs visit Beijing annually. China also trains Latin officers in its staff academies. China's arms sales to, and imports from, the region are a second type.[160] It sells a relatively small amount of weaponry and military equipment to Latin America—approximately $150 million per year of helicopters, artillery, armored personnel carriers, vehicles, K-8 trainer aircraft, radars and command and control equipment, antiship missiles, and light assault weapons—while buying avionics and antitank and anti-air missiles from Brazil. Some of the Sino-Brazilian aerospace cooperation is also military-related. It is alleged that China may also have some access to former Soviet-built military intelligence communications facilities in Cuba, but this has not been established. All in all, China's military-security presence in Latin America is gradually growing.[161] But it has certainly not yet reached a level where Washington needs to be seriously concerned.

Commerce is by far the most important dimension of China's presence in Latin America. Trade has been growing almost exponentially, reaching $242 billion in 2011. This is a dramatic increase of more than twenty times since 2000, and the growth seems to be accelerating. It jumped 31.5 percent from 2010 to 2011. China is now the No. 1

trading partner of many Latin nations, having supplanted the United States. Brazil dominates regional trade with China, accounting for almost 40 percent of the total. In 2010 China surpassed the United States as Brazil's largest trading partner ($56 billion). Two-way trade has grown dramatically in recent years, but Latin America still accounts for only about 4 percent of China's total foreign trade. Although Brazil is China's largest export market in Latin America, it ranks only as China's twentieth largest trading partner.

In terms of trade composition, though, it is heavily concentrated and not well diversified. The trade is dominated by Chinese purchases of raw materials and agricultural commodities; fully 70 percent of Brazil's exports to China are in two commodities (iron ore and soybeans). China imports large amounts and a wide range of minerals, energy supplies, and raw materials from Latin America. Purchases of oil (refined and unrefined) from the region are also growing: Venezuelan President Hugo Chavez promised in Beijing in April 2009 to quintuple his country's daily deliveries from 200,000 to 1 million barrels per day. Brazil's oil exports to China increased to 200,000 barrels per day in 2010.

China's voracious appetite for raw materials has contributed to high global prices for these commodities (and has provided a significant revenue stream for Argentina, Brazil, Chile, and Peru). Today China consumes about 40 percent of the world's coal, 25 percent of the nickel, 25 percent of iron ores, 20 percent of copper ores, and 14 percent of aluminum. China is the world's leading importer of iron ore and No. 2 of copper. It also buys large amounts of agricultural products, fish, and wine from the region, along with accounting for 40 percent of global soybean imports. About 80 percent of China's imported fish meal comes from Peru and Chile, while 80 percent of its sugar comes from Cuba. Argentina is also a significant source of meats and leather goods for the Chinese market.

In return, Latin countries purchase a range of manufactured goods, especially electronics (largely cell phones and computers). Large Chinese exports of textiles, footwear, and other low-end consumer goods have hit several Latin economies hard, particularly Mexico and Argentina. There is also evidence of China's dumping these goods on Latin markets, taking advantage of Market Economy Status (MES) accords China has managed to sign with fifteen Latin countries. Many of these countries signed these accords unwittingly, as Chinese diplomats told them they were a "normal" part of bilateral "strategic partnerships." In fact, MES status exempts China from countervailing dumping duties. As a result, Mexico and Argentina have had to institute unilateral safeguards against the flood of Chinese goods since 2007. Fully 50 percent of all Argentine antidumping and countertrade measures were directed against China that year, and it rose to 90 percent in 2008. Gradually, China is beginning to move up the technological ladder in its regional trade in Latin America, trading in autos, motorcycles, aircraft and aircraft parts, electronics, and agro-, bio-, nano-, and information technologies. As it does so, it may begin to alleviate the competitive dynamic in low-end manufactured goods.

To facilitate trade, China has signed bilateral FTAs with Chile, Peru, and Costa Rica. Creative trade financing is also an interesting new area. Beijing struck a $10 billion arrangement with Buenos Aires that permits Argentina reliable access to Chinese currency to pay for its imports from China. This deal follows similar ones Beijing has struck with South Korea, Indonesia, and Belarus.

China is also increasing its direct investment in the region, becoming the second-largest destination for Chinese ODI after Asia. The Ministry of Commerce reported $7.3 billion in 2009, of which the vast majority of the financial flow was into tax havens in the British Virgin Islands ($1.61 billion) and the Grand Cayman Islands ($5.36 billion).[162] The total stock of Chinese ODI in the region at the end of 2009 was $30.5 billion.[163] The Economic Commission for Latin America and the Caribbean (ECLAC) provides higher figures, however, reporting that Chinese ODI into the region was $15 billion in 2010.[164] This represents approximately 10 percent of the total foreign investment in the region. To date, most of it has been in the mining, energy, and agricultural sectors. Given China's hunger for natural resources, and Latin America's fairly well developed infrastructure, there is also potential for joint ventures in manufacturing. China's purchase of real estate—particularly farmland—is also likely to grow. As a result of these synergies, ODI into the region is likely to continue to grow at a steady pace in future years.[165]

China provides some aid to Latin countries as well. Exact figures are hard to come by, but one study reported that Beijing contributed

$26.7 billion between 2002 and 2007.[166] This figure seems high, however, and no doubt it partially involves Chinese commercial investments in the region. Although no official figures have been released by the Chinese government, during a visit to Washington, the director general of Latin American and Caribbean affairs in the Foreign Ministry observed that the real figure is "less than $2 billion per year."[167] He indicated that much of it comes in the form of preferential loans and grants and that most of the assistance in the hemisphere goes to Caribbean countries, in the form of hard infrastructure (buildings, stadiums, transportation), human resource training, and agricultural assistance.[168]

In all of these dimensions, China's footprint in Latin America and the Caribbean is growing, and growing quickly. China's regional diplomacy is fully in service of its commercial interests. Through this rapidly expanding footprint, though, Beijing is wary of Washington—and Washington is keeping a close eye on China's activities in the region. Even though the Monroe Doctrine has been consigned to history, Washington continues to view the region as its "backyard" and keeps a close eye on China's multidimensional thrust into the region. Beijing is aware of this and has gone out of its way not to establish a military presence in the region or draw too close to certain regimes. For example, it has kept its distance from the Chavez regime in Venezuela; has not been directly involved in supporting insurgencies, socialist movements, or far-left-leaning governments; has maintained a very low level of arms sales in the region; has not established any kind of military presence in the region; and, while being supportive of Havana, has kept its ties with Cuba at a relatively low profile.

Irrespective of the United States, China's presence in Latin America is only going to continue to grow over time. Whether Beijing's burgeoning foothold will continue to be welcomed, though, remains an open question. Public opinion polls show a steady decline in China's favorability ratings in the region since 2007. In 2011, the BBC found that only 55 percent of Brazilians and a paltry 23 percent of Mexicans polled held positive views of China.[169] Its image in Mexico has long been negative, owing to economic competition and unbalanced trade (in 2009 Mexico imported $31.9 billion in goods from China, while exporting only $2.2 billion), and similarly mixed views are now commonplace in

Argentina, Chile, Peru, and Colombia. As in Africa, China's declining image is largely the result of its investments in the natural resource and raw materials sectors, and dumping of low-end manufactured goods on Latin markets. The growing impression across the developing world of China as a mercantilist trader and neocolonial extractor is going to be a difficult image for Beijing to cope with.[170]

A Cautious Diplomatic Power

China has come a long way in its diplomatic dealings with the world, but it remains a cautious diplomatic actor—and one that uses diplomacy largely in pursuit of its priority goal of economic modernization as well as offsetting threats to its national security. It prefers bilateralism to multilateralism. On balance, I would assess China's bilateral relations with other countries around the world as mixed. Only with Africa can they be said to be strong (and even in this case there are recent signs of strain). Everywhere else, China finds itself enmeshed in ambivalent and strained relationships. This is, of course, not the picture one gets from reading Chinese state propaganda or listening to the speeches of its leaders or diplomats. But when one assesses all of the regional relationships discussed above, one sees clear signs of growing frictions.

This is perhaps a natural condition for a growing world power. As China's presence and interests spread, it is naturally going to generate some suspicion and friction. This is quite new to China and is going to be a challenge for diplomats to manage.

In addition to China's bilateral and regional relationships, it is also being called upon to be more involved in "global governance" issues—to which we now turn in the next chapter.

4

China and Global Governance

Global governance is a Western concept. The West emphasizes "governance," while China emphasizes the "global" dimension. We care more about equality of participation than about governance.

—Chinese scholar, 2011[1]

China cannot even manage itself—how can it manage the world?

—Chinese scholar, 2011[2]

For China, the most populous country, to run itself well is the most important fulfillment of its international responsibility.

—China's White Paper on Peaceful Development, 2011[3]

AS CHINA'S POSITION AS a major power grows and its global influence spreads, the question of its contributions to "global governance" arises.[4] Western nations increasingly expect Beijing to proportionately contribute to a broad range of transnational challenges collectively affecting the international community—in the words of Robert Zoellick, to become a "responsible [international] stakeholder."[5] China's contributions to global governance are also seen by Westerners as a litmus test of whether Beijing is emerging as a "status quo" or "revisionist" power.[6]

Does China shoulder its fair share, "free ride," or selectively contribute to global governance? Does it seek to uphold or overturn the existing international system? Does it play by the existing rules of existing institutions, or does it seek to establish new rules and alternative institutions? Does Beijing believe there are common international "public goods" that it should contribute to, or does it only pursue narrow national interests?

These are some of the questions being asked about China and global governance. Underlying all of them are more fundamental questions—not only about China, but about what constitutes global governance. Today there is a prevailing sense that the post–World War II order is in crisis and its institutions are in need of fundamental reformation, to reflect new geoeconomic and geopolitical realities. A redistribution of global power is under way, from West to East and from North to South. In this fluid and dynamic context, global institutions and the rules of the game are being renegotiated.

The Origins of Global Governance

Global governance can be simply defined as "the collective management of common problems at the international level."[7] One of the earliest treatises on the subject, by the noted international relations scholar James N. Rosenau, termed it simply "governance without governments."[8] In 1995 the Commission on Global Governance (a group of prominent international figures) similarly defined it as "the sum of the many ways individuals and institutions, public and private, manage their common affairs.... It is a multi-level collection of governance-related activities, rules, and mechanisms, formal and informal, public and private, existing in the world today."[9] In academic discourse, the concept of global governance grew out of the field of international political economy, but it has since evolved into other fields of international relations. This is because of the increasing number of transnational issues that have arisen on the international agenda, as well as the rise of nongovernmental actors in world affairs.

Global governance institutions can be traced back to the nineteenth century, as European states sought to deal with issues stemming from the industrial revolution that involved cross-border jurisdictions: regulating commercial activities, establishing health standards for travelers, rules for shipping in rivers and waterways, postal links, and the newly invented telegraph.[10] The International Telegraph Union was established in 1865 and the International Postal Union in 1874, two of the world's first multilateral regimes.

Thereafter, global governance took shape in The Hague. A series of conferences organized there at the turn of the twentieth century began the process of institutionalizing commercial dispute arbitration, establishing the Permanent Court on Arbitration in 1899. The Hague conferences included, for the first time, non-European states (among them China, Japan, and a number of Latin countries) and each enjoyed an equal voice and seat at the table—establishing the twin principles of universality and legal equality of states. The Hague conferences also, for the first time, promoted the novel ideas of common interests of mankind and the codification of international law.

The next phase of global governance was the League of Nations. Primarily concerned with preventing the outbreak of another world war, the league also undertook to establish new standards and institutions for health, labor, and justice. Eventually, however, the League foundered on the U.S. Senate rejecting American participation and the inability of the league to prevent or roll back Japan's invasion of Manchuria in 1931, Italy's invasion of Ethiopia in 1935, the Spanish civil war, and Nazi Germany's remilitarization and annexation of its eastern neighbors. The Western economic depression of the 1930s also contributed to the league's failure, as many members withdrew and retrenched into nationalism. Despite these shortcomings and the league's ultimate failure, its creation nonetheless moved the concept of global governance forward. It also established some institutions that survived the league, such as the International Court of Justice (ICJ).

Literally out of the ashes of the Second World War, global governance was resurrected in the form of the United Nations and "San Francisco Treaty System" in 1945. The UN has subsequently been the principal mechanism for global governance over the past half century.[11] It has done much to codify expected and accepted norms and rules of international behavior across a wide range of functional issue areas. The UN's constituent agencies all regulate transnational interactions in their respective functional domains (UN Development Programme, International Labor Organization, Food and Agriculture Organization, International Atomic Energy Agency, International Civil Aviation Organization, International Maritime Organization, International Telecommunications Organization, UN High Commissioner on Refugees, Universal Postal Union, World Health Organization, UN Educational, Scientific and Cultural Organization, and the World Meteorological Organization). The Bretton Woods institutions of the

World Bank, International Monetary Fund (IMF), Organization of Economic Cooperation and Development (OECD), and World Trade Organization (WTO) similarly monitor and regulate international commerce and finance and provide development assistance. A series of regional development banks (such as the Asian Development Bank and Inter-American Development Bank) and organizations (such as the Organization of American States, African Union, and Association of Southeast Asian Nations), with their subsidiary and associated organs, all add further layers to the global governance institutional architecture.

Notwithstanding the important roles played by the United Nations in governing these interactions and addressing a wide range of humanitarian conditions since its inception, the concept of global governance has gained momentum since the 1990s, when the bipolar Cold War order was replaced by a less predictable, more anarchical, but interdependent global system. The distinguishing characteristic of the emerging system became known as "globalization." Though the term originally denoted economic interdependencies, as famously described by Thomas Friedman,[12] it soon evolved to include a broader range of functional issues that penetrated across sovereign national borders: global climate change and biodiversity; peace, security, and conflict resolution; development and commerce; human rights; public health; transnational crime, etc.

At the same time, largely in reaction to the Rwandan genocide of 1994 and the Serbian genocide against Kosovars in 1998–99, humanitarian atrocities inside nation-states joined this broader menu of globalized challenges to international "order." This led to the concept of the collective "Responsibility to Protect" (R2P) against mass "genocide, war crimes, ethnic cleansing, and crimes against humanity"—which led to the report of the International Commission on Intervention and State Sovereignty in 2000, its adoption by UN members at the 2005 World Summit, and reaffirmation in United Nations Resolution 1674 in 2006.[13] China worked closely with the United States to shape this concept and these documents.

To be sure, the global governance agenda exhibits a strong Western liberal cast. It has both a philosophical and institutional history rooted in Western liberal societies, civil law, and democratic polities. In the well-chosen words of global governance expert G. John Ikenberry, "At its most basic, liberal internationalism offers a vision of an open, rules-based system in which states trade and cooperate to achieve mutual gains. Liberals assume that peoples and governments have deep common interests in the establishment of a cooperative world order organized around principles of restraint, reciprocity, and sovereign equality."[14] In the international relations literature, global issues were married to the notion of "norms" and adherence to standards of state behavior in international "society" (the English School). This normative behavior is sometimes referred to as "soft law," as norms frequently form the basis of international laws.

As Western nations and international relations scholars pushed liberal "norms" of global governance, their views were challenged by a series of developing nations (led by those in Southeast Asia) that upheld state sovereignty and rejected many of the liberal assumptions.[15] State-centric and authoritarian governments such as China reject liberalism wholesale and view it as a ruse for Western intervention. For them, domestic order trumps international order. Such advocates countered that "Asian values" were distinctive from Western liberal values.[16] A similar strain was heard from the "Beijing Consensus" and "China Model" schools of thought.

China's Record in Global Governance

It is in this context that we examine China's evolving approach to, and role in, global governance and international institutions. I argue that there has been an evolution in Beijing's behavior over time: from opposition to this order from the 1950s–1970s, to a generally passive position during the 1980s–1990s when it sought membership in international institutions and wished to learn the rules of the road, obeying them to a large extent, to a more selective and activist position in international institutions during the early 2000s, when Beijing became more confident and outspoken, to a more recent, moderately revisionist posture since 2008 that seeks to selectively alter rules, actors, and the "balance of influence" largely from *within* existing institutions—while simultaneously trying to establish alternative institutions and norms of global governance and redistribute power and resources within the international system.

The world has generally witnessed China evolving from a passive to more activist actor, reflecting both its growing power and confidence. As Canadian scholar Gregory Chin aptly describes it, "Beijing is not looking to overturn the international system; rather, it is acting more like a moderate revisionist power—one that prefers gradual reform of the international order."[17] Chinese scholar Ren Xiao similarly describes China's role as a "reform minded status-quo power," which has benefited from the existing global system and international institutions but still seeks to change "unjust and unreasonable components" of the system.[18] This recent tendency should not be overstated, as China still remains very reluctant to become engaged on many issues and still displays a distinct "selective multilateralist" posture. While assiduously and tenaciously guarding its own corner to protect national interests in the international institutional arena, China also pursues and has long articulated a foreign policy agenda that favors multipolarization, equality in international relations, and empowerment of developing nations. This is hardly a hidden agenda. Now, with Beijing's sense of its own growing international influence, along with other rising powers and the fluidity of the international system, the world is beginning to witness some modest steps by China to weaken the power and influence of the West and strengthen the South.

One area where China is pushing this agenda is in global finance. Since central banker Zhou Xiaochuan first floated the idea on March 23, 2009, China has increasingly called for reform of the international monetary system and has floated the idea that the dollar should be phased out as the world's principal reserve currency, while the *renminbi*, together with a basket of currencies, should replace dollar hegemony. Even the World Bank expects the U.S. dollar to lose its solitary dominance in the global economy by 2025, as the Euro and *renminbi* establish a new "multicurrency" international monetary and reserve system.[19] This may be a long-term trend, but 61 percent of the world's $5.3 trillion in currency reserves was still denominated in dollars in 2011, according to the International Monetary Fund.[20] Until 2005 the RMB was pegged to the dollar, but in that year, under significant pressure from the United States, Beijing shifted to a "managed float" system based on a basket of major foreign currencies, although the RMB still moves mainly in response to the dollar. Since that time through

2011, the nominal RMB exchange rate appreciated approximately 25 percent against the dollar.

Thus we see both continuity and change in China's approach to international institutions and global governance. Yet China continues to display and practice a distinct "transactional" style of diplomacy, carefully weighing national costs and benefits, rather than contributing to global collective "public goods." There also exists ambivalence in Western discussions: although many call for a *more* internationally engaged China in terms of contributing to security and economic development, others are not at all comfortable with China developing and expanding its military reach and aid programs into various parts of the world. They would prefer China to remain a benign regional actor and not become a global power. Thus there is an essential contradiction embedded in Western discourse concerning China's role in global governance: philosophically many support it, but practically many do not wish to see it.

Asian nations seem less concerned with China's global contributions and are generally not caught up in this discourse. Rather, Asian states seek a peaceful neighbor and productive commercial partner in China. They are far more worried about Beijing's behavior in the regional neighborhood than in far-flung parts of the world. This said, many of China's neighbors do carefully monitor and warily watch Beijing's expanding role in Asian regional institutions. Paralleling the increased activism that some observers note in global institutions since 2008, Asians perceive an increased assertiveness in China's behavior in regional regimes during the same period. As a Singaporean diplomat observed to me in 2009, "China used to be content to sit in the back seat of the regional multilateral car and let ASEAN [the Association of Southeast Asian Nations] drive, but now they have moved to the passenger's seat, taken the map out of the glove box, and are telling us how to drive! It is only a matter of time before they try and take over the steering wheel."[21] When I visited Singapore one year later, I met with the same official and asked him if this had happened yet. He sarcastically but realistically replied, "No, it seems that they [China] prefer to sit in the back seat, give directions, and be chauffeured."[22]

China has used its newfound global financial power to become more active in the G-20, World Bank, International Monetary Fund (IMF), and other regional development banks. China has also leveraged the new financial status to increase its share of voting rights in the IMF, and to have Justin Yifu Lin appointed as the World Bank's chief economist, Cai Jinyong as head of the World Bank's International Financial Corporation, and Zhu Min as deputy managing director of the IMF.

Other developing nations in Africa and Latin America hold more mixed views of China and global governance. On the one hand, they welcome China's development assistance and contributions to security stabilization and peacekeeping. On the other hand, some view China as pursuing a mercantilist and resource-depleting posture in their regions. Developing nations also tend to view China as a fraternal developing nation and one that, like them, was historically subjected to colonial and imperialist exploitation and incursions at the hands of Western powers. South-South fraternalism binds Beijing together with many other developing nations that are suspicious of the whole concept of global governance, viewing it as a ruse for Europe and the United States to intervene in sovereign affairs and perpetuate their underdeveloped status.

There is, consequently, no common understanding among Western, Asian, and developing nations on the question of China and global governance. Indeed, there is no common perception in China either. As we saw in Chapter 2, there is both animated debate and deep skepticism in the international relations community in China toward both the general concept of global governance (全球治理) and, specifically, Beijing's contributions.[23] In fact, the concept of *global governance* did not enter the official lexicon of the Chinese government until 2009, when it was first used in a speech by State Councilor Dai Bingguo at the G-8 + 5 summit meeting in Italy, when Dai used the term "global economic governance" (全球经济治理).[24]

A Responsible Major Power?

Much of the skepticism in China about global governance is linked to the question of whether or not China is a "responsible major power" (负责任的大国). Some scholars, such as Peking University's Wang Jisi and Renmin University's Shi Yinhong, understand the concept of "responsibility" in terms of contributing to global "public goods."[25] But a number of other commentators sharply criticize the concept of being a "responsible power" as simply a new means by which the United States and the West seek to control China's behavior and retard its rise—replacing "containment" and "hedging" with "responsibility." In the words of the deputy director of the Department of Policy Planning in China's Ministry of Foreign Affairs, "The West now tries to regulate China's international behavior by demanding China share responsibilities and acknowledge the rationality and legitimacy of the current system, and to influence China's internal affairs and development by bringing it into the current international system.... The underlying assumption of the 'responsibility theory' is still that China might 'irresponsibly' use its national strength; hence whether China is a responsible country should be defined and judged by other countries."[26] The former president of the China Institute of International Studies and Ambassador to Britain, Ma Zhengang, shares this view: "Once the veil on the 'China responsibility theory' is removed, the essence of the argument is clearly revealed: China is an 'irresponsible' country.... The basic approach is to restrain and regulate China...In emphasizing 'China's responsibility' toward the international system, the United States is attempting to request China to coordinate with the United States and other Western countries and act according to U.S. wishes as well as transform itself according to U.S. criteria."[27] Another critic writing in the journal of the International Department of the CCP is also starkly critical: "The very concept of 'great power responsibility' is flawed as all it does is serve the global hegemon by compromising the sovereignty of other states, holding these states accountable to so-called 'universal' values that were invented by an exclusive group of dominant states, which ensures that a nation's relative power remains the key determinant of its position in the international order."[28]

These perspectives are pervasive. Global governance is met with much skepticism in China. Another common view is that China has so many domestic problems that it does not have the luxury of contributing much to global governance. A variant of this line is that China's bureaucracies are not well configured to address global issues. As Vice Foreign Minister Cui Tiankai observed in an interview with the author: "We are not fully ready yet for global governance. Some government departments are not ready. We are still preoccupied with domestic problems. U.S. leaders have a global perspective, but our leaders are thoroughly preoccupied with domestic issues."[29]

Nonetheless, despite this rationale, China cannot ignore the issue of global governance or international calls to contribute more to global "public goods" as it continues to rise. China has certainly been a (major) beneficiary of the post–World War II Bretton Woods system and institutions.[30] As such, it has occasionally been accused of being a "free rider" on that system—but, at the same time, it is more and more involved in international institutions and global governance. Chinese scholars actively debate how much "responsibility" their country should shoulder in world affairs. As one scholar noted: "We should be cautious in taking responsibility. At the same time, we can't do everything, but we cannot do nothing—we have to carry our own weight."[31] Officially, China's official White Paper on Peaceful Development states: "As countries vary in national conditions and are in different stages of development, they should match responsibility with rights in accordance with their national strength.... For its part, China will assume more international responsibility as its comprehensive strength increases."[32]

The call by Robert Zoellick for China to become a "responsible international stakeholder" was an effort to redefine the terms in which China thinks of its role in the world, as well as how the world thinks about China. In essence, the Western strategy toward China from the 1970s through the 1990s was premised on *integrating* China into the existing international institutional system, so as to both strengthen the system by giving China a deserved "place at the table" but also to "socialize" China into the prevailing rules and norms of the system. As such, it was accepted that a variety of international institutions that collectively made up the global system—from developmental to financial and monetary, to health and welfare, to security and other dimensions—should contribute their institutional resources *to China* so as to help it develop and simultaneously socialize it into the existing norms of international behavior. The strategy definitely treated China as an *object*, both as a recipient of resources and as a nation to be molded and shaped normatively. Zoellick's speech implicitly argued that this stage of Western strategy—and of China's own behavior—had come to an end. China was now a "member of the club," completely integrated into the international institutional landscape. As such, the paradigm had shifted from (to paraphrase John F. Kennedy) "what the world can do for China" to "what can China do for the world?" Zoellick was *not* arguing that China should somehow "save the world," but he was suggesting that the phase of *institutional integration* was over, and now a new phase of *normative integration* had opened.

Zoellick's statement further implied that China's integration was only partial (via institutional membership) and that, even though China obeyed most international rules and norms, its compliance was selective and shallow. That is, its role was not what some scholars contrasted with "deep integration"—full assimilation of the values that reflect the norms underlying the rules and regulations of the Western liberal system.[33] This would accord with the findings of IR social constructivist theorists who argue that states generally tend to pass through two stages of socialization into the norms of international institutions: (1) an initial stage where states comply with existing norms, but only as a conscious, instrumental calculation (essentially "feigned compliance" and role playing); and (2) a second stage whereby the state deeply internalizes the norms, and complies with them because the internalization has occurred to such an extent that the state's identity is transformed.[34] China still seems stuck somewhere between the first and second phases. Zoellick was therefore suggesting that China needed to move beyond being a beneficiary of the global liberal system to becoming a more entrenched "responsible stakeholder" in, and contributor to, it. To do this, however, requires a state to make more than tactical adjustments, truly absorbing norms and thus taking on new identities where behavior stems from value-based orientations and not rational cost-benefit calculations.[35]

But China continues to reflect discomfort with liberal norms. As Ann Kent, an Australian specialist on China's participation in international organizations, observed: "Most theories of compliance are based on the assumption of shared liberal norms, both international and domestic, and a common understanding about the principles of conduct necessary to uphold them. These understandings are not shared by China, which does not accept the universality of liberal norms."[36] If anything, in the words of Tsinghua University scholar Yan Xuetong, "China seeks to develop differentiated—rather than uniform—norms of global governance."[37] Nor, Yan observes, is China comfortable with the existing global governance institutions developed by the West after World War II, instead seeking to replace—rather than reform—them. Yan argues that "In the future, China will prefer to establish new institutions, rather than reform existing ones—it is easier to build a new building than to remodel an old building."[38] Katherine Morton, a specialist on China and global governance at the Australian National University, thus concludes, "For those who look to China to share more responsibility in the world, prepare for a very slow process."[39]

In the rearrangement of multilateral roles and responsibilities currently under way in international diplomacy, China is certain to have an important impact. To understand China's likely impact and its current preferences for global governance and world order, it is vital to recall what China's experience has been with the postwar liberal international order to date.

China's Road to Global Governance

The experience of the PRC's participation in global governance is intertwined with the evolution of its multilateral involvement in international organizations. This is not to say that China does not contribute to global governance both unilaterally and bilaterally.

Unilaterally, China makes an important contribution to global governance by effectively governing itself. This is a key point often neglected by observers and critics. To feed, clothe, house, educate, and employ 1.4 billion people—one-fifth of the world's population—is a significant contribution to global stability. Lifting more than 200 million people out of absolute poverty over the past quarter century is another significant contribution and accomplishment. Maintaining China's own territorial integrity and security is another; should China break down or break up, it would spew crime, refugees, and perhaps lethal matériel outside its borders. But beyond what China contributes to global governance through governing itself, we must also note the aid and overseas development assistance (ODA) contributions China makes to other developing nations.

Bilaterally, China has signed a large number of treaties and agreements with foreign governments that govern various spheres of activity and interaction. Through these reciprocal obligations, China contributes to upholding rules and procedures of international order.

But it is in China's participation in multilateral international and regional organizations where Beijing's major impact on global governance is felt. Until the PRC's admission to the United Nations at the Twenty-sixth Session of the General Assembly in 1971, China was largely kept outside of the international institutional order. From that time to the present, China's overall experience with the international institutional order has been one of *integration*. Over the course of four decades (1971–2011) China moved from outside the global institutional order to inside. But it has not been a seamless transition. I would describe the integrative process as having passed through four broad phases.

Upon entry into the UN, throughout most of the 1970s, and during the first phase Beijing started as a *system challenger*. It challenged the existing order and the institutions that had excluded its participation over the previous two decades. Even after admission to the UN, Beijing regularly denounced the international system as unequal and unfair, often refused to participate in voting as a kind of protest, and advocated reform so as to increase the role and voice of developing countries. At the same time, Beijing was a stern critic of "superpower hegemonism." Deng Xiaoping's speech to the UN General Assembly in 1974, which unveiled Mao's "theory of the three worlds," was indicative of this revisionist phase, as were a number of fiery speeches given by China's UN delegate and Foreign Minister Qiao Guanhua. China's stance in the UN during the late Maoist era (1971–1976) reflected the radicalization of foreign policy under the Gang of Four's influence. Although Beijing's rhetoric during this first phase was radical, its diplomatic behavior inside the UN was actually quite passive. Its favored voting preference in the Security Council was either nonparticipation or abstention (although in the General Assembly it usually voted with the bloc of developing nations). At first, China elected to participate in only eight UN specialized agencies—including the UN Education, Scientific, and Cultural Organization (UNESCO), the UN Environment Program (UNEP), Food and Agriculture Organization (FAO), International Labor Organization (ILO), International Civil Aviation Organization (ICAO), and World Meteorological Organization (WMO)—and selectively studied joining others. By 1977 China was a member of only twenty-one intergovernmental organizations (IGOs).

With the death of Mao, overthrow of the Gang of Four, and full ascension to power by Deng Xiaoping and other reformist leaders in 1978, China's stance in the UN and international bodies shifted to a *system studying phase*. This indicates a shift from Beijing's advocacy of changing the international system to upholding it. To some extent, China toned down the rhetoric about the Third World and superpower hegemony; but it simultaneously increased its anti-Soviet rhetoric while softening attacks on the West and the United States. In terms of international organizations, China remained passive and studious. From 1977 to 1984 it joined only eight more IGOs (although participation in nongovernmental organizations, NGOs, jumped from 71 in 1977 to 355 in 1984). Importantly, this included the three main Bretton Woods institutions of the World Bank, IMF, and General Agreement on Tariffs and Trade (GATT),[40] as well as the Asian Development Bank (ADB). During this second period (1978–1984), China mainly sought to study and learn how these international institutions operated.

This apprenticelike period led to a lengthy third phase from 1985 to 2000 that can be described as a *system exploitation phase*. During this time, China further integrated into the international institutional order and learned very well how to benefit from it by extracting resources. For example, China became the largest recipient of World Bank loans and projects, surpassing India. By the end of 2009 the World Bank had cumulatively committed a total of $46.06 billion in loans, involving 309 projects, to China.[41] From 1986 to 2007 China received $19.25 billion in loans and grants from the ADB.[42] Beijing learned to milk a wide variety of other multilateral agencies for aid, loans, and investment—surpassing all other nations in the world.

As Beijing learned how to play the system, its presence and voice also grew. Numerically, China progressively joined more and more IGOs (fifty-one by 1996) and NGOs (1,079 by 1996), representing the nation's increased integration into the system. In addition to joining more institutions, during the 1990s China also acceded to a number of international treaties and conventions. Of particular importance was its accession to key international security and arms control treaties. By signing these treaties and joining these regimes, China took tangible steps to indicate it was becoming a "status quo" power and system-maintaining power. The costs to its international image of not joining and instead remaining outside the system were too high for China to bear. Moreover, scholarly studies show that two other factors were important. The work of Rand Corporation analyst Evan Medeiros indicates that pressure from, and bilateral negotiations with, the United States were important—but Ann Kent of the Australian National University and Harvard's Alastair I. Johnston argue that Chinese officials became "socialized" into understanding and supporting the norms of underlying regional and international regimes.[43] Finally, China's own national security interests played a role, as Beijing did not want nations with nuclear weapons on its borders (with the Indian, Pakistani, and North Korean detonations, it failed to achieve this goal).

Diplomatically, during this period Chinese leaders and officials began to appear at and address numerous international gatherings to discuss issues on the global governance agenda. In these speeches, China was unfailingly supportive of multilateral efforts to address global issues, but the speeches and position papers also continued to emphasize state sovereignty, greater multipolarity, and redistribution of power from North to South, and they were often critical of the United States. Thus, on one hand, China sought to act as a status-quo, system-supporting power by working *through* international organizations, but on another it continued to evince discomfort with the way the system was configured. This ambivalence was also apparent in China's voting record in the United Nations. In the Security Council, from 1989 to 1996 only 17 percent of the time did China's votes coincide with those of the United States, and in the General Assembly China continued to exhibit strong solidarity with developing countries.[44]

Hence during this third period of international institutional interaction, we see a China that was technically more integrated in terms of its growing membership and participation in international and regional bodies, legally and normatively more integrated through its growing accession and adherence to international treaties and accepted practices, a major beneficiary of the resources international institutions had to offer, and more proactive in international institutions, but still extremely uncomfortable with the Western bias in the system.

Although China is to be credited with behavior increasingly befitting a "responsible power" during this period, China's continuing ambivalence with the existing institutional order is equally apparent.

This ambivalence continues into the fourth, *system altering*, phase, of China's evolving relationship with international institutions and global governance (2000 to the present). The fourth phase is characterized by expanded membership and deepening participation in international institutions. In this phase we see a much more proactive China that is more comfortable in and seeks to use international institutions more to its benefit. One example is the World Trade Organization Dispute Settlement Body (WTO/DSB), where China overcame its aversion to multilateral adjudication and became one of the most active *initiators* (filers) of complainant cases.[45] But beginning around 2008, we also see a China that is proactive in pushing for change in some IGOs to reflect Beijing's long-stated commitments to multipolarity and enhancing the influence of developing countries. Over the past decade China has continued to join IGOs and NGOS and participate in ad hoc regimes. According to the official *People's Daily*, by the end of 2008 China was a member of more than 130 IGOs and twenty-four UN specialized agencies, and signatory to more than three hundred multilateral treaties.[46]

It is now evident that China is fully integrated into the international institutional architecture. It remains outside of very few major IGOs, really only the Organization of Economic Cooperation and Development (OECD). As it integrated, Beijing's confidence grew and its participation became more self-assured. The diplomats and representatives China posts to these organizations now uniformly receive high marks for their knowledge, preparedness, and sophistication. They master the technical details and operating procedures of institutions and are assertive in setting and shaping agendas. As one U.S. congressional study observed: "China is thorough, exceedingly well prepared and well organized about executing its responsibilities as an institutional member. It does its homework and raises detailed, substantive questions about matters which not only affect China's interests, but also on issues of purely institutional relevance. This includes questions about operational issues and structures, staffing and office locations, and a range of administrative issues."[47] This meticulousness is a far cry from the aloofness and apparatchik-like behavior of previous years.

As an illustration of China's evolving role in international institutions, let us examine Beijing's behavior in the United Nations over time.

The United Nations

The most important international institution for China is the United Nations. Ironically, after being shut out of it for so long, China has become one of the world's strongest advocates of the UN, as it is founded on the basis of both of China's most cherished diplomatic principles: state sovereignty and universal equal representation. At the same time, it also enjoys the status of being one of the Permanent Five (P-5) members of the UN Security Council (along with Russia, the United States, France, and the UK), which confers major power status (and veto power). Inside the Security Council, China has become much more active, although it still often adopts a wait-and-see posture, waiting to see how the other P-5 members vote before revealing its own hand. It is much more cautious about wielding a veto in the Security Council, although Beijing has (by a wide margin) been the least frequent veto user among P-5 member states. In the 25 years from 1971 to 1996, China cast 21 vetoes, but from 1996 to 2011 it used only five.[48] The issues of Taiwan and Tibet will reflexively trigger a veto from Beijing, although it works hard not to let these issues get anywhere near voting stage. Oftentimes China expresses its "principled opposition" by voting an abstention instead of an outright veto; Beijing has the distinction of casting more than half of all abstentions among the P-5. But the primary pattern of China's Security Council voting in recent years has been that of a partner rather than a spoiler. Although usually reflexively aligning itself with Moscow, on many issues China worked to forge consensus with other members and—whenever possible—to vote in common with the United Kingdom, United States, France, and Russia (over the past decade there has been frequent unanimity). This included sensitive cases such as Sudan, Myanmar, Zimbabwe, Iran, North Korea, and Libya. For example, in February 2011 China joined the rest of the Security Council in imposing an arms embargo on Libya as well as a travel ban and freeze of assets on the Muammar el-Qaddafi regime (although it abstained on the resolution authorizing a no-fly zone and air strikes). But this experience burned Beijing, as it led to NATO air strikes on

Qaddafi forces, ultimately overthrowing the regime and taking his life. China did not believe it had authorized the use of force, but NATO interpreted the UN resolution in this way. This experience led Beijing, together with Moscow, to veto similar UN resolutions against the Syrian regime in 2012. Working to forge common positions with the other P-5 states, Beijing also frequently succeeds in hard negotiating to moderate and water down resolutions and sanctions. This gives China the appearance of being cooperative, but at the same time forging compromise positions more in line with China's own interests.

The Libyan case is indicative of how Beijing's position on sanctions has evolved over time. Once completely allergic to sanctions (and having been on the receiving end of them), China has grown to endorse them in certain cases and under certain conditions. It still views sanctions as a "last resort" and always argues in favor of dialogue and diplomacy instead of coercive or punitive measures. But in the cases of Iran, North Korea, and Libya, China has endorsed and voted in favor of sanctions. At the same time, Beijing was successful in watering them down so as to strip out some of the more coercive clauses and to target governments and not populations. Beijing also insists that *all* sanctions must be authorized by the UN and not adopted by individual states or groups of them.[49] Since sanctions were adopted, however, China has a mixed record on implementation. It has been accused of trying to sell arms to Libya, being a transit point for weapons shipments into and out of North Korea, laundering funds for Iran through Chinese banks and permitting its oil companies to operate there—all in contravention of UN sanctions Beijing endorsed.

In a positive development, China reversed its previous opposition to "humanitarian intervention" and in 2005 came to accept the "Responsibility to Protect" (R2P) principle, that is, the collective responsibility to protect civilians from genocide and other crimes against humanity. Although a Western initiative, Former Foreign Minister Qian Qichen sat on the UN panel that drafted the R2P language at the 2005 World Summit, and China voted in favor of Security Council Resolution 1674 in 2006, which formally adopted the principle.[50] Nonetheless, China remains reticent to invoke R2P except in extreme cases or when it finds a consensus among other Security

Council members (as with Libya in 2011).[51] In the Libyan instance, China voted in favor of resolutions to protect civilians but exercised its veto in the Syrian case.

China is also rhetorically supportive of, but practically reluctant in, engaging in Security Council reform. An official statement by the Foreign Ministry reads: "China firmly supports necessary and reasonable reform of the Security Council to increase its representativeness and transparency and make it better serve Member States. The reform must give priority to increasing the representation of developing countries, particularly African countries, and must reflect the trend toward democracy in international relations so that small and medium-sized countries will have more opportunities to be involved in Security Council decision making."[52] Even though China is in favor of expanding the Security Council in this manner, it is *not* in favor of expanding the number of *permanent* members. China has made it clear that it will not countenance Japan, India, Brazil, or Germany gaining this status. Nor has Beijing done much to forge consensus on Security Council reform.[53]

China has also become a significant contributor to UN peacekeeping operations (UNPKO). Having contributed nearly twenty thousand personnel over the past twenty years and with approximately two thousand currently deployed, China is the largest contributor of all Security Council P-5 nations (yet No. 16 overall). In 2009, Beijing paid only about 4 percent of the UNPKO operating budget (approximately $300 million).[54]

By accepting R2P in principle, endorsing and generally enforcing sanctions, contributing to UN peacekeeping missions, favoring Security Council reform, holding to a "conformist" UNSC voting record, and being deeply involved in all UN specialized agencies and commissions, China has arguably taken on the image and role of "system maintainer" and "responsible power" in the United Nations. Beijing has certainly come a very long way from its aloof and often doctrinaire posture of the past, and is one of the most vocal champions of the United Nations.

Yet, this positive trend should not be overstated: China still displays concerted ambivalence in several respects. It remains reluctant to penalize small and developing states when they transgress international rules and norms, and it continues to deal extensively with governments that much of the rest of the world shuns: North Korea, Iran, Syria, Sudan, Uzbekistan, Zimbabwe, Myanmar, and Qaddafi's Libyan regime. In the cases of North Korea, Iran, Sudan, and Libya, China has been caught violating UN sanctions.[55]

Even though more engaged than in the past, it must also be said that China remains a cautious actor in the Security Council, usually acting defensively to limit and water down the more far-reaching objectives of others (notably the United States). As Michael Fullilove, director of the Lowy Institute in Australia, concluded in his study of China in the UN, "China continues to define its national interests narrowly and pursue them with an uncompromising resolve. *China wants respect, but not responsibility.*"[56] He also sees some slippage in China's positions on a series of key indicators in recent years (post-2005), what he describes as the "stakeholder spectrum," where China is distancing itself more and more from Western positions. It also continues to exhibit a certain free-rider orientation. For example, China's financial contributions to the UN are not commensurate with the nation's economic clout. Although it possesses the world's second-largest economy, China is only the seventh-largest contributor to the UN operating budget (at 3.2 percent), ranking it behind the United States (22 percent), Japan (19.47 percent), Germany (8.66 percent), the UK (6.13 percent), France (6.03 percent), and Italy (4.89 percent), and just ahead of Canada (2.81 percent) and Spain (2.52 percent).[57] China's relatively paltry contribution is far from being commensurate with the nation's economic strength and international stature.

China also exhibits a certain schizophrenic persona in the UN: in the General Assembly China is more rigid and doctrinaire, and in the Security Council Beijing is more pragmatic and flexible. This is evident in China's voting patterns. I surveyed all of China's votes in the Security Council from 1994 to 2006 (858) and in the General Assembly from 1996 to 2007 (786).[58] Security Council votes do not reveal much, as there is a very high propensity to vote in common with other members. Much effort is put into formulating wording for resolutions that can be acceptable to all parties. Accordingly, from 1994 to 2006, China voted 93.1 percent identically with the United States, 94.5 percent identically with the UK, 95.2 percent identically with France, and 94.4 percent with Russia. By contrast, General Assembly voting patterns are much more revealing. During 1996–2007, China voted 80.2 percent identically with Brazil, 80.3 percent identically with India, 85.4 percent identically with Iran, and 70.7 percent identically with Russia, but only 45.3 percent identically with France, 44.3 percent identically with the UK, and a paltry 11.7 percent of the time identically with the United States.[59] By showing the extreme divergence between Beijing and Washington (and to a lesser extent with France and Britain) in these voting patterns, we see more clearly China's discomfort with—and opposition to—Western positions.

Thus, on balance, as in so many other aspects of China's international behavior, its posture in the UN is a contradictory work-in-progress. China remains a conflicted nation and a partial power. But Beijing's behavior in the UN demonstrates just how far China has come in its diplomacy over the past three decades, and also just how far it has to go before it can truly be judged a "responsible power." As China's ambassador to the UN Wang Guangya observed in a 2008 interview with the author at the UN Mission in New York:

> China has this identity, this mentality, as being a big major power on the one hand, but it is still a poor and economically backward country. Therefore on many world issues—economic and environmental issues, issues such as sustainable economic development—China still considers their position and our concern is closer with the G-77. I think that this is a complex identity for China, but I also feel that over the last four or five years, in the UN itself, China has played a role that is as a bridge between the major powers on one hand, and between the developing powers on the other.[60]

More broadly, scholars who have studied China's participation and behavior in multilateral organizations identify a series of patterns in Beijing's behavior.[61]

The first school of thought is that China has integrated well, is willingly assimilating itself into the international order, and on the whole is absorbing the norms of international behavior. A second school finds China to be much more pragmatic and selective in its participation—what some describe as a "supermarket approach" of selectively purchasing what it needs. This line of analysis posits that China's participation is only tactical and not fundamentally philosophical. A third school of thought contends that China does not accept the existing liberal order and is simply biding its time until it can overturn the system, or more likely "hollow it out from within." There is probably truth in each of these perspectives. Let us now turn to examine China's positions and postures on a select range of global governance issues.

Nonproliferation and Arms Control

Since the mid-1990s, China has joined and participated in nearly all the relevant international treaties and regimes concerned with non-proliferation and arms control: the Biological Weapons Convention (1984), UN Arms Control Register (1991), Non-Proliferation Treaty (NPT, 1992), Seabed Arms Control Treaty (1992), Comprehensive Test Ban Treaty (1996), and Chemical Weapons Conventions (1997). In the mid-1990s, the Chinese government also joined the Zangger Committee (the implementing organ of the NPT to control the export of nuclear materials) and promulgated its own export control regulations, the Nuclear Suppliers Group (NSG), provided verbal and written commitments that it would adhere to the Missile Technology Control Regime (MTCR), and unilaterally proclaimed a nuclear weapons No First Use (NFU) pledge. These accessions to treaties and regimes were significant not only because they represented the foundations of the global security architecture but also because China had been accused of proliferating nuclear weapons technologies, chemical weapons precursors, and ballistic missiles and missile components and had continued atomic testing until 1996.

Officially, Beijing stands firmly opposed to enlargement of the international nuclear weapons club. To this end, it serves a vital role in convening the Six Party Talks on North Korea's nuclear program. Beijing will not likely abandon this role, but at the same time it is reluctant to squeeze North Korea with harsh sanctions (although it has signed on to the UN sanctions). China is also a member of the sextet of nations (UN Security Council Permanent Five plus Germany) working to bring Iran into compliance with all IAEA (the UN's International Atomic Energy Agency) requirements and to halt what is widely assumed to be a nascent nuclear weapons program. But Beijing is resistant as well to toughening and enforcing sanctions against Tehran, given its large commercial, energy, and military interests there. China has carried out nuclear technology cooperation with Pakistan, which may have benefited Islamabad's nuclear weapons program.

Although opposed to proliferation of nuclear weapons technologies, China also used its participation in the NPT 2005 and 2010 Review Conferences to lobby against states whose nuclear doctrines permit the first use of nuclear weapons (e.g., the United States), end deployment of nuclear weapons on the territories of other states, and abandon the policy of providing a "nuclear umbrella" to other states.[62]

With respect to nuclear arms control, China has been involved in the UN Conference on Disarmament in Geneva for many years, calling in particular for a ban on all nuclear weapons, a Fissile Material Cutoff Treaty (FMCT), as well as the nonmilitarization of outer space. But other than in this venue, Beijing has not entered into nuclear arms reductions bilaterally or multilaterally. It has long argued that the two major nuclear weapons states—the United States and Russia—must drastically reduce their arsenals down to China's level before Beijing will consider joining such discussions. If Washington and Moscow can indeed agree on a new strategic arms treaty that brings their warhead stockpiles down to a thousand or less on each side, then pressure will mount for China to enter into trilateral or multinational (with France and Britain) negotiations. At present, China is thought to have somewhere between 250 and 500 nuclear warheads—although, as is discussed in Chapter 7, this could double or even triple as new intercontinental-range missiles (the DF-31, DF-41, and JL-2) join the arsenal of China's strategic forces over the next few years.

China's nuclear arsenal has long been based on a doctrine of minimum deterrence and second-strike capability, and Beijing publicly proclaims an NFU doctrine. Thus it possesses a relatively small but growing nuclear arsenal. The PLA's Second Artillery (which includes the nuclear forces) engaged over the past decade in a significant modernization of its missiles, arming them with warheads of increasing accuracy (possibly multiple) and moving from liquid- to solid-fueled rockets.

China's positions in other arms-control regimes also reflect divergence from the position of the United States. During the negotiations over creating an inspection and verification organ under the Biological Weapons Convention (BWC) Protocol, China joined with Russia to restrict "challenge inspections" and recognize the "right of all parties to the *peaceful* use of biological agents and toxins."[63] China has similarly sought the "peaceful right" to chemical technologies and to limit the scope of an inspections regime in the Chemical Weapons Convention (CWC). In both cases Beijing seeks to soften, block, or roll back efforts to create highly restrictive export-control regimes.

Thus, China's positions in various nonproliferation regimes are not entirely consistent: in the BWC and CWC it sides with developing countries, while in the NPT and Zangger Committee it tends to side more with developed countries. Part of the reason for this divergence could have to do with China's own status as a nuclear power. The NPT grants China special status as a nuclear power, placing it in a small club of recognized nuclear states, even though the BWC and CWC apply the same restrictions on all members. So, here again, we see a China that seeks to preserve its own status as a major power while simultaneously protecting its identity as a supporter of developing countries.

INTERPOL and International Crime

Transnational crime is now a serious issue of global governance, one that truly requires transnational cooperation. It is particularly acute in Asia. This takes a variety of forms: money laundering; extortion, embezzlement, and racketeering; drug trafficking; small arms smuggling; kidnapping and human smuggling; sex trade networks; illegal gambling; maritime piracy on the high seas; etc. No country in Asia is immune from these phenomena, although Japan, China, and Thailand seem to be the worst affected. Chinese triads and tongs and Japanese *yakuza* are legendary and continue to dominate the organized crime scene in Asia, but new transnational networks have also sprung up in Northeast, Southeast, South, and Central Asia. Many of these issues are in fact global in nature. Certainly those affecting financial and cyber security are having an impact on China.

China realized early on that it stood to benefit by joining INTERPOL (International Police), which it did in 1984.[64] Although necessarily quiet, INTERPOL has enjoyed many successes. One secret to its success is its ability to share information, for national police forces and security services to act quickly and in tandem yet retain sovereignty. INTERPOL operates internationally but has no transnational forces of its own. With China it works with an organ of the Ministry of Public Security known as the National Crime Bureau of China (NCB). This organ is responsible for domestic coordination with provincial and local police forces, railway and airport security, the People's Armed Police, and other special forces that guard particular installations. The Ministry of State Security has links with INTERPOL as well. In certain crises or special situations, as in the run-up to the 2008 Olympic Games in China, a special multiagency task force is established to interface with INTERPOL. In 1995 China hosted the 64th INTERPOL Assembly in Beijing, which attracted 600 delegates from more than 130 nations.[65] After the meeting, Minister of Public Security Tai Siju reported that the conclave had allowed China to sign bilateral cooperation accords with twenty more nations and that with INTERPOL China was able to assist in solving seven hundred major criminal cases.[66]

China's participation with INTERPOL has had its successes and troubles. Managing security for the Olympic Games in 2008 was a notable success. Only one random incident marred the games, the stabbing of an American tourist by a disgruntled Chinese citizen at the Drum Tower in Beijing. After assailant Tang Yongming committed the crime and leapt to his death, his name and fingerprints were run through INTERPOL databases—only to confirm that he had no prior criminal record and the case was random. China had good reason to worry about terrorist attacks at the Olympics, given the repeated attacks against civilians carried out in Xinjiang Autonomous Region and other provinces (including Beijing itself) by East Turkestan Independence Movement (ETIM) operatives. ETIM is formally listed with INTERPOL as an international terrorist group. But the games were successfully held, with no attacks.

The cracking of the "Goldfish" drug smuggling operation in the early 1990s was another notable success story. Chinese triads in Shanghai and Hong Kong were placing packets of high-grade heroin in the bellies of goldfish before their shipment to San Francisco. Simultaneous raids in Shanghai, Hong Kong, and San Francisco cracked the case.

This was the first instance of China's close cooperation with the U.S. Drug Enforcement Agency (DEA).

More problematic have been cases that involve extradition of fugitives sought by the Chinese government. According to Xinhua News Agency, in 2008 more than five hundred fugitives who were collectively accused of stealing RMB 70 billion fled abroad.[67] In 2007 the *China Daily* cited sources in the Ministry of Public Security saying that more than eight hundred fugitives wanted for economic crimes were overseas.[68] For some reason, though, China had not previously sought to sign bilateral extradition treaties with other states. It signed the first with Spain in 2006, but over the next two years it signed more than a hundred bilateral "justice assistance protocols" and thirty extradition treaties.[69] By 2011, China had agreed to extradition treaties with thirty-seven countries,[70] though China and the United States do not yet have one in place. Many Western countries have been reluctant to repatriate individuals sought by Chinese judicial authorities for fear that they will be tortured or subjected to capital punishment. This includes a number of ethnic Uighurs picked up in the al-Qaeda training camps in Afghanistan after September 11, 2001.

The most notorious case was that of Lai Changxing, the mastermind of a multibillion-dollar smuggling operation in Xiamen, Fujian Province, during the 1990s. Lai's company, Yuanhua, was a front for smuggling luxury cars, petrochemicals, designer watches, cigarettes, and other goods to and from Hong Kong. At one point Lai's company was said to be responsible for importing one-sixth of the nation's oil imports, while Lai ordered the building of an eighty-eight-story skyscraper, a new airport, and a new soccer team for Xiamen. He doled out Mercedes-Benzes and packets of cash to officials. In 1999 Lai fled to Canada after being accused of operating an organized crime ring responsible for smuggling RMB 53 billion ($8.2 billion) worth of goods and official bribes. The case became the largest in the PRC to date, with approximately three hundred municipal and provincial-level officials implicated. In 2000, a Chinese court sentenced fourteen to death, twelve to life in prison, and fifty-eight to other prison terms for their involvement.[71] But Lai was safely ensconced in Canada—where he sought refugee status (which was not granted). After eleven years of battling extradition, on the eve of deportation in 2001, Lai's lawyers appealed to the Canadian Supreme Court that his return to China would surely result in his execution. The court agreed to delay his deportation on this basis, until the Canadian government finally acquiesced a decade later in 2011 when the federal court in Ottawa agreed to Lai's extradition on the grounds that the criminal allegations against him were indisputable.

Lai's return to China removed a lengthy thorn in the side of China-Canada relations. Canadian officials insist that the extradition was carried out entirely according to decisions made by the courts and the Immigration and Refugee Board, *not* because the government of Prime Minister Steven Harper was trying to get back in the good graces of Beijing following several years of strained relations. As one official said, "We don't want the Chinese thinking our system works like theirs."[72] Lai was given a life sentence for operating his smuggling ring and an additional fifteen years for bribery by the Xiamen Intermediate People's Court, which commented (via Xinhua News Agency), "The sums involved are unusually large, and the details are extraordinarily serious, meriting the double sentence."[73]

Chinese police have also worked well with Southeast Asian authorities to crack several drug smuggling rings, with American authorities to break up several child smuggling networks, and with British and French officials to expose trafficking in migrant workers. In these and other cases, China is an active member and positive contributor to INTERPOL.

Public Health

Public health has risen up the global governance agenda, particularly since the Severe Acute Respiratory Syndrome (SARS) outbreak in China in 2003.[74] China today accounts for 10 percent of the world's cases of extremely drug resistant tuberculosis (XDR-TB) and is a source of Avian influenza (H5N1).[75] HIV/AIDS has also spread quickly in China, with an estimated 740,000 currently living with the disease and 26,000 having died from it in 2009.[76] Of course, China has black marks on its public health record for having covered up the SARS outbreak in 2002–03, the spread of HIV/AIDS and discovery of "AIDS villages" in Henan Province in 2005, and the Enterovirus 71 (EV-71) outbreak in 2008. Taken together with other cover-up scandals concerning tainted milk, lead toys, river poisonings, and deadly explosions, the proven propensity of China's central and local leaders to try to hide public health threats is not encouraging.

China has an important role to play in global health governance merely by maintaining a careful watch over—and publicizing—such transmittable diseases at home. At the same time, the international community must maintain a watchful eye on China. Since the aforementioned cover-ups, the Chinese government has admitted its failings and taken steps to improve reporting and public awareness. The State Council established leading groups and working committees on HIV/AIDS prevention and control, promulgating a series of regulations for China's health, public security, and tourism bureaucracies to follow. The National People's Congress revised the Law on the Prevention and Control of Infectious Diseases (which originally came into effect in 2004). For the first time, this legislation specifically targets willful transmission of HIV/AIDS and other life-threatening communicable diseases and pandemics. By 2008 the Chinese government had ramped up funding to combat HIV/AIDS to RMB 994 million (approximately $142 million).[77]

Internationally, China became a member of the World Health Organization (WHO) in 1972, displacing Taiwan. From then to 2004, the WHO provided China with "various technical assistance valued over $100 million."[78] Over time China's representatives to the WHO also participated actively in the bureaucratic procedures of the organization. In 2008 the WHO launched a five-year WHO-China Country Cooperation Strategy, the first ever to be signed jointly by WHO and the Chinese government. The strategy outlines a medium-term framework for cooperation between WHO and China to improve national health development. Since the SARS, HIV/AIDS, and H5N1 cover-ups, Beijing has experienced much closer scrutiny from the WHO, as well as contributing more data to the Geneva headquarters and opening its domestic health care system to closer scrutiny from WHO officials based in China.

China and the Global Environment

There is probably no other dimension where China's domestic governance has more of an impact on global governance (negative and positive) than environmental governance. China's own domestic environmental pollution contributes significantly to global climate change and environmental degradation. Conversely, China is becoming a world leader in production and usage of noncarbon alternative energy sources and has a clear national plan (which is being implemented) to reduce carbon intensity and diversify its sources of energy over the next thirty years. China has also been an active participant in global environmental governance forums since it first participated in the UN Conference on the Human Environment in 1972. Thus, as with many other dimensions of China's participation in global governance, there are both domestic and international aspects, as well as dimensions where China is a serious laggard and others where it is at the forefront of innovation.

One must begin by considering China's national environmental degradation and impact on the international environment. China now holds a number of dubious environmental distinctions.[79] In 2007 it surpassed the United States as the world's largest emitter of carbon dioxide. In 2009 China's share of global CO_2 emissions was measured at 6,319 million tons, 21.4 percent of the total.[80] With continuing annual economic growth of 8 percent, by 2020 China will be spewing 14.2 billion tons of greenhouse gasses into the atmosphere. China's sulfur dioxide (SO_2) emissions are also the highest in the world. As a result, China chokes in air pollution, which accounts for sixteen of the world's twenty most air-polluted cities and twenty of the world's thirty worst cases.[81] Acid rain (a combination of SO_2 and nitrogen oxide) is also a serious problem and is pervasive in northeastern and southeastern China, affecting the Koreas and Japan to the east and Hong Kong to the south. Polluted rivers in southern China that flow into the Mekong similarly affect downstream Laos and Vietnam. Air pollution from Guangdong Province now similarly envelops Hong Kong and Macao; some even blows northeast over Taiwan.

Water contamination is also pervasive, with an estimated 70 percent of Chinese rivers and lakes contaminated. According to China's Ministry of Environmental Protection, 43.2 percent of state-monitored rivers were classified as grade 4 or worse in 2010, meaning their water was unsuitable for human contact.[82] Two-thirds of China's 660 largest cities are reported to be water-stressed, where most of the water supply depends on groundwater pumped from aquifers—which are drying up and being depleted because of rapid salinization of soil (the situation is particularly acute on the North China Plain).[83] According to the World Bank, an estimated three hundred million rural residents are exposed to nonpotable water,[84] while another study estimated that 90 percent of urban groundwater is contaminated.[85] China's own Geological Survey estimates that half of the country's groundwater is contaminated.[86] Many rivers and arteries have experienced serious lead, mercury, and other chemical spills. In 2005, the Songhua River, which flows through northeastern Heilongjiang Province, registered benzene levels 108 times higher than national standards as a result of an upstream chemical plant explosion—resulting in an eighty-kilometer-long downriver toxic slick of an estimated 100 tons of benzene. Up to 90 percent of China's grasslands are degraded, with desertification now afflicting one-third of China's landmass; forest resources are being depleted (also contributing to ozone depletion); and China's wetlands have reportedly been reduced by 60 percent.[87]

Glacial melt on the Qinghai-Tibetan Plateau is another serious problem. Himalayan glaciers are melting at a rapid rate, having already shrunk by 21 percent. This prospect has profound and dangerous implications as the Hindu Kush glaciers feed all seven of Asia's great rivers (the Yellow, Yangzi, Mekong, Salween, Indus, Ganges, and Brahmaputra), affecting the Indian subcontinent, Myanmar and Indochina, and eastern China. If there is one transnational environmental issue in Asia calling out for multinational collaboration, it is this one.[88]

To deal with its pervasive environmental degradation, China is taking a number of proactive steps. The first dimension is legal and regulatory. Since the passage of the first Environmental Protection Law in 1979, China has passed more than forty environmental protection laws and a large number of state regulations.[89] In 2007, the National Development and Reform Commission of the State Council enacted the National Climate Change Program, a comprehensive endeavor that affects a variety of production, consumption, and environmental systems in China.

However, as in so many other areas in China, there is no shortage of laws and regulations—but rather, insufficient and arbitrary enforcement. Together with the National Development and

Reform Commission, Ministry of Land and Resources, Ministry of Water Resources, Ministry of Agriculture, Ministry of Science and Technology, and the State Forestry Administration, the Ministry of Environmental Protection is the lead central-level organ charged with overseeing and enforcing this legal-regulatory framework, and they all have provincial and subprovincial representation. These organs now evaluate localities not only on their GDP output but also on their "green" contributions as well. Environmental consciousness, activism, and organizations are also growing concomitantly. According to official estimates, more than three thousand environmental NGOs now operate nationwide,[90] activating civil society involvement and empowering nascent citizen organizations on the issue.[91] The environment, in fact, probably has the greatest potential to trigger widespread unrest and political protests.

As a result of the severity of China's environmental crisis and growing energy shortages, the government and private industry have taken a broad range of initiatives to cut emissions and transition the economy to alternative renewable sources.[92] At the UN Summit on Climate Change in September 2009, Hu Jintao announced a series of initiatives that included reduction of CO_2 emissions to 1.5 billion tons by 2020 (a 17 percent reduction in carbon intensity over 2005 levels), expanding forests to cover 40 million hectares, and increasing the share of nonfossil fuels in primary energy consumption to around 15 percent by 2020.[93] Twenty-seven new nuclear power plants are currently under construction (with thirteen already in operation). This will go a long way toward meeting the 85 percent increase in electricity demand expected by 2020. New building construction is similarly supposed to meet high energy-efficiency standards. The government has also set high efficiency standards for coal plants, shutting down many older plants and mines that are producing less than 30,000 tons per year, while also trying to eliminate personal burning of bituminous "soft" coal during winter. Biofuels are being promoted (China is now the world's third-largest ethanol producer). China's solar energy industry showed strong growth, in 2007 becoming a $12.9 billion industry and the world's largest producer of photovoltaic cells, before declining sales and exports hit the industry after 2008. Even with the drop-off in sales and revenue, the top Chinese solar firms—Suntech Power, Yingli Green Energy, and Trina Solar—are setting industry standards worldwide and forcing their foreign competitors to struggle or go bankrupt.[94] Wind power is another of China's comparative advantages. In 2009 China surpassed Germany as the world's top wind turbine producer, is now the world's fifth-largest consumer of wind power (generating 16 gigawatts in 2009), and by 2011 accounted for 21.8 percent of all the installed capacity of wind energy in the world.[95] However, the lack of transmission infrastructure in this sector has left a significant amount of capacity underutilized.

The final aspect of China's contribution to environmental global governance comes via its participation in international environmental regimes and adherence to their agreements. As noted earlier, China has been a participant in every notable intergovernmental environmental conference since the UN Conference on the Human Environment in Stockholm in 1972, soon after the People's Republic gained its seat in the UN.[96] China has signed and ratified numerous environmental treaties, including the Kyoto Protocol and the International Convention on Biological Diversity. It participated in the 1992 Earth Summit, the 2009 Copenhagen Conference on Climate Change and follow-up conferences in Cancún, Mexico, and Durban, South Africa. China's position at Copenhagen did not win it any praise from developed countries—or, for that matter, from many small developing countries—but it was more forthcoming at Cancún and Durban, agreeing to multilateral carbon emission cuts and an agreement to adopt a universal legal agreement on climate change. Previously, at Copenhagen, Beijing had refused to adopt any specific targets for industrialized or developing countries, refused to support a call for a binding international treaty, and was unwilling to endorse any kind of international verification regime, or register its own national goals in a binding international document. In the eyes of many, Beijing sabotaged a successful outcome at Copenhagen.[97] What China did do was to try to ally with developing countries to put the onus of responsibility and resources on developed countries. It continued to stress sovereignty over global cooperation, and China allied with developing countries against developed countries on a key global governance issue.[98] It is uncertain if the global criticism China received for its stance at Copenhagen induced Beijing to be more flexible in Cancún and Durban; but whatever the reason, its more positive positions are welcomed by the international community.

China and Global Governance in Perspective

Considering all of these cases, a picture with three dimensions emerges. The first is a China that is progressively more and more engaged in international institutions and on global issues, and generally positively so. The second is a China that remains highly ambivalent—and essentially distrustful—of calls from the West to contribute more to global governance. And third, we see a China that is consistent in its view that the existing international system is unequal and unfair, and clear in its support for developing countries to assume a larger voice and greater resources in the system. These are not mutually exclusive.

More generally, in China's international institutional and global governance behavior we see a nation insisting on being treated with the respect of a modern great power, but still clinging to its identity as a poor developing country. China seeks to shield other developing countries from what it sees as the inequities and "power politics" of developed countries. Chinese personnel in international institutions are technically very well prepared and are highly disciplined, but they still rarely go beyond the brief sent to them from Beijing. China is more confident and active in international organizations but still exhibits a "defensive" posture in many negotiations. It is a nation that knows what it is against but not necessarily what it is for, and one that finds it easy to say no but still difficult to say yes. Philosophically, China does not really support the liberal concepts of global governance and public goods, but it is increasingly sensitive to the implications for a global image of its role in global governance. China frequently uses multilateral institutions to constrain and dilute American power and influence, using "multilateralism" as a means to achieving "multipolarism."

These commonalities in China's positions and posture are manifest across a range of international institutions and global governance issues. Its full *normative* integration into the international system remains a work-in-progress, and at the end of the day it is most likely to be only partial at best.

Finally, I would argue that, to some degree, China's future contributions to global governance will be conditioned by its political culture. Chinese political culture has (at least) three distinguishing features that will shape its approach.[99]

The first is a Hobbesian one, whereby most Chinese believe they live in a highly unpredictable and predatory domestic environment. This extends to their view of the international environment, but perhaps even more so because externally there are many non-Chinese actors who are seen as trying to take advantage of China in an anarchical world. In such an environment, every interaction is seen as power-maximizing and zero-sum. Trust is at a minimum, and therefore, in the Chinese worldview, collective action cannot possibly be based on common ideals or values. A lack of commonly shared social values—in the aftermath of the Cultural Revolution and three decades of go-go growth—has produced a society of individual indifference and lack of collective responsibility. As a result, a moral void pervades Chinese society. What this means for China and global governance is clear: a society composed of self-seeking, power-maximizing individuals who are dismissive of domestic social responsibilities and public goods are certainly in no position to embrace arguments concerning international responsibilities and public goods.

The second constraint is a "transactional" feature deriving from the central role played by *guanxi* (reciprocal obligations) in Chinese society. Every day, everywhere, everyone in China turns normal social interactions into transactional ones whereby reciprocal provision of goods and services is the norm. It is hard-wired into the DNA of Chinese culture, society, and business. This is one important reason corruption will *never* be controlled or eliminated in China, because Chinese expect business to be done on the basis of favoritism and personal ties. As a result of *guanxi* culture, there is no such concept as "public goods" (the key to global governance). Everything is bartered all the time (and Chinese constantly calculate the qualitative or monetary equity of every exchange). In such a transactional social-business culture, Chinese are constantly looking for a tangible personal benefit from any interaction or transaction. Every action and investment of resources is weighed in terms of cost and benefit: What is to be tangibly gained from the investment? One does not do things for the simple betterment of the community (public goods). This transactional mentality also helps to explain China's cost-benefit approach to diplomacy, whereby every diplomatic situation is carefully weighed on a narrow national opportunity-cost basis.[100]

The third element of Chinese political culture that will constrain China's contributions to global governance has to do with how state-society relations are viewed. In China, there exists a universal belief in a *strong state* that provides for society (or at least *should* do so). Part of this is due to the PRC's sixty-year-plus experience with socialism, but it also goes back much further, to the imperial Chinese state.[101] Unlike the European and Anglo-Saxon tradition, there is no underlying concept of a Lockean social contract whereby citizens comply with the law because they accept the underlying norms of the law or contribute their individual earnings to the state via taxes so as to provide for the common good. Many Chinese do not understand why they must pay individual or corporate taxes; they do their best to avoid paying them and just assume that, somehow, the state will accrue resources and provide public services to society. This is beginning to change somewhat, as citizens now realize that tax avoidance is difficult—and therefore they are beginning to examine what they (collectively) are getting for their tax payments.

Thus, behind China's ambivalence and distrust of global governance lie these orientations deeply engrained in Chinese political culture. These three features are all reinforcing. Taken together with the suspicions that global governance is just the latest American or Western "trap" to retard China's growth and manipulate it internationally, as well as China's views about the inequities of North-South relations, the world should not expect China to become a full-fledged "responsible international stakeholder" anytime soon. Beijing's contributions will likely remain selective and limited.

5

China's Global Economic Presence

We need to have firm confidence, capitalize on favorable conditions and factors, and continue to grasp and make the most of this important period of strategic opportunities to promote steady and robust economic development, and continue to enhance China's overall strength and its international influence.

—PREMIER WEN JIABAO, Work Report to the National People's Congress, 2012[1]

I don't care how many tons of oil we can ship home, what I do care about is stock price.

—LOU JIWEI, Chairman, China Investment Corporation, 2009[2]

BY MANY MEASURES CHINA is a global economic powerhouse. As of 2011 China:

- Possessed the world's second-largest economy, with a GDP of $5.87 trillion;
- Had the highest average annual growth rate in the world over the preceding two decades (10.2 percent in constant price terms), accounting for about 40 percent of global economic growth;
- Was the world's largest energy consumer;
- Was the world's largest merchandise exporter and second-largest merchandise importer, third-largest trader in services, and second-largest trading nation overall;
- Was the second-leading recipient of (committed) foreign direct investment (FDI) in the world ($105.7 billion), and fifth largest global contributor of outbound direct investment ($60.5 billion);

- Had four of the world's top ten banks in terms of capitalization;
- Possessed the largest foreign exchange reserves ($3.2 trillion);
- Had the world's largest number of millionaires (1,020,000) and billionaires (115); and
- Was the largest foreign holder of American government debt ($1.6 trillion).

But scratch beneath the surface and its global position is not as strong as it seems. Although it is a trading superpower, its exports are still dominated by generally low-end consumer products. According to the WTO, in 2009 fully 93.6 percent of China's exports were manufactured goods.[3] China's financial services sector and knowledge-intensive industries still lag behind Western and other East Asian nations. It has few leading multinational corporations and poor brand presence in international markets. Although growing, China's overseas direct investment (ODI) and overseas development assistance (ODA) both remain limited compared with those of other major powers. China is only the world's fifth-largest overseas investor ($60.5 billion in 2011), and its ODA (estimated at $2.5 billion) does not even rank among the world's top ten donor nations.

By these measures, China remains a partial economic power. This becomes apparent when examining four discrete dimensions of China's global economic footprint discussed in this chapter: its global trade profile, position in global energy markets, overseas direct investment and multinational corporations, and aid programs.

The Trading Superstate

The world has never witnessed a trading power like China. The United States' and Japan's foreign trade did not expand nearly as fast or as broadly as has China's. The government privileged foreign trade as an important pillar of its overall development and growth strategy ever since Deng Xiaoping announced the opening of Special Economic Zones (SEZs) in the early 1980s and Premier Zhao Ziyang unveiled the coastal development strategy in 1988. Since then China's coastal provinces have become one big export platform and China's share of world trade has grown several times over. In 1980 it accounted for just 1 percent of world trade flows; today it is over 8 percent. It surpassed Germany as the world's largest exporter in 2009 and now accounts for more than 9 percent of global exports. China no longer runs as large an overall global trade surplus ($155 billion in 2011) as in the past, but it still continues to experience enormous surpluses with the United States and the European Union.[4]

China has certainly become the workshop of the world. Currently it is the world's largest producer of household and office furniture sets, machine tools, lubricant oils, lithium ion batteries, Christmas ornaments, footwear, cameras, computers, televisions, tape recorders, instrumentation, cloth and nylon fibers, textiles, plastics, stainless steel, washing machines, watches, mobile phones, and other consumer durables. In 2014 China is projected to overtake Australia as the world's largest wine producer by volume.

China's main trading partners have been steady in recent years but are beginning to change. It continues to primarily target the developed world with exports, although exports to the developing world are rapidly expanding and it has grown increasingly dependent on the developing world for imports of raw materials and natural resource inputs to its own economy. This evolving mix is evident among China's top ten trading partners (Table 5.1).

TABLE 5.1 China's Top Trade Partners (2010)

Rank	Country/Region	Volume ($ billions)	% Change Over 2009
1	United States	385.3	29.2
2	Japan	297.8	30.2
3	Hong Kong	230.6	31.8
4	South Korea	207.1	32.6
5	Taiwan	145.4	36.9
6	Germany	142.3	34.8
7	Australia	88.3	46.5
8	Malaysia	74.2	42.8
9	Brazil	62.6	47.5
10	India	61.8	42.4

Source: PRC General Administration of Customs, China's Customs Statistics.

What this table does not indicate is that, collectively, the European Union (EU-27) is still, by far, China's largest trading partner— accounting for € 395.129 billion in 2010 (approximately $550 billion at 2010 exchange rates).[5] Other regions' trade with China is also growing rapidly. In 2010, China-ASEAN trade surged 37.5 percent to $292.78 billion, after a Free Trade Area was launched at the beginning of the year, its trade with Africa similarly grew 33 percent (over 2009) to $110 billion, while with Latin America it surged 51.2 percent to reach $178.6 billion. Overall, the regional distribution of China's foreign trade is evident in Figure 5.1.

China's regional trade profile will also be affected by the growing number of free trade agreements (FTAs) it is forging with other nations. In addition to ASEAN, by 2011 China had FTAs with thirteen nations, had five more under active negotiation (with the Gulf Cooperation Council, Australia, Iceland, Norway, and South Africa), and was undertaking feasibility studies for FTAs with India, South Korea, Switzerland, and a trilateral one with Japan and South Korea.[6] China has also signed bilateral investment treaties with 129 countries and double taxation avoidance agreements with 96 countries.[7]

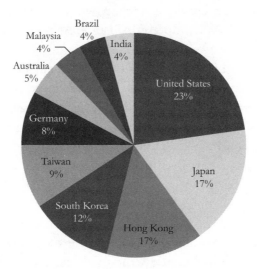

FIGURE 5.1 Composition of China's Regional Trade Partners, 2010 ($ Billion)

Source: PRC General Administration of Customs, *China's Customs Statistics*

Another facilitating feature is Market Economy Status. This is a designation under the WTO, but granted by sovereign states. MES affords a measure of protection against imposition of antidumping duties. China is the victim of dozens of antidumping cases filed against it every year (largely by the European Union, United States, and India). In 2009 it was the object of 40 percent of total antidumping investigations and 75 percent of countervailing duties (tariffs) in the world.[8] Absent MES, China will continue to be hit with such suits—so Beijing tries hard to secure this status. As of 2009, ninety-seven nations had granted China MES status—but not the major developed economies. This has been particularly contentious in China-Europe trade relations.[9] The United States has also declined to grant MES to China (although China will automatically qualify in 2016 under the terms of its accession to WTO).

China's exports are also supported by a variety of state subsidies and trade promotion measures. Of the 120 "national champion" SOEs that the government promotes and protects, many are among China's primary import-exporters. This includes all of China's state oil companies and big energy and commodity firms. China's state banks (four of which rank among the top ten in the world in capitalization) enjoy a cozy partnership with China's SOEs, lending them money at low state-prescribed interest rates and never calling in debts.

The Chinese government has also used its currency, the *renminbi* (人民币), to support trade. Unlike most advanced economies, China does not maintain a market-based floating exchange rate but instead keeps the rate artificially depressed by intervening in the currency markets. This means that China is, in effect, subsidizing its exports through keeping an artificially low currency value. In a bid to internationalize the RMB, the government has also gradually expanded to 70,000 the number of Chinese firms authorized to settle international transactions in RMB, with some analysts predicting that it is just a matter of a few years before 20–30 percent of China's total trade is in *renminbi*.[10] China has also structured creative financing arrangements with a number of countries to settle transactions either in RMB or via barter trade. China has granted five nations (Argentina, Indonesia, Japan, Pakistan, and South Korea) and Taiwan access to currency swap lines to pay for traded goods, where China's Central Bank provides RMB in exchange for the currency of the swapping country.

In these and other ways, China's government goes much further than other nations in supporting exports. A variety of tariffs and nontariff barriers similarly restrict imports. In this regard China has followed the classic "East Asian developmental state" model.[11]

In terms of the composition of foreign trade, as noted above, China is the "workshop of the world," accounting for production of a significant proportion of the world's manufactured goods. This has primarily been composed of low-end manufactures, but this product mix and reputation is changing, as China seeks to move up the value chain in line with the goals of the Twelfth Five-Year Plan.

As China moves up the technological ladder and tries to improve indigenous innovation, its share of global patents and trademarks will increase. One notable breakthrough was the 2010 unveiling by China of the world's fastest supercomputer, stealing the top spot from the United States, which had held the distinction for many decades. The Tianhe-1A is capable of 2,507 trillion calculations per second—1.4 times faster than its nearest American competitor—and was developed by the National Center for Supercomputing in Tianjin.[12] But then it was subsequently revealed that most of the chips and components to build the computer were built by Intel and NVIDIA, a U.S computer animation company.[13] Despite years of efforts and uncountable investment, China has fallen short of its decade-long goal to build the world's leading semiconductor industry, as it still imports the vast majority of microchips for the products it assembles. Experts estimate that China's best chip factories remain two to three generations behind world leaders such as Intel.[14] This is another indication of China being a partial power.

China's imports are dominated by a mixture of raw materials and natural resources coming from the developing world, while the developed world supplies China with high technologies, machinery, and specialized equipment. The increasing importance that raw materials and natural resources play in the composition of China's imports cannot be overstated. This requires consideration of China's energy profile.

China's Energy Needs

China has an insatiable appetite for energy of all kinds, which is growing by the year and decade. In 2009 it became the world's largest total energy consumer, accounting for nearly half of the world's growth in energy consumption over the previous decade. Driving this demand is heavy industry and the needed inputs: oil, electricity, iron ores, and other natural resources.

Although doing its best to tap domestic reserves, China is increasingly dependent on overseas sources of supply. It can meet much of the domestic hydropower and electric energy demand with domestic supplies, but this is not the case with oil. The dramatic growth in oil demand and imports is the backdrop to international expansion of China's national oil companies (discussed below). In 1993 China crossed the threshold to being a net importer and is now the world's second largest after the United States. By 2010 China was dependent on imports for more than half of its total consumption—4.8 million barrels per day (bb/d) of 9.2 million bb/d that year (costing the country $138.5 billion). The growth of China's oil consumption has been at about 8 percent per year since 2002.[15] During the first half of 2011, dependence on foreign crude imports actually surpassed that of the United States for the first time, reaching 55.2 percent (for the United States it was 53.5 percent in the same period).[16] The International Energy Agency projects that by 2030 China's oil demand will rise to 16.6 million bb/d and its imports will reach 12.5 million.[17]

To protect itself against market fluctuations and possible interruptions of supply, China began building a strategic petroleum reserve in 2001. It is taking form in phases, to be completed by 2020, when it should have one hundred days of reserve supply. China's first national oil reserve base in Zhejiang Province was completed in 2007, with a storage capacity of 5.2 million cubic metric tons. This is one of four such bases (two in Zhejiang and one each in Shandong and Liaoning) that became operational at the end of 2008, providing China with a strategic oil reserve of around 10 million tons, or the equivalent of about thirty days of imports. Construction of another oil storage facility in Xinjiang is also believed to have been completed. Under the second phase of China's national oil reserve plan, scheduled for completion in 2020, a further eight oil bases will be constructed in Jiangsu, Guangdong, Gansu, and Liaoning.

The lion's share (47 percent) of China's oil imports now comes from the Middle East.[18] In 2009, Saudi Arabia was the largest supplier to China, followed by Iran, Oman, Iraq, and Kuwait.[19] Sub-Saharan and North Africa has become China's second main regional supplier, led by Angola, Sudan, and Libya. China imports relatively little oil from Nigeria (1.29 million tons in 2010), but there is potential for growth since Nigeria possesses the world's fifth-largest reserves and is currently the eighth-biggest oil exporter worldwide. Chinese oil companies have been aggressively bidding for ownership stakes in Nigerian oil and gas fields. They are similarly active in other African states: Ghana, Gabon, Guinea, Sierra Leone, Liberia, Madagascar, São Tomé, and Uganda. In Latin America, Venezuela is China's most important energy supplier. During a state visit to Beijing in 2009, President Hugo Chavez announced a doubling of exports from half a million to one million barrels of crude oil per day; however, Venezuela's crude has high sulfur content and thus requires considerable refining. China has also tapped Brazil for oil, and some of its acquisition methods are very creative. In 2009, China announced a $10 billion loan from the China Development Bank to Brazil's state oil firm Petrobras, in exchange for ten years of crude oil deliveries of 200,000 bb/d. China's global oil suppliers are illustrated in Figure 5.2.

The majority of China's oil imports arrive via sea. Fully 77 percent passes through the strategic chokepoint of the Straits of Malacca between Malaysia and Singapore.[20] As a result of this dependency—which Hu Jintao has reportedly described as China's "Malacca dilemma"—China is working hard to connect to a network of oil pipelines that traverse Central Asia and the Caucasus Mountains. China's key to tapping into this network is the new 2,228-kilometer Sino-Kazakh pipeline, which opened in 2006 and by 2011 was transporting its full capacity of 10 million tons of oil into China per year. This pipeline gives China some above-ground options that will lessen its dependence on seaborne transport. Another cross-border pipeline connects China's Northeast to Russia's Far East (Daqing to Skovorodino); it opened in January 2011. It will deliver 300,000 bb/d to China between 2010 and 2030, which is

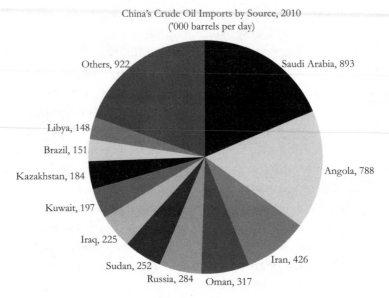

FIGURE 5.2 China's Crude Oil Imports by Source, 2010 ('000 Barrels per Day)
Source: FACTS Global Energy

guaranteed under a $25 billion loans-for-oil deal consummated between the two countries in 2009.[21] The two sides are discussing a similar natural gas agreement, and in August 2010 they signed a separate $6 billion loan-for-guaranteed-coal-deliveries deal over the next quarter century.

Russia, the world's second-largest oil exporter,[22] figures prominently in China's energy-import plans.[23] So does neighboring Kazakhstan. Not only does the aforementioned pipeline link China through Kazakhstan to rich supplies in countries surrounding the Caspian and Black Seas, but China is also tapping directly into Kazakh reserves—currently controlling equity stakes in an estimated 7 billion barrels and absorbing nearly half of Kazakh oil exports in 2010.[24] China is also energetically laying new cross-border rail lines into Kazakhstan, which can carry oil and liquefied natural gas (LNG).

China's National Oil Companies

Leading China's global hunt for oil and gas have been its three major national oil companies (NOCs): China National Petroleum

Corporation (CNPC), China National Offshore Oil Corporation (CNOOC), and China Petrochemical Corporation (Sinopec). China Chemical Corporation (Sinochem) is also a major player in refining and natural gas exploration, and is beginning to get into oil exploration and production, although it is not yet considered to be in the same league as the Big Three.

These energy giants are what the Chinese call *jituan* (集团), or conglomerates, and all have their headquarters adjacent to one another along the Second Ring Road in Beijing (informally known as 集团路, or "Conglomerate Row"). CNPC and Sinopec are the two largest state-owned enterprises in China. Together with CNOOC, the three made up 24.1 percent of total sales revenue, 23.5 percent of profits, and 40 percent of taxes collected among 123 major SOEs in 2007.[25] By 2010 Sinopec and CNPC had grown to become the fifth- and sixth-largest multinational corporations in the *world*, as measured by revenue and ranked on the *Fortune* Global 500 list. Only Wal-Mart, Royal Dutch Shell, ExxonMobil, and BP ranked higher, with China's power giant State Grid ranked right behind in seventh place (CNOOC was ranked 162nd and Sinochem 168th).[26]

The origins of these energy conglomerates vary, which accounts for their different operations today. Sinopec and CNPC date back to the Soviet-style state ministry monopolies of the 1950s, the Ministry of Petroleum Industry and Ministry of Chemical Industry. CNPC was specifically tasked with onshore production of oil and gas, while the Sinopec Group was created to focus more on refining, marketing, and petrochemical manufacturing.[27] There was also an explicit geographical division of labor: CNPC controlled Northern China, Sinopec the South, with CNOOC dominating offshore production. In 2000–01 all three had initial public offerings (IPOs) to raise capital and establish front companies that could operate abroad.[28]

CNOOC has a history and corporate culture quite different from CNPC and Sinopec. It was created first in 1982 as part of the "reform and opening" program specifically to interface and partner with foreign oil companies. It absorbed the offshore assets of the Ministry of Petroleum Industry and was assigned the specific task to explore for oil and gas offshore in conjunction with foreign oil companies. As a result, CNOOC had a government mandate to go global long before the other NOCs.

Because of the earlier start, CNOOC had a better understanding of international resources, practices, management, and laws. Today it still has the largest number of international partnerships among the NOCs.

In 1998, as part of a large-scale radical reorganization of State Council ministries and agencies initiated by Premier Zhu Rongji aimed at streamlining and rendering loss-making SOEs more efficient and profitable, all three NOCs were incorporated. They were given more leeway to conduct business on a profit-and-loss basis and to operate more globally. The idea was to create a clearer division of labor among entities responsible for certain dimensions of "upstream" (exploration and production) and "downstream" (refining and marketing) operations, thereby introducing elements of competition and greater efficiency with a long-term view to creating internationally competitive energy companies that could garner a larger share of international extraction, production, refining, and marketing. Prior to the reorganization, CNPC dominated onshore upstream operations, Sinopec led refining, CNOOC dominated offshore exploration, and Sinochem was primarily an oil trader. After the reorganization, CNPC gave some of its upstream assets to Sinopec, and Sinopec turned over some of its downstream assets to CNPC.[29] Maintaining government ownership and investment was thought to be a comparative advantage vis-à-vis many "oil majors."

The reorganization worked. Although a seeming oxymoron, the new system has been aptly termed "oligopolistic competition."[30] It eliminated and streamlined cumbersome, domestically focused Soviet-style bureaucracies, transforming them into more agile and internationally oriented multinational corporations (although Sinopec and CNPC retain ministerial rank status, CNOOC is a general bureau in the State Council).

CNPC has evolved to become an integrated, internationally active, broad-based energy company with a number of businesses covering oil and gas upstream and downstream operations, oilfield services, engineering and construction, equipment manufacturing and supply, capital management, finance, and insurance services.[31] Even though CNPC's strengths were always in exploration and production, it has begun to branch out into downstream businesses. Acquisition of Singapore Petroleum in 2009 was a clear step in this direction. CNPC has dramatically expanded its overseas assets and operations, purchasing access rights to oil fields in countries as diverse as Algeria, Angola, Azerbaijan,

Canada, Chad, Indonesia, Iran, Iraq, Kazakhstan, Niger, Nigeria, Peru, Qatar, Syria, Sudan, Thailand, Turkmenistan, and Venezuela. It has long-term LNG contracts with Australia. CNPC held hydrocarbon assets in twenty-nine countries by the end of 2010, with 684,000 bb/d of overseas oil equity production,[32] and was the fourth-largest oil-producing company in the world with revenues for 2010 totaling $240.19 billion and a profit of $14.36 billion.[33] Despite its growing global footprint, CNPC still accounts for almost 60 percent of China's domestic production of oil and 80 percent of gas output.

Sinopec has also diversified and grown dramatically. Today it is an integrated energy and chemical company involved in exploration and trading of petroleum and natural gas and related products. Sinopec is still the largest refiner in China, but it has increasingly gone global with significant upstream investments in Algeria, Angola, Australia, Ecuador, Iran, Russia, and Saudi Arabia. Sinopec was the first Chinese oil company to undertake (via partnership with BP) deep-water exploration off Angola and is exploring for gas in Saudi Arabia.[34] In 2009 Sinopec's purchase of the Swiss-based oil exploration company Addax Petroleum for $7.19 billion was the largest takeover of a foreign firm by a Chinese company.[35] In 2010 Sinopec acquired 18 percent of Chevron's deep-water gas project in Indonesia. It has purchased oil sands exploration rights in Colombia and Canada, as well as stakes in Brazilian, Swiss, Russian, and Kazakh energy companies. It has a large refining presence in Iran. In 2010 Sinopec's revenue ballooned to $273.4 billion, turning a profit of $76.2 billion.

Sinopec has not always enjoyed a positive reputation. In 2009 one of its senior officials, Chen Tonghai, was convicted of taking more than $28 million in bribes and sentenced to death. In 2011 it came to light that Sinopec's Guangdong branch office had been on a buying and drinking binge of 1,176 bottles of expensive French wines worth $245,000 (including some Chateau Lafite Rothschild costing $2,100 per bottle).[36] News of the scandal quickly spread across the country on the internet, causing public ridicule. One result was that Sinopec's chairman, Su Shulin, was removed and transferred to a new job as a deputy Party secretary and governor of Fujian province (Su was replaced by CNOOC's chairman, Fu Chengyu). Sinopec was also the object of violence at one of its facilities in Africa. In April 2007 a raid by a Somali rebel group on a drilling site in eastern Ethiopia's Ogaden desert left seventy-four dead, including nine Chinese oil workers, and seven Chinese were kidnapped. The rebels, the Ogaden National Liberation Front, later released the seven abductees.

From the start, CNOOC's specialization in offshore drilling operations gave it a comparative advantage internationally. More recently, CNOOC has shown special interest in developing onshore oil sands reserves. In 2011 it acquired the cash-strapped Canadian oil sands producer Opti Canada for $2.1 billion, after Opti filed for bankruptcy protection. Canada has the world's second-largest estimated oil sands reserves, of approximately 175 billion barrels. After completing the purchase of Opti Canada, CNOOC's chief financial officer, Zhong Hua, commented, "We have ample cash in hand and will continue to pursue other acquisition opportunities that are in line with our company's strategy."[37] His prediction was soon validated when, in 2012, it made a $15.1 billion bid for the Canadian energy firm Nexen (the largest Chinese overseas investment bid to date). Natural gas has also been a constant part of CNOOC's portfolio, and the company is taking this global. CNOOC holds numerous supply contracts with Australia, Indonesia, Qatar, and other countries.[38] But over the years, CNOOC has also diversified, into downstream businesses such as fertilizer production, power generation, engineering, financial services, and logistics.[39] Today CNOOC is active all over the world. Between 2002 and 2010 it acquired assets in Angola, Argentina, Brazil, Canada, Equatorial Guinea, Indonesia, Iraq, Kenya, Myanmar, Nigeria, the Philippines, Uganda, and the United States. CNOOC has not always been successful in its foreign bids, failing most notably in its attempt to acquire the American company Unocal in 2005 for $18.5 billion in cash. CNOOC withdrew its bid after substantial pressure from the U.S Congress and public controversy. "We learned we need to be more prudent in terms of public relations and political lobbying when dealing with such a big deal," reflected CNOOC's then-chairman Fu Chengyu after the failed bid.[40] Largely because CNOOC does not have a domestic onshore dimension to its business, net revenues lag far behind CNPC and Sinopec (in 2010, CNOOC's revenues totaled $52.4 billion, with profits of $7.23 billion); but in terms of *growth* in profits, production, and reserves, CNOOC greatly outperformed Sinopec and CNPC in 2010.

Finally, Sinochem is also emerging as an international energy player. It is the successor to China Import Company, which was created in 1950 to trade with the Soviet Union and the socialist bloc. During the 1970s it became responsible for exporting crude oil, but it also diversified operations into chemical production. Today Sinochem remains an SOE with business in agriculture, energy, chemicals, real estate, and finance. It is China's largest integrated agricultural company, producing fertilizers, pesticides, and seeds. In addition to being China's largest chemical company, Sinochem ranks as China's fourth-largest oil company.[41] In 2011 it ranked 168th on the *Fortune* Global 500 list, earning $49.53 billion in revenues and $7.98 billion in profits.

Since the global financial crisis erupted in 2008, China's NOCs have taken advantage of their liquidity to ramp up their overseas investments. Altogether, during 2009–10 the NOCs purchased assets in the Middle East, Canada, and Latin America, with about $28 billion invested for direct acquisition of oil and gas assets from other companies. In 2010 the NOCs invested nearly $16 billion in oil and gas development in Latin America alone.[42] In 2010 PetroChina (a subsidiary of CNPC) chairman Jiang Jiemin announced that the firm was prepared to invest $60 billion abroad in coming years.[43] During 2008–2010 Chinese NOCs also secured bilateral oil-for-loan deals with several countries amounting to more than $90 billion.[44] The NOCs' overseas mergers and acquisitions in the petroleum sector accounted for 13 percent of all M&As in the sector worldwide in 2009,[45] rising to 20 percent in 2010.[46] Sinopec was the largest dealmaker in 2010 with $13.1 billion in takeovers, followed by CNOOC's $5.8 billion.[47]

As this profile of the NOCs' international investments indicates, no corner of the globe has escaped their eye. In surveying opportunities for operations, China energy experts note several criteria that the NOCs consider.[48] Like other resource-seeking oil companies, they favor countries with large oil reserves; hence their preference for Saudi Arabia, Angola, Iraq, Russia, Brazil, and Venezuela. They have also exhibited a preference for sources in Eurasia where oil can be transported by pipeline, thus avoiding the potential strategic vulnerabilities of tanker transport by sea. Chinese NOCs also prefer to go into countries where the competition from international oil companies (IOCs) is limited (although this is changing). This strategy often leads Chinese

NOCS to partner with countries that are international political pariahs ("rogue states" such as Sudan, Syria, Libya, Myanmar, and Iran), where IOCs have lower exposure. These rogue partnerships caused much diplomatic controversy for the Chinese government internationally, and even some prominent Chinese scholars and officials have criticized the NOCs for "hijacking" Chinese foreign policy.[49] Like the IOCs, Chinese NOCs also prefer countries that have high-quality, light, "sweet" crude oil, so as to reduce refining costs. Refineries in China are known to have very limited capacity to refine heavy sulfuric oil; thus the NOCs (Sinopec in particular) are building refineries in these countries (notably in Venezuela and the Sudan). Additional motivations for the NOCs overseas investments are to diversify sources of supply so as to reduce the risk of overdependence on a few key suppliers; to partner with IOCs so as to gain technical know-how and managerial experience; to decrease political risk; and to develop an integrated international supply chain.[50] But perhaps the main reason for investing overseas is to grow reserves and profits. Like other oil companies, in order to survive they need to constantly replace the reserves they use up.

In terms of ensuring supply, in the mid-2000s there was a growing global perception that China was trying to "lock up" or "tie down" long-term, exclusive, monopolistic relationships with suppliers. But several studies examining these deals find this not to be the case.[51] In any event, China does not import all the oil it pumps abroad; it sells a lot on the international market. Brookings Institution energy expert Erica Downs estimates that in 2007, for example, China's NOCs sold at least 40 percent of their foreign oil production on the spot market and did not send home any of the oil pumped by NOCs in Azerbaijan, Russia, Syria, or Tunisia.[52] Other reasons for selling oil abroad are that Chinese NOCs can get higher prices on the international market, and some of the crude may be "sour" (thick and high in sulfur) and in need of further refining. Also, China has logistical limits to what it can import (Chinese storage tanks are usually near capacity).

China's NOCs have truly gone global in recent years, dramatically expanding their footprint around the world, but they still pale in comparison with ExxonMobil, BP, and Royal Dutch Shell and other established Western oil majors. But Chinese NOCs have ambitious plans to catch up. In the process of going global, they have transformed from classic narrowly focused state-owned enterprises into globally competitive comprehensive energy firms. Flush with cash and willing to outbid competitors, they are garnering new sources of supply. If they can increase their overseas downstream assets in refining, delivery, and marketing, global consumers may soon be filling their petrol tanks at Chinese service stations.

China's Global Mining Operations

Oil is hardly the only natural resource or energy commodity China actively seeks abroad. Chinese companies are literally scouring the earth for a variety of minerals and metals, timber, thermal coal, copper, gold, iron ores, manganese ores, chromium ores, and other natural resources.

As its appetite for raw materials surged, global commodity prices also spiked. This is one area where China definitely *does* influence global trends. This was particularly the case in 2008–09, when China went on a buying binge in order to stockpile a variety of commodities: iron ore, aluminum, copper, nickel, tin, zinc, canola, and soybeans.[53] The surge in imports tailed off somewhat in 2010 but rebounded in 2011. In 2010 China accounted for an astonishing 40 percent of global copper demand, driving prices to nearly $9,000 per ton.[54] The State Reserve Bureau, which manages the nation's strategic stockpiles, announced that the intentional policy of stockpiling had resulted in a world-record 3.18 million tons of imported refined copper being imported during 2009.[55] Its imports of gold more than quadrupled from 2009 to 2010, totaling more than 220 metric tons and making China not only the world's leading gold producer but also the biggest importer.[56] Chromium ore imports surged 492.4 percent from 2002 to 2009, stimulated by China's production of stainless steel and other fabricated metals.[57] China's iron ore imports more than doubled between 2003 and 2007.[58] In 2009 China imported 628 million tons of iron ore, 68 percent of total world exports.[59] At one point that year, China had ordered so much foreign iron ore that ninety fullyloaded freighters idled outside Chinese ports waiting to off-load for as long as two weeks, because port storage facilities were overflowing.[60]

Unlike China's oil industry, where three or four state NOCs monopolize business, China's mining industry is more decentralized and includes both state-owned and private companies (many are hybrids of the two). Unlike the oil companies, many are provincial-level rather than national-level firms. China Minmetals Corporation is the largest and most significant actor in the industry. Like the NOCs, it is a state corporation with bureaucratic origins in the pre-reform planned economy, but it is attempting to remake itself into a modern multinational.[61] Minmetals is now the sixth largest metals corporation in the world, operating in twenty-six countries, with 168,000 employees and total assets of 200 billion RMB ($31.29 billion).[62]

Like Minmetals, China Non-Ferrous Metals Mining Corporation and China Metallurgical Construction Corporation are fully state-owned and operated. But there are also a number of hybrid state-owned corporations that operate with considerable—if not total—corporate autonomy; Baosteel, Chinalco (China Aluminum Corporation), Shougang (Capital Steel) Group, Jinchuan Group, Shenhua Group, Sinosteel, Tonghua Iron and Steel, and Wuhan Iron and Steel are the largest and best known. All are active abroad. Then there are a number of provincial-level corporations, which benefit from provincial government investment and can be considered "provincial-owned enterprises," but which also operate with a high degree of corporate autonomy. Notable examples include Jiangxi Metals and Minerals International Trade Corporation, Henan International Mining Company, and Hunan Non-Ferrous Metals Holding Group (acquired by Minmetals in 2010).

Rather than simply buying minerals and raw materials on the international commodities markets, China's mining companies are going global by taking a page out of the NOC playbook: direct purchases from foreign suppliers, acquisitions of mines abroad, term leases of mines or smelters, joint ventures with foreign mining companies, M&As of foreign mining companies (in whole or in part), and agreements with foreign governments for multiyear supply arrangements. Minmetals, Chinalco, and the Shenhua Group are leading the charge in overseas investments. Although China's mining companies have begun to internationalize their operations and 24 percent of the nation's outbound direct investment in 2010 was accounted for by the mining industry (according to the Ministry of Commerce),[63] Chinese companies' share of global mining investments remain paltry, accounting for less than 6 percent of global transactions in 2010.[64]

Not all of China's attempted overseas mining acquisitions have been successful. The most notable failure was Chinalco's 2009 $19.5 billion attempted investment in the British-Australian mining giant Rio Tinto. In the widely reported case, Chinalco's bid was rejected by Rio's Australian shareholders after political pressure grew from the public and the Australian government. Chinalco could be forgiven for assuming that their bid would be successful, as just the previous year they executed a joint acquisition (with American partner Alcoa) in purchasing a 12 percent stake in Rio Tinto. With Chinalco defeated in its acquisition bid, Rio decided to merge its iron ore operations with rival BHP Billiton.

All in all, China's footprint in the global mining industry is more a matter of reputation than reality. That is, China is known for gobbling up resources all over the planet, but the reality is that the vast majority of its imported minerals and metals (90 percent plus) comes from direct purchases from suppliers or from international commodity markets. Its share of, and control over, global production resources (e.g., mines) is really minuscule compared to those of national governments and leading international corporations. This fact does not minimize the importance of the enormous volume of natural resources China needs and is importing, with the concomitant impact on global commodity prices. But the often-heard accusation that China is trying to lock up international mineral production is far from accurate. Buy up, yes; lock up, no. China's mining firms also have a proven record for negligible environmental management and poor labor conditions.

The one commodity where China is accused of mercantilist and monopolist behavior is in so-called rare earth elements, a category of seventeen metallic elements used in high-technology applications as wide ranging as automobile catalytic converters and hybrid engines, compact discs, cell phones, computer display screens, communications systems, missile guidance systems, laser-guided weapons, and high-temperature superconductivity. China is the world's leading producer of rare earths, controlling 95 percent of existing global production and producing more than 120,000 tons in 2010.[65] What is controversial is that China has restricted exports of domestically mined rare earths, which (given its semimonopoly status) severely affects foreign manufacturers of high-tech equipment. Beginning in 2009 China began restricting exports of a number of these mineral elements by substantially lowering preset quotas for exports to the European Union.[66] As a result, the EU—together with the United States and Mexico—filed a case with the World Trade Organization arguing that China's near monopoly on production combined with its unilaterally restricted exports was discriminatory behavior violating WTO free trade rules by applying export quotas. In July 2011 the WTO agreed, ruling against China.[67] China then denied it was intentionally restricting exports and manipulating the international market by arguing that its production and export quotas were appropriate and fair, and it appealed the ruling.[68] In January 2012, China lost the appeal before the WTO Appellate Body.[69] This was a prime example of China's state-dominated mercantilist trading practices bumping up against international regulators.

Overseas Direct Investment

The third area of China's global economic footprint, ODI (对外直接投资), is a more recent phenomenon. For more than three decades, China has been one of the world's top *recipients* of foreign direct investment (absorbing a total of utilized FDI of more than $1 trillion between 1979 and 2010[70]), but now the situation is reversing. The Chinese government sits on a whopping $3.2 trillion in foreign reserves, and many Chinese companies are awash in foreign currency and under strong government encouragement to "go out" and establish an international presence. China's ODI has been steadily growing since 2003 but has spiked significantly since 2008, as it became the world's fifth-largest foreign investor in 2010.

Going Out to Go Global

To understand China's ODI, one must begin with the origins of China's "going out" (走出去) or "going global" (走向世界) policy. Usually, only the first of these two terms is used, but both are often translated as "going global."

Jiang Zemin was instrumental in formulating and developing the "going out" policy. The earliest indication of the policy came in some internal speeches Jiang gave in mid-1992 in the lead-up to the Fourteenth Party Congress that autumn.[71] In one indicative sentence in his report to the Party Congress, Jiang said, "We should grant to enterprises and to science and technology research institutes the power to engage in foreign trade, and we should encourage enterprises to expand their investments abroad and their transnational operations."[72] From 1993 to 1996, Jiang continued to give internal speeches encouraging overseas investments, particularly in developed countries. But on July 26, 1996, after returning from a state visit to Africa, Jiang gave an important speech in Tangshan that for the first time explicitly encouraged Chinese firms to "go out." At the end of 1997, he again spoke of the policy explicitly when receiving representatives at the National Foreign Investment Work Conference. In 1997, in his speech to the Fifteenth Party Congress, Jiang again touted the policy—but this time he coupled it with a call to "bring [investment] in and go out" (引进来, 走出去) and "take advantage of both markets" (domestic and foreign). Jiang also briefly signaled: "We should form large internationally competitive companies and enterprise groups through market forces and policy guidance."[73] This was a reference to creating modern conglomerates (大集团) out of inefficient, loss-making, socialist state-owned enterprises. Then Jiang made the most forceful public call to date for the going-out policy: "Implementation of the strategy of 'going out' is an important measure taken in the new stage of opening up. We should encourage and help relatively competitive enterprises with various forms of ownership to invest abroad in order to increase export of goods and labor services and bring about a number of strong multinational enterprises and brand names."[74] In 1998 Jiang stressed the going-out strategy at several more conferences, particularly encouraging China's SOEs to explore markets in Africa, Central Asia, the Middle East, and Latin America.[75] Finally, Jiang discussed the strategy at a Politburo meeting on January 20, 2000.[76]

With these authoritative statements by China's leader, and with the nation preparing for its accession to the WTO in 2001, Premier Zhu Rongji followed suit by referring to the going-out policy in his annual report to the National People's Congress. Zhu's speech is considered to have marked the official launch of the policy. His imprimatur catalyzed the State Council bureaucracy to get busy formulating specific rules and regulations governing Chinese enterprises' outbound investments.

A series of state decrees were issued between 2000 and 2002 to regulate and encourage firms to invest overseas. It was decreed that proposed investments by Chinese companies abroad should be reviewed and approved by the government. The Ministry of Commerce (MOFCOM) was to review all cases where a Chinese business entity was to be incorporated abroad, while natural resource development projects with investment exceeding $200 million and nonresource investments over $50 million had to be approved by the State Council's National Development and Reform Commission (NDRC).[77] In July 2004 MOFCOM and the Ministry of Foreign Affairs jointly issued the first *Guidelines for Investments in Overseas Countries' Industries* and the *Overseas Investment Guidance Catalogue*, where recommended industry sectors were listed together with all 68 priority recipient nations. In March 2005, the list was updated to include 28 more countries.[78] This document dramatically reformed and simplified the ODI approval process. Another new set of ODI guidelines was released by MOFCOM in 2011, giving preferential treatment to certain industries and providing specific guidance for investing in 115 countries.[79] Going global and increasing ODI was also emphasized in the Eleventh (2006–2010) and Twelfth Five-Year Plans (2011–2015). Commenting on the Twelfth Plan, one NDRC official envisioned that Chinese ODI would diversify away from concentrating on natural resources toward a more broad-based set of industries: telecommunications, automobiles, agriculture, electronics, research and development, and service industries (finance, insurance, logistics, tourism, event management, and other professional services).[80]

China has also been busy using government instruments to promote ODI. When leaders travel abroad they now usually bring an entourage of businessmen along—not only looking to buy from the recipient country, but also to invest in it. Another tactic is the bilateral investment treaty. As of June 2011 China has successfully signed BITs with 127 nations (notably missing from this list is the United States, although negotiations are under way).[81]

Like most Chinese policies, the going-out policy for ODI has evolved over a considerable period of time and did not occur overnight. Indeed the rhetoric preceded the phenomenon. This had at least as much to do with the pressures of domestic market capital saturation as with government invocations to go out.

Generally speaking, over time China's ODI has passed through several phases of development.[82] Prior to the "reform and opening" (改革, 开放) policy launched in 1978–79, China had no ODI to speak of (nor inbound FDI, for that matter). As part of the new opening to commerce with the outside world, the government not only encouraged foreign trade but also authorized a select number of SOEs and some provincial and municipal enterprises to invest abroad. During the period from 1979 to 1985 there were 189 approved foreign investment projects with total investment amounting to about $200 million.[83] During 1986–1991 regulations were relaxed somewhat and the number of approved projects increased sixfold and total investment quintupled to $1.2 billion. Nonetheless, this amount was negligible by global standards. The next phase (roughly 1992–2000) showed gradual growth of ODI. After a brief spike in 1992 during which it shot up to $4 billion, statistics show an annual average of about $2.3 billion for the remainder of the decade. During this period the State Council designated 120 state-owned industry groups "national champions" and gave these companies the charge of leading the internationalization of Chinese enterprises. Firms that received this designation were provided high-level political support, financial subsidies, more management autonomy, greater profit retention rights, and information from the government on possible foreign investment targets.[84]

Starting around the turn of the century, China entered the current stage of ODI development. With strong government support, a great upsurge and diversification of overseas investment ensued. As a result of government encouragement and deregulation, in 2001 China's ODI shot up to $6.9 billion—more than six times the previous year's total. As Figure 5.3 indicates, there was a brief fallback in 2002 before a continuing and substantial upward trend began in 2003, holding to this day.

By 2010 MOFCOM statistics indicated total ODI flows of $68.81 billion and an accumulated total ODI net stock of $317.21 billion.[85] MOFCOM further reported that 12,000 "domestic investing entities" had established 13,000 overseas enterprises in 177 countries. The 2011 figures actually fell off somewhat to $65.1 billion for the year.[86] Coastal provinces Liaoning, Zhejiang, Shandong, Guangdong, and Shanghai are the top five investors abroad, but interestingly, MOFCOM statistics for 2010 show that provinces accounted for

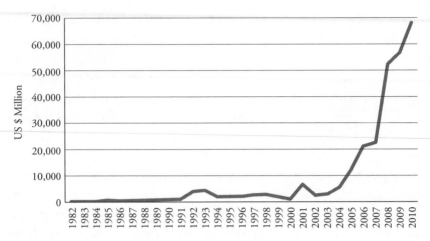

FIGURE 5.3 China's ODI Flows (1982–2010)
Source: UNCTAD Statistics Database; includes only nonfinancial ODI

only *one quarter* of China's total ODI ($17.7 billion out of a total of $68.8 billion) in ODI—starkly revealing the dominant position of central level SOEs, which accounted for 75 percent of total ODI ($42.4 billion)![87]

Although the growth of Chinese ODI over the past decade has been sharp, it must be remembered that it started from a low base and still falls far short of that of the United States and other major industrialized nations. By contrast, American firms invested $328.9 billion abroad in 2010, nearly five times more than China. In aggregate, the United States has an accumulated stock of $4 trillion, twenty times larger than China's, while Japan's is three times larger; China's level is comparable to those of Denmark and Taiwan.[88] As British economist Peter Nolan notes in his book *Is China Buying the World?* China's ODI stock by 2009 was only 27 percent of that of the Netherlands, 17 percent of Germany's, 13 percent of France's, 14 percent of Britain's, and only 5 percent of that of the United States.[89]

But this is all changing rapidly. Studies by the Rodium Group in New York predict somewhere between $1 and 2 *trillion* will be invested by China overseas by 2020.[90] Another consulting firm, A Capital, predicts a surge of $800 billion in Chinese ODI from 2011 to 2016.[91] For its part, MOFCOM predicts more modest 17 percent annual growth in ODI during 2011–2015, achieving an accumulated stock of $560 billion at the end of the period and roughly $1 trillion by 2020.[92]

Various factors will affect these trends. The first is saturation of investment capital in the domestic market, driving companies to look overseas for new opportunities. This "push" factor will combine with the "pull" element of host countries' preferential investment policies and climates. Many countries in the world are desperately looking for inbound investment and are taking a page out of the Chinese playbook in offering a range of foreign investment incentives. Access to easy bank credit and state funding is another facilitating factor. China's insatiable demand for raw materials is only going to continue to grow—thus accelerating the existing investments in foreign oil and mining. However, as China begins to transform its ODI mix to increase the manufacturing component, it will build more production plants abroad, and these will require tapping into existing logistics and supply chains or creating new ones. This will stimulate a greater Chinese multinational downstream presence. China's M&As will continue to grow, particularly in the financial services sector.

As overseas infrastructure construction has gained in China's ODI portfolio, China has become a major exporter of labor. From 1978 to 2009 China dispatched a total of 4.91 million workers abroad, according to the chairman of the China International Contractors Association.[93] By the end of 2009, China had 772,000 workers working in 190 countries abroad.[94] Of these, 71.2 percent were working in Asian countries.[95] In 2010 Chinese construction firms signed overseas contracts worth $134.4 billion, according to the association. This is set to grow—including into new North American and European countries.[96]

Finally, there is a rising probability of increased capital flight on the part of firms and individuals nervous about investment opportunities in the domestic Chinese economy. For all these reasons, China's ODI can only be expected to increase worldwide in the years to come.

In terms of the *type and modalities* of China's overseas investment, even though "greenfield" (start-up) investments are increasing, mergers and acquisitions remain the preferred modality for Chinese overseas investment. China has now become a leading M&A player globally. The global consulting firm PricewaterhouseCoopers estimates that Chinese companies concluded 188 outbound M&A deals in 2010 worth

$38 billion,[97] although the rival consulting firm Deloitte & Touche put the registered deal value for the year higher at $62 billion.[98]

Despite spiking in volume and value, China's M&As have not thus far been very successful. One report estimates that 90 percent of China's three hundred overseas M&As in 2008–2010 were unsuccessful, with companies losing 40–50 percent of their value after the acquisition.[99] As the OECD notes, this is particularly the case in the technology, communications, and natural resource sectors since they are a quick means to acquire advanced technology, sales networks, established brand names, and other strategic assets overseas.[100] But Chinese firms are particularly inexperienced in operating in developed country markets, so M&As remain an easier path for them than trying to set up a factory or business from scratch. Most Chinese multinational corporations (MNCs) have very few multilingual staff experienced in working in cross-cultural environments (if any), and they are inexperienced with local business practices, professional relationships, environmental practices, and laws. For these and other reasons, it is much easier for a Chinese MNC to simply buy a share of an established foreign firm in order to gain all of these elements and offset their deficits in one stroke. Therefore, the majority of M&As were concentrated in North America and Europe in recent years.[101] For example, when Lenovo acquired IBM's PC business in 2004, it inherited 1800 foreign R&D and management staff—attributes Chinese MNCs are notoriously short of—and former IBM staff were placed in half of Lenovo's global corporate structure.

Examining the most recent data (2010), we can see more clearly the geographic dispersion and sectoral composition of China's ODI. Table 5.2 indicates the top ten destinations of China's ODI.

Note that the top four destinations for China's ODI in 2010 are tax havens or what might be described as "pass-through" locales: Hong Kong, the British Virgin Islands, Grand Cayman Islands, and Luxembourg. Where the ODI goes from there is anybody's guess. This may suggest that China uses these financial safe havens as "hubs" to invest in Asia, Central and Latin America, and Europe respectively. These pass-through destinations aside, Australia continues to be the largest recipient of Chinese ODI (because of the mining industry). China's official data show that Asia continues to draw the lion's share of China's ODI (65 percent),

TABLE 5.2 Top Ten Destinations of China's ODI in 2010

Rank	Destination	Amount
1	Hong Kong	$38.5 bn.
2	British Virgin Islands	$6.11 bn.
3	Grand Cayman Islands	$3.49 bn.
4	Luxembourg	$3.20 bn.
5	Australia	$1.70 bn.
6	Sweden	$1.36 bn.
7	United States	$1.30 bn.
8	Canada	$1.14 bn.
9	Singapore	$1.11 bn.
10	Russia	$875 mn.

Source: 2010 Statistical Bulletin of China's Outward Foreign Direct Investment.

followed by Latin America (15.3 percent), Europe (9.8 percent), North America (3.8 percent), Africa (3.1 percent), and Oceania (2.7 percent).[102]

In the years ahead, we can expect China's ODI to Asia to remain strong, and likely increase in the United States and Europe. Its investments elsewhere in emerging economies (Africa, Central Asia, Latin America, the Middle East) will continue to be dominated by the natural resources and energy sectors (70 percent plus), although in some regions China is trying to diversify into sectors such as automobile and appliance manufacturing (Brazil, the Middle East, North Africa).[103]

Since the onset of the 2008 global financial crisis and the 2011 European sovereign debt crisis, the EU has witnessed a mini tsunami of Chinese investments washing across the continent.[104] China's investments in Europe jumped to $6.8 billion in 2010, a 102 percent increase over 2009 and accounting for 10 percent of China's total worldwide ODI during the year, according to Vice Minister of Commerce Chen Jian.[105] In 2011, according to MOFCOM figures, Chinese investment in the EU surged an additional 94 percent over 2010 to $8.28 billion.[106] The ongoing European economic and debt crisis has made the continent a particularly attractive target for Chinese investors. Chinese companies have invested in a range of European ventures. Examples abound. The British car company MG Rover was purchased by Nanjing Automobile Corporation. Geely bought Volvo. Operation of the Greek port of Athens was granted to China Ocean Shipping Company (COSCO) for thirty-five years. PetroChina took a stake in the British oil refiner Ineos, giving it a strategic foothold in European energy markets. The Norwegian chemical conglomerate Orkla sold $2 billion of its assets to China National Blue Star. Sany, China's mammoth producer of heavy construction equipment and cranes, made a run at several smaller European firms. The Czech auto company Skoda (a subsidiary of Volkswagen) is producing cars with partner Shanghai Auto in the Czech Republic. Great Wall Motor set up a similar plant with a Bulgarian partner to manufacture small cars to serve the low-end Balkan and East European market. Chinese banks such as ICBC prowl the continent looking for bargain buy-ups of small and medium-sized national banks.

Germany has been a primary target for Chinese takeovers. The approximately 3.7 million *Mittelstand*—small and medium-sized companies—that anchor the German industrial economy and are the engine of the nation's exports are particularly attractive to Chinese firms, as they are family-owned and hence preferable to dealing with corporate boards and stockholders.[107] Examples include Sany's purchase of German machinery maker Putzmeister, Xuzhou Construction Machinery's buying a minority stake in Schwing (another machinery manufacturer), LDK Solar's purchase of the solar panel manufacturer Sunways, Hebei Lingyun's purchase of Kiekert (the world's largest manufacturer of car door latches), and Zhejiang-based Joyson Investment Holdings' buying out the automotive electronics supplier Preh.

This wave of investment and M&As has caused pundits to ponder the two extremes of whether China is "taking over Europe" or "saving Europe."[108] The European Council on Foreign Relations observes that it has provided employment while simultaneously causing angst and adding to the already poor European public perception of China.[109] Even though Chinese money is pouring into Europe, not all investments have gone well. A motorway linking Warsaw to the German border went bust and became a *cause célèbre* for critics of Chinese investment.[110]

A similar dynamic is at work in the United States. Following the blocked bids by CNOOC to buy Unocal and Huawei to acquire

Nextel Sprint, 3Com, and 3Leaf, Chinese firms were hesitant to try to invest in the United States. Only 1 percent of foreign investment in the U.S. comes from China. But this is changing. As a 2011 study by the New York consulting firm Rodium Group indicates, China's combined greenfield investment and acquisitions skyrocketed almost tenfold from $589 million in 2007 to $5.35 billion in 2010.[111] Chinese firms have now invested in thirty-seven of the fifty states. Texas, New York, Virginia, Illinois, and California are the most attractive destinations for Chinese investments to date, but states such as Delaware, New Jersey, Michigan, Georgia, Ohio, and Idaho are advancing up the list. Idaho, for example, has a number of attractive attributes for Chinese investors, from open space to abundant minerals and mines, to green technology energy firms, an investment-friendly state government and a governor who has been visiting China for more than three decades.[112] But in Idaho, as elsewhere, potential Chinese investment brings with it a great deal of suspicion on the part of locals and politicians.[113] For its part, the U.S. Department of Commerce has tried to calm nerves and officially welcome Chinese investments into the United States.[114] Such reassurances have not convinced China's government or companies that the American door is truly open; their fingers have been burned before and they face substantial suspicions and regulatory barriers to entry.[115] Some companies (such as telecom giants Huawei and ZTE) are investing substantial funds in lobbying to try to improve their image on Capitol Hill.[116]

China's Sovereign Wealth Fund

Another interesting dimension of China's ODI is the role played by its national sovereign wealth fund, China Investment Corporation (CIC). CIC was formed in 2007 by the central government to manage some of what was then $1.4 trillion in foreign exchange reserves.[117] CIC was set up with $200 billion in initial capitalization. The idea behind the setup was simple: to diversify investment beyond buying foreign bonds and thereby to realize a greater return on investment than U.S. Treasuries. Initially, $90 billion of CIC's funds were allocated to overseas investments, with $110 billion for investment in the domestic financial sector, according to Jin Liqun (chairman of the CIC Supervisory Board). Of the latter, two-thirds were equity investments in China's four major banks.[118] Initially, most of CIC's overseas investments are portfolio investments, but over time it has become more direct investment into companies.

Not all went well for CIC initially. As the international financial crisis gripped in 2008–09, CIC took a big hit. Its overseas investments of $4.8 billion in 2008 earned a *negative* 2.1 percent return, according to CIC's annual reports.[119] By 2009, it had lost 40 percent of its $5.6 billion investment in Morgan Stanley and 70 percent of its $3 billion stake in the Blackstone Group.[120] Undeterred by netizen outrage in China for squandering the "people's money," CIC forged ahead and invested an additional $1.2 billion into Morgan Stanley and diversified into a number of other global investment opportunities. Altogether CIC made $35.7 billion in new investments overseas in 2010, and they paid off: CIC turned a profit of $41.6 billion in 2009 and $51.5 billion in 2010.[121] But CIC's investments went south again in 2011, reporting a loss of 4.3 percent in its overseas investment portfolio.[122] North America remains the largest destination for CIC's direct and portfolio investments overseas (41.9 percent), followed by the Asia-Pacific region (29.8 percent), Europe (21.7 percent), Latin America (5.4 percent), and Africa (1.2 percent).[123]

In addition to CIC, the State Administration for Foreign Exchange (SAFE) has an overseas investment arm. SAFE Capital owns at least $300 billion in overseas assets.[124]

Building Multinational Corporations with Chinese Characteristics

Chinese multinational corporations have suddenly burst onto the world scene. Although the vast majority still lack global brand recognition, Chinese multinationals are rapidly expanding their international operations and revenue streams. In 2001 there were only twelve Chinese companies on the *Fortune* Global 500 list; a decade later, Chinese companies (including four headquartered in Hong Kong) totaled sixty-one. Collectively, the sixty-one Chinese MNCs had combined annual revenue of $2.89 trillion and estimated overall profit of $176.1 billion in 2010.[125] Of the fifty-seven mainland companies, forty-nine are SOEs. China now ranks third on the global list, only slightly behind Japan.

Even though indicative of the growing clout of Chinese corporations, ranking on the *Fortune* Global 500 list does not mean that a company is internationally active and a real MNC. The list is based on a company's total revenue. When one examines the assets and operations of these Chinese corporations it becomes clear that the vast majority operate almost exclusively domestically. In other words, many leading Chinese corporations do not operate overseas and thus cannot be considered real multinationals, and many of those that have done so still hold a majority of domestic assets. State Grid, for example, ranks as the world's seventh-largest company by revenue, but only thirty-second among all Chinese corporations in foreign assets. For the majority, the domestic market still predominates, and many companies have yet to go global. Conversely, in some industries, domestic market saturation is driving them to do so.

What does it take for Chinese corporations to successfully go global, and what are the major impediments? Which companies have succeeded thus far, and what strategies have they adopted? Which ones have done poorly, and why?

Although there is no single model for success, there are a number of commonalties needed for MNCs to compete in today's globalized and highly competitive world. Obviously, a company must be able to operate and deploy resources on a truly global basis (not just regionally)—including sales and distribution channels, production facilities, supply chains, logistics networks, R&D centers, and employees. In particular, it must have a genuinely multinational management staff that possesses a "global mind-set" and is capable of operating in multiple cultures and languages. It should possess globally recognizable brands and invest substantially in advertising to maintain and grow "brand presence." It must have the ability to leave behind management practices that are successful at home and adopt new practices that work abroad. It should have well-defined human resources programs for recruitment, promotion, rotation, retention, midcareer training, and clear performance indicators. It must have well-thought-through strategic plans for geographical expansion and foreign market penetration. It must have a clear understanding of its comparative advantages, strengths, and weaknesses, and find a strategic market niche. A successful multinational should know and obey the regulatory and legal environments of foreign countries, be transparent, adopt "best practices," maintain strict accounting procedures, and institute genuine corporate governance and oversight. Successful multinationals are aware of the difficulties of M&As and prefer strategic alliances and partnerships that may be a better mode to leverage comparative advantages and thus expand a global footprint. They must also understand external-internal linkages of foreign MNCs; that is, many potential corporate partners abroad also seek to grow their business inside other countries.

How do Chinese multinational corporations tend to stack up against these criteria? On the whole, not well. Chinese multinationals are found to be lacking in virtually every category, although there are some successful examples of a few firms that have done better.

Very few Chinese firms can truly operate globally. Haier, Huawei, and the national oil companies Sinopec, CNOOC, and CNPC are really the only ones that have truly global capital, operations, and sales. Many of the other companies to be discussed here (banks, auto companies, natural resource companies, IT) really only invest in and operate on some continents, and they are far from possessing global production, marketing, distribution, logistics, supply, R&D, and HR networks.

The Achilles' heel of Chinese multinationals is human resources—particularly management. Every assessment of Chinese multinational corporations notes this to be a fundamental weakness. As one study starkly noted: "A lack of global management experience and skills is a fatal weakness of Chinese companies in going global. Cross-cultural understanding is a huge gap."[126] A study by McKinsey & Company, the global multinational consulting firm, estimated that only 10 percent of Chinese college graduates meet the requirements of international companies.[127] The McKinsey study also estimated that Chinese multinationals will require 75,000 global managers by 2020 (up from a pool of only three to five thousand in 2005). As a result, Chinese are flooding into foreign MBA programs and business schools in China—such as the Guanghua School of Business at Peking University and the China-Europe International Business School (CEIBS) in Shanghai—which are showing swelling enrollments. Distance-learning MBAs tailored to the China market, such as those pioneered by New York University and George Washington University, are also taking off. Some Chinese companies are beginning to take advantage of the global financial downturn by hiring laid-off staff (preferably young) in New York and London.[128] By the end of 2010, the *China Daily* reported that Chinese companies operating overseas had hired a total of 800,000 foreign employees.[129]

Despite the fact that Chinese-made goods flood world markets, only a handful of its multinational corporations (Haier "white goods," Lenovo computers, Geely automobiles, Huawei telecommunication equipment, Hisense televisions, Li-Ning sportswear, Tsingtao beer, and Air China) have established any kind of international brand recognition. At the 2010 World Cup in South Africa, Yingli Solar made its debut on the periphery of the soccer pitch. But, as of 2010, not a single Chinese company has managed to crack the *Business Week/Interbrand* international ranking of the "100 Best Global Brands."[130] Chinese brand reputation has also been damaged by several product scandals in recent years: tainted milk, lead-painted toys, malfunctioning electronics. Conscious of the country's low global brand recognition, in December 2009 the government undertook a short-lived campaign to brand China itself. Themed "Made in China, Made with the World," the Ministry of Commerce bought advertising airtime on CNN and other international networks and took out ad space in major foreign newspapers. But the initiative backfired. Domestic bloggers and media in China criticized the ad campaign as perpetuating the stereotypical image of China as the "workshop of the world,"[131] when in fact Chinese companies are trying to cultivate a global image of producing higher-tech and higher-quality goods. As a result of the criticism, the ads were pulled from the air within a week.

Instead of being global in perspective and able to easily adapt to foreign practices, Chinese companies and their management display an inability to escape their own national corporate culture and business practices. Chinese businesspeople are overly accustomed to the peculiarities of Chinese business culture, which emphasizes interpersonalization rather than institutionalization of relationships, where personal connections (关系) operate horizontally across businesses but in a strict vertical hierarchy within them; a short-term orientation toward profit in business decisions; lack of transparency and oversight; a personal comfort level with only Chinese people (including overseas Chinese); and a high degree of corruption. Moreover, Chinese companies are politicized. That is, many have Communist Party cells, secretaries, and members embedded within the firm. In 2010, half of the CEOs of China's 109 "national champion" firms under government control were appointed by the Organization Department of the CCP.[132] This is true of multinational corporations as well. As the newspaper of the Central Party School pithily observed in an article about establishing party branches in companies operating abroad, "Where there are people, there are Party organizations and Party activities."[133] Conversely, Western business culture could not be more different, emphasizing teamwork and management-staff cooperation, patience and long-term plans, transparency and oversight, multiculturalism, prosecution of corruption, institutionalization of relationships, and being apolitical.

Some Chinese firms develop business plans and strategies to globalize, but the majority do not.[134] They tend to be driven by pent-up cash in search of a place to invest (in a saturated domestic market), a strong mandate by the government to go out (with incentives to do so and penalties if they do not), naiveté about the complexities of foreign countries, impatience with cumbersome foreign regulatory environments, a desire to maximize profits as quickly as possible (rather than producing steady revenue streams), and a management tendency to frequently change decisions and directions. As a result, they often fail to do their homework to develop detailed plans for global market entry. These tendencies are not conducive to strategic planning.

Chinese firms also tend not to carry out due diligence on their competitors abroad, and as a result they often overlook weaknesses of foreign firms. This is one of the principal causes of Chinese failures in M&As. Nor do they tend to know the strengths of their international competition, not only their product quality (the "hardware"), but especially how foreign firms work with local communities ("software"). This is something that Japanese firms learned to do well during the 1980s in the United States and Europe, but it is something most Chinese firms have yet to figure out.

Although Chinese firms do tend to have clear performance indicators and incentive programs and do provide good job security, they do not score as well in incentivizing initiative in the workplace or investing in retraining personnel. Chinese firms—like the Chinese government—are extremely hierarchical. This makes for, among other things, a climate of risk aversion and disincentives to take initiative. Being entrepreneurial (which the Chinese certainly are) is different from being innovative and creative. Chinese organizational culture stresses discipline and conformity. Because of this preference for hierarchy and clearly defined workplace roles, Chinese tend not to adapt well to flat management structures which prize decentralization and individual initiative. Moreover, the Chinese notion of teamwork is similarly hierarchical (following leaders' instructions), rather than embracing the more egalitarian and collegial norm prevalent in Western organizations. These proclivities result in repeated culture clashes in Chinese M&As with Western companies.

The practice of midcareer (re)training is similarly new to Chinese MNCs, whereas it is intrinsic to most Western corporations. Chinese firms tend to train a worker for a precise skill and job, which the person is expected to do indefinitely; many Western firms adopt much more dynamic personnel policies emphasizing self-improvement, retraining, and job mobility within the firm. Oftentimes this is done within the firm through holding training courses for new job skills, but also via midcareer management training outside the firm—called "executive education." This is a big business in Western countries, led largely by business schools, public policy schools, and professional schools of international affairs. A one-month stint in an "Executive Ed" program at the Wharton School, the Kennedy School, INSEAD, the London Business School, or many other institutions offers an "escalator effect" for corporate management. Chinese companies, on the other hand, have no such organizational culture in the corporate world, although midcareer training has become *de rigueur* in the CCP and government.[135]

Chinese companies also demonstrate difficulties adapting to foreign legal, regulatory, tax, and political environments. Transparency and corporate governance are not exactly attributes associated with Chinese companies whose decision-making processes are usually opaque, whose business practices are frequently corrupt, and whose accounting procedures are often fraudulent. They do not have in-house legal counsel knowledgeable about foreign legal and regulatory environments, and they often run afoul of local politicians who are suspicious of Chinese investments.

These characteristics have negatively affected Chinese multinationals' ability to operate abroad, thus driving many into M&As as a means to get around these impediments. They have had a negative impact not only on business opportunities abroad but also on Chinese companies trying to list on foreign stock markets. Many Chinese companies were found to have filed fraudulent information with securities regulators prior to their IPOs in the United States.[136] A series of scandals rocked the industry in 2010. One frequently used Chinese tactic is the "reverse merger," whereby Chinese firms tried to gain listing rights but avoid the scrutiny of an IPO by taking over a shell company already listed on the New York Stock Exchange or NASDAQ. Dozens of Chinese companies that entered the United States via reverse mergers have been accused of fraud and falsified accounting.[137] In 2010 the U.S. Securities and Exchange Commission (SEC) launched an investigation into the accounting practices of Chinese firms that had tried to list in the United States, and found at least twenty-five had fraudulent accounting in their filings.[138] As a result of these investigations, a number of Chinese companies delisted, reversing their reverse mergers, and withdrew from the United States before having to pay large penalties to the SEC. Altogether twenty-two companies reportedly delisted and bought back their stock in 2011, according to the Chinese newspaper *International Herald Leader*.[139]

Even though M&As are the preferred modality for Chinese MNCs to go global, there have been multiple failures. Most Chinese MNCs are not yet comfortable making their management staff truly multinational, and M&As are thus an intensified form of corporate culture shock. Simple logic may argue that corporate weaknesses can be offset and complementarities exploited through a merger, but the fact is that cultural differences are usually brought into sharp relief and the "fit" is frequently awkward. Everything from management styles to HR management methods to simple interpersonal communications may not mesh well. Once these frictions become evident, stark choices in management motifs and organizational cultures present themselves and the goal of a synergistic merger can quickly give way to a hostile takeover. Both sides lose, and the potential advantages of partnership are squandered.

The incompatibility in corporate cultures, the nonglobalized nature of Chinese MNC management, and lack of understanding of foreign regulatory and legal environments have been the biggest problems, resulting in many failed ventures. Many also run into difficulties with foreign environmental standards.[140]

Finally, in looking for foreign partners, Chinese MNCs run up against the "reciprocity problem." That is, many foreign multinationals (with whom Chinese MNCs seek to partner) have either been operating in China for a number of years or seek to get into the market. Those with an already established in-country presence have most likely experienced years of Chinese red tape, investment obstacles, and very frustrating experiences (even if they became profitable). Those that have not established a presence want an *entrée*. In both cases, they look to the Chinese MNC to make life easier for them *inside* China. For them, there is an informal *quid pro quo*: you help us in China, we help you abroad. The problem is that many MNCs in China have a bifurcated corporate structure—domestic and international—thus producing a situation where the left hand and right hand do not communicate well with each other. Moreover, it is not necessarily the Chinese partner firm that is responsible for improving a foreign company's situation or solving their problems in China; it is domestic governmental authorities. For these reasons, there is often a mismatch of expectations between Chinese and foreign MNCs.

Consequently Chinese MNCs face a number of impediments in going global.[141] They have a steep learning curve. Over time, they will no doubt learn and adapt—as Chinese in all professional pursuits seem so capable of doing—but these aforementioned obstacles are not insignificant. China's MNCs are still taking baby steps in global business.

China's TCL Group's experiences with France's Thomson-CSF and Alcatel are excellent illustrations of these problems. Thomson was one of the world's largest television and integrated circuit manufacturers, while Alcatel was one of the leading telecom companies. The TCL Group began as one of China's largest appliance manufacturers but sought to diversify into electronics. In 1986 the company developed China's first hands-free speakerphone, and in 1993 it moved into the color television production business. By 1998 TCL was developing a strategy for overseas expansion. The first step came in 1998 when it purchased a Hong Kong–owned Vietnamese color TV manufacturer, quickly becoming the third-largest producer in Vietnam. In 2000 it entered the Indian market, producing TVs as well as a broader range of home appliances and electronics. In 2002 TCL took its first tentative steps into the West, when it acquired a majority share in the German firm Schneider Electronics AG. This initial move into the European television market was followed in 2003 by acquiring majority shares in RCA TV in the United States. Instantly TCL went from being unknown in the international TV production industry to gaining valuable footholds in the EU and United States. The 2004 joint venture with Thomson's color television division (in which TCL controlled 67 percent of the new entity called TTE) was the next step for TCL, followed quickly by a purchase of 55 percent of Alcatel's shares for €55 million ($67.7 million at the time). With these, TCL instantly became the world's third-largest manufacturer of TVs and seventh-largest mobile phone manufacturer. TCL's strategy was based on not only expanding market share but also gaining the most modern technologies. By acquiring Alcatel, TCL hoped to secure core 3G technologies in network and wireless access systems.[142]

Instead of becoming the largest TV manufacturer and one of the biggest mobile phone producers, the joint venture saw both deals founder. TTE lost nearly $300 million in the first year of operation and $419 million in 2006. The TCL-Alcatel joint venture went on to lose more than the ill-fated Thomson venture. Although TCL did gain the rights to Alcatel's 2G and 2.5G technologies, its 3G technologies were actually owned by a different Alcatel joint venture with Japan's Fujitsu (and hence off-limits to TCL). As the industry transitioned to 3G, the TCL venture had no comparative advantage. It made similar wrong production decisions on televisions; thinking that flat-screen plasma digital TVs did not have a future, they continued to produce the liquid crystal model.

But in both cases, TCL's problems went much deeper than production decisions: the cause of difficulties derived largely from differing corporate cultures and management styles. Both senior management and production line staff left in large numbers. In the TTE case the issue of overtime compensation—indeed, the concept of overtime itself—became contentious. The French employees were not accustomed to working overtime, but Chinese management thought they should do so and without extra compensation. In the Alcatel case, TCL had no strategic plan to grow the company beyond acquiring the brand name, European market share, and hopefully 3G technologies. TCL management was also too flexible and loose in their decision-making style, while Alcatel and Thomson executives were much more deliberate and procedural. They believed in detailed, carefully crafted strategic plans that would be meticulously followed, while Chinese management apparently cared little for procedures or plans and altered decisions, marketing strategies, and production plans almost daily.

As a result of these clashing corporate cultural styles, TCL's takeovers of these two leading French firms were disastrous failures. Following its blunders, TCL reflected, regrouped, and retreated from international equity ventures. Instead, it focused on manufacturing trendy handheld devices for export (mainly tablet PCs). By 2011 it had recovered from its French forays and was again turning a handsome profit.[143]

To be sure, some Chinese companies have done better than others. Sectors where they fared less well are electronics, banks, petroleum, and steel. Four sectors where Chinese firms have done better are telecommunications, automobiles, appliances, and computers. Let us examine these successful cases briefly in turn, and illustrate each sector with several successful companies.

Telecoms

The global telecom industry is very crowded, very competitive, and very dynamic. Huawei is one of the few Chinese firms to have successfully gone global by the aforementioned criteria, and it is thus considered by many to be China's most successful multinational corporation.[144] In 2012 Huawei overtook Swedish rival Ericsson and became the world's largest manufacturer of telecom equipment, producing everything from switches and routers to smart phones and tablet computers.[145] Huawei reported revenues of $28 billion in 2010, $32.4 billion in 2011, and aims to reach $50 billion by 2015. Headquartered in Shenzhen, Huawei now operates in 140 countries.

Huawei was founded in 1987 by Ren Zhengfei, a former People's Liberation Army officer with twenty-five years of service in the PLA's engineering and logistics corps. Ren built the company from an initial investment of 21,000 renminbi (about $3,300 at the current exchange rate) and manufacturing digital switches into a multibillion-dollar global telecommunications giant.[146] Ren's corporate strategy and secret is an old one: to produce better-quality equipment than the competition at (much) cheaper prices, and provide 24/7 technical service to customers.

But Ren's military origins and the company's original links to the PLA have clouded its reputation in Europe, Australia, and the United States, where a number of Huawei's attempted acquisitions and investments were nixed on national security grounds by government authorities. The fear is that Huawei's equipment could pilfer industrial secrets, eavesdrop on communications or shut them down during a conflict, and hack networks.

For its part, Huawei claims that it is a "collective enterprise" and an employee-owned company with 120,000 staff, having no ties with either the Chinese government or military. Its 2010 Annual Report states that "Huawei Holding (the parent company) is solely owned by employees of the company, without any third parties, including government bodies, holding any of its shares."[147] Nonetheless, Huawei's corporate structure and accounting remain opaque and its links to the PLA remain in question. In an effort to calm such concerns, Huawei began in 2012 to offer foreign governments "security guarantees" that include foreign government access to the company's source codes and security checks of equipment and software.[148]

Despite national security concerns in some developed countries, Huawei has been able to expand its corporate footprint globally. When I interviewed him in São Paulo, Huawei's chief executive in Brazil described the company's strategy as a "Maoist strategy of surrounding the cities from the countryside."[149] This was an allusion to the Chinese communists' military strategy against the rival Kuomintang army during the civil war (1945–1949), but in this context it meant, the executive recounted, the company plotted its global expansion in three phases: (1) first establishing itself in Asia, Africa, and Latin America; (2) then expanding into Europe; and (3) finally gaining a foothold in North America. Phase 1 has been very successful, with these regions accounting for $23 billion in global revenue during 2008 (75 percent of Huawei's total revenue). The 2010 Annual Report indicates that the 75–25 (global vs. domestic sales) revenue stream has continued.

Phase 2 of Huawei's global growth strategy is also essentially complete, as it now supplies all of Europe's major telecom operators (including Vodafone, Deutsche Telekom, France Télécom, Telefónica, and British Telecom) and is currently turning its attention to North America. Despite failed attempts to acquire the U.S. firms 3Com, 3Leaf, and Sprint Nextel, Huawei is redoubling its efforts in the United States and Canada. The company has tried to learn from these failures by improving its government relations and lobbying in Washington, D.C.[150] But an October 2012 House Intelligence Committee report recommended banning Huawei from operating in the United States. Also, rather than trying to acquire other companies and gain a foothold in systems routing or infrastructure, Huawei seems to be pursuing a strategy centered on research and development. The company established its first R&D center in Plano, Texas, in 2001; by 2011 it was operating seven R&D centers and twelve offices employing fifteen hundred Americans. Huawei reports that its investment in R&D in the United States has grown by 66 percent per year since 2001, reaching $62 million by 2011.[151] Globally, Huawei spent $2.6 billion on R&D in 2010, with approximately half of its global employees engaged in R&D.[152] Huawei's chief executive in France, Leo Sun, claims that the company owns more than eighteen thousand patents and devotes more than sixty thousand personnel to this endeavor, making it "the biggest R&D force in the world."[153] This is one of Huawei's secrets to success.

Huawei has clearly emerged as one of China's leading-edge multinationals, eclipsing other domestic competitors that are trying to go global. In many ways, Huawei is *the* model for other aspiring Chinese firms. It is poised for further growth, particularly if it can shake off the image problem of alleged ties to the Chinese military.

Auto Companies

Just as international auto companies have been working hard to establish footholds and expanded market share in China, the world's largest and fastest-growing auto market, so too are Chinese vehicle manufacturers vying intensively for sales abroad. China has a horde of auto companies all trying to go global.[154] Some have made headlines—such as Tengzhong Heavy's bid for General Motors' Hummer line, Geely's acquisition of Volvo's passenger car production, Beijing Auto's attempt to acquire

Opel (owned by GM), and several Chinese companies' attempts to purchase Sweden's Saab out of bankruptcy (which ultimately failed). In 2005 Shanghai Auto (SAIC) and Nanjing Auto rescued the British icon MG Rover, which had declared bankruptcy and laid off six thousand workers, for a purchase price of only $101 million.

Despite the crowded field, little by little Chinese vehicle manufacturers are establishing themselves around the world and expanding market share. Exports of cars produced in China are also rising rapidly: 280,000 units in 2010 and 487,900 units in 2011. Chinese auto companies are doing best in Latin America and Europe, and increasingly well in North Africa and the Middle East. As of 2011, China's auto firms still accounted for less than 2 percent of the global auto trade.[155] Having gained a foothold, China's auto producers are trying to expand their footprint. Expansion into Africa, Europe, Central Asia, and Latin America are the priority targets. Yet, it will not be easy, as foreign competition remains stiff and government quotas on imports exist in many countries.[156]

Chery has China's largest overseas sales, selling 192,000 small passenger cars abroad in 2010.[157] Chery does much of its manufacturing abroad, with sixteen factories and an impressive network of 1,153 dealerships in eighty countries.[158] Its first plant opened in Egypt in 2006, and since then it has established production lines in sixteen countries.[159] Many of these production lines actually assemble knock-down kits shipped from China. Chery is betting on the Latin market at present, investing heavily in Brazil and Uruguay; it hopes to sell 150,000 to 170,000 cars in Brazil by 2013.[160] Unfortunate for Chery, in 2011 the Brazilian government drastically increased taxes on the auto industry, forcing Chery to halt construction of its $500 million plant there.

Geely, a Zhejiang-based firm, is only China's tenth-largest automaker, but it made international headlines with its 2010 acquisition of the Swedish trademark luxury car Volvo, purchasing the company from its owner Ford Motor Company for $1.8 billion.[161] This was China's biggest overseas auto acquisition to date. One year after the takeover, the new venture turned a $190 million profit.[162] Geely's turnaround strategy was not only to continue to build and sell Volvos around the world but to start production and expand sales in China. New factories have been built in Shanghai, Sichuan, and Liaoning provinces, with an established network of 117 dealerships in eighty-three Chinese cities. Geely announced in

February 2011 that it hopes to sell 200,000 cars in China annually by 2015; the company is well on track to achieve and exceed this goal, having sold 100,881 Volvo vehicles in China during the first quarter of 2012.[163] China's luxury car market is booming and is predicted to reach one million units annually by 2015. Geely's Volvo line hopes to have a significant segment of that market share. The company is also ramping up its production abroad—already establishing factories in Russia, Ukraine, Malaysia, and Indonesia—with plans to have fifteen worldwide by 2015.[164]

Appliances

The international household appliance sector is ready-made for Chinese multinationals. By 2006, an IBM study found that Chinese companies were the largest global manufacturers in twenty-eight of thirty-two home appliance product categories (although predominantly for the domestic market).[165] Haier Corporation has done the best and is way out in front of the competition, but other manufacturers such as Hisense are gaining international market share.

Taking its name from the Chinese transliteration of a former German partner, the Liebherr Group (*li bo hai er*, 利勃海尔), Haier dates its origins to the 1920s but really took off in the mid-1980s. Managing Director Zhang Ruimin turned the company around and has taken it global. Headquartered in Qingdao, Haier produces a range of household goods.[166] Its products include air conditioners, mobile phones, computers, microwave ovens, washing machines, refrigerators, and televisions—but it is best known for its "white goods" (refrigerators and washing machines), in which Haier had the world's largest market share in 2010 (6.1 percent).[167] It has virtually cornered the market for miniature refrigerators (very popular among American college students living in dormitories), window air-conditioning units, and small fast-cycle washing machines (popular in small European and Japanese households).

Haier's global growth strategy passed through four stages. It first expanded into Southeast Asia (Indonesia, Thailand, Malaysia, and the Philippines) in 1996–97 and was the first Chinese manufacturer to open a production facility in Japan for sales to that domestic market. Haier then took aim at the United States, bringing it into direct competition with established giants Whirlpool, GE, Maytag, and Frigidaire. In 2005, it even tried—but failed—to take over Maytag (which was bought by rival Whirlpool). Starting with an initial $30 million investment in 1999, the United States has become one of the company's most successful markets. Because of its product quality, tailored products (such as the mini-fridge and compact air-conditioning units), and low cost, Haier was able to establish a foothold in the American market. As part of its strategy, Haier also sought not just to *sell* to Americans but to *employ* them as well. In 2000 the company opened a production facility in Camden, South Carolina, which now employs six hundred Americans. Haier's profile in the United States was also enhanced by official partnership with the National Basketball Association (NBA). The company purchased a prominent midtown Manhattan building (the former Landmark Greenwich Bank Building) for its North American corporate headquarters.

Beginning around 2002–2005, Haier began the third phase of its expansion by moving into South Asia, the Middle East, and Africa—establishing plants in Pakistan, Jordan, Tunisia, Algeria, Nigeria, Egypt, and South Africa. The fourth phase began in 2009, with the move to establish production facilities in Europe and Latin America (Italy and Venezuela). By 2011, Haier had established twenty-nine manufacturing facilities, sixteen industrial parks, and eight R&D centers on all continents, sales staff of 58,800, and total revenues over $20 billion.[168] With marketing slogans such as "convenience for a modern lifestyle" and "smarter life for a better planet", Haier is at the cutting edge of both practical and green products. Haier has staked its strategy and success on an old-fashioned business principle: quality. It has also done what few other Chinese multinationals have done: hire foreigners into its senior management and marketing staff. For all these reasons, Haier is taking aim to overtake industry leaders Samsung and Sony (numbers one and two respectively).

Computers

It is well known that China is the world's largest manufacturer of personal computers, but almost all firms manufacturing there are foreign in origin. Only Chinese home appliance manufacturers like those noted above (TCL, Huawei, Hisense) have ventured into the handheld computer marketplace. Lenovo is the exception to the rule.

Founded in 1984 by the Chinese Academy of Sciences Institute of Computing Technology, Lenovo has become China's top-selling computer brand and the world's third-largest vendor of PCs (accounting for 10.4 percent of market share in 2010). In December 2004 the Lenovo Group made its boldest move, by buying IBM's worldwide PC division for $1.75 billion. Instantly, Lenovo was catapulted into being one of the top three PC suppliers in the world. Although risky, the acquisition was successful. It provided Lenovo with established trademarks such as the Think Pad, management talent and business units experienced in international industry, pioneering R&D centers in the United States such as Research Triangle Park in North Carolina, and overseas marketing and distribution channels. Lenovo's stock price instantly rose by 60 percent in the six months after the IBM takeover.

But all did not go smoothly. Within four years, Lenovo's market share had slipped to 4 percent, with sales plummeting during 2008–09. This was due to a combination of sluggish corporate demand (Lenovo had particularly targeted bulk company sales) during the global financial crisis, the declining appeal of the desktop computer (in favor of the laptop), and competition resulting from Apple's introduction of the iPad and MacBook Air. As a result, Lenovo turned its attention away from the North American market and instead focused its sales strategy on emerging economies and China itself. The recalibration worked. Sales in China, Russia, India, Central Europe, and Latin America rose sharply. By the end of 2010, Lenovo had recovered a 10.2 percent market share globally, while domestic sales accounted for 46.4 percent of its earnings.[169]

Having turned things around, Lenovo is now embarked on multiple fronts to take on Apple, Acer, and HP.[170] Its launch of LePhone and LePad are direct and undisguised challenges to Apple's iPhone and iPad. Time will tell whether China's largest personal computing firm can compete in an intense global marketplace.

Backlash and Risk

These relative success stories of Chinese multinationals are just part of the picture of the overall growth in overseas operations and direct investments. As Chinese companies go global and establish a broader and deeper footprint in various parts of the world, they will inevitably encounter difficulties. The backlash has already begun. It has taken different forms in different regions.

In developed countries Chinese investments are questioned mainly on national security grounds. In America, the government's Committee on Foreign Investment in the United States (CFIUS) scrutinizes attempted Chinese mergers, acquisitions, and investments, such as the 2005 CNOOC-Unocal deal and an earlier attempt by Hong Kong's Hutchison Whampoa to manage the port of Long Beach. Australian citizens and politicians are similarly questioning the wisdom of massive Chinese investments in the country's mining sector. Opposition to the attempted 2009 Chinalco purchase of part of the mining behemoth Rio Tinto is only the most well-known case of rising Australian antipathy.[171] The Australian government similarly nixed a bid from Huawei to upgrade the nation's broadband network (on grounds of national security). Minmetals' attempted acquisition of the mining firm Noranda raised similar opposition in the Canadian parliament. A 2011 attempt by a Chinese developer to buy 300 square miles of desolate Icelandic wilderness supposedly to develop a luxury resort for $200 million located near sensitive NATO radar and reconnaissance installations, raised eyebrows in North America and Europe—owing to the island's strategic position in the north Atlantic.[172] When the bid by Chinese businessman Huang Nubo was rejected by the Government of Iceland's Ministry of Internal Affairs, his reaction was that "the denial reflects the unjust and parochial investment environment facing private Chinese enterprises abroad."[173] Leading European think tanks have begun to question the wisdom of China's purchase of European sovereign debt as well as its bourgeoning purchases of prime real estate, infrastructure, and manufacturing investments.[174]

Anti-China sentiment is also rising in developing countries.[175] In 2004 three Chinese engineers working on the Gwadar port construction project in Pakistan were killed by a car bomb, and the next year two more Chinese engineers were kidnapped (one died in a botched rescue attempt). In 2005, eleven Chinese railway workers were murdered at a construction site in northern Afghanistan. Also in 2005, eight Chinese workers were kidnapped in Iraq. Five oil workers were kidnapped—and released—in Nigeria in 2007. In the same year seven more were kidnapped (and also released) in Ethiopia. Nine Chinese oil workers were assassinated in Somalia in 2008. Nine more were kidnapped and killed in western Sudan in 2009. Three more oil workers were kidnapped in Yemen in 2010. In 2010 gunmen kidnapped a Chinese worker in Chad. In October 2011 thirteen Chinese crew members were murdered on a cargo vessel in the Mekong River. Three Chinese workers and their translator were kidnapped by FARC guerrillas in Colombia, also in 2011. Twenty-nine Chinese road builders were kidnapped by rebels in South Sudan, with an additional twenty-five kidnapped in Egypt's Sinai, during January 2012.

Kidnappings and killings are not the only forms of anti-China backlash in developing countries. In Kyrgyzstan angry crowds besieged a Chinese-owned shopping mall, ransacking Chinese shops and terrorizing shopkeepers.[176] Similar demonstrations against the influx of Chinese goods and workers have occurred in places as diverse as Spain, Italy, Fiji, and Yemen. In several cases, Chinese enterprises were the target of looting and arson. Demonstrations broke out in Zambia against Chinese companies' environmental damage in national parks, as well as targeting mining ventures for labor abuses and the general influx of Chinese shopkeepers and goods.[177] Similar sieges occurred at Peruvian mines.[178] Chinese merchants in Russia report being regularly blackmailed lest their businesses encounter "trouble."

These examples only indicate that China is now experiencing what many Western countries have long found in operating around the world: it is part and parcel of being a global commercial power. But in China's case, there seem to be two unique features. There is resentment over domestic unemployment, due to low-cost Chinese goods proliferating in countries where Chinese merchants offer easy targets for the discontent. Second, China's vast mining of natural resources in Africa and Latin America raise historical memories of colonialism and exploitation.

To be sure, Chinese companies, citizens, and government are all aware of—and deeply concerned about—these phenomena. A discussion has emerged in the Chinese media about how to anticipate and prevent such occurrences.[179] Some argue that China should develop long-range military capacity to cope with such contingencies. Says Tao Jian, president of China's University of International Relations: "The [2011 Libya] incident is evidence that China needs to develop its long-range weapons arsenal and improve security for its nationals living abroad.... China should utilize its military might, such as its new and first aircraft carrier, in this endeavor."[180] Another scholar at the China Institutes of Contemporary International Relations (under the Ministry of State Security) argues that China "set up some kind of private armed force. If China had a private security company in Libya, like the U.S. 'Blackwater Security Company' in Iraq, Chinese investors would not have had to flee from Libya and they would not have lost so much money."[181]After twenty-nine Chinese workers were kidnapped in Sudan in January 2012, one Chinese contributor to Sina Weibo (China's leading microblogging site) vented: "Now we have an aircraft carrier, fourth-generation war planes, and the second highest gross domestic product—do we still have to tolerate this?"[182]

One thing is certain: such incidents will occur as China continues to go global. It is part and parcel of being a global power.

China's Overseas Aid

Another aspect of China's overseas economic presence is foreign aid. Although a developing country and recipient of foreign aid itself, China has been an aid donor abroad since the 1950s. Although China has received considerable international criticism for its lack of transparency and "no strings attached" policies, in many ways the aid programs are an untold success story. China has made important contributions to developing countries in the areas of medicine and public health (particularly in tropical diseases), tertiary and vocational education, agriculture, and hard infrastructure. Some instances of China's overseas aid are very well known—such as the Tanzania-Zambia (Tanzam) Railway and the Karakoram Highway linking China and Pakistan—but much is not well known. Until China released its first (and only) White Paper on Foreign Aid in April 2011, no systematic data were available from the government. Because China is not a member of the OECD, it does not have to comply with or contribute data to the OECD's Development Assistance Committee. Indeed, if it did, much of China's foreign assistance (对外援助) would not even be counted as such.[183] Much of the aid does not meet the OECD criteria because it straddles the line between aid and overseas investment, involves private companies, and gives loans that often do not have a grant element over 25 percent.

According to China's White Paper on Foreign Aid, China uses three types of foreign aid financing and eight forms of foreign aid.[184] Financing includes grants, interest-free loans, and concessional loans. The latter are granted by the Export-Import Bank of China and raised on the stock and bond markets. The Export-Import Bank also offers short-term credits to Chinese companies involved in delivery of aid-related goods and services abroad, and longer-term credits for foreign recipients of this aid. The China Development Bank offers commercial loans and lines of credit to recipients, including the China-Africa Development Fund (these types of financing are considered by the OECD as "Other Official Flows," rather than conventional ODA). The eight types of China's foreign aid are:

- *Complete projects.* Presently accounting for 40 percent of China's foreign aid expenditure, these projects come in four forms: agriculture projects, public facilities, infrastructure (including power and telecommunications),[185] and industrial facilities.
- *Goods and materials.* This includes machinery, equipment of various kinds, medical devices, transport vehicles, food, and medicine.
- *Technical cooperation.* This involves training in a variety of fields and dispatch of Chinese technicians to recipient countries.
- *HR development cooperation.* This involves various types of in-country or in-China training programs for government officials, medical personnel, educators, etc.
- *Chinese medical teams working abroad.* Since 1963 China has been dispatching medical teams abroad. By the end of 2009, China claimed to have sent twenty-one thousand medical workers abroad, who treated 260 million patients. In 2009, sixty such teams were working in fifty-seven countries.
- *Emergency humanitarian aid.* China has become quite active in recent years contributing postdisaster assistance in Asia, Africa, and Central and Latin America.
- *Overseas volunteer programs.* Since 2002 China has been dispatching youth volunteers and Chinese language teachers abroad. They work primarily in the education and health care fields.
- *Debt relief.* By the end of 2009 China had signed debt relief protocols with fifty countries, canceling 380 debts worth RMB 25.58 billion.

In Africa alone China claims to have completed 900 projects, built 2,233 kilometers of railroads, 3,391 kilometers of highways, 42 stadiums and 54 hospitals; dispatched more than 18,000 Chinese medical and public health personnel and 350,000 technicians, trained 30,000-plus Africans from various sectors, and offered 34,000 government-funded scholarships to African students.[186]

In providing aid and financing in these areas, China has always practiced a "no (political) strings attached" policy. That is, it does not practice "conditionality" by tying aid to domestic governance. This has caused a great deal of controversy and consternation among other donor countries, the OECD, the World Bank, regional development banks, the IMF, human rights groups and nongovernmental organizations, and even recipient countries. This is because China's aid often undercuts the goals and conditions of good governance and best practices—while rewarding some of the world's worst dictators and most corrupt and repressive regimes.

In terms of the distribution of China's foreign aid, China's White Paper indicates that the lion's share goes to Africa (45.7 percent), followed by Asia (32.8 percent), Latin America (12.7 percent), Oceania (4 percent), and others (4.5 percent).[187] Statistics from the *China Statistical Yearbook* put the figure for total aid disbursements at roughly $970 million per year from 2003 to 2006.[188] But China's official foreign aid expenditure in 2009 was RMB 13,296 or $2.08 billion.[189]

These figures place China's aid levels not even among the top ten international donor nations. This is another indicator of China punching below its weight, not carrying proportionate international responsibility, and being a partial power. By contrast, the United States remains the world's largest donor state, providing $31 billion in aid in 2010.

Yet much is not known about China's aid program. In fact, we know more about China's military budget than its aid budget. A considerable amount of China's overseas assistance is concealed in other ministerial budgets (Ministry of Health, Ministry of Education, Ministry of Agriculture, Ministry of Foreign Affairs, Exim Bank, China Development Bank, etc.), while the Ministry of Commerce remains the lead agency. Also, China's categories of aid expenditures do not conform to international standards.

In terms of the ODA decision-making process, this too is quite opaque.[190] The institutional epicenter of both the decision-making and the implementation processes is the Ministry of *Commerce*—which says much about how China conceives of foreign aid—where the line between assistance and profit-making commercial activity is frequently blurred. Although recipient countries no doubt convey their "wish lists" to Beijing, aid is very much used proactively by the Chinese government to support and reward certain countries for certain reasons. Access to natural resources, business opportunities, and diplomatic priorities (including competition with Taiwan) all affect the aid that China provides. The Ministry of Foreign Affairs is therefore more actively involved in the process than MOFCOM officials admit.

China's aid program thus has multiple motivations and involves multiple actors. What is bureaucratically unusual is that, unlike other major donor countries, the process is run by the Ministry of Commerce rather than the Ministry of Foreign Affairs—and this is somewhat instructive as to how the Chinese approach the issue. This is not necessarily to imply that Chinese aid is not benefiting recipient countries, as it is doing a *lot* of good, and China should thus receive more credit than it does from the West and other donor states. China's ODA is also a significant contribution to global governance and is an instrument in the government's soft power toolbox. China sees its aid as a tangible form of "South-South cooperation."

For all these reasons, China's aid is noteworthy—even if it is controversial at home. One likely reason for the lack of transparency, Chinese interlocutors told me, is that if the public knew about China's aid abroad the government would be criticized for neglecting domestic poverty alleviation. If the nation could become more integrated into the international donor community,[191] particularly the OECD's Development Assistance Committee, it would do much to alleviate the existing deficit of transparency; but it may also expose corrupt practices at variance with international norms and standards.[192]

Prospects

In this chapter we have examined four distinct aspects of China's economic footprint abroad: trade, energy, investment, and aid. Of all the aspects of China's international presence examined in this study, this is the dimension where the global impact is greatest. Yet we have also seen that even in this economic dimension, China's footprint and influence is not that deep or great. It certainly is in terms of trade and global energy markets, but it is not particularly affecting the world in investment or aid. China's ODI and ODA figures are comparable to relatively modest industrial countries. Undoubtedly, the world can expect China's overseas investment to grow considerably in coming years. China will also continue to draw a large and increasing share of global energy supplies and natural resources. But its aid levels are likely to remain near where they are today. China is certainly an economic superpower and the world's second-largest economy, yet its domestic economy still faces many challenges to move up the value chain, maintain employment, continue to grow GDP, and broaden its international impact.

6

China's Global Cultural Presence

We should bring Chinese culture to the world, develop cultural soft power compatible with China's international standing, and increase the influence of Chinese culture in the world.

—PRESIDENT HU JINTAO, 2011[1]

China should actively engage in public diplomacy in order to comprehensively develop its soft power and further boost its international appeal and influence.... This is both a pressing task and a long-term strategy.

—FOREIGN MINISTER YANG JIECHI, 2011[2]

China political system is not attractive and they have no attractiveness as a model. China has little soft power.

—LEE KUAN YEW, 2011[3]

IN ITS SEARCH FOR status as a global power, China has discovered the importance of international image and soft power.[4] But, in this arena too, we witness a large and growing number of China's cultural activities abroad—but very little influence on global cultural trends, minimal soft power, and a mixed-to-poor international image in public opinion polls. As in other spheres examined in this book, China also remains a partial cultural power.

The Chinese government has launched a concerted effort to improve its global image and ramp up its cultural presence around the world—pumping an estimated $7 to $10 billion per year into its "overseas publicity work." The Seventeenth Central Committee of the CCP even devoted a whole plenary session in October 2011 to the issue of *culture*, with the final plenary communiqué declaring that it was a national goal to "build our country into a socialist cultural superpower," claiming that "it is a pressing task to increase the state's cultural soft power and enhance the international influence of Chinese culture." But the communiqué went on to lament, "The task of maintaining the state's cultural security is even more arduous."[5] President Hu Jintao's own sharply worded speech to the Plenum seized on the issue of protecting China's "cultural security" domestically, asserting that China was under cultural assault from abroad: "We must be sober enough to see that international hostile forces are intensifying the strategic plots to Westernize and divide us (西化分化), and that the ideological and cultural sectors are the main areas through which they commit long-term infiltration. Given this, we must thoroughly perceive the seriousness and complicated nature of ideological struggle, always sound alarms, remain vigilant, and take forceful measures to be on guard and respond."[6] Since Hu put "cultural security" on the national agenda, various elements of China's national security apparatus have been put on alert to guard against corrosive cultural penetration from abroad.[7]

Meanwhile, the government is pouring huge resources into multiple efforts to broaden China's cultural reach, public diplomacy, and soft power abroad. The State Council launched its "Cultural Industries Revitalization Plan" on September 26, 2009. The man and the institution in charge of the effort—Wang Chen, director (minister) of the State Council Information Office—noted: "With the ever intensified competition between countries in the area of national cultural soft power, the role of external communication has increased in importance. It helps China develop into a powerful nation."[8] Premier Wen Jiabao and other leaders have also emphasized the role of culture as a source of China's national strength and international competitiveness. In his government work report to the 2010 National People's Congress, Premier Wen stated, "Culture is the spirit and soul of the nation and a determining factor of whether it is truly strong or not."[9] CCP Politburo Standing Committee member and Propaganda Department Director Liu Yunshan noted in 2009, "It has become an urgent strategic task for us to make our communication capability match our international status. In this modern era, those who gain advanced communication skills, powerful communication capabilities, and whose culture and values are more widely spread, is [*sic*] able to effectively influence the world."[10]

The fact that culture is also big business is not lost on the Chinese. To this end, Minister of Culture Cai Wu proclaimed that "We aim to establish a batch of world-famous cultural brands."[11] In 2006 the State Council adopted the *Outline of the National Plan for Cultural Development During the 11th Five Year Plan*.[12] By 2010 the total value output of China's "cultural industries" was estimated at more than 1.1 trillion RMB ($170 billion), accounting for 2.75 percent of gross domestic product (GDP).[13] The government has plans to make culture a "pillar industry." This includes exports of a variety of "cultural products" (文化产品): heritage goods; books, newspapers, and periodicals; other printed matter such as maps, brochures, and designs; recorded and audiovisual media (including film, television, radio); visual arts; and performing arts.

Outside of China and around the world, journalists and scholars have also been paying more attention to China's soft power push.[14] Some observers believe China possesses much soft power, while others believe it possesses little.

The "father" of the concept, Harvard Professor Joseph S. Nye, defines *soft power* as the "ability to shape preferences of others" and "to get others to want the outcomes you want."[15] Hard power usually involves some level of coercion or threat of force to deter or compel desired behavior. Soft power, by contrast, relies on cooptation rather than coercion. It is the intrinsic ability of a country to attract others. As such, writes Nye, soft power "grows out of a country's culture, political values, and foreign policies."[16] Soft power is thus highly normative in nature. It is like a magnet that pulls and draws others to a nation simply because of its powerful appeal by example. It is thus largely about the capacity of a *society* to *attract* others, rather than a *government* to *persuade* others.

This is the main distinction between soft power and public diplomacy. Soft power largely originates from *society*, while public diplomacy is an instrument in the hands of *governments*. To be sure, the latter can contribute to the former, but public diplomacy will be much less effective without intrinsic soft power. No matter how well resourced by government, if the message is not sellable the messenger will have difficulty selling it.

China's Discourse on International Image, Soft Power, and Public Diplomacy

The concept of soft power, usually translated in Chinese as *ruan shili* (软实力),[17] has percolated in Chinese academic discourse for two decades. The first academic article on the subject was published in 1993 by Professor Wang Huning, who was then at Fudan University; his academic career turned political soon thereafter when he became a close advisor to former President Jiang Zemin and his successor Hu Jintao.[18] After a decade hiatus, the concept fully entered Chinese academic discourse around 2003–04, largely in response to the Chinese translation and circulation of Nye's popular book *Soft Power*. President Hu's references to soft and cultural power in his keynote address to the Seventeenth Party Congress in 2007 did much to stimulate interest in and publications on the subject: "The great rejuvenation of the Chinese nation will definitely be accompanied by the thriving of Chinese culture.... We must enhance culture as part of the soft power of our country.... We will further publicize the fine traditions of Chinese culture and strengthen international cultural exchanges to enhance the influence of Chinese culture worldwide."[19]

Academic and newspaper articles on soft power spiked sharply in the years following Hu's speech. Several universities and research institutions have sponsored conferences and forums on the subject. Fudan University, Beijing University, Tsinghua University, China Foreign Studies and Culture University, the Central Party School, and the China Institutes of Contemporary International Relations (CICIR) have all convened soft power symposia.

There is also a parallel and rapidly growing interest in the subject of public diplomacy (公共外交).[20] Journalism and media departments in Chinese universities have established majors in public diplomacy, a quarterly journal entitled *Public Diplomacy* was launched by the Chinese People's Political Consultative Congress (CPPCC) in 2010, the CPPCC at provincial and municipal levels was instructed in 2011 to establish public diplomacy offices and activities, the Ministry of

Foreign Affairs established an Office of Public Diplomacy in 2010, and even a Museum of Public Diplomacy was established in eastern Beijing in 2008.

There is growing recognition in China that the components of its international image are subjects worthy of academic study as well as foreign policy practice.[21] Interviews with a variety of Foreign Ministry and other governmental officials at the central and provincial levels all indicate they are paying increasing attention to both domestic and international opinion. This is usually done in departments and universities concerned with mass communications, media studies, and broadcasting rather than IR or diplomacy institutions.[22] This is an interesting insight into how Chinese authorities and academics think about the issue, i.e., national image is something to be *marketed* via the media rather than built by society or promoted via diplomacy. The most thorough study of China's international image building to date was edited by Zhou Mingwei, director-general of China's Foreign Languages Press. The FLP has a long tradition of trying to "tell China's story to the world," dating to the establishment of the People's Republic. For many decades it was a straightforward state propaganda organ, employing foreign "fellow travelers" with socialist and pro-CCP sympathies, but under Zhou's direction the FLP has more recently sought to remake itself as a more serious international publishing house and publish more sophisticated books and magazines about China. A tall and dapper man, Zhou himself has had an extensive career in interacting with foreigners, first as spokesman for the Shanghai Municipal Government, then in the Taiwan Affairs Office of the State Council, and since 2005 as head of the FLP. Under his aegis, the press has been transformed from a propaganda organ into a large publishing conglomerate (集团) that produces a variegated range of media products.

Zhou's edited volume *National Image* is a comprehensive analysis and blueprint of China's international image "construction" (国际现象构建), and it is one of the few studies that attempt to analyze China's global image on the basis of foreign public opinion surveys. The study is also unique for its critique of what China lacks in its international image.[23] Zhou and his colleagues advise China to promote three "core images" images abroad: *ancient China*, *modern China* (including economic development, political system, and cultural modernization), and *peaceful China.* They also recommended establishing a "China Brand Strategy Leading Group" under the State Council, which would be composed of representatives of twelve government ministries and agencies. Despite the attention paid to marketing China, Zhou's tome is woefully lacking in *specifics* of the *content* of China's messages to be advanced abroad. This reflects a lack of awareness in China of what really constitutes the nation's potential soft power.

The question is *not* what is *unique* about China, but what is (potentially) *universal* about China. This is the essence of soft power: to possess national attributes that transcend one's own country and appeal to others. Here, China seems to have few responses other than "peace and harmony."

China's "soft power deficit" becomes even clearer when one more closely examines the soft power discourse in China.[24] Professor Men Honghua of the Central Party School led a team of scholars to measure a variety of indicators (such as China's presence in international media, literature, film, etc.). They concluded that Chinese cultural products had little appeal abroad.[25] Although most scholars agree on the growing role and importance of soft power in the world today, they are in sharp disagreement as to what should constitute China's soft power. All Chinese analysts seem to be in agreement that *culture* is a key element.[26] But that is where the consensus ends. Some also believe that politics, economics, and foreign policy should be taken into account. Even those who advocate the "culture as the core" approach divide into two camps.

Men Honghua is indicative of the first camp, which can be described as the "values as culture" school. Professor Men is one of China's leading scholars of soft power; he has published numerous articles and is editor of the important book *China's Soft Power Strategy.* In his writings and interviews with the author, Men stressed the universality of four core Chinese values: 和 (peace and harmony), 德 (morality), 礼 (etiquette), and 仁 (benevolence).[27] "These values are the greatest contribution of China to global culture," Men claimed.[28] But in a separate interview with me, Professor Men seemed much less confident about the *existence* of Chinese values. He lamented that they had been "destroyed" during the Cultural Revolution. "We have lost our values—we do not have any common values at all. There is a vacuum of values in China. Nor do we have an ideology," he observed.[29]

Yu Xintian may be the most well-known advocate of the second soft power-as-culture school, which might also be described as the "ideological cultural" or "propaganda as culture" approach.[30] Madame Yu is the former president of the Shanghai Institutes of International Studies and a well-known policy intellectual. In her writings, she criticizes those scholars who take what she calls a "pure culture" approach, those who stress only China's history and Confucian classics.[31] "Many scholars are lost in the fog of pure culture," she argues.[32] Instead, she advocates that a contemporary ideology (当代意识形态) of "socialism with Chinese characteristics" and China's "peaceful development road" should play prominent roles in China's soft power. In an interview with the author, Madame Yu elaborated on her thinking about soft power.[33] First, she distinguished her definition from Nye's by arguing that soft power is "uncountable and immaterial," whereas hard power is "countable and material." For example, *ideas* about economic models should count as soft power in her view—but not economies (which can be statistically measured) per se. "Ideas, systems, culture, values, and the quality of people constitute soft power," she explained. Public diplomacy, she argued, should be distinguished from soft power as well, asserting: "It is a type of diplomacy. It is one—but only one—way to strengthen soft power. It is a concrete means to promote soft power." Finally, Madame Yu was critical of the Chinese government's "cultural going out" (文化走出去) policy: "It is natural (cultural exchange)—why do we need to promote it?" she observed.

Others argue that even though China does possess unique cultural values, they should not be exported and transposed onto others. As the veteran diplomat and well-respected intellectual Wu Jianmin observed, "Chinese culture is so powerful—it is the core of our soft power. But we do not seek to transform others with it. We believe deeply in 和而不同 (seek common ground while reserving differences) and we have understood for 2,000 years that cultural diversity is a reality that cannot be changed."[34] But former Ambassador Wu also laments that contemporary China is lacking in new values. "We need to build up a *new* mainstream culture, but this will take generations. Currently, Chinese society has an identity crisis (信用危机), an intellectual and moral vacuum, so we need to reinvent our culture," he observed.[35]

A second but small cohort, represented by analysts such as Yan Xuetong of Tsinghua University, believe that China's political system is important—even the key—to China's soft power.[36] For Professor Yan, China's political soft power includes capability (能力) and legitimacy (合法性), but he thinks that at present both are weak. Professor Yan laments this fact, arguing that China must perfect its "political model" (政治模式) so that it is not only strong internally but also appealing to other nations.[37] Yan Xuetong and a colleague even undertook a comparative study of U.S. and Chinese soft power, finding that China's is approximately one-third that of the United States.[38] When asked what accounted for China's soft power deficit vis-à-vis the United States, Yan replied, "China's soft power is weaker than the U.S. mainly in the aspect of its political system. China's development has only provided economic success but not political and social success. Culture is a resource like the military or economy, but political power is the capability to make use of those resources—without political power we cannot utilize our soft power."[39]

A third cohort emphasizes China's development experience, particularly its economic growth, as the core of its soft power. This is usually referred to as the "China Model" (中国模式), the "Chinese Experience" (中国经验), "Chinese Path" (中国道路), or "Chinese Example" (中国例子). The Chinese government has not officially endorsed these concepts, although they are very popular in intellectual discourse. If anything, the government has disowned the idea on the grounds that every country's "development path" is unique to national conditions, cannot be transferred, and should not be exported across borders. Yet the notion persists, and writings on the subject have mushroomed in recent years.

Two events stimulated discussions of the "China Model" in China. The first was the reaction to *The Beijing Consensus*, published in 2004 by Joshua Cooper Ramo.[40] In his short study, Cooper Ramo essentially argued that China's unique blend of authoritarian politics and a mixed state/market economic model offered the developing world an appealing alternative to the "Washington Consensus" of democracy and free market capitalism. The second event was the global financial crisis that gripped the world economy after 2008, causing much global soul-searching about the viability of the

Western capitalist model, but triggering much hubris and vindication in China concerning its state/market development model.

Thus, the soft power discourse in China cleaves into three camps, emphasizing *culture, politics,* and *economic development.* But all three schools lament China's *lack* of soft power. This is a common underlying theme in all the literature. As Professor Men Honghua of the Central Party School despairingly observed to me: "Though we talk a lot about soft power (in China), actually we are very weak in it."[41] In another interview with the author, Tsinghua University's Yan Xuetong linked China's soft power deficit to China's lack of a clear international identity: "China's international identity has a serious problem. Our credibility as a developing country is ridiculous! Who are our friends? North Korea, Iran, Myanmar, Sudan, Zimbabwe, Venezuela! We have a big [image] problem. We do not have a *priority identity*. We have no main identity in the world, so we cannot prioritize. Who are we? We should identify ourselves as a quasi-superpower; if we do so, we can clearly define our national interests."[42]

Well-known journalist and *People's Daily/Global Times* opinion writer Ding Gang also laments China's lack of soft power, but for different reasons: its mediocre product quality, low brand recognition and poor global advertising, no exportable religion, a poor commercial reputation owing to the gift-giving *guanxi* business culture, academic bribery to attain degrees abroad, and nonuniversal China-specific popular culture.[43] Professor Pan Zhongying of Renmin University is another soft power expert. He spent a year at the Brookings Institution in Washington comparing American and Chinese soft power and returned home critical of the role that research institutes play in China. He criticized them as all being government organs rather than operating as real public think tanks, and he accused "researchers" of mainly being "propagandists."[44] Huang Renwei, vice president of the Shanghai Academy of Social Sciences and another leading contributor to China's soft power discourse, places the blame for China's "soft power deficit" on three other causes: "China's soft power is small in quantity and low in quality. First there is a serious deficit in China's culture—compared with Western countries, China's culture is in a weak position. Second, there is a lag in democracy in our politics and feudalism still limits our democratic political development. Third, our strong sense of nationalism is an impediment."[45] Although Huang Renwei is pessimistic about China's soft power compared with the West, in another publication he and his Fudan University coauthor Pan Zhongqi argue that China enjoys a "geo-cultural space" to expand its soft power in Africa, Central Asia, and Latin America.[46] Huang and Pan argue that China particularly needs to develop "Chinese style universal values."

These examples provide a flavor of China's academic soft power discourse. There is widespread recognition of the importance of soft power, but equally widespread recognition that China lacks it. Much of China's poor international image and lack of soft power has to do with its government propaganda machine.

China Presents Its Face to the World

China transmits a variety of messages abroad—many intentionally, some unintentionally. For the government, and indeed for many scholars as well, there is a confusion and conflation of soft power, public diplomacy, and external propaganda (对外宣传). They do not tend to grasp the basic distinctions that Nye makes between society-generated soft power and government-generated public diplomacy and propaganda. As Vice Foreign Minister Fu Ying (who has herself devoted considerable time and professional attention to the subject) observed, "We use the terms soft power, public diplomacy, and external publicity interchangeably."[47]

There is a prevailing belief in Chinese officialdom that information *must* be managed, if not controlled, by the government. This belief grows out of the way the government and ruling Communist Party have always treated information and news domestically: it is to be controlled and managed so as to intentionally project and transmit intended messages and images to target audiences. The Chinese propaganda system has a long history and is very deeply institutionalized, although recent commercialization of the media has eroded control to a certain extent.[48] The "external propaganda system" (对外宣传系统) morphed out of the domestic propaganda system in the early 1990s, and since that time a clearer demarcation between internal (对内) and external (对外) propaganda work has been established. Also, as a reflection of the increased sensitivity to China's foreign image, the CCP Propaganda Department has switched to calling itself the "Publicity Department" in English (although its Chinese name remains the same). Even though external propaganda work became a significant bureaucratic and financial undertaking of the Chinese government over the past two decades, the PRC has long targeted foreign audiences with propaganda, state-directed messages, and "people-to-people diplomacy."[49]

Intentionally Transmitted Messages

The Chinese government and CCP puts strong stock in slogans, known as *kouhao* (口号), domestically and externally. *Kouhao* (usually compounds of four, eight, sixteen, twenty-eight, or thirty-two characters in length) are often used as propaganda devices. This has long been intrinsic to Chinese communist political culture. *Kouhao* are meant to simultaneously motivate the intended recipient audience and summarize the content of a specific policy. Although many governments and politicians use catchy slogans to describe policies, what I describe as "slogan politics" (口号政治) and "slogan diplomacy" (口号外交) are particularly used in communist-style political systems. *Kouhao* are not only supposed to convey policy and indoctrinate recipients, but the main purpose is to force uniformity of thought and language. Therefore, the appropriate response within the Chinese political system when hearing a *kouhao* is to parrot it back—to literally repeat it—so as to reflect internalization and acceptance of it. In Chinese this is known as the act of *biaotai* (表态), "to declare where one stands."[50] Thus, to *biaotai* to a *kouhao* is a ritualistic and significant political act, the essence of loyalty to the regime. Although many *kouhao* are neither well understood nor accepted, people nonetheless play the game by parroting the slogan—so as not to get into trouble for political deviance. This is a prime example of what the late Sinologist Lucian Pye referred to as an act of "feigned compliance." For Professor Pye, much of Chinese political culture is all about the ritualistic political theater of feigning (pretending) compliance to authorities.[51] To *biaotai* does not mean that one actually believes or complies with a given *kouhao* or government policy; it is an expression of compliance through verbal conformity. It is a political ritual of pretension.

This is all-important to bear in mind when evaluating messages transmitted domestically and abroad. The problem for China, however, is twofold. First, such slogans are usually designed with domestic audiences in mind and thus do not translate well linguistically or politically across borders and cultures. Second, foreigners are expected—but are usually unwilling—to *biaotai* to a Chinese foreign policy *kouhao*. Thus, many of the Chinese government's messages abroad fall on deaf ears and simply fail to resonate with foreign audiences—linguistically, culturally, or politically. This is China's problem. Much of its culture and propaganda is seen as *sui generis*, its values are viewed as amorphous, its political system as undesirable, and many aspects of China's society and economy either do not appeal or lack transferability across borders.

Over the years, the Chinese government has propagated a large number of slogans, statements, myths, and messages abroad. The most well-known of these is the "Five Principles of Peaceful Coexistence" (和平共处五项原则).[52] Ever since first promulgated in 1954, the Five Principles have been used in Chinese diplomatic documents and, one way or another, are repeatedly regurgitated under new formulations. They have been embedded in a series of official Chinese Government foreign policy *kouhao*: "New International Order" (1988),[53] "New Security Concept" (1998),[54] "China's Peaceful Development Road" (2005),[55] "China's Peaceful Rise" (2005),[56] China's "Strategic Partnerships" (1996–), etc.

In addition to these, in recent years China has sought to project two newer slogans/concepts abroad: its "Peaceful Development" and "Harmonious World." The concept or *kouhao* of "peaceful development" (和平发展) is an outgrowth of Deng Xiaoping's concept of peace *and* development. First put forward in 1985, Deng offered his concept as an alternative to Mao's notion of superpower competition and the inevitability of world war, arguing instead that the world had entered a new era of peace and development and that China needed peace externally in order to pursue development internally.[57] Enshrined in an important 2011 government White Paper, Deng's concept demonstrated remarkable staying power in China's official lexicon and guiding ideology, even long after his death in 1997.

During 2002–2007, Zheng Bijian (a leading CCP theorist, executive vice president of the Central Party School, and chairman of the

China Reform Forum) spearheaded a movement to coin a new term to reassure the outside world about China's growing power and presence. As noted in Chapter 2, Zheng's *kouhao* was "peaceful rise" (*heping jueqi*, 和平崛起). During these five years Zheng Bijian was a one-man global advocate of China's peaceful rise, and the *kouhao* attracted widespread attention at home and abroad. Zheng published a lead article on the subject in the prestigious American policy journal *Foreign Affairs*, made it his theme in the keynote address to the 2005 Boao Forum (China's answer to the World Economic Forum), and used it in countless speeches and articles. Zheng felt that the peaceful rise *kouhao* was a useful counterpoint to the other two main China theories he encountered on visits to the United States: the "China Threat Theory" (中国威胁论) and the "China Collapse Theory" (中国崩溃论).

Despite highest-level support from President Hu Jintao and the Party Politburo to both research and propagate the concept, Zheng and his colleagues at the Central Party School ran into resistance from a range of scholars and officials (primarily in the Ministry of Foreign Affairs) who were particularly uncomfortable with using the term "rise" (崛起). The opposition argued that the term would contribute to existing alarm in the West about China's rise (which was already the standard term used in numerous "China threat" publications), was not consistent with Deng Xiaoping's admonition to "bide time and keep a low profile" (韬光养晦) in world affairs, and did not adequately take account of China's status as a developing country. For these reasons Zheng's thesis and campaign ran into trouble in 2005. By the time President Hu Jintao gave his keynote address to the Seventeenth Party Congress in 2007, "peaceful rise" had been dropped altogether in favor of a return to "peaceful development," and Zheng was eased into retirement.[58] It is thus ironic that the *one* slogan that did gain traction abroad was abandoned.

In addition to peaceful development, the other cornerstone of China's international messaging in recent years is the concept of "harmonious world" (和谐世界). Put forth most systematically by President Hu at the United Nations in 2006, a harmonious world should have four principal attributes: effective multilateralism with a strong role for the United Nations, development of a collective security mechanism, prosperity for all through mutually beneficial cooperation, and tolerance and enhancement of dialogue among diverse civilizations.[59] Like peaceful rise theory, "harmonious world" theory posits that China's rise will not threaten or disrupt the existing global order. Despite President Hu's explanation of the harmonious world *kouhao* and significant efforts by the Chinese government to popularize the concept since 2006, the idea has failed to resonate abroad. The 2009 survey *Soft Power in Asia*, from the Chicago Council on Global Affairs, specifically asked respondents in Japan, South Korea, the United States, Indonesia, and Vietnam if they had heard of the "harmonious world"; large majorities of the publics polled had heard nothing or little of the concept.[60]

Over the years, China also sought to publicize a variety of messages to foreign audiences: that military modernization is "purely defensive" and threatens no one, China is a "peace loving country," it is a developing country, it is a "responsible [international] power," it has endured a "century of shame and humiliation" (1840s to 1949), and China has a great and long history as a civilization. Pursuit of peace is a particularly repetitive theme. As State Council Information Office Director (Minister) Wang Chen told delegates at the Fourth World Forum of China Studies in Shanghai (the forum itself is a major external propaganda exercise with funding from the CCP Propaganda Department): "We Chinese have embraced the philosophy of peace for 2,500 years as *the* most valuable value. We value peace *more than any other people in the world* [emphasis added]. Since 1840 China has been invaded repeatedly by foreign countries—so we know keenly about peace."[61]

These messages are all officially sanctioned and transmitted by a variety of government organizations. Thus, bearing in mind the important distinction between soft power and public diplomacy, the messages all fall into the latter realm.

The Messengers

China uses a range of governmental, semigovernmental, and nongovernmental institutions and instruments to practice its public diplomacy, external propaganda, and soft power promotion abroad.

The State Council Information Office

The nerve center and leading organ in this sprawling system is the State Council Information Office. The SCIO is commonly known in Chinese as both the *Guo Xin Ban* (国新办) and *Wai Xuan Ban* (External Propaganda Office, 外宣办). The reason for the two names is that it straddles two bureaucratic systems: the party and the state. It is formally under the State Council but also overseen by the CCP's External Propaganda Leading Small Group (or EPLSG).[62] This bureaucratic duality is what the Chinese describe as "one organ, two signboards" (一个机构两块牌子), a reference to the white placards that hang outside the gates of all Chinese institutions (in this case giving the appearance of two institutions, but in reality with only one inside). As such, the SCIO is the administrative office for the EPLSG, playing a coordinating role in the media area similar to that performed by the Central Foreign Affairs Office (CFAO, 中央外办) for the Foreign Affairs Leading Small Group (外事领导小组)[63]; but the SCIO is more empowered and far better resourced than the CFAO. It has a much larger staff, considerably larger budget, and a great deal more bureaucratic clout.

The SCIO is currently directed by Minister Wang Chen (王晨). A rotund man with a soft face but serious demeanor, Wang came to the SCIO following a career in journalism with the *Guangming Daily* (where he worked his way up through the ranks to become editor-in-chief from 1995 to 2000). Following a brief stint as vice minister of the CCP Propaganda Department in 2001, Wang was then appointed executive editor of the *People's Daily*, the mouthpiece of the Communist Party, from 2002 to 2008. From there he was moved to the SCIO to spearhead the party's external propaganda work.

Mention of the *Guo Xin Ban/Wai Xuan Ban* often brings a concerned look to the face of many Chinese, particularly intellectuals and journalists. This is because it is a key watchdog organ overseeing the media in China.[64] Located in an old Soviet-era building, it looks and plays the part of the Ministry of Truth in George Orwell's *1984*.[65] The SCIO shares this oversight role with the CCP's Propaganda Department, the State Council's Ministry of Industry and Information Technology (the agency responsible for regulation of the postal service, internet, wireless and broadcast communications, production of electronic and information goods, and the software industry), the State Press and Publishing Administration (which oversees the book and periodical industry), and the State Administration for Film, Radio, and Television.

In addition to its main oversight role and coordination of all of China's external communications, the SCIO is a "messenger" in its own right; it has spokesmen, holds press conferences,[66] publishes magazines and books, produces films, coordinates compilation and publication of all government White Papers, and carries out other activities. It has even developed an "app" (application) for cell phones, to provide one-stop shopping for all Chinese government White Papers and other forms of PRC publicity.[67] External propaganda toward Taiwan, Hong Kong, and overseas Chinese communities is shared with the Central Committee's United Front Work Department.[68] Propaganda aimed at foreigners resident in China and short-term visitors such as tourists and businessmen is also a priority.[69] The SCIO is involved as well in control of internet content, and it must approve all applications for websites.[70] But its main job is to define the messages to be propagated abroad and keep the plethora of other involved institutions and media "on message."

In this role, the SCIO convenes an annual conference where it promulgates guidelines for the coming year. This process began following President Hu Jintao's 2007 report to the Seventeenth Party Congress (which stressed soft power).[71] The annual plan includes "planned exhibitions, publications, media activities, exchange programs, 'Years of China' festivals abroad, and other activities," according to SCIO Vice Minister Jiang Weiqiang, who called it "our soft power strategy."[72] The plan itself is secret at the time of adoption but is subsequently published in the *China Media Yearbook* (中国新闻年鉴).[73] At the 2011 National Foreign Publicity Work Conference, SCIO Minister Wang Chen boasted that because of successful external publicity (propaganda) work, the world was gaining a much better understanding of China and its global image was improving.[74] At the previous year's conference Minister Wang emphasized: "Realizing a leap in our country's international media development and style is a necessity. The purpose is to improve international society's understanding of China, to know China, and the necessity of explaining China to the world; actively participate in international cultural competition; recognize the necessity of enhancing our country's soft power; defeat the Western monopoly of public opinion; and contribute to advancing the fair and equitable distribution of international information."[75]

This is how the SCIO sees its mandate. In pursuing it, the State Council Information Office oversees and coordinates a plethora of other institutions in China's soft power bureaucracy. Let us examine the main ones.

Ministry of Foreign Affairs Information Department and Office of Public Diplomacy

The MFA Information Department is another frontline organ in explaining Chinese government policies to the world. This is done primarily via its spokespersons. The Ministry of Foreign Affairs was the first to have a spokesman (established in 1983), who now holds regular (twice weekly) "news conferences."[76] Although these briefings do convey information publicly, many foreign journalists based in Beijing do not consider them very useful. The spokespersons often dodge and do not answer questions from the press corps, and usually they just provide boilerplate responses. Even worse, their statements are sometimes peppered with nationalistic and sharp rhetoric (e.g., "The Chinese government and people demand that XX reflect on and correct its erroneous actions, and stop hurting the feelings of 1.3 billion Chinese people"). Hectoring language like this does not advance China's soft power.

From the perspective of China's spokespersons, they are just trying to do their job. The Foreign Ministry's chief spokesman during 2008–2011, Ma Zhaoxu, reflected in an interview with the author:

> Improving China's soft power is a strategic goal, and public diplomacy is one of the most important tools to achieve this goal. Public diplomacy is not only a tool, but an integral part of diplomacy itself. Frankly, we Chinese like to focus on our own business, but we cannot close the door. We need to tell the world what China is and what our goals and wishes are. Frankly, I find it very difficult explaining China to foreigners—not only because public diplomacy is new for us, but because of historical, cultural, and value differences between China and the Western world.[77]

On another occasion, Spokesman Ma claimed that "China's foreign policy is one of the best in the world in terms of its substance—the problem is in explaining our policy effectively to the world."[78]

One of the Information Department's main duties is to oversee all foreign journalists in China. The issue of foreign correspondents definitely fits into China's soft power and public diplomacy. As of early 2010, there were 647 registered foreign correspondents from 415 news organizations and fifty-four countries registered in China. The vast majority are Beijing-based, with 114 from twenty-one countries resident in Shanghai, and a few based in Guangzhou, Chongqing, and Shenyang.[79] These 647 individuals do much to shape the world's image of China. Thus, managing them and contributing to their work is (or *should be*) a key priority for the Chinese government. However, one would not always know it, as the government often seems to constrict their work rather than facilitate it.

It is true, as many longtime resident foreign correspondents attest, that working conditions for these journalists have improved over time. Gone are the days when foreign journalists could not travel outside Beijing without the express permission of the MFA and local Foreign Affairs Offices, and without personal "minders" (this system was abolished in 2008). Travel to Tibet is still highly restricted (though possible with advance permission), but for the rest of the country journalists now just buy a ticket, get on a plane or train, or drive to their destination. Journalists also comment that they enjoy expanded access to diverse sectors of society, and to a limited extent government officials at various levels. Another improvement is the government's facilitation of access to crisis locations, notably the 2008 Wenchuan earthquake, the "AIDS village" in Henan, and the 2009 ethnic riots in Urumqi, Xinjiang. Although foreign journalists report that such facilitation was short-lived, these were unprecedented efforts by the government to allow foreign coverage of these events; in every case, it resulted in more complete on-the-spot reporting.

Despite improvements over time, foreign journalists in China are still subject to a range of obstacles and impediments not found in most other societies.[80] All office and private telephones are monitored. Email is also monitored, and in 2010 a series of journalists' accounts were hacked. Cameras outside offices and residences monitor the comings and goings of people, and hidden microphones inside monitor conversations (this is true for many foreign diplomats and businesspeople as well). News bureau local staff must be hired through the Diplomatic Service Personnel Bureau (although this requirement loosened slightly in 2009–10). It is assumed that many of them are "planted" by the Ministry of State Security (MSS), and all are supposed to regularly report to the MSS. Correspondents are often "tailed" by undercover personnel, frequently harassed, and sometimes beaten up. Television correspondents are subject to particular scrutiny, sometimes having their cameras smashed and film confiscated or erased. Correspondents have poor access to central government and CCP organs and officials, there is no opportunity to interact with China's top leaders, there is virtually no access to the military, and access to court proceedings is forbidden. Requests for interviews routinely go unanswered. Questions at the biweekly MFA press conferences are often met with boilerplate responses, the spokespersons from other government organs rarely hold "press conferences" if ever, and the premier of the State Council gives a press conference only once per year (at National People's Congress). There is a general lack of transparency concerning policy making and statistical reporting from all government organs. And the Foreign Correspondents Club of China (FCCC) in Beijing is not officially recognized as a legal or legitimate entity by the MFA and Chinese government.

In addition to these specific harassments and complaints, foreign print journalists in China observe that their articles are being scrutinized more than ever for their content. If the authorities do not like the slant or substance of a journalist's writings, the MFA calls the person in for a "tea chat" and sometimes implies that his or her visa may not be renewed (foreign journalists must apply for reaccreditation annually). Occasionally, individual journalists or bureau chiefs are summoned to the Foreign Ministry for admonishment over "unfriendly articles." In early 2011, in the wake of the "Arab Spring" uprisings in the Middle East and North Africa (dubbed the "Jasmine Revolution" in China), the security services unleashed an unprecedented crackdown on foreign journalists in China—tracking, detaining, harassing, and beating them, hacking into their computers, and threatening their expulsion from the country.[81]

Needless to say, these continuing impediments to normal reporting constrain the work environment for foreign correspondents in China, and inevitably they cause frustration and lead to embitterment on the part of some. It may be no coincidence that some journalists write very critical books about China after completing their tours. Thus, through these tactics, the Chinese government is turning a very valuable potential soft power and public diplomacy asset into a liability. Foreign journalists are still intrinsically viewed as enemies rather than potential partners by Chinese government authorities. This is unfortunate, as these journalists are able to reach global audiences that the Chinese government will *never* reach (and with credibility), no matter how many resources it pours into external propaganda and public diplomacy work.

Technically, the MFA considers its Information Department to be part of the "public diplomacy system" (公共外交制度), as distinct from the external propaganda system.[82] Since 2010 the MFA is paying increasing attention to public diplomacy as part of China's broader soft power and external publicity push. Foreign Minister Yang Jiechi gave an important speech in September 2011 signaling the new importance attached to public diplomacy work: "Public diplomacy is considered an important means of developing soft power.... This will give us a greater say in international affairs, help ensure the smooth implementation of China's development strategy and foreign policy...and put an end to misunderstanding, prejudice, and suspicion towards China in the international community."[83]

In October 2009 the MFA established its Office of Public Diplomacy (公共外交办公室) within the Information Department (新闻司). It is directed by Wei Xin, who returned from China's embassy in Washington in 2008 to head up the new office. The office has a staff of forty-five personnel (half diplomats, half administrators). But it is clearly an institution in search of a mission. "We are trying to figure out what to do," Wei admitted in a 2010 interview.[84] "We are trying to increase awareness of public diplomacy within the ministry, are encouraging embassies abroad to talk more to local media, we help draft our officials' and ambassadors' speeches, but are trying to broaden our work," she continued, then lamenting: "We are not very good at public diplomacy, of telling our positions to the world. It is important to tell the world what we are doing, but we don't know how to tell our own story effectively. In some cases the policy itself (which we must explain) is an impediment—no matter what we say, the policy will not change."

Interestingly, Wei indicated that her office sees half of their job as conveying China's foreign policy to internal Chinese audiences, and half to external audiences. Wei's boss at the time, Zhang Zhijun (now vice minister of foreign affairs), elaborated the dual mission: "We are being watched not only by people outside China, but also inside China. So we need to explain to both communities. But our main challenge is how to explain and get our message across to the rest of the world."[85] Foreign Minister Yang Jiechi concurred in an interview with the author: "We not only have to explain our policies to the world, but also to our own people. We also need to listen to our own people, to monitor the internet, and to learn our citizens' views by many means. But we don't need opinion polls to know what they think about a lot of things—like Taiwan and Tibet."[86]

Clearly, China has much work to do in conceptualizing and executing its public diplomacy, but the effort is under way.[87]

Media

Media expansion overseas has been a major component of China's going out (走出去) strategy. Its media are embarked on a major international expansion in order to win greater market share, make money, and improve China's image around the world (all at the same time). Tens of billions of *renminbi* are being poured into the main media outlets to enhance their international presence. No official investment figures have been announced, but one media scholar claimed that as much as 60 billion RMB ($8.79 billion) was pumped into the "Big Four" Beijing media outlets in 2009: Xinhua News Agency, Central China Television (CCTV), China Radio International, and the *China Daily*.[88] As a result, in early 2010 all four unveiled new launches of their global product lines.

China's media expansion has taken a number of forms. One is toward creating huge media conglomerates resembling News Corp, Time Warner, Bloomberg, and Viacom—a process known as the "big fish swallowing the small" (大鱼吞小鱼). By 2007 China had ten major media conglomerates (大媒体集团).[89] Indeed, the media have much scope for consolidation, as they expanded rapidly in recent years. In 2007 China had 3,127 public television stations, 140 pay TV channels, 2,432 radio stations, 1,938 newspapers, 9,468 magazines, more than three million websites, and almost 250,000 books published.[90] Of these, only a small fraction are broadcast or printed for foreign audiences. Some of the bigger media groups are quite profitable. The Shanghai Media Group (SMG), one of China's biggest state-run media conglomerates, earned about $1 billion in revenue and $100 million in profit in 2008.[91]

In terms of foreign outreach, an important initiative was the decision to convene the first-ever World Media Summit in Beijing in October 2009. Dubbed the "Olympics of the Media Industry" and hosted by Xinhua News Agency, it attracted representatives from 170 foreign media organizations and seventy countries, attending the three-day session in the Great Hall of the People.[92] The summit itself was a significant effort on the part of the government to influence foreign media opinion. Whether it accomplished its intended result is another story, with one foreign attendee grumbling, "They just don't get it. It was one big propaganda exercise!"[93]

Other forms of China's global media blitz involve specific organizations: the Xinhua News Agency, China Central Television, China Radio International, *China Daily* and *Global Times* newspapers, and others.

Xinhua News Agency

Xinhua News Agency is China's official state news service and a Communist Party Central Committee organ. It is a large and sprawling organization reaching throughout the country and around the world. Bureaucratically, with the brief exception of 1980–1982, when it was placed under the direct administrative control of the Central Committee and CCP Propaganda Department, Xinhua has always officially been an organ of the State Council.

From its inception, Xinhua has had a dual role: to report news and to disseminate Party and state propaganda. This is true both domestically and internationally. The division between these two functions is not always distinct, although straightforward news reporting has increased and improved during the reform period. Headquartered at 57 West Xuanwumen Street in central Beijing, Xinhua's international operations date back to Mao's 1964 instruction to "span the world."[94] Altogether Xinhua now has approximately three thousand journalists, of which four hundred are posted in 117 bureaus abroad, with plans to expand to 180 bureaus by 2020.[95] In 2010 Xinhua's North American headquarters took out a twenty-year lease on the top floor of a forty-four-story skyscraper at 1540 Broadway, in the middle of Times Square in New York City—symbolizing its ramp-up in international operations.[96] In addition to opening new bureaus, Xinhua is strengthening the staffs of existing ones (particularly in the North American, European, and Asian markets) and diversifying its product line beyond traditional news reporting to substantially beef up web presence, video and audio streaming, and multimedia.[97]

Xinhua has set up its own online twenty-four-hour English-language news channel, known as China Network Corporation (or CNC World). It went live on a limited basis on July 1, 2009, and became fully operational on a real-time, 24/7 basis one year later.[98] "CNC will offer an alternative source of information for a global audience," Xinhua's President Li Congjun claimed at the launch ceremony.[99] The channel is broadcast via satellite, cable, mobile phones, the internet, and outdoor screens as well as indoor shopping malls. For all practical purposes, this is television, but it reaches many more people than television. Beginning in January 2011, CNC World began to reach all of Europe, the Middle East, and North Africa (complementing its satellite coverage throughout Asia and North America).[100] Xinhua's move into the world of TV has proven quite controversial inside China's media industry because it directly challenges the monopoly that CCTV previously had over foreign television broadcasting. CCTV reportedly tried to bureaucratically block Xinhua's new venture every step of the way.

Xinhua is also aggressively entering the cell phone video market. In 2009 this service began to provide viewers with 3G-quality imagery. The idea is to dispense news and information directly to the individual before it can be gotten from television or more traditional sources. To meet expansion plans, the Audio and Video News Department at

Xinhua is aggressively hiring new staff—tripling the Beijing force to three hundred in 2009 alone.[101] By the end of 2009 Xinhua had videographers in *every* international bureau.[102]

Xinhua's global expansion is motivated by several factors (they are not mutually exclusive). The first is financial: to make money. Xinhua sees a particular target of opportunity to "compete head-to-head" with the main Western newswires (AP, UPI, Thomson Reuters, Bloomberg, etc.) and become a "real world international news agency."[103] The idea is to file mainly descriptive news reports, unfiltered with Chinese perspective, and to develop a client list based on marketing a cheaper product than the big Western wire services. Currently, Xinhua has 80,000 paying institutional subscribers, which produces a strong revenue stream but also constitutes a source of news and information to publics in the developing world where there are precious few domestic sources. The second motivation is to launch a series of "China features" to better tell China's story to the world. These would be written by domestic staff in China but marketed abroad. This shows Xinhua's role in China's soft power push. According to Xinhua Executive Deputy Editor-in-Chief Zhou Qisheng, "Xinhua's expansion into overseas markets is closely related to China's expansion of its soft power abroad—we cannot just rely on economic power alone!"[104] Zhou summed up Xinhua's role as twofold: "First, we explain world affairs to Chinese; second, we explain to the world what goes on in China—to report the 'real China' to the world."[105] Finally, the strategy is to turn Xinhua into a modern multimedia conglomerate. Xinhua aspires to play in the "premier league" with the likes of News Corp, Viacom, and Time Warner. Once its online TV presence expands, possibly broadcasting on airwaves as well, then it will compete in the global marketplace with CNN, BBC World, Al Jazeera, Deutsche Welle, and other 24-hour channels. Xinhua's website (www. chinaview.cn) is already the primary Chinese government-sponsored weblink for information about China.

CCTV

China Central Television (CCTV) has also gone global.[106] It launched its first twenty-four-hour English channel, CCTV International

(CCTV-9), back in 2000, and now broadcasts in six languages. CCTV-9 entered the American cable market in 2002, as part of a deal that allowed AOL Time Warner and News Corp access to cable systems in Guangdong Province in southern China. CCTV claims a large viewership for these channels.[107]

On all of these channels, CCTV is trying to alter the traditional stilted and propagandistic flavor and to expand its global presence.[108] CCTV-9 was the first to undergo a face-lift in early 2009. In January 2012 new production facilities were set up in Nairobi, Kenya (the first international broadcaster, CCTV claimed, to have established broadcast facilities on the continent), in order to "provide to the world daily programming *of* Africa *from* Africa."[109] One month later CCTV unveiled its ambitious "CCTV America" initiative from newly built studios in downtown Washington, D.C. The new facility went live in February 2012, but not without multiple glitches and hitches. The Washington operation, CCTV says, will become the global hub of its news gathering and broadcasting operations.[110] CCTV claims that it hired anchors and correspondents with experience at the BBC, Bloomberg, CNN, and other international channels (although none were familiar to global viewers). Although tailored for the U.S. market, some programming will be beamed throughout the Americas.

CCTV is also trying to diversify programming, airing a variety of feature programs aimed at showing foreign viewers images of China. There has also been an attempt to include expert commentary on the "Dialogue" program, which is hosted by Yang Rui or Tian Wei. The two hosts present contrasting faces to the world. Yang is an aggressive (often impolite) male interviewer, while Tian Wei is the opposite: female, attractive, suave, polite, inquisitive, and intellectual. While Yang Rui often gives a negative and nationalistic image to foreign viewers, Tian Wei offers a softer and more inquisitive face of China to international audiences. Yang Rui fancies himself "China's Mike Wallace" and has consciously studied the late American anchor's aggressive on-camera style. He badgers and is often offensive to on-camera guests. When I asked him why this is so, he curtly replied: "Hard politics, hard talk."[111] In 2012

Yang Rui made international news himself with a slanderous anti-foreign rant on his micro blog:

> The Public Security Bureau wants to clean out the foreign trash. To arrest foreign thugs and protect innocent girls, they need to concentrate on the disaster zones in [student district] Wudaokou and [drinking district] Sanlitun. Cut off the foreign snake heads. People who can't find jobs in the U.S. and Europe come to China to grab our money, engage in human trafficking and spread deceitful lies to encourage emigration. Foreign spies seek out Chinese girls to mask their espionage and pretend to be tourists while compiling maps and GPS data for Japan, Korea and the West. We kicked out that foreign bitch and closed Al Jazeera's Beijing bureau. We should shut up those who demonize China and send them packing.[112]

CCTV's English service plans to grow to fifty bureaus worldwide, from the thirty in 2011. CCTV-4's satellite channel is also planning to expand. This is all part of an ambitious global plan to build CCTV into a global television giant.[113] A press release put out when launching CCTV America claimed, "In time, CCTV News aims to join BBC World News, CNN International, Al Jazeera English and other broadcasters in establishing a strong global television news presence. CCTV News' editorial standards will be in keeping with other world broadcasters: pursuing quality, accuracy, balance, and alternative views."[114] Ma Jing, director general of CCTV America, added: "We uphold traditional journalistic values. We consider accuracy, objectivity, truthfulness, and public accountability more important than anything else. We will strive to provide good journalism, high-quality television, and alternative views."[115]

Time will tell if these stated ambitions are realized. Thus far, though, it is clear that certain subjects remain off-limits and reportage is biased. Over time, CCTV may find its way into more global living rooms. But being beamed into living rooms is only the first (easy) step; gaining and keeping viewer market share—particularly in the West—is much more difficult. CCTV and Xinhua television are making some inroads in Africa, but penetrating other markets around the world is proving more challenging. Ultimately, though, it is the credibility and substance of reporting that will attract viewers. No matter how fancy and improved the packaging of programs, if the content continues to reveal Chinese government bias and propaganda overtones, it will not be competitive (or persuasive) in the highly competitive global media market.

China Radio International

China is also stepping up its penetration of foreign airwaves. China Radio International (CRI), formerly known as Radio Beijing, was founded in 1941 as a wartime propaganda tool against Japan, but it has also now gone global.[116] CRI is government-owned and -subsidized and broadcasts 1,520 hours of programs each day globally in fifty-nine languages, transmitting on twenty-seven broadcast frequencies, maintaining thirty-two overseas bureaus.

CRI is trying hard to penetrate the local AM market in the United States, buying airtime in many smaller localities across the country, but also in bigger cities such as Honolulu, Los Angeles, and Houston. By moving into local U.S. markets, according to one description, "Chinese music is replacing country music."[117] It now broadcasts one or two hours per day in more than twenty American and Canadian cities.[118]

In terms of programming content, CRI's content is increasingly diverse and moving away from being a government mouthpiece. According to CRI Director Xia Jixuan, when I interviewed him at CRI headquarters near the Babaoshan National Cemetery in western Beijing, "Since the 1990s we have been trying to figure out how to transform ourselves from a propaganda machine to being a broadcasting organization."[119] Accordingly, CRI programs include regular news bulletins and in-depth news analyses, as well as a variety of engaging feature programs. Director Xia also says that CRI "tries to transmit Chinese values such as collectivism, harmony, benevolent rule, even democracy. We want to project a comprehensive image of China abroad—not just about our economic growth. To only do that is distorting."[120]

Newspapers

Two primary English language newspapers are targeted at international audiences: *China Daily* and *Global Times* (*Shanghai Daily* is limited to a local readership). Of the two, *China Daily* is the older, is better established, and has the larger circulation. But *Global Times*, a spin-off of the *People's Daily*,[121] is stealing market share. Both newspapers also run very informative websites.

China Daily undertook a major "relaunch" on March 1, 2010, aimed at clawing back domestic readership from *Global Times* and broadening its international appeal. The relaunch resulted in a complete makeover for the paper, leaving it much more readable and informative. *China Daily* was founded in 1981 and now has a global circulation of more than 400,000 (280,000 domestic, 50,000 in Hong Kong and Macao, and 100,000 overseas).[122] *China Daily* is aggressively marketing in the United States, inserting supplements into the *Washington Post*, *New York Times*, and other mainstream papers, setting up coin sale boxes on the streets of major cities, and launching direct mail campaigns.

The *Global Times* Chinese edition came out in 1993, but the English edition appeared only in April 2009. The Chinese edition is widely popular, with a 2.8 million circulation (40 percent subscribers, 60 percent newsstand sales); it is known for nationalistic and firebrand articles. One of the most popular is "Strong Nation Forum" (强国论坛), which regularly publishes diatribes against the United States and Japan. The English edition is less nationalistic and is informative with an imaginative format. By the end of 2009, after only eight months in operation, the English *Global Times* was averaging between 70,000 and 100,000 sales per day.[123]

Global Times exhibits considerable editorial independence from government policies, but its editorial management still has links to the official propaganda system. For example, senior international editor Ding Gang is simultaneously an editorial writer for the Communist Party's official *People's Daily* and a longtime party journalist, thus personifying the close links between the two papers. When I asked him about linkages to the propaganda system and government censorship of *Global Times*, Ding replied that it exists but is "indirect."[124] The rest of the editorial and writing staff are very young (in their early twenties) and inexperienced. Still, they are putting out a fine product in a short time, which has gained great popularity in China, but *Global Times* remains handicapped by its nonexistent distribution network abroad.

China Daily remains more staid and government-oriented, although the 2010 relaunch did much to improve its presentation format and readability. The business section and coverage of China's foreign investment are particularly good, offering information unavailable elsewhere. *China Daily*'s deputy editor-in-chief claims the paper has five main priorities in reporting: "What is happening in China; why is it happening; what are the future trends; what is the impact on the outside world; and how Chinese people perceive the outside world."[125] Editor Qu particularly sees *China Daily*'s main mission to improve foreign understanding of China: "There are many misconceptions about China abroad—foreigners think China is all like Shanghai and Tibet. There are, in fact, many faces to China."[126]

Although newspapers like *China Daily* and *Global Times* are important two-way windows for the world to look into China and for China to explain itself to the world, the fact is that global citizens still primarily get their information about China from foreign newspapers and multimedia. This fact irritates Chinese authorities no end, as they believe there is an inherent foreign media bias against China (see the discussion at the end of this chapter).

Books and Periodicals

China's book industry is enormous. Although the publishing industry is struggling around the world, China has always had an insatiable domestic market. From 2005 to 2010 a total of 34 million books were published in China, according to the General Administration of Press and Publications.[127] Of these, only a small fraction are in foreign languages or intended for foreign markets (2,063 in 2009).[128]

The book publishing industry in China has long been monopolized by a handful of state (and provincial) presses, and distribution is dominated by the Xinhua bookstore monopoly chain. Importation of foreign books is similarly monopolized and strictly controlled by the China National Publications Import and Export Corporation, which falls under the watchful eye of the SCIO. However, in recent years the domestic publishing industry has begun to allow some private publishing houses to operate, and censorship and control over topics and titles is looser in the provinces. If an author wishes to publish on a sensitive topic, he or she is advised to go with a provincial publisher (this is true for translations of sensitive foreign books as well).

At the national level, the recent trend is twofold: commercialization and conglomeratization. Some of the biggest publishing groups are beginning to list on the stock market. An example is the giant China Publishing Group (CPG), which raised RMB 1.8 billion ($264 million) in its 2010 debut on the Shanghai stock exchange. The group is also indicative of the trend toward conglomerates in China's publishing industry, where "big fish eat the small."

Chinese books in foreign languages are also monopolized by CPG's counterpart, China International Publishing Group (CIPG). It oversees seven separate presses inside China (FLP, New World Press, Sinolingua, China Pictorial Publishing House, Dolphin Books, New Star Press, and Blossom Press). These outlets are all undergoing reform. As CIPG official Huang Youyi observes, "In the past we exported mostly books about traditional Chinese culture, but Western readers are more interested in contemporary China."[129] The problem, again, is foreign distribution, as these books are not marketed well abroad. But clearly the CIPG Group and Foreign Languages Press have moved away from their former propaganda personas into more variegated product lines and, as a result, are making money. CPG President Nie Zhenning put it succinctly: "We will not just be there to propagate Chinese culture, but also to run a commercial business."[130]

China still publishes relatively few foreign-language periodicals. The main popular domestic magazines, such as *Caijing*, do not have foreign-language editions (although many popular foreign magazines, notably *Vogue*, *Bazaar*, *Cosmopolitan*, *GQ*, *Men's Health*, *Newsweek*, *Elle*, and *Golf*, have launched Chinese-language editions). Nor do many research institutes of universities publish academic journals in foreign languages.

The mandate of reaching international audiences thus falls to the hardy perennial Foreign Languages Press, now part of the China International Publishing Group (CIPG). FLP today publishes fifteen magazines in eleven foreign languages. FLP's budget increased fourfold from 1999 to 2009 and many new publishing and multimedia initiatives were launched during this time. Future plans include tailoring each magazine to specific regional audiences, rather than publishing one generic issue worldwide.[131] But CIPG Director Zhou Mingwei (a sophisticated individual experienced in international affairs) complains that all of its publications, particularly magazines, face significant hurdles in foreign distribution: "Even if we publish interesting publications, we have difficulty getting it to readers."[132] Another future priority is to target Latin America and Western Europe, areas where understanding of China is weak, and continue trying to meet rising demand in Africa.

Exchange Organizations

China maintains several semiofficial organizations that are involved in bringing foreign personages to China and taking Chinese delegations abroad. The most well-known is the Chinese People's Institute of Foreign Affairs (CPIFA), founded in 1949. It is affiliated with the Ministry of Foreign Affairs (MFA). CPIFA concentrates on interacting with international elites—primarily retired officials—but also influential opinion shapers abroad, and it has done much good work to further mutual understanding in the area of international relations over the years. CPIFA both responds to requests made from Chinese embassies abroad to invite individuals and delegations and initiates invitations on behalf of the MFA or on its own. Its work has been heavily concentrated on the United States, with increased attention to Europe and Asia in recent years.

Another exchange organization is the Chinese People's Association for Friendship with Foreign Countries. Founded in 1954, its mission is similar to CPIFA's, but it is not as active. Two other civilian exchange organizations merit mention: the China Association for International Friendly Contact and the China Reform Forum (CRF). The former is a front organization for the CCP's International Department (discussed in Chapter 3),[133] while the latter is affiliated with the Central Party School. Both are quite active in hosting visitors from abroad, with the former focusing on foreign political parties and affiliated institutions (consistent with the International Department's mission), while CRF concentrates on inviting experts in international affairs.

The People's Liberation Army (PLA) maintains two similar outreach organizations: the China Institute of International Strategic Studies (CIISS) and China Foundation for International Strategic Studies (CFISS). Both are directly affiliated with the PLA General Staff Department's Second Department (responsible for intelligence). Both do analysis for the PLA General Staff and serve as the principal conduit for inviting foreign security specialists to China. CIISS and CFISS also perform the dual role of explaining Chinese positions on various strategic and military issues to foreigners (a form of public diplomacy) and, at the same time, collecting views and intelligence from foreign experts and officials (which are fed into their intelligence system).

Several of China's IR research institutes (think tanks) perform this same dual role. The most important of these are the CICIR, attached to the Ministry of State Security; the CIIS, attached to the Ministry of Foreign Affairs; and the Shanghai Institutes of International Studies (SIIS), which is attached to the Shanghai municipal government. To a lesser extent, the China Academy of Social Sciences and Shanghai Academy of Social Sciences perform these same roles, but on a much broader range of issues.[134] These institutions are all discussed in Chapter 3. In 2009 the Charhar Institute was established, with a specific focus on public diplomacy and improving China's image abroad.[135] It operates more as an association than an institute, with a range of members across the country and abroad.

Oversight

Taken together, this sprawling network of institutions constitutes the constellation of China's propaganda, media, and public diplomacy actors. It is indeed a large and expansive community. As such, it is not easy to coordinate their actions or effects. Although the SCIO does attempt such coordination, and it promulgates an annual set of guidelines, in reality each organ exercises considerable autonomy. Budgets are decentralized as well. As previous studies on Chinese propaganda and censorship have found, control in today's China does not come from above; it comes from "within."[136] In this way self-censorship and staying on message are exercised within every organization, at several tiers of officialdom. Taken together, the totality of these actors and their programs is impressive in number, if not in quality.

Beyond the State: China's Expanding Global Cultural Footprint

Beyond state-directed efforts, China's global cultural and social presence is diffuse. It includes a variety of elements: history, high culture and popular culture, the fine and performing arts, film, literature, intellectual achievements, inventions and innovation, product brands, tourism, sports, music, science, education, language teaching, religion, social values, major international events such as the 2008 Olympic Games or the 2010 World Expo in Shanghai, and even animals (pandas), all are part of China's global cultural presence. Indeed, some of these dimensions are promoted and marketed by the government and thus fit into its public diplomacy, but other elements are more autonomous and better fit Joseph Nye's definition of soft power. Let us consider some examples of each.

History and Civilization

Clearly, China's more than five thousand years of uninterrupted history and cultural tradition are seen by many in China as the country's ace in the deck of its soft power cards. This is indeed ironic, as for many years of the People's Republic of China (1949–1978) the Communist government both denied and attacked its historical past (particularly during the Cultural Revolution). Since the 1990s, however, there has been a concerted effort made to embrace the past at home and project it abroad. Countless temples have been restored; tombs and excavations designated UNESCO World Heritage Sites; and China's great sages (Confucius, Mencius, Lao Zi) venerated. In 2010 the epic film *Confucius* (孔子) packed movie theaters in China, competing head-to-head with *Avatar*. A statue of Confucius was even briefly erected on the eastern side of Tiananmen Square in 2011, only to be inexplicably removed one month later during the night. China's legacy of scientific and technological inventions bolsters its cultural heritage.[137] This historical and cultural appeal is particularly strong in Asia, but the Chinese government has done its best to market it around the world.[138]

Part of the rationale to promote China's past is related to the government's effort to gain the support of the world's 40 million overseas Chinese, politically, diplomatically, economically, and culturally. This has long been the case in Beijing's diplomatic war with Taipei, as well as seeking to attract large sums of their remittances and investments to the "motherland." But it is also about garnering political support for the CCP and linking the PRC regime to China's historical legacy in the hearts and minds of the diaspora.

Often China's traditional heritage is marketed abroad as part of a series of "Year of China" festivals staged in a number of countries. A good example was the October 2009–February 2010 "Europalia-China Arts Festival." The festival traveled through Belgium, the Netherlands, France, Germany, and Luxembourg; included a thousand artists and performers; organized fifty exhibitions; and held three hundred performances.[139] Sometimes specialized exhibitions are mounted. A large number of imperial art exhibitions from Beijing's Palace Museum, terra-cotta warriors from Xian, or other historical sites have traveled abroad. Increasingly, however, they are mixed exhibitions that combine traditional and contemporary arts. As Minister of Culture Cai Wu indicated when I interviewed him, "We need to be more comprehensive in how we present ourselves and not only focus on our history. The greatest feature of Chinese culture is its diversity."[140]

Many overseas exhibitions are mounted by the Ministry of Culture's China Arts and Entertainment Group, now a large state-owned enterprise formed in 2004 out of the merger of China Performing Arts Agency and China International Exhibition Agency.[141] The State Council Information Office is also involved in staging exhibitions abroad. Altogether, China participated in 120 cultural exhibitions in more than forty countries in 2008.[142] But from a financial standpoint, these exhibitions are not profitable, and in fact, says Minister of Culture Cai Wu, they are loss-making: "The annual income of China's overseas commercial performances has not reached $100 million, which is even less than a single popular foreign circus."[143]

One particularly notable exhibition intended to project China's civilization abroad (as well as foreign nations in China) was the 2010 World Expo in Shanghai. An extravaganza of unprecedented scale in the history of World Expos,[144] Expo 2010 showcased the city of Shanghai along with many of the best aspects and best practices of China's urban planning, science and technology, innovation, architecture, the arts, and local governance. Of course, many foreign countries also mounted their own pavilions to highlight their accomplishments. The Chinese government spent a whopping $45 billion in preparation for the six-month extravaganza that attracted a record 73 million people from across China and around the world, and drew rave reviews from visitors and the media.

An even more impressive example of China showcasing itself to the world was the 2008 Olympic Games. The games were beamed via television all around the globe; audiences worldwide watched the impressive opening and closing ceremonies, and China's superb athletes winning the most gold medals. Having attended the games, I can attest that not only did the athletic events inside the $500 million "Bird's Nest" Olympic Stadium, Water Cube, and Olympic Park attract large and enthusiastic crowds, but the host city of Beijing also greatly benefited. The government invested a stunning $30 billion in upgrading infrastructure and sprucing up the city, and an overall total of $42 billion in hosting the games.[145] It was altogether a very impressive display.

Education and Research

Higher education is a distinguishing element and conveyor of any nation's culture and soft power. It has been a key component of America's soft power appeal for decades. Great Britain, France, Canada, and Australia also capitalize on their universities' prestige to attract large numbers of foreign students. China has similar aspirations and is beginning to catch up.

Chinese students have been going abroad for higher education since the mid-1970s, but particularly since the period of "reform and opening" began in 1978. Altogether, for the 2010–11 academic year, the Ministry of Education reported 620,000 Chinese students studying in foreign universities, a remarkable 93 percent of whom were self-funded![146] With the newfound wealth of their families, Chinese students have become a major revenue stream for Western universities and boarding schools. Altogether, the Ministry of Education reports that a total of 1.39 million students studied abroad between 1978 and 2008—but shockingly, only one in seven (230,000) had returned to China as of 2005.[147]

Meanwhile, the numbers of foreign students coming to study in Chinese universities continue to climb, showing particularly dramatic growth since 2007. Collegiate education in China is a very big and lucrative business. In the 2010–11 academic year 265,090 foreign students studied in China.[148] By far, South Korea tops the list by sending a total of 64,232 students to China, followed by the United

States (18,650), Japan (15,409), Vietnam (12,247), Thailand (11,379), and Russia (10,596). Although the United States came second, nearly 12,000 were short-term (language) students, whereas the others in the top five were much more heavily weighted toward year-long study.[149] During President Barack Obama's state visit to China in November 2009, he announced that the United States had set a goal of sending 100,000 American students to China over the next five years (the so-called "100,000 Strong" initiative). Over time, there has been a shift away from foreign students from developing countries to those from developed countries. Ultimately, education officials at the China Scholarship Council and Ministry of Education estimate that China will receive 500,000 foreign students by 2020.[150]

Being educated in China will have a major long-term impact on these individuals' views of China, after they return to their native countries and move up the professional ladder. They will be sensitized to Chinese views, customs, preferences, habits, values, policies, etc.—and they will have a variety of connections, known as the all-important *guanxi* (关系), with their Chinese classmates for life.

For foreign students coming to study in China, the government is also increasing the amount of scholarship support offered. The China Scholarship Council (国家留学基金管理委员会) offered a total of approximately 17,500 scholarships for 2009–10, allocated as follows: 1,500 for the Americas, 3,000 for Europe (including Russia), 5,000 for Africa, 8,000 for Asia.[151] In May 2010 the council announced it would earmark 10,000 scholarships for American students as part of the 100,000 Strong initiative. Altogether, the Chinese government gave out $117 million (800 million RMB) in scholarships to foreign students in 2009–10, with provincial governments furnishing an additional 110 million RMB, according to the Ministry of Education.[152] The percentage of scholarships handed out to Africans is rising the fastest, up 15 percent from 2008 to 2009. Still, government scholarship support accounts for only about 8 percent of foreign students in China (公费留学生), while 92 percent are still self-funded (自费留学生).[153]

The number of foreign students in China is set to increase as Chinese universities improve their global standing. Several of China's elite universities have their sights on moving up the table of global rankings.[154] The World University Rankings for 2010–11, issued by the internationally recognized British *Times Higher Education Supplement,* ranked the University of Hong Kong twenty-first, Peking University thirty-seventh, and Tsinghua University fifty-eighth globally.[155] Hong Kong University of Science and Technology Business School's MBA Program was ranked in the top ten globally (number nine) by the *Financial Times* in 2010.

The Chinese government is making a major investment in higher education during the 2010–2020 decade, with the aim of both improving "indigenous innovation" at home and international competitiveness abroad. The government aims to create a handful of world-class universities. In October 2009, nine leading Chinese universities combined to form what they called the "C9" (China Nine), intended to become China's Ivy League.[156] In his 2010 work report to the National People's Congress, Premier Wen Jiabao said that this targeted educational investment is meant to make China a global leader in several technological spheres in order to "capture the economic, scientific, and technological high ground"—singling out biomedicine, nanoscience, quantum control, energy conservation, information technology, aerospace, and oceanography."[157] China is already producing more graduates in engineering and the sciences than other countries, while it surpassed the United States as the world's top producer of Ph.D.s in 2008. Yet China still lags significantly behind developed countries in approved patents (an important measure of innovation), although it now ranks second in the world (after the United States) on research and development spending in science and technology, allocating $139 billion in 2011.[158]

Despite these ambitious goals and the impressive achievements of China's science and technological development, there remain serious impediments to its becoming a world-class power in science and technology. In its 2010 report the Ministry of Science and Technology ranked China thirteenth in "worldwide scientific influence" but offered a number of sharp critiques of the nation's scientific shortcomings.[159] As Zhao Zhiyun, the principal researcher and author of the report, put it: "Currently, there is a bad trend in China's science policy. It is geared toward a desire for quick returns. The priority should be for China to encourage a curiosity for pure science, and promote exploring unknown worlds. We must strengthen basic scientific research in order to promote original technological innovation, because China cannot find its place in the new economic order merely by following or imitating technologies developed elsewhere."[160]

The need for basic (as opposed to applied) research has plagued Chinese policy throughout the communist period, and even during the Nationalist era.[161] There are at least four explanations why China has not fostered a basic research environment.[162] The first is political. To do basic research (in all fields) necessarily means going beyond politically proscribed boundaries. The CCP continues to place various restrictions on free thought and inquiry, particularly in the humanities and social sciences. Second, the culture of academic corruption in China is corrosive and widespread. Academic plagiarism, favoritism, and false credentialism are rampant, and intellectual property rights theft is endemic. Third, innovation requires open-minded and open-ended intellectual exploration, not rote memorization of knowledge. Chinese educational pedagogy has yet to escape the latter and embrace the former. Fourth, it requires being thoroughly linked into global intellectual and professional networks. In so many areas of the sciences, humanities, and social sciences, Chinese scholars remain trapped in a domestic discourse in Chinese and do not engage in—or contribute much to—international scholarly discourse or publications in the global language of English (Chinese scholars are even curiously absent from the global debate in contemporary China studies concerning their nation's rise in world affairs).

On all of these scores, China impedes its own scientific and technological development. Despite these continuing impediments, Chinese intellectuals are benefiting from globalization and their nation's "open door." International knowledge and expertise have flowed into China for three decades—but it is flowing *out* of China to a far lesser extent. In some fields, particularly in the natural and medical sciences and in economics, Chinese scholars are contributing to the global knowledge pool and are better linked into global scholarly networks, oftentimes engaging in collaborative research and coauthoring publications. Yet if one looks carefully at these publications one frequently finds that the Chinese scholar is based *abroad* and not in China. There is also a significant shortage of truly collaborative research and publications between Chinese scholars *in* China and those abroad. After thirty years of scholarly *exchanges* with China, there remains a dearth of real *collaboration*.

Confucius Institutes

One of the most notable aspects of China's growing global cultural footprint is its establishment of "Confucius Institutes" (university level) and "Confucius Classrooms" (secondary level) to promote Chinese language and culture around the world. Confucius Institutes (CIs) are modeled on Germany's Goethe Institute, France's Alliance Française, Spain's Instituto Cervantes, and to a lesser extent the British Council.[163]

There has been a strong surge in the establishment of CIs around the world in recent years—a trend that is showing no sign of abatement. International demand is strong, with an estimated 40 million students learning Chinese globally in 2009.[164] According to Xu Lin, the lead official overseeing the CI effort, more than 400 institutions in 76 countries have expressed interest in establishing a CI or CC,[165] and China's goal is to establish 1000 CIs and CCs worldwide by 2020; the nation will provide 3000 scholarships to do so.[166]

The first full CI was established in Seoul in November 2004, following a prototype in Tashkent in April 2004. By the end of 2011 more than 350 CIs and 500 CCs were operating in 105 countries, according to Xu Lin.[167] These numbers compare very favorably with the British Council (230 offices, with 138 English language and British culture teaching centers), France's Alliance Française centers (1,140 in 138 countries), Germany's Goethe Institutes (128 in 76 countries), and Spain's Instituto Cervantes (38 in 23 countries) worldwide.[168]

Confucius Institutes are overseen by the Office of the International Language Council, or Han Ban (汉办), which is directly under the Ministry of Education but affiliated with eleven other ministry-level bodies.[169] Xu Lin is the executive director. The Han Ban was originally set up in 1987, on the suggestion of State Councilor Zhu Muzhi, and was primarily oriented at that time to recruiting and paying for African students to study in China. North America and Asia were priority regions for establishing CIs and CCs from 1995 to 2005, but since that time CIs have gone global by expanding into Europe, and more recently Latin America, the Middle East, and Oceania.

There are five main models of CIs: between a Chinese university and a foreign university, between a Chinese middle school and a foreign middle school, between a Chinese university and overseas community organizations, between local governments in China and their foreign counterparts, and between a Chinese university and foreign enterprises.[170] The purpose of the CIs and CCs is primarily to teach Chinese language and culture abroad, and on occasion to stimulate business partnerships. In addition to teaching the Chinese language, CIs and CCs offer classes on Chinese medicine, history, culture, society, martial arts, theater, flower arranging, paper cutting, and occasionally contemporary topics.

In terms of funding, Han Ban usually contributes a start-up contribution of $100,000 followed by an annual subsidy to the foreign partner and hopes to operate on the basis of matching funds.[171] Some, however, receive $100,000 to $250,000 or more per annum.[172] In theory, Han Ban seeks to provide only three years of seed funding, with the foreign institution absorbing 100 percent of operating costs thereafter, but Executive Director Xu Lin admitted when I interviewed her at Han Ban headquarters in Beijing that "Some Confucius Institutes cannot do that, and we continue to finance them after three years."[173] On top of this subsidy, Han Ban usually directly pays a large percentage or all of the salaries and overseas living stipends of the Chinese teachers sent to teach in CIs and CCs abroad. The total official Han Ban budget for CIs in 2010 was $137,761,000.[174] Even though the annual budget is quite large and due to grow even more, Xu Lin claims that Han Ban has to fight to maintain its allocation from the Ministry of Finance against those who ask, "Why give foreigners money when there are so many poor Chinese?"[175]

Although an organ of the Chinese government, thus far the Han Ban has been quite careful *not* to advocate Beijing's political agenda or pressure CIs abroad through political strings attached to their grants. But in the United States, some Confucius Institutes have come under the watchful eye of the FBI, which suspect that they may become bases of intelligence collection (although there is no evidence of this to date). Of perhaps greater potential concern is the impact on teaching Chinese studies in Western universities. So far this has not been a problem, as the CIs have generally not sought to influence China curricula in other departments. The generally apolitical and hands-off nature of CIs thus far is notable and commendable. Nonetheless, concerns have been voiced that faculty brought from China do convey a certain national perspective on cultural subjects taught, which are frequently at variance with foreign perspectives.

It is also curious that China has yet to discover the potential of making large endowments to universities and think tanks abroad (something rival Taiwan mastered long ago). But it probably will not be long before Beijing does so. It is only a matter of time before China endows a "Deng Xiaoping Center for Chinese Studies" or something similar in foreign universities. If and when this occurs, it will also be interesting to see if Beijing seeks to attach political strings to such endowments. If so, then it will likely learn the same lesson Taiwan has learned over the years: that many foreign institutions are unwilling to accept funds on these grounds and will permit only limited influence over public programming.

Literature

China's global literary presence is also gradually expanding. Many Chinese fiction writers have become well known abroad and had their works translated. Gao Xingjian won a Nobel Prize in Literature (after leaving China), as did Mo Yan in 2012. Ha Jin enjoys widespread appeal (especially in the United States) for several of his books. Han Han does as well. Jiang Rong's *Wolf Totem* was published by the Penguin Group (although it did not sell well).[176] Despite the growing presence of Chinese authors overseas, the linguistic and financial impediments to further international recognition remain large.[177] As one article noted, "The hard truth is that while Chinese art and cinema have managed to impress Western audiences, Chinese literature is yet to carve its own niche in the global gallery of contemporary literary greats."[178] Not a single Chinese author cracked the top 250 best-selling books in the UK in 2010, and one expert estimated there were none in the top 2,500.

Another example, although not entirely positive, was the October 2009 Frankfurt Book Fair (Frankfurter Buchmesse), where China was that year's guest of honor.[179] The world's premier book fair attracted about 300,000 visitors, 10,000 journalists, and 7300 exhibitors from more than 100 countries. The organizers worked for fifteen years to secure China as the honored guest. Frankfurt offered Beijing a golden opportunity to expose the global literary and publishing community to a much wider range of lesser-known Chinese authors and various published and electronic products. China spent an estimated $7.5 million on the event and dispatched more than 2000 publishers, artists, writers, and poets. As an indication of the importance that the Chinese and German governments attached to it, German Chancellor Angela Merkel and Chinese Vice President Xi Jinping opened the event.[180]

The fair must be considered a net success for China in exposing and expanding its literary presence abroad, but it did not come without blemishes. In the run-up to the fair, the international writers association PEN organized a symposium that resulted in a major political confrontation and walk-out by the Chinese delegation because organizers invited and gave the stage to two leading dissident authors (Bei Ling and Dai Qing). "We did not come to be instructed about democracy!" huffed delegation leader and former ambassador to Germany Mei Zhaorong, as he led the walkout of the Chinese delegation.[181]

The fair itself went more smoothly on the surface, but behind the scenes there continued to be serious wrangles (both bureaucratic and physical) between the organizers and Chinese government authorities over format, topics, speakers, media coverage, and participants. For its part, China drew different lessons: "The Frankfurt Book Fair gave us a warning that cultural diplomacy is a war without bullets," observed *Global Times* commentator Chen Xuegen.[182]

Frankfurt was an example of the growing trend of China's heavy-handed attempts to control events and agendas outside of the country. In 2012 the Chinese embassy in Washington, D.C., tried to get the Smithsonian Institution's Hirshhorn Museum to cancel a scheduled exhibition by the famous performance artist Ai Weiwei. Numerous other examples exist of Chinese authorities trying to intimidate foreign institutions from sponsoring events involving dissident artists.

Art

China's presence in the international art market is growing very rapidly. This is true not only of the global appetite for Chinese art but also of the impact of wealthy Chinese purchasers of Western art and artifacts. According to the *Hurun Wealth Report*, a Chinese *Forbes*-like publication that tracks private wealth in China, as of 2012 there were 1,020,000 millionaires, and they are investing in art.[183] Private art auction houses in London, New York, Hong Kong, and elsewhere report a surge in private Chinese buyers flush with cash. Citigroup estimates that Chinese buyers accounted for 23 percent of the $61 billion in global art sales in 2011.[184]

Chinese purchases are particularly active in Hong Kong, where auction market turnover skyrocketed 300 percent from 2009 to 2010. For the first time in its history, Sotheby's in Hong Kong topped $1 billion in auctions and private sales of 7800 works of art in 2011.[185] Chinese buyers accounted for half of all auction purchases at the Hong Kong venue in 2009.[186] In 2011, Sotheby's and Christie's together made $1.8 billion in Hong Kong sales.[187] At Christie's 2010 spring auction in New York, an anonymous Chinese bidder paid a world record $106.5 million for Pablo Picasso's 1932 portrait of his blonde mistress *Nude, Green Leaves, and Bust*.[188] At Sotheby's spring 2011 sale, a Chinese buyer paid $21.3 million for Picasso's *Femme Lisant (Deux Personnages)*.[189] In the spring 2010 auction at Poly International (a Beijing auction house) one calligraphic hand scroll fetched an international record for a Chinese art object, claiming a $64 million price tag.[190] In 2011 at an auction in Toulouse, France, a Chinese buyer shelled out a new French record of $31 million for a scroll from the imperial Palace Museum collection.[191]

Not surprisingly, wealthy Chinese buyers are snapping up Chinese paintings and artifacts, in a nationalistic effort to return such pieces to the "motherland," but they are also buying much more broadly. "They bought across the board, in every category, at every financial level," opined one leading art critic commenting on the Christie's 2010 auction.[192] With deep pockets, these buyers are bidding two or more times the asking price—introducing an inflationary element into the market. Commenting on the rapidity with which the buyers are quickly establishing control over the global art market, Christie's Chinese art specialist Theow Tow observed, "We are witnessing a tectonic change."[193] Asian art critic Souren Melikian similarly observed: "Like all beginners proudly using their financial muscle, some Chinese buyers occasionally display an enthusiasm not fully warranted by the objects.... Eventually, discernment will come. The Chinese learn fast. They will soon achieve total domination in the field of their own art, financially and otherwise."[194]

Domestically, China has emerged as the third-largest international art market after the United States and UK.[195] By 2010 China had become the world leader by auctioning $8.3 billion in art and artifacts, according to Artprice.com,[196] accounting for 33 percent of all art sold worldwide.[197] The major Western art auction houses salivate over the potential sales *in* China, but to date they are permitted to operate only in Hong Kong. However, Christie's got on the bad side of the Chinese government for trying to auction two rare animal heads from Yves Saint Laurent's huge Chinese art collection following his death in 2009. The objects had been looted from the Yuanmingyuan, which was sacked and razed by British and French forces in 1860. The Chinese government threatened Christie's and demanded that the objects be returned to China. When Christie's refused, the objects were put up for auction, where a Chinese businessman bid $40 million for them (but failed to pay for the objects). Having defied Beijing by proceeding with the auction, Christie's was put on Beijing's black list. As a way to get back in good graces with the Chinese government, Christie's agreed to mount a special exhibition on "Transrealism" in New York, co-sponsored by the Ministry of Culture's Center for International Cultural Exchange. The show brought twenty-nine works by seventeen carefully selected artists vetted by Beijing, with Christie's covering all costs. Christie's has much at stake, in potentially operating not only on the Chinese mainland but even in Hong Kong.

The global appetite for contemporary Chinese art is also voracious. In 2007 five of the ten best-selling living artists at auction were Chinese-born.[198] Artists such as Zhang Xiaogang, Xu Bing, Zhang Huan, Zao Wouki, Li Songsong, Zeng Fanzhi, and others are making a lot of money on their works. Zeng's paintings often fetch $1 million apiece, while Zhang's total auction sales have totaled an impressive $56 million as of 2007.[199] Zao Wouki sold a painting for $8.8 million at Sotheby's 2011 Hong Kong auction.

Ai Weiwei, one of China's leading art icons, has attracted an international following for his art, architectural design, (political) activism, and social commentary. He contributed to the design of the "Bird's Nest" Olympic Stadium in Beijing, has had a number of individual shows in Europe and North America, and has appeared often in the international media. Because of his satirical and direct criticism of the Chinese government, Ai Weiwei has been repeatedly harassed by the Chinese government and security services in recent years. He was taken into custody in November 2010 and charged with a $2.4 million tax evasion bill in 2011. Although he was subsequently released to a form of house arrest, Ai's detention and continued harassment is another black mark on China's global soft power.

An interesting twist in China's global art presence has been its efforts to track "looted treasures," precious art and cultural relics that left the country over the previous two centuries and now sit in museums and private collections around the world. China is particularly indignant about (and anxious to repatriate) art and artifacts taken from the Imperial Palace Museum (Gugong) collection,[200] and the ruins of the Old Summer Palace (Yuanmingyuan). According to China's Cultural Relics Association, more than ten million Chinese cultural relics were taken from the country between 1840 and 1949, including 1.5 million objects from the Yuanmingyuan, which are now located in more than two thousand museums in forty-seven countries.[201] Beginning in 2009 China began to dispatch "inventory teams" to the United States, Europe, and Japan to catalogue collections in leading museums and, when they could gain access, private collections.[202] Chinese observers are showing up at international auctions at Christie's, Sotheby's, Bonhams, and other major auction houses—often bidding on pieces, but sometimes just noting their location. The State Administration of Cultural Heritage, the official organ charged with protecting and retrieving cultural relics, has begun to offer cash rewards for individuals who return objects to China.[203]

Finally, following many years of renovation and delay, China opened its National Museum on the east side of Tiananmen Square in 2011. The world's largest museum, it showcases several millennia of Chinese artistic and cultural history. Although the archaeological and artistic objects on display are very impressive (much more impressive than those on display in the Palace Museum on the north side of the square), it quickly becomes apparent that the historical presentations are highly selective, conforming to Chinese communist historiography.[204] One theme that is hammered home to visitors is the traditional "unity" of Han Chinese and non-Han ethnic minorities. Another concerns overcoming "feudalism." Then, as one moves to the north wing of the museum, which presents modern history, viewers are pervasively subjected to the theme of Western imperialist incursions, exploitation, and the "century of shame and humiliation." As I viewed the exhibition "The Road to Rejuvenation" in June 2011 just after its opening and on the eve of the ninetieth anniversary celebrations of the CCP, the narrative of past foreign aggression and Chinese aggrievement was omnipresent. So was the concomitant explanation that the CCP has rebuilt Chinese society and restored the nation's rightful place in the world—presenting the image of a phoenix rising from the ashes. Missing, however, were displays on sensitive and dark periods in the Party's past. For example, there was a complete gap in coverage from 1956 all the way to 1964 and the detonation of China's atomic bomb. This includes, of course, the period of the Great Leap Forward, when upward of thirty million people perished. Then there was a sole photo of Red Guards in Tiananmen Square during the Cultural Revolution, but otherwise nothing from 1964 to 1976 and the death of Mao. In essence, there was a two-decade gap in PRC history—during which Mao wrought havoc on the nation. Such official historical amnesia is not conducive either to China's own national identity or to its international image.

Fashion and Design

China is the world's largest apparel manufacturer, but it has yet to make an impact on international *haute couture*. A handful of Chinese fashion designers have established brands and reputations known outside of China. Shanghai Tang, Vivienne Tam, Sue Wang, and Betty Charnuis are the best known, but all now reside and headquarter their businesses outside of China. As *Vogue* reported, China has a growing coterie of fashion designers who aspire to go global, but thus far it remains an aspiration.[205] It is only a matter of time, though, before Chinese designers make a global impact, as there is so much artistic creativity and financial resources available.

The same applies to architecture. Although Chinese architects have designed some unique buildings in China's booming cities—notably

Shanghai—they have yet to (be commissioned to) design notable structures abroad. Indeed, some of China's most eye-catching architecture, such as the CCTV Building and National Opera in Beijing, were designed by foreign architects. This may be changing, though. Chinese architect Wang Shu was awarded the 2012 Pritzker Architecture Prize, the most prestigious international prize in the profession. Wang, the first Chinese architect resident in China (I. M. Pei, who was born in China, won the prize in 1983), was given the prize for a series of his designs, including the Ningbo Contemporary Art Museum, the Ningbo Historical Museum, the Xiangshan campus (near Hangzhou) of the Chinese Academy of Art, and the library at Suzhou University. Wang's work is known for its abstractness, unorthodox angular shapes, integration with the natural surroundings, and an earthy industrial quality.[206]

Film

Chinese films and directors are beginning to attract international attention. The domestic film industry is booming, but its international presence remains limited. China produced 456 feature films in 2009, placing it numerically third in the world behind the United States and India.[207]

Chen Kaige and Zhang Yimou are perhaps the best-known Chinese directors, famous for *Yellow Earth, Ju Dou, Farewell My Concubine, Raise the Red Lantern, Red Sorghum, The Story of Qiu Ju, Hero, House of the Flying Daggers, To Live*, and other films popular with foreign audiences. Another famous director, Wang Xiaoshuai, has won awards at the Berlin and Cannes Film Festivals and was honored with the Order of Arts and Letters from France's Ministry of Culture in 2010. Wang's 1993 film *The Days* was the only Chinese language film included in the BBC list of the hundred greatest-ever films.

China's contributions to the international film circuit is sure to increase. As such, this will have an impact on how China is culturally perceived abroad. Nonetheless, compared to Hollywood's global impact, China has a long way to go to catch up. For example, in 2010 the United States produced more than five hundred films and its domestic box office netted $10.3 billion, while overseas takings collected an additional $19.3 billion (accounting for 30 percent of the global total)—whereas Chinese films earned only about $2 billion domestically in 2011 and had negligible earnings abroad.[208] Yet China's cinemas are expanding rapidly—adding three new screens per day, faster than in any other country in the world.[209]

Many Chinese commentators bemoan the lack of an international impact of the Chinese film industry. One factor is creativity. A Chinese expert on soft power observed, "We have *gongfu* [martial arts] and we have pandas, but we could not make a film like *Kung-fu Panda*!"[210] *Kung-fu Panda* grossed more than $100 million at the Chinese box office. Censorship also remains a significant constraint on Chinese filmmakers. China's most famous filmmaker Zhang Yimou observes: "There are a lot of movies I knew from the start would not pass the censors. The way you make movies in China is to know what will make it past the censors and what won't make it. In front of censorship everyone is equal. My films may be subject to more scrutiny. Leaders in charge tell me in private that my films will be looked at more closely because I have bigger audiences, both in China and overseas."[211] Zhang Yimou's latest film, *Curse of the Golden Flower*, a story about the Nanjing Massacre, cost $94 million to make and was nominated by the Chinese government (foreign governments are allowed to nominate one film per year) for the 2012 Academy Award for best foreign film. Although it was the highest-earning Chinese film of 2011, it still finished far behind foreign films *Transformers 3* and *Kung-fu Panda 2* in Chinese box office earnings.

If China cannot produce world-class films, then it attempts to acquire studios that can. During 2011 several Chinese investors expressed interest in purchasing equity shares in British and American film companies. Several leading Hollywood studios have been targeted for purchase by Chinese investors.[212] During Vice President Xi Jinping's visit to Hollywood in February 2012, a multimillion-dollar joint-venture deal was announced between DreamWorks Animation, the creator of *Kung-fu Panda*, and Chinese partners (China Media Capital, Shanghai Media Group, and Shanghai Alliance Investment).[213] Chinese companies are also trying to capitalize on the foreign film market. In 2012 the Dalian Wanda Group purchased the huge American movie theater chain AMC Entertainment for $2.6 billion. China's film industry is trying to go global—but, as in other dimensions surveyed in this chapter, it is trying to *buy* soft power rather than *build* it.

Tourism

With their rising wealth and disposable income, Chinese citizens are going abroad as tourists in unprecedented numbers. And they are spending money—lots of it!

The China National Tourism Administration (CNTA) estimates seventy million Chinese tourists traveled abroad in 2011 (of this total, fifty million visits took place to Hong Kong, Macao, and Taiwan, meaning that the real number of Chinese tourists traveling to foreign countries was twenty million).[214] With only 3 percent of citizens now holding passports, there is substantial potential for growth in the years to come. China has signed "approved destination status" (ADS) agreements with 134 countries, enabling group tours, with a number of foreign tour companies mounting direct marketing campaigns in China. As a result, its tourists are fanning out all around the world. Southeast Asia and Europe remain the most popular destinations, but the United States is gaining ground quickly as a result of the 2008 ADS accord. In 2011, 1.36 million visited the United States, while 3 million visited Europe.[215]

Global tourism plummeted as a result of the global financial crisis in 2009, but Chinese tourists picked up the slack. China's middle and upper classes are globetrotting in growing numbers and spending their incomes lavishly. Many are seeking to buy property abroad and are preparing to emigrate. A 2011 study by the Bank of China and *Hurun Report* (publisher of China's list of the wealthiest) reports that 60 percent of those possessing RMB 10 million ($1.6 million) or more have begun the process of emigration or are planning to do so.[216]

When abroad, Chinese tourists stay at high-end luxury hotels, frequent trendy boutiques, and purchase a variety of luxury goods. The UN World Tourism Organization ranks Chinese tourists as the fourth-biggest spenders worldwide,[217] while Global Refund (the firm that offers tax rebates on tourist purchases) reports that Chinese tourists spend more on average than any other nationality.[218] The China National Tourism Administration estimates Chinese tourists spent

$69 billion abroad (including Hong Kong, Macao, and Taiwan) in 2011.[219] The U.S. Department of Commerce and U.S. Travel Association ranked Chinese tourists seventh as spenders in the United States during 2010, at $5 billion.[220] Although tourism to the United States usually requires a months-long process for applications, it remains a destination of choice for many Chinese tourists. In 2011, 1.1 million Chinese tourists visited the United States, a figure due to double by 2014, according to the U.S. Department of Commerce. Hawaii and the West Coast are the most popular destinations, with many travel agencies now offering packages to the Hawaiian Islands. More and more, wealthy Chinese tourists are looking for unique travel experiences, rather than uniform group travel. Boutique hotels and secluded resorts are in. Meanwhile, large American hotel chains have begun to cater to Chinese tourist tastes; Starwood and Hilton now offer amenities such as in-room slippers and tea kettles, Chinese-style breakfasts with congee and fried rice, a Chinese-language welcome letter, and access to Chinese-language satellite television stations. American retailers of luxury goods such as Tiffany's, Bloomingdale's, Bergdorf Goodman, and Saks Fifth Avenue have all added Mandarin-speaking staff to their Manhattan and Beverly Hills stores.[221]

Chinese are spending large amounts of cash on luxury goods in major cities around the world.[222] Paris has become a prime shopping attraction for many Chinese tourist groups, the last stop on a multicity, multination European bus tour. The average Chinese shopper in Paris spends €1,300 on shopping, according to Global Blue (a French tax rebate company). Galleries Lafayette in Paris reports that the typical Chinese tourist spent €1,000 in two hours of shopping during 2009, 87 percent of it on fashion items, including shoes and handbags.[223] The number of Chinese tourists to France in 2010 rose to 550,000, and they spent €650 million ($890 million).[224] In 2009, Chinese tourists surpassed Russians as the highest-spending non-European visitors to France.

Nouveau riche Chinese are also developing an appreciation for fine French wines, buying up vineyards in Bordeaux[225] and importing red wines (Chinese have a particular affinity for reds over whites). China has overtaken the UK and Germany as the top export market for Bordeaux wines.[226] Ansel Travel, a Paris-based firm that brings 15,000 visitors to Europe every year, arranges tailored tours of Château Lafite Rothschild, St. Emillion, Chateau Margaux, and other elite Bordeaux vineyards, where it is not uncommon for the Chinese visitors to snatch up cases of expensive wines valued at $800 per bottle.[227] Chinese are buying Bordeaux wines not only by the bottle and case, but also by the vineyard. Cofco, the owner of Great Wall wines, bought the Château de Viaud vineyard in 2011.[228] But, as *Financial Times* wine aficionado Jancis Robinson observes, "They all make the classic mistake of newcomers to the region of choosing their acquisitions on the basis of the beauty of the château building rather than on the wine's appellation."[229] Some Chinese need travel only as far as Hong Kong to buy their imported wines: Sotheby's Hong Kong reported sales of $52.5 million in valuable vintages during 2010, accounting for 59 percent of all wine sold at auction worldwide that year, surpassing its sales in New York and London together![230]

Chinese tourists also love Germany. In 2010 Chinese visitors to Germany topped one million for the first time, an increase of 33 percent over 2009. They visit the "magic cities" of Hamburg, Munich, Cologne, and Leipzig, taking tailored "castle tours" along the Rhineland and through Bavaria. Frankfurt and Berlin are favored shopping destinations, with Chinese visitors now outspending Russians on Berlin's upscale Friedrichstraße. In 2010 they spent €234.4 million ($311.6 million) in Germany, accounting for the lion's share of tax-free retails sales.[231]

They have also discovered Italy, in an ironic reversal of Marco Polo's forays seven centuries earlier. Tuscany, the birthplace of the Renaissance and home to stunning scenery, fine wines, and food, is a destination of choice for Chinese tourists. Florence experienced a 50 percent increase in Chinese visitors during 2010. Altogether, the Italian embassy in Beijing issued 81,000 tourist visas during 2010 (a 30 percent increase over 2009, reported Italian Ambassador Attilio Massimo).[232] The Tuscany region caters to Chinese tourist tastes by establishing customized services under a multiprogram "China Project," which adopts tailored maps and iPhone applications to encourage Chinese to navigate the region in couples or small groups.

Chinese are also known to be impulsive shoppers. "Chinese tourists are different from Japanese tourists, who make out shopping lists before trips—Chinese just buy what they fancy!" says Li Meng of the China International Travel Service.[233] A DFS Galleria outlet on Singapore's famed Orchard Road reported on a day in 2009 when a 400-member tourist group from Wenzhou spent $300,000 in an hour, wiping the shelves clean of Louis Vuitton and other luxury products, while the Bulgari outlet reported that 70 percent of Chinese tourists spend $10,000 in groups of two or three per visit on average.[234] When I encountered one such group on Orchard Road in 2011 I queried one shopper (in Mandarin) what he was buying, and to my surprise, he responded: "We can't buy enough—we'd buy the world if we could!" Stores in Tokyo's Akihabara and Ginza districts note similar shopping patterns, with visiting Chinese purchasing several thousand dollars' worth of electronic or designer goods in a matter of minutes. Japan's tourism agency estimates that Chinese visitors spend more than twice as much as British or American tourists.[235] One vendor in Akihabara, a warren of tightly clustered electronics shops, exclaimed: "Chinese are the saviors for us! I have never seen any foreign tourists spend as much as Chinese."[236] In New York 1200 Chinese tourists dropped an estimated $6 million in one week during the 2010 Chinese New Year holiday, according to Zheng Wenqing of the New York Tourism Board's China office.[237]

Chinese are also very brand-conscious shoppers, purchasing Louis Vuitton, Gucci, Armani, Burberry, and other name brands. The World Luxury Association (an international nonprofit specializing in luxury brand market research) estimated that China itself will have the world's largest luxury goods market by revenue by 2015. A study by the global consulting firm Bain & Company calculated that Chinese shoppers spent $17.4 billion on luxury goods in 2011.[238] Despite strong growth in the domestic market, many Chinese *nouveau riches* still prefer to shop abroad. In 2011, the association estimated Chinese tourists spent $50 billion on luxury goods in Europe alone, four times that spent in the domestic market.[239] Compared with Europe or the United States, domestic sales of luxury goods in China remains small; but they are growing rapidly.

Chinese luxury tastes vary. Jewelry is in particular demand, with shoppers dropping large amounts on gems and precious metals. China is now the world's second-largest gold consumer. Some are buying luxury cars, particularly sports cars. Casinos in Singapore, Nice, Monaco, and Las Vegas also report an upsurge in high-rolling Chinese gamblers. Macao is now the largest-grossing gambling mecca in the world, having eclipsed Las Vegas in 2009. Others, as described above, are buying art.

Many Chinese have focused their energies and incomes on buying property abroad. As the global financial crisis hit in 2008–2010 and domestic real estate prices soared, Chinese investors fanned out across the globe in search of prime real estate.[240] Mainland Chinese property investors have already replaced those from Russia and the Middle East as the "busiest buyers with the deepest pockets, looking for trophy assets and pushing up prices," report some brokers.[241] Unlike clients from Russia and the Middle East, however, these buyers are not looking to live in the properties themselves but instead are seeking appreciating assets and steady rental income. Because citizens need to get approval from local authorities in China to invest more than $50,000 per year overseas (a frequently ignored regulation), many wealthy Chinese skirt restrictions by maintaining foreign bank accounts. Most of the buyers pay cash to minimize the paper trail.[242] Real estate brokers across the world recount Chinese buyers arriving at closing meetings with suitcases literally stuffed with cash.

The real estate buying binge is truly worldwide: beachfront properties on Indian Ocean islands, Balinese retreats, Hong Kong midlevel flats, single-family homes in Canada and the United States, New York high-rise condos, Hawaiian villas, and Australian and French vineyards. In Japan, Chinese buyers are snapping up rural forests and mountainous land, causing concern in traditionally conservative rural areas.[243] Meanwhile, London estate agents reported a surge in Chinese purchases of properties in the high-end districts of Mayfair and Belgravia, where few flats sell for under £1 million,[244] as well as Knightsbridge and Canary Wharf.

New York City is another good example. Manhattan realtors report a huge increase in inquiries from wealthy Chinese interested in luxury residential properties, some in the $30 million–plus range. "They see the apartment, they make the offer, and right away fly back to China. Cash deal," one real estate agent recalled.[245] Chinese residential purchases are only the tip of a larger iceberg of Chinese commercial investment in New York. Chinese banks poured more than $1 billion into real estate in

New York City during 2010, including funding redevelopment projects such as the Atlantic Yards in Brooklyn, the Alexander Hamilton bridge, the Number 7 subway line extension, a Park Avenue building housing J. P. Morgan Chase and Major League Baseball headquarters, and the Metro-North Railroad station at Yankee Stadium. Chinese companies are taking out leases at prestigious addresses such as the Empire State Building and One World Trade Center.[246] All of this has occurred very rapidly and very stealthily without publicity, note commercial real estate analysts.

Not all Chinese tourists are wealthy and sophisticated. Some leave a negative impression for their poor manners. "Talking loudly, spitting, refusing to queue up, smoking in non-smoking areas, and disregarding traffic lights" is commonplace, observed one *China Daily* article.[247] In 2006 thousands of Chinese tourists were caught on camera at Disneyland in Hong Kong littering, spitting, smoking, and being ill-mannered—images that were subsequently published in Chinese newspapers and on the internet, provoking a national discussion on the manners of Chinese tourists abroad.[248] The China National Tourism Administration and nine other government departments launched a nationwide campaign and issued fifteen guidelines to educate people to mind their manners when they travel abroad:[249]

1. Do not spit in public.
2. Do not litter in public places.
3. Line up and do not jump queues at public venues.
4. Do not take photos when a sign says "no photos."
5. Do not talk in loud voices.
6. Do not polish your shoes with bed linen or hotel towels.
7. Do not smoke in non-smoking areas.
8. Wear proper clothes.
9. Do not strip down to the waist (for men) when it is hot.
10. Do not wear pajamas in supermarkets or on the street.
11. Do not remove shoes or socks in airport terminals.
12. Men should observe the "ladies first" rule.
13. Flush toilets after using.
14. Do not block other pedestrians by walking side by side on sidewalks.
15. Do not force foreigners to pose for photographs.

The Chinese government is taking these steps to try to improve the image of Chinese tourists traveling abroad.

Somewhat related to tourism is the issue of Chinese emigration to other countries. Accurate statistics do not exist, but Chinese have emigrated abroad in huge numbers over the past two decades. Everywhere they go, they draw on their entrepreneurial roots to establish businesses. For example, the Italian city of Prato, a medieval enclave near Florence in Tuscany, was overwhelmed by a decade of 100,000 Chinese immigrants turning it into an offshore manufacturing base of counterfeit designer goods with "Made in Italy" labels (which is technically true, but they are not licensed by Italian luxury goods companies).[250] Similar stories abound in Southeast Asia, Africa, Europe, and Latin America.

Sports

Sporting prowess is another example of a nation's soft power and international reputation. International sporting competition is also an element in geopolitics. During the Cold War, the United States and the former Soviet Union took their global rivalry into the Olympics and other sporting venues. So did East Germany, demonstrating how concentrating resources (including steroid enhancement) in selected sports such as swimming could produce a world-class sporting champion.

The PRC has certainly absorbed these lessons. Not only did China reap substantial international prestige by hosting the 2008 Olympic Games in Beijing, but its athletes topped the gold medal table (securing 51) and came second in overall medals (100). Chinese athletes dominated a number of events. At the 2010 Winter Olympics in Canada, China finished ninth overall but won five gold medals (both records for China). Pairs figure skaters Shen Xue and Zhao Hongbo won gold, breaking the monopoly held by Russian skaters since 1964. At the 2012 summer games in London, Chinese athletes garnered 88 overall medals and 38 gold (second in both categories).

Chinese athletes have also begun to attract global attention in other sports. NBA professional basketball is the prime example, led by former Houston Rockets star Yao Ming. In 2010 Ed Wang became the first Chinese-born player to be drafted from a U.S. college (Virginia Tech) and play in the U.S. National Football League (NFL). There are no Chinese soccer players in Europe's premier leagues yet, but it is only a matter of time. Meanwhile, Liu Xiang has become a world-class hurdler, and Chinese female tennis aces Zheng Jie and Li Na are competing at the top of their game (reaching the semifinals of the 2010 Australian Open, with Li Na winning the 2011 French Open). Feng Shanshan became the first Chinese female golfer to win the 2012 LPGA championship.

Despite these notable sporting achievements on the world stage, China's professional sports leagues are particularly underdeveloped and riddled by corruption and match-fixing scandals.[251] China's best athletes are forced to train with national teams, and thus professional or collegiate leagues do not serve as the talent incubator or brand-name generator that they do in the West.[252] Thus far this approach to fostering national athletic talent seems to have paid benefits in individual sports, but not (yet) in team sports.

Considering the Impact

Taken together, China's global cultural soft power footprint will continue to expand. To be sure, there are other elements of Chinese culture projected abroad that we have not considered, such as cuisine and music. But in all of these areas, China is more deeply etching itself in the consciousness of people around the world. Yet the overall impact of China's global cultural presence should not be exaggerated. Compared with the United States, for example, China lags far behind in most categories. Moreover, much of Chinese popular culture abroad is targeted at the overseas community and never reaches non-Chinese audiences. It is an insular discourse in Chinese, by Chinese, and for Chinese. But in this *Huaqiao* (overseas Chinese) community, Beijing has successfully competed with rival Taiwan's deep roots—winning political support from Chinese abroad.

Misunderstood or Disrespected China?

Chinese officials, scholars, and average citizens frequently express frustration over foreign (particularly Western) misunderstanding of China. In public and private sessions, officials frequently voice the view that China is misunderstood abroad and subject to deeply rooted bias and prejudice in the West. "We have a credibility problem," pithily observed Zhu Yinghuang, former editor-in-chief of *China Daily*.[253] Politburo member and China's chief information czar Liu Yunshan (who oversees all aspects of information, media, and culture) observed in a meeting with the author: "In the international media, there is an imbalance of power. People speak of a 'digital gap,' but there is also an information gap. It will take us a long time to overcome it. We lack the power to influence the outside world, but we need to increase our use of words and speech to gain the initiative, we need experts abroad to speak about China in a more objective way, and we need more transparency."[254] At a National People's Congress press conference in March 2010 Foreign Minister Yang Jiechi also lamented foreign misunderstanding of China: "We hope the world appreciates China's uniqueness and national circumstances, and people stop looking at the country through tinted glasses, and abandon stereotyped perceptions, particularly bias. I like both oil paintings and traditional Chinese paintings. It is definitely wrong for one to judge Chinese paintings using the criteria of oil paintings."[255] On another occasion, Foreign Minister Yang wrote: "Prejudice, misunderstanding and suspicion are still commonplace in international perceptions of China, which is mainly due to differences in values and ideology, lingering Cold War mentalities, and uneasiness over China's rapid growth. These tendencies are embodied in the 'China threat theory,' the notion that China must assume more 'responsibility,' and in assertions that China is getting 'tough' or 'arrogant.'"[256]

Foreign Minister Yang is not alone in holding these views. I repeatedly encountered it in my interviews and research. So I would always ask my Chinese interlocutors, "What is it *exactly* that foreigners do not understand about China, and what are the sources of this misunderstanding?" Frequently I would receive perplexed looks to my question, as if simply asserting the misunderstanding was sufficient. Often the question would produce a stock response that foreigners do not respect China's "national conditions" (国情) or "Chinese characteristics" (中国特色), or that they simply did not respect its policies (中国政策) or ways of doing things (中国作风). Tibet and the Dalai Lama were frequently cited as examples of this tendency. In other words, to not *agree* with Chinese official policy or to be critical of it is seen as *misunderstanding* China. Not a single official I interviewed offered a concrete example of something that is misunderstood about China different from not agreeing with government policy.

But some officials did try to account for the sources of misunderstanding. For example, CPPCC spokesman (and former SCIO director) Zhao Qizheng observed in an interview: "Today, in the West, there are still misunderstandings of China in mainstream media and societies. China is seen as 'communist' or 'authoritarian' or a 'police state' or assister of 'rogue states.' Concerning China's foreign relations, Western countries still have distorted perceptions of China.... The causes of Western misunderstanding of China are many. Ideology is one source. Others include conflicts of interest, such as trade relations."[257] I also interviewed several of Zhao's colleagues in the SCIO on the question of foreign misunderstanding of China. Director (Minister) Wang Chen observed: "In our foreign publicity work, we want to create a favorable international opinion environment. China does not export its ideology to other countries, but we cannot accept others to impose theirs on us. China has embarked on a different path from others, but China is not well respected or understood abroad."[258] Similarly, SCIO Vice Director Qian Xiaoqian observed:

> China's image abroad is frequently distorted. Some countries still view China from an ideological perspective. China is still seen as a communist dictatorship. The reason is because they compare China with the former Soviet Union, although there are some fundamental differences. China and the CCP are in no way a copy of the former Soviet Union.... Another problem is that opinion abroad is dominated by Western media—even in Africa and Latin American countries, the local media use reports from Reuters, BBC, CNN, and other Western media. There is an implicit belief of superiority in this reporting. Another reason is the practice of Western journalism that is sensationalistic and it tries to tell stories. This compromises truthfulness and authenticity of reports. Often these reports are negative and cast China in a bad light.[259]

Vice Foreign Minister Madame Fu Ying, one of China's most sophisticated diplomats, also has some tough words concerning Western prejudice about China. Meeting with some European journalists (in her capacity in charge of European affairs), she asserted: "The West is too arrogant and must stop lecturing us and trying to change China. Unless you can accept China as it is, there is no basis for a relationship."[260] In another interview with the author, Madame Fu lamented: "Our difficulties are with the media psyche in Western countries. They are often biased against China. Engaging them is not an easy thing. It makes the Chinese feel there is a Western conspiracy against China."[261] The current minister of culture, Cai Wu, used to be the SCIO director from 2005 to 2008 (and previously minister of the CCP/ID). He has a lot of experience in public diplomacy and speculated about Western press coverage of China: "The American media is mostly biased about China, presenting only our problems, and often in a biased way. In contrast, the U.S. is featured frequently in the Chinese media and the reports are largely objective and positive. We know the American political system, economic situation, and social life—but it is not reciprocal."[262] When asked about Western misunderstandings of China, the director of China Radio International, Xia Jixuan, named six misconceptions. "We are a communist country; we live under dictatorship; ideology is important; China will collapse like the USSR; people in China are unhappy; China is only an economic power," opined Director Xia.[263] Senior Colonel Liu Mingfu, a senior officer at the PLA's National Defense University, wrote a whole book on American myths about China. Entitled *The China Dream* (中国梦), Liu identifies in particular four principal myths propagated about China in the West: (1) the "China rise" theory (中国崛起轮), (2) the "China collapse" theory (中国崩溃论), (3) the "China threat" theory (中国威胁论), (4) and the "China responsibility" theory (中国负责论).[264] Liu's best-selling book analyzes and attempts to debunk these theories and other concepts prevalent in Western discourse, which he argues are essentially the product of Western ideological bias and wishful thinking. SCIO Director Wang Chen noted in March 2010 that the four were "old theories" (to defame China), but recently three new ones had appeared: the "China arrogance theory," "China pride theory," and "China unreasonableness theory."[265]

These selected quotations from a variety of bureaucratic sources are good illustrations of how and why Chinese officials and scholars think their country is misunderstood and discriminated against abroad (mainly in the West). No doubt there *is* lack of understanding in the West about China, as it is a highly complex and opaque country, and it is difficult for Western media and scholars to penetrate it. Yet this is not to say that Western reporting on China is generically biased per se. My own reading of the mainstream Western media on China is that they are quite accurate, if often critical. But in Chinese culture and official thinking, criticism equals misunderstanding, and agreement equals understanding. In Chinese society and culture, to be criticized publicly is one of the worst things that can happen to anyone, as the person loses face. Western scholarship on China is also quite accurate and highly detailed—much more than an average newspaper reader could absorb. Moreover, my own considerable experience in public speaking across the United States and around the world indicates that there is *not* intrinsic prejudice against China (except what I encountered in the Czech Republic). Quite to the contrary, there seems to be an insatiable thirst for information and explanation about China. Curiosity is the norm. Ignorance and a low level of understanding China do certainly exist, but more often than not they translate into curiosity and desire to know and learn more.

Chinese officials and pundits, however, certainly have their work cut out for them in more effectively explaining their country to the world. Many of China's policies rub up against basic foreign (especially Western) sensitivities, particularly concerning its political system, treatment of human rights, minority policies, and "legal" practices. Imprisoning high-profile dissidents and artists such as Liu Xiaobo and Ai Weiwei hardly helps China's international image. Moreover, Party and government policy making is often opaque and nontransparent (despite improvements). Its society is complex and hard to reach. Restrictions on foreign news reporting in China remain severe, leaving these aspects more rather than less difficult to comprehend. Also, as noted earlier, the language of China's officialdom often does not translate well across national boundaries. It often comes across as hollow slogans with unintelligible content.

China's Soft Power Remains Very Soft

I therefore conclude that China's soft power and global cultural appeal remain very limited. As Joseph Nye observed, "What China seems not to appreciate is that using culture and narrative to create soft power is not easy when they are inconsistent with domestic realities."[266] Soft power is also not something that can be bought with money or built with investment. As the many indicators in this chapter illustrate, the Chinese government is approaching soft power and public diplomacy as it constructs high-speed rail or long-distance highways: by investing money and expecting to see development. Soft power is not built this way. It is *earned*.

Ultimately, as noted at the beginning of this chapter, there is not much the Chinese *government* can do about this soft power deficit, absent a significant loosening of its political controls. When asked by SCIO Minister Wang Chen what I thought China should do to improve its soft power, I responded: "Just get the government out of your own people's way. China has an enormously talented society—just let it speak for itself." I could literally see the difficulty Minister Wang had trying to digest this advice, as his job involves repressing and channeling China's creative sectors (in addition to showcasing them).

Soft power appeal, as we noted at the outset of this chapter, comes almost entirely and intrinsically from *society*—not from government. As much as China craves the international recognition of winning Nobel Prizes, until 2012 not a single Chinese residing in China has won one (except imprisoned dissident Liu Xiaobo, recipient of the 2010 Peace Prize). All eight Nobel Prize winners in the sciences who are of Chinese descent are American citizens, and (until Mo Yan in 2012) the sole awardee for literature won after immigrating to France. The Nobel deficit, I would suggest, is directly traceable to China's political system, which stifles creativity. It is also true that the country's political system is part of its soft power deficit. Other countries do not want to *be* like China, and China is not a magnet attracting others to it. China's attributes may be unique, but they do not hold universal appeal. And no matter how well the government resources the "messengers," if the message is not intrinsically appealing no amount of investment can sell it. At present, China does not have the universal appeal necessary to possess soft power. Moreover, its public diplomacy (or "external propaganda work") remains clumsy, rhetorical, propagandistic, and relatively unsophisticated. One might even say that China's public diplomacy actually *hinders* its soft power!

These cannot be gratifying conclusions for China's soft power and public diplomacy practitioners. China's efforts to improve its international image will continue, but it is very much an uphill battle. The nation's soft power deficit is another indicator that it is a partial power.

7

China's Global Security Presence

China's participation in world security cooperation is by no means enlargement of a sphere of influence or territorial expansion.... The Chinese military's outreach for international security cooperation is not intended to impair the international system, but to become a player and builder of the system, providing additional public goods to the international community so that the benefit of security can be truly shared by all.

—CHINESE MINISTER OF DEFENSE LIANG GUANGLIE, 2011[1]

Over the past decade China's military has benefited from robust investment in modern hardware and technology. Many modern systems have reached maturity and others will become operational in the next few years.

—UNITED STATES DEPARTMENT OF DEFENSE, 2011[2]

THUS FAR CHINA'S GLOBAL security presence has not evolved in the "traditional" great power manner of establishing alliances, acquiring bases and dispatching troops abroad, building global power projection capabilities, sailing its navy around the world, coercing others, or fighting in conflicts directly or via surrogates. At the same time, China has been steadily improving and expanding its military capabilities over the past two decades and, by some measures, can be considered to possess the No. 2 military in the world today. Although strengthening its capabilities, the PRC has thus far limited its military deployments to China's own sovereign territory, its Asian maritime littoral, or under international peacekeeping missions in other regions. In other words, the Chinese military has not yet gone global. To be sure, it remains an Asian regional military power and strategic actor to be reckoned with, and its strengthened strategic posture is affecting the balance of power throughout the Asia-Pacific region—but China remains far from being a global military power or strategic actor. Despite the impressive progress in its military modernization in recent years, it should be remembered that China's global military footprint actually remains very limited. It has no foreign bases or troops stationed abroad (except under UN auspices) and Chinese civilian and military officials frequently reiterate that, as a matter of principle, China will never build bases or garrison forces abroad. Other than cyber warfare, its space program, and intercontinental ballistic missiles, it has no global power-projection capabilities. To be certain, these are not insignificant capabilities, but China's air and ground forces cannot operate away from China's immediate periphery, and the naval forces have very limited deployment capacity beyond China's "near seas" (近海). When China had to evacuate 35,000 civilians from Libya in 2011, it had to rely completely on leased ships, ferries, and civilian aircraft from neighboring countries—as it did not have the air or naval capacity to deploy that far and did not possess military base arrangements in the Mediterranean region.

Thus, in the military/strategic realm (as in others considered in this book), China is a *partial power*. But this posture could be changing, as military capabilities improve, domestic nationalistic pressures grow, and the nation's security interests become more globalized. China's international commercial presence and energy needs are redefining the nation's security interests. Rising dependence on imported oil and other natural resources is fundamentally reshaping China's energy security strategy. This has major implications for national security strategy, frontier defense, importance of offshore territorial claims, and development of the navy.[3] As we witnessed in Chapter 2, there are rising domestic voices (including in the PLA) urging China to act like a big power and become more assertive in protecting its interests abroad. In terms of capabilities, we see the People's Liberation Army Navy (PLAN) beginning to sail outside of its immediate littoral waters into the western Pacific, Indian Ocean, and beyond (but still infrequently and in relatively small numbers, largely to make symbolic port calls).[4] The most notable example of the PLAN's out-of-area operations has been as part of the multinational naval force carrying out counterpiracy operations off the coast of Somalia in the Gulf of Aden. As of 2011, China had deployed eight task forces of twenty ships that had escorted 4000 vessels (40 percent under foreign flags) in this operation.

At present, China's global security interests remain modest, but they are gradually expanding commensurate with all other aspects of China's domestic modernization and global involvement. Although China's conventional military capabilities and presence remain minimal to nonexistent globally, in other multilateral and "nontraditional security" (nonmilitary) areas China's global security presence is steadily increasing.[5] The Gulf of Aden operation is a prime example. After refusing to participate for many years, China now also engages in joint exercises with foreign navies and militaries. The PLA has a robust military exchange program with foreign nations, including training a large number of foreign officers and service personnel in Chinese military academies. Chinese military, paramilitary, and civilian personnel are now regularly involved in disaster-relief operations around the world—as nearby as Japan and Southeast Asia and as far away as Haiti and Chile in the Western Hemisphere. Perhaps the most noteworthy example of China's contributions to international security comes via its contributions to UN Peacekeeping Operations (UNPKO). In all of these ways China contributes to, and participates in, international security activities.

The Contradictions of China's Global Security Presence

China's capacity to contribute to meeting global security challenges is inextricably tied to its own conceptualization of an enlarging global role as well as the world's growing expectations of it. As we saw in Chapter 2, China remains very conflicted about its international identity and responsibilities. Contributions to international security are, in fact, a subset of the broader question of China's contributions to global governance more generally (as was discussed in Chapter 4). In fact, the security sphere is a challenging area (if not *the* most challenging) for China to establish a global presence, simply because its *capabilities* are more limited than in other areas. It is also constrained by self-imposed policies about foreign intervention and having no military bases or forces abroad.

Comparatively speaking, China possesses greater capacities to contribute to global financial and economic stability and growth, to development assistance in developing countries, to global climate change, to global public health, to global innovation and technological development, to global energy supplies. In all these areas and others, China's capacity to influence global patterns and global governance is *greater* than in the traditional military security area (although these subjects are all now considered to be part of "nontraditional security"). The international community—particularly the United States—expects a continuously growing Chinese contribution to addressing international global governance challenges commensurate with the nation's new power, size, expanding global interests, and influence. Just as these governments will expect more out of China, two other things are equally certain.

First, there will remain substantial unease in some countries—particularly the United States and in Asia—about China's growing global security role and military capabilities. Nascent concerns over an emerging "China threat" will continue to exist, and will likely grow proportionately to China's increased military capabilities and power-projection capabilities. There already exists considerable unease around the world about China's rapidly growing global economic presence, and most notably its voracious appetite for energy and raw materials. Once a larger military/security footprint is married to an already expansive economic-energy footprint, the anti-China angst will only intensify. Thus, China's rising international activism is a double-edged sword: if it is done in tandem with Western nations or under the sponsorship of the United Nations or other recognized regional organizations, Western publics and governments will generally be accepting—even encouraging—of China's activism. But if China is unilaterally active—or acts together with what are considered "rogue states"—then it will not be welcomed.[6] If China is relatively inactive in contributing to global security, then it will be criticized for free riding and not living up to its responsibilities as a major power.

Thus there is a paradox: for China to contribute more to international security cooperation it must enhance its capabilities (particularly air and sea lift); yet as China develops such capabilities it will generate concerns on its periphery and around the world. If China continues to increase its capabilities but shirks responsibility to contribute to cooperative global security, then a classic "security dilemma" will arise, with other nations viewing China suspiciously. Moreover, if China continues to develop its military capabilities while remaining outside of alliances with the main status quo states in the international system (NATO and those allied with or having strong security ties to the United States), this will further contribute to the image of selfish and potentially dangerous power.

There is also a second certainty, namely that China itself will remain conflicted about international contributions to global governance generally and specifically about international security cooperation. Although there has been a positive trend in recent years toward expanded Chinese contributions to both, there remains a profound ambivalence and skepticism within the Chinese government and expert community concerning the wisdom of external entanglements and deep suspiciousness about so-called global governance. This will hold China back from being a good global citizen.

Thus, when considering the potential for China's involvement in the international security arena in the future, these factors will all influence, constrain, or embolden China's choices and involvements. Most likely, the world will witness exactly what it has been witnessing over the past decade: a steadily modernizing Chinese military with progressively expanding power-projection capabilities, a China that is more involved in global security at the diplomatic level and on low-cost nontraditional security issues, and a China that remains internally conflicted about the wisdom of deeper involvement in global governance and expanding its global security and military footprint. At the same time, Beijing will go on selectively contributing to global security governance within its capacities, and usually under United Nations auspices.

Military Modernization

Of the various dimensions of China's global security presence, the one of greatest interest and import is its rapidly developing military capabilities. For more than three decades the nation has pursued a sustained and comprehensive military modernization effort. It has not been a "crash course," although official expenditures on the military have (in percentage terms of annual increase) exceeded even China's stunning economic growth rates (defense expenditures have averaged 12.1 percent per annum since 1989). Measured in terms of percentage of GDP or percentage of state expenditure, however, defense spending is much more modest—1.4 percent and 8.5 percent respectively on average. To put this in perspective, the United States spends nearly 5 percent of its GDP on defense, while the former Soviet Union spent more than half of its state budget on the military during the height of the Cold War. To be sure, the USSR's excessive military expenditure and distortion of its national economy in favor of the military-industrial complex were two of the principal reasons (the Chinese concluded) that the Soviet Union collapsed.[7]

Even though China has learned this lesson from the former Soviet Union and is not excessively investing in defense, nonetheless its aggregate defense spending is significant. It is now the second largest in the world ($106 billion in 2012), as depicted in Figure 7.1.[8] In addition, China's declared internal security budget totaled $112 billion in the same year.

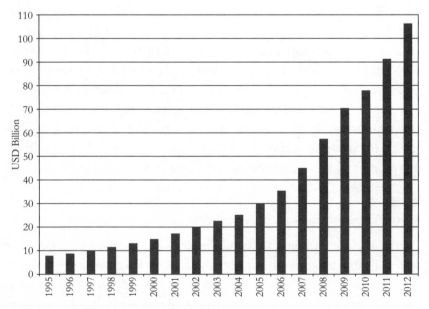

FIGURE 7.1 China's Annual Defense Budget

Total military expenditures are in excess of these official figures (probably about 15 percent higher), as China buries many defense-related expenditures in other state budgets.[9] This is not unlike many other governments in this regard, but the opacity of China's military budget system makes it impossible to accurately estimate total military expenditure. What is known, though, is that since 1999 more and more off-budget expenditure has gone on-budget. This was the result of a series of fiscal reforms launched by Premier Zhu Rongji, most notably "zero-based budgeting." Under this accounting procedure, state institutions cannot roll over unspent funds to the next fiscal year (a longtime practice in the Chinese government and military). Other important bureaucratic reforms were also undertaken at this time that produced greater coherence and discipline in the budgeting process. These importantly included the Central Military Commission/State Council/CCP Central Committee triple directive ordering the military to get out of business activities and turn over their commercial assets to State Council control. Without extra commercial income, the PLA became more dependent on government allocations, and opportunities for corruption decreased significantly. The Ministry of Finance also strengthened and centralized its power and oversight of the budgeting process (including more pervasive auditing of accounts).

As a result of this sustained investment, the PLA has been rapidly improving its capabilities across the board—personnel, training, logistics, facilities, and weaponry. These improvements accelerated during the first decade of the twenty-first century, with the PLA fielding new weapons systems, although the modernization has been a steady process since the 1980s.

Catalysts

Along the way, five instructive experiences catalyzed the process. The first was the PLA's humiliating performance in its attack on Vietnam in 1979. In this debacle, Chinese forces were unable to bring air or naval power to bear on its neighboring adversary, and ground troops were unable to undertake even a modest cross-border incursion because of geographical, logistical, and command impediments. Instead of "teaching Vietnam a lesson" (the intended justification for the attack), it was

Vietnam that administered the lessons. China lost an estimated 42,000 casualties in *one month* of warfare![10]

The second experience was witnessing how the United States prosecuted the 1991 Gulf War. With that awesome display of firepower, long-range air strikes, stealth, precision-guided munitions, electronics, computers, satellites, intelligence, and battlefield mobility, the PLA realized that a "revolution in military affairs" (军事革命) had occurred in the United States. The fact that the U.S. military could prosecute such a conflict half a world away while China could not even undertake a modest cross-border operation left PLA generals scratching their heads as they realized just how far behind their military had fallen.

The third experiences were the 1995 and 1996 Taiwan Strait missile crises, when China threatened Taiwan by firing short-range ballistic missiles into the sea near the island. China was trying to affect the outcome of the island's first direct presidential election and intimidate Taiwan's independence movement. These aggressive actions spurred the United States to deploy two aircraft carrier battle groups to the region in response. From these actions, China learned that it possessed only blunt instruments of attack (ballistic missiles) but not the full spectrum of air, sea, ground, and electronic assets necessary to actually prosecute a conflict over Taiwan. Thus commenced an effort to compensate for its weaknesses and build a full-spectrum attack capability.

In 1999 China had a fourth instructional experience when it witnessed the role of sustained airpower employed by NATO forces against Serbian targets (and one mistaken target of the Chinese embassy in Belgrade). Many of these bombing raids were carried out by long-range stealth bombers launched from the continental United States. This reemphasized the importance of stealth technologies and precision-guided munitions in contemporary warfare.

Since 2001 China witnessed how U.S. and multinational forces prosecuted counterinsurgency operations in Iraq and Afghanistan, using special operations forces (SOFs), unmanned aerial drones, stealth helicopters, and other unconventional capabilities. These wars made the Chinese realize that the United Sates and others were not only able to attack from afar but were also willing to put large numbers of boots on the ground and take casualties.

These five instructive experiences are joined by two other specific drivers for China's military modernization: Taiwan and the pursuit of comprehensive power. The rise of the Taiwan independence movement and the administrations of former Presidents Lee Teng-hui and Chen Shuibian on Taiwan during the 1990s provided a very specific mission around which the PLA oriented modernization: its doctrine, training, and weapons procurement. Secondly, military modernization was viewed by the Chinese leadership and government (as well as the military) as simply one piece of overall "comprehensive national power" (综合国力)." "A major aspect of being a strong national power is, I think, a strong defense," observed Defense Minister Liang Guanglie in a *People's Daily* interview in 2010.[11] Thus, the specific "threat" of Taiwan independence and the more generic desire to build a world-class military to match other aspects of China's development aspirations have been the primary drivers of military modernization in China. The importance of bureaucratic politics should also be noted, the role played by institutional actors in China's military-industrial complex.[12] Like all developed countries with indigenous military production capacity, various Chinese governmental organs, commercial enterprises, research-and-development laboratories, and universities constitute its military-industrial complex and have institutional and financial stakes in the military modernization process. Geography is also a factor affecting China's defense calculations and responsibilities. China has borders with fourteen other countries totaling 22,000 kilometers, and a coastline of more than 18,000 kilometers.[13] This geographic reality has a profound impact on the force structure of the People's Liberation Army.

As a result of these factors, over the past twenty years every dimension of China's military capabilities has been significantly upgraded. This includes, importantly, not only the "hardware" of weapons but also the "software" of professionalization of personnel, logistics, mobility, training, communications, intelligence, etc. China's electronic, space, and cyber capabilities have made particularly notable progress. Its weapons systems—from tanks to intercontinental ballistic missiles, aircraft to ships—have all enjoyed real qualitative improvement. Old generations of weapons systems have been retired and new ones brought on stream. Many of these new weapons systems were on display in Tiananmen

Square on October 1, 2009, to commemorate the sixtieth anniversary of the PRC. Qualitative advances have been made throughout the military; the fighting capacity of all services has been increased; and the command, control, and "jointness" of PLA forces have been improved across the board. As the 2011 annual U.S. Department of Defense report on the Chinese military noted: "Following [this period of] ambitious acquisition, the decade from 2011 through 2020 will prove critical to the PLA as it attempts to integrate many new and complex platforms, and to adopt modern operational concepts, including joint operations and network-centric warfare."[14]

Let us look more carefully at recent improvements and current Chinese military capabilities and missions.

The Evolving Military Mission

All militaries configure their forces on the basis of a combination of four principal factors: military doctrine, potential threats, indigenous resources, and sources of supply. Together, these factors constitute fighting capacity and military mission. In the case of the PLA, they have evolved considerably over time.

In terms of doctrine, during the Maoist era China imagined that if it were to have to fight a war it would be done on Chinese soil; hence the "people's war" (人民战争) doctrine to wage a guerrilla campaign of attrition and "lure the enemy in deep and drown them in a sea of people." This strategy did not obviate the need to fight conflicts on China's borders: in Korea (1950–1953) and against Taiwan (1955, 1958), India (1960–1962), and the Soviet Union (1969). By the late 1960s these border contingencies were married to a new kind of threat: the need to prepare to absorb a nuclear strike from the Soviet Union on China's cities and nuclear installations. This triggered a massive urban civil defense program and a crash program to upgrade China's own nuclear deterrent.

In 1979, under the direction of Marshals Su Yu and Ye Jianying, China shifted its doctrine slightly to one of "people's war under modern conditions" (在现代条件下的人民战争), which authorized more attention to be paid to modern weaponry instead of solely relying on the sheer number of ground forces. This was one of the lessons learned from China's 1979 war with Vietnam. During 1985–1991 this evolved further into the doctrines of "local war" (局部战争), and then from 1991 to 2001 to "local war under high-technology conditions" (高技术的条件下的局部战争). These were euphemisms for preparing for conflicts on China's maritime periphery against opponents (Taiwan, the United States, Japan) that possessed more modern weaponry. After 2001 the doctrine was modestly modified to "local war under high technology and *informationalized* conditions" (高技术与信息化条件下的局部战争), which included a terminological addition that took note of the important role played by information technologies in modern warfare. In 2004 President and Chairman of the Central Military Commission Hu Jintao gave the important doctrinal speech "Understand the New Historical Missions of Our Military in the New Period of the New Century" (新世纪新阶段我军历史使命), which put forward a much more variegated set of new military missions, including maritime security, space security, and cyber security.[15] Hu's directive remains the operative PLA doctrine to this day, although his successor as commander-in-chief, Xi Jinping, will likely enunciate a new doctrine in due course.

Thus the PLA's linguistic and practical doctrine has evolved as a result of potential contingencies and the force structure needed to wage different types of conflicts against different types of adversaries. However, from 1996 until very recent years (since approximately 2008) there was a singular primary driver for Chinese military modernization: Taiwan (and, by extension, the United States). As noted above, the 1995–96 Taiwan Strait crises taught the PLA that it possessed a largely single-dimensional strike capacity: ballistic missiles. To actually prosecute a conflict against Taiwanese and U.S. forces, it would require many other capabilities. Nor were ballistic missile deployments sufficient in number or accuracy to ground Taiwan's air force, knock out other high-value targets, and keep American aircraft carrier strike groups at bay. The PLA needed to attain capabilities that could launch precision strikes against high-value command, control, and political targets; undertake special operations sabotage attacks against key military and civilian infrastructure targets on Taiwan and adjacent islands; ground Taiwan's air force by saturating airfields, runways, and aircraft shelters with ballistic or cruise missiles; "deafen and blind" Taiwan's command, control, communications, and intelligence infrastructure through a combination of missile strikes and electronic and information warfare attacks; bottle up and blockade Taiwan's navy in ports at Tsoying, Su'ao, Jeelung, and Kaohsiung (also effectively blockading civilian shipping in and out of the latter two ports, thus stifling the island's merchandise trade and energy imports); take control of the airspace over the Taiwan Strait and Taiwan island in order to launch amphibious landings and airdrops of paratroopers; create a *cordon sanitaire* around Taiwan to force the U.S. Navy to operate well away from the island and the Taiwan Strait (so-called sea and area denial); harass logistical supply lines of U.S. forces in the western Pacific; attack U.S. carrier strike groups (possibly with ballistic missiles); and deter U.S. (and Taiwan) forces from attacking targets on mainland China.

After a decade of intense investment and training, the PLA has made considerable progress in acquiring most of these capabilities. But it still lacks the capacity to mount an all-out conventional assault on the island, which would include landing hundreds of thousands of troops and being able to enforce a total naval blockade of the island as well as prevent American intervention. These capabilities still remain five to ten years away, in the view of knowledgeable analysts. Nonetheless, the "cross-strait balance" between Taiwanese and mainland forces has become something of a fiction, as the mainland's military capabilities now far outstrip Taiwan's.[16] The PLA has acquired dominance across a wide spectrum of capabilities across the strait. Moreover, many of the naval, missile, air, and electronic warfare assets that the PLA has acquired affect U.S. military calculations as well. The Chinese have pursued and acquired expanded littoral capacity—the capability to operate farther and farther from its coastline into the western Pacific, thus making it extremely risky for foreign forces to operate under wartime conditions in a broad area up to three hundred nautical miles from the Chinese coastline. This deterrent capacity is known as "area denial and sea denial" (AD/SD) in Pentagon parlance.

Having attained its goal of possessing a broad spectrum of war-fighting capacity against Taiwan and increasingly along its periphery, and consistent with the PLA's 2004 doctrinal *New Historic Missions of the PLA in the New Century and New Era* noted earlier, the Chinese military is turning its attention to possessing a broader range of military assets and capabilities to meet a wider range of traditional and nontraditional security threats (非传统安全威胁) and contingencies farther and farther away from China. As the U.S. Pentagon put it in its annual 2010 *Report to Congress on Military and Security Developments Involving the People's Republic of China*, "Earlier this decade, China began a new phase of military development by articulating roles and missions for the People's Liberation Army that go beyond China's immediate territorial interests. Some of these missions and associated capabilities...appear designed to improve the PLA's ability for extended-range power projection, although China's ability to sustain military power at a distance today remains limited."[17] Nongovernmental analysts are also increasingly of the view that the PLA is now preparing for missions beyond Taiwan— particularly related to energy security and expanded naval operations.[18] If this is true, the PLA may be on the cusp of going global.

For its part, the Chinese military and government rarely publicly discuss the rationale for military modernization, deployments, contingencies, or strategy. What is usually provided are boilerplate assertions by the defense minister and other officials that "China unswervingly adheres to a defense policy defensive in nature."[19] Reading China's biannual defense White Paper offers some further clues to understanding the PLA's thinking about the immediate and general security environment. For example, the 2010 version provides an official overview of how China views the international security environment:

> China is still in the period of important strategic opportunities for its development and the overall security environment for it remains favorable.... China has vigorously maintained national security and social stability, and its comprehensive national strength has stepped up to a new stage. China is meanwhile confronted by more diverse and complex security challenges.... Therefore, it faces heavy demands in safeguarding national security.... Pressure builds up in preserving China's territorial integrity and maritime rights and interests. Nontraditional security concerns, such as existing terrorism threats, energy, resources, finance, information and natural disasters, are on the rise. Suspicion about China, interference and countering moves against China from the outside are on the increase.[20]

The Chinese Defense White Paper tellingly depicts a nation and a military that perceive a complex and ever more unstable security environment. The existing and potential threats to China's national security still primarily relate to the PRC's perception of Taiwan independence and other sovereign territorial interests (now often termed China's "core interests"). The United States continues to loom large in Beijing's strategic calculations as well. But what is notable is more mention of nontraditional security challenges—ethnic separatism, counterterrorism, energy security, financial stability, cyber security, nuclear proliferation, environmental security, public health, natural disasters, transnational crime, and regional "hot spots." This diversified security agenda is notable for China, which has traditionally defined its national security interests in terms of internal stability plus threats from external military powers. Today, the former is still the case, but the latter has declined and been replaced in Beijing's worldview by a broader menu of nonstate security concerns.

Capabilities

Considering the current capabilities of the PLA, one is impressed by many developments.[21] In reviewing these specific capacities of different service sectors of the Chinese military, it is important to bear in mind that military capabilities are based on far more than weapons.[22] Most knowledgeable experts would note that "software" is at least as important as "hardware"—that is, the skills of personnel, intelligence collection, the logistics chains, communications, training, and other nonkinetic dimensions of militaries are at least as important as the lethal capabilities of weaponry. This is important to note because the Chinese military has thoroughly absorbed this lesson in its modernization program. It has invested heavily—if not primarily—in these software dimensions. In other words, the PLA has understood that "professionalization" is a fundamental precursor to "modernization."[23]

It is also worth noting the advances made in the hardware dimension, particularly China's own ability to produce increasingly sophisticated weaponry. For decades, China's defense industries have lagged far behind the state of the art (except in ballistic missiles) and been beset by numerous domestic and international impediments. Domestically, the military-industrial complex was a classic Soviet-style monopoly operating according to set plans with no market incentives and little integration with the civilian technological economy. Since the creation of the General Armaments Department in 1999, bureaucratic obstacles have been broken down and market mechanisms introduced (such as competitive contract bidding). These reforms have spurred a variety of important technological and production breakthroughs. Externally, since 1989 China has been under an arms and defense technology embargo from the United States, European Union, Australia, Canada, Japan, and South Korea. Although this embargo has definitely impeded innovation and progress, China's defense industries have benefited significantly from Russian assistance. Post-Soviet Russia has supplied China with its most advanced fighters (Su-27s, Su-30s), destroyers (Sovremenny), submarines (Kilos), tank technology (T-99), and assistance to ballistic missile modernization, satellites, and other high-tech systems. At its peak (2001–2007), Russia was supplying China with approximately $3 billion in weaponry per year. But beginning in 2008, sales began to taper off considerably—reduced to under $1 billion per year. There were several reasons for the reductions. First, contracts and production cycles had come to their natural conclusion and were not renewed. Second, there was an active debate and increasing caution in the Russian military and national security community about the strategic wisdom of arming China. Third, China's defense industries began to acquire indigenous capabilities they previously did not possess. Finally, Chinese arms producers pilfered Russian technology on a large scale.

For all of these reasons, Russian suppliers began to get cold feet and reduce their supplies to China while Chinese buyers began to ask for more. As one Russian arms seller observed:

> The nature of the relationship has changed. They used to meet with us and acted very grateful for what we were teaching them and acted very respectfully and looked upon us as their mentors. Now their demeanor is very abrasive and arrogant. They just tell us "do what we tell you and do not ask questions"—sort of like the way they talk to American officials on economic matters. The more they buy from you—in our case military hardware—the more they think they have the right to order you around.[24]

These comments are reminiscent of the fallout in Sino-Soviet relations during the late 1950s.

Despite rising Russian reservations, China's defense industries have already absorbed the "lift-off" technologies and expertise they have long sought. Though they no doubt would benefit greatly from purchases from advanced foreign suppliers (and the existing U.S. and EU arms and technology embargoes *do* hurt) and being integrated into international defense networks, China's military-industrial complex is no longer the "sick child" of the Chinese economy or the Achilles' heel of the PLA.

The Ground Forces

China possesses the world's largest military forces (2.3 million), of which 1.6 million are in the ground forces.[25] In addition, the PLA has a reserve force of about 600,000 (primarily demobilized ground forces) and can draw on the paramilitary People's Armed Police (PAP) force of approximately one million and nationwide militia numbering in the tens of millions. About half of ground force deployments remain concentrated in north and northeast China, while approximately 400,000 are deployed in the three military regions opposite Taiwan.

The ground forces underwent a substantial streamlining and downsizing during 1995–2005 in an attempt to reduce costs, improve readiness, and eliminate redundancies. Since 1985 PLA ground forces have been reduced by half. Group Armies (GAs) remain the center of the main force deployments, with eighteen currently deployed in China's seven military regions. GAs vary in size from 30,000–50,000, but for practical command purposes they are composed of divisions (10,000–12,000 personnel) and brigades (approximately 5000–6000 personnel). The legacy of large-scale GAs derives from the Soviet influence on the PLA, but in recent years an effort has been made to reduce the actual size of units under command (particularly down to the brigade level).

This reform is intended to improve mobility, jointness, and combined-arms capabilities. An increase in transport helicopters has also contributed to the ground forces' mobility. Five military regions now have ground force rapid reaction units (RRUs, known in Chinese as 快速反映部队) deployed in them, while the PLA Air Force (PLAAF) has three RRUs, and the PLAN Marine Corps has two rapid reaction brigades. The goal is that every Group Army will possess at least one RRU. Each RRU has about 35,000 soldiers and is theoretically capable of deploying anywhere in the nation within forty-eight hours. To improve rapid reaction deployment capacity, the PLA needs long-range transport aircraft and transport helicopters (still unattained capacity). Thus far these RRU forces have not deployed outside of China, although they are theoretically capable of doing so to neighboring countries if necessary. There exists *no* capability to rapidly deploy these forces anywhere else in the world. Even the ground forces that China contributes to UN peacekeeping efforts are generally transported via chartered commercial aircraft. Similarly, when China evacuated 35,000 civilian personnel from Libya in 2011 (where 75 Chinese companies had fifty contracts for major projects worth $18.8 billion[26]), it did so entirely by leasing commercial planes, ferries, and boats in neighboring countries. Although it was a very impressive display of financial firepower, and China should be credited with being able to mobilize and mount such a large-scale civilian evacuation operation, it nonetheless left many pundits in China grumbling that the nation needed to possess and use long-range military aircraft and naval ships for such occasions.

The educational levels of ground force officers and conscripts has also increased, with the goal of all rank-and-file soldiers being required to hold a high school equivalent degree and all officers required to hold a university equivalent degree. Importantly, a noncommissioned officer (NCO) corps has also been established in the PLA. This has been an effort to emulate Western armies that use NCOs for small unit leadership, and devolve decision making downward and thus increase battlefield flexibility. In the PLA personnel are also appointed as NCOs if they possess particular technical skills. There are approximately 800,000 NCOs in the ground forces today, accounting for nearly half of the rank and file.[27] Even though the ground forces have received lesser priority in recent years—as the naval, air, and missile forces received more—they remain the backbone of the PLA.

The PLA ground forces field a full range of equipment, including tanks, armored personnel carriers, artillery, surface-to-surface and surface-to-air missiles, helicopters, and unmanned aerial vehicles. The inventory numbers are large, but the quality is very uneven and much of the hardware remains antiquated. For example, of the 7,050 main battle tanks, 5,100 are of 1950s–1980s vintage. The remaining 2,000 tanks are composed of the T-96 through T-99 series (so denominated to reflect that they first came into production in 1996 and 1999 respectively), which are as good as those in some NATO countries. The ground forces also possess a large number of towed and self-propelled artillery (12,000 plus), armored personnel carriers (2,700), armored infantry fighting vehicles (2,390), antitank weapons (7,200), air defense guns (7,700), surface-to-air missiles (approximately 300), a variety of helicopters (more than 500), and other conventional land systems.[28]

In all of its weapons procurement choices nowadays, the PLA is opting for mobility and "combined arms" campaigns where different types of forces are integrated. Although it is difficult to imagine a foreign nation attempting to launch a land invasion and air attacks on the Chinese mainland, the PLA continues to train and prepare for just such a contingency. But unlike the old people's war doctrine of "luring the enemy in deep," PLA ground and air defense forces today are ready to engage the enemy at the frontier or beyond.

The PLA Air Force

Following decades of production problems, inefficiencies, and large-scale mothballing of antiquated aircraft, the PLA Air Force has made qualitative improvements in recent years. Most of the approximately 1,600 combat aircraft in China's inventory are still so-called second-generation fighters, while approximately 25 percent are of a modern world-class standard. The fighter inventory mainly includes older versions of the J-7, J-8, and Q-5, although the modern multirole J-10 and J-11 have now entered production in significant numbers. The PLAAF's most advanced fighters are the Su-27s and Su-30s purchased from Russia (about seventy of each). The indigenously built J-10 went into serial production around 2000 after two decades of design and manufacturing difficulties, and there are now approximately 260 deployed. The FB-7A (also known as the JH-7A) is an all-weather medium-range fighter-bomber, in service for a decade. On January 11,

2011, in the midst of a highly publicized visit by former U.S. Secretary of Defense Robert Gates, the PLAAF unveiled and flight-tested a new prototype stealth fighter (the J-20).[29] A delta-wing, single-pilot, twin-engine strike fighter powered by cloned Russian engines, this aircraft could be operational by 2017–2019. But if the problematic history of the J-10 is indicative, the J-20 will encounter many manufacturing problems before it is deployed. In addition to this range of fighters, the PLAAF also flies approximately 100 helicopters (in addition to those in the ground forces), 600 or more transports, 10 tankers, 82 bombers (all of old Soviet design but many with upgraded capabilities), 290 reconnaissance aircraft, 8 airborne warning and control (AWAC) aircraft, and about 200 training aircraft.

Another recent development is the PLAAF's interest in acquiring force-multiplier capabilities, particularly AWACs and in-flight refueling tankers. The PLAAF now possesses these capabilities, although in both cases in limited numbers. China has converted Russian Il-76 transports into an indigenous AWAC (of which it now possesses 8–10). The PLAAF has been known to possess in-flight refueling tankers (converted H-6 bombers) since they were seen flying over the 50th anniversary of the PRC parade in 1999, and they were on display again at the 60th anniversary parade on October 1, 2009 (which I witnessed). In the intervening decade, much progress has apparently been made in mastering in-flight refueling (a difficult maneuver). Growing numbers of tanker and fighter pilots have now gotten to grips with this procedure. At present the J-8 and J-10 fighters are capable of being refueled in-flight; the new Il-78 tankers bought from Russia can refuel the Su-27, Su-30, and J-11s, while the Chinese military media claimed that some J-8II aircraft were, for the first time, successfully refueled over water in the East China Sea.[30]

Finally, the PLAAF fields about eighty bombers of various versions of the old Hong-6. Although this plane entered production in the 1970s (having been copied from the Soviet Tupolev Tu-16 medium-range bomber), recent versions have all been upgraded for extended-range flight, possessing new electronic and electronic counterwarfare (EW and ECW) systems, able to operate in all-weather conditions, and carrying new air-to-air and air-to-ground attack cruise missiles that can strike targets up to 120 kilometers away at a speed of 0.9 Mach.

Some may also be configured for reconnaissance purposes and some reconfigured for refueling. The H-6 itself cannot be refueled in-flight. The older versions are thought to have a range of approximately 8,000 kilometers, although the newer versions may be longer-range.[31] If China is to develop a bona fide global power projection and strategic strike capability, it definitely needs to develop a modern and stealthy long-range bomber.

Thus, like the rest of the PLA, the Air Force is in transition from dated to more modern equipment, with significant progress made since 2000. This progress comes despite a decades-long history of chronic problems and failures in China's aircraft-manufacturing industry and because China has remained cut off from access to American and European weapons systems since 1989. To be sure, Russia did much to fill this void—particularly by providing "off the shelf" (already assembled) Su-27 and Su-30 fighters, but also design technologies. Thus, since about 2005 analysts have witnessed some qualitative breakthroughs in Chinese indigenous military (and civilian) aircraft production. In terms of power projection and "global reach," it must be said that the PLAAF does not possess them. Only the H-6 has extended range much beyond continental China, although with in-flight refueling some of China's fighters can now "loiter" and maintain presence over the East and South China Seas. One analyst estimates that as many as 410 of China's most modern fighters can now be refueled in-flight,[32] which if true gives the PLAAF a nascent capacity to carry out integrated air-sea campaigns up to 250–300 nautical miles from shore. But this estimate is doubtful, and in terms of real power projection beyond China's immediate periphery, this capability remains many years away for the Chinese air force.

The PLA Naval Forces

In terms of power projection, the PLAN has made the greatest advances and become a privileged service in recent years. This is the case for three principal reasons: because of the military demands of a Taiwan contingency, because of the desire to eventually establish a blue water presence throughout the western Pacific and Indian Ocean, and because of the attributes of China's shipbuilding industry. Russia has helped with supplying key destroyers, submarines, and the best supersonic antiship cruise missiles available in the world. Thus, broad military doctrine has combined with specific war-fighting scenarios and industrial capacity to make the PLAN a favored service.

The PLAN's mission has traditionally been for coastal defense—a "green water" navy that operates only up to 200 nautical miles from shore. This range includes the so-called first island chain, encompassing the Kurile Islands in the north down through Japan, the Senkaku and Ryuku Islands, Taiwan, and some of the South China Sea. But this is changing, as China is building ships and submarines with operating ranges up to 700 nautical miles and beyond. The PLAN is now a "limited blue water" navy that operates out to the second island chain, which encompasses all of the South China Sea down to Indonesia and East Timor. A third future stage will be to become a Pacific "blue water" navy that can operate to and beyond the third island chain of Guam, Australia, and New Zealand anywhere in the western Pacific Ocean. A fourth stage of development would be for the PLAN to be truly a "blue water" navy able to operate throughout the Pacific. A final fifth stage would be to have the capability to operate in any sea or ocean worldwide. The PLAN is presently in the second stage: acquiring a limited blue water capability. As it does so, it is establishing a presence in sea lanes of communication (SLOCs), dominated by the U.S. Navy for the past half-century. As such, China's growing maritime range and ambitions are altering the balance of power in the western Pacific. We are also witnessing the PLAN more frequently sailing farther and farther into the Pacific as well as through the Straits of Malacca into the Andaman Sea and Indian Ocean. Perhaps most noteworthy, as noted above, the PLAN has contributed to the multinational antipiracy force in the Gulf of Aden off the coast of Somalia. This has been an unprecedented sustained presence since 2009.

China's growing dependence on maritime trade and energy imports is fueling reconceptualization of China's maritime needs, ambitions, and capabilities. More than 90 percent of China's merchandise trade and 95 percent of its oil and gas imports travel by sea. China also derives significant income from the sea. In 2006, maritime industries accounted for $270 billion in economic output (nearly 10 percent of GDP).[33] This figure apparently includes China's shipbuilding industry, now the world's largest in terms of dead weight tonnage (DWT) annually. Qualitatively, South Korean and Japanese shipyards still produce better ships, but China is quickly catching up (although the global industry declined significantly in 2011–12). The design and construction of Chinese vessels is of world standard, but their shipbuilders have experienced many problems producing quality subsystems for merchant and naval vessels, hence having to rely heavily on imports for propulsion systems, navigation and sensor suites, and on-board weapons systems.[34] The energy import imperative is serving as a catalyst for the shipbuilding industry and tanker fleet, as presently Chinese tankers only carry half of China's oil imports.[35]

In terms of immediate naval doctrine, since the 1990s the PLAN has been building capabilities to meet two broad scenarios. First, it needs an offensive capability (particularly amphibious and subsurface) for prosecuting an all-service military campaign against Taiwan. Second, it requires a defensive capability to deny outside naval forces (notably the U.S. Navy) from being able to operate inside the first island chain, particularly around Taiwan. Both of these capabilities and missions have essentially been achieved, although the U.S. Navy remains confident that it could operate as needed should a conflict erupt. This said, the U.S. Navy does recognize the significant potential complications posed by new PLAN reach and capabilities. A particularly notable one is China's development of the DF-21D antiship ballistic missile (ASBM)—the so-called carrier killer—which flies at hypersonic speeds (Mach 5) and has a range of 1,500 kilometers. Former U.S. Commander-in-Chief of Pacific Forces (CINCPAC) Admiral Robert Willard reported to Congress in December 2010 that the missile had achieved "operational capability."[36] According to the U.S. Department of Defense, it has a range of 1,500 kilometers and is armed with a maneuverable warhead.[37] The PLAN possesses a broad range of other accurate and lethal antiship cruise missiles, but simply deploying ASBMs is certainly a significant deterrent against U.S. aircraft carrier battle groups.

Beyond the Taiwan scenario and China's expanding area of operation into the western Pacific, the longer-term driver for naval development will be China's insatiable appetite for energy imports. This is discussed in greater length in Chapter 5. Suffice it to note here that China has been a net oil importer since 1993, importing half of its total consumption of crude today (of which 40 percent comes by sea). Most of this comes from Africa and the Persian Gulf through the India Ocean and Malacca Straits, creating what President Hu Jintao reportedly described as China's "Malacca Dilemma" (the potential for supplies to be disrupted at this key strategic chokepoint in time of conflict). Moreover, China depends on maritime transportation for fully 90 percent of its imports and exports. As such, it will increasingly need to develop a naval doctrine focused on patrolling SLOCs and the transit waterways.[38] This SLOC-based naval mission might be termed a "commercial and resource" mission. But there is evidence of discussions in the Chinese naval community for building a global fleet presence.[39] The degree to which these discussions go beyond simply that—discussions—and translate into actual doctrine remains to be seen. But there is no shortage of speculation concerning China's expanding naval footprint around the globe.[40]

Turning from doctrine to capabilities, China's naval inventory today includes 78 principal surface combatant ships, composed of 13 destroyers and 65 frigates. In addition, there are 211 patrol and coastal combatant craft, 73 mine warfare vessels, 210 amphibious landing ships and craft, 205 logistics and support ships, and 71 submarines.[41] Many ships (particularly frigates) have been retrofitted and upgraded over time, but many new ships have also been commissioned. A limited number of these vessels can be considered blue water (open ocean) capable; the vast majority still constitute a coastal force that operates in green water, as described above. The most advanced destroyers are the four Russian Sovremenny-class guided missile destroyers (known as Hangzhou class). Each carries eight SS-N-22 ("Sunburn") sea-skimming antiship missiles, which are among the most advanced in the world. The Sunburns were designed specifically to penetrate the defenses of U.S. Navy Aegis destroyers and aircraft carrier battle groups. The PLAN has also commissioned two new Luhai-class guided missile destroyers, the *Shenzhen* and the *Yantai*. Displacing nearly 7,000 tons, these indigenously produced ships are a smorgasbord of imported armaments and equipment; they are powered by Ukrainian gas turbine engines and carry German electrical systems, French radars, Russian sonars, Russian helicopters, and Italian torpedoes. They also incorporate stealthlike features on the bridge, similar to the French Lafayette-class frigates. The PLAN also possesses two Type 052 Luhu-class destroyers, which are composed of a similar set of hybrid systems. Several new, very modern destroyers are in sea trials or under construction, including many with stealth attributes. Besides these vessels, the rest of the PLAN's 57 surface combatants are older, but retrofitted, Luda-class destroyers and Jiangwei and Jianghu-class frigates.

China's long-awaited first aircraft carrier began its sea trials in August 2011. Formerly named the *Riga*, the former Soviet-era Kuznetsov-class carrier was to be the most advanced carrier in the Soviet fleet.[42] The Ukraine purchased it from the Soviet Union just before the USSR's collapse in 1991 but was unable to finish construction and subsequently stripped the ship of its weapons and engines and put it up for sale. A Chinese company bought it from the Ukraine in 1998 for $20 million. The carrier was then towed to dry dock in Dalian, where it underwent a decade of retrofitting. Slightly larger than the Charles de Gaulle class of French carriers but considerably smaller than the Nimitz class of American carriers, the *Liaoning* is 300 meters long, weighs 60,000 tons, can cruise up to 31 knots, and has a sloped ramp for launching planes (it will likely carry 25–35 planes). Adding an aircraft carrier to the PLAN fleet has been a long-dreamed-of goal. Lt. General Qi Jianguo, assistant chief of the General Staff, told the Hong Kong *Commercial Daily* that, "All of the great nations in the world own aircraft carriers—they are symbols of a great nation."[43] General Li went on to note that, "Even after the aircraft carrier was deployed, it would definitely not sail to other countries' territorial waters." But he added: "We are now facing heavy pressure in the oceans—whether in the South China Sea, East China Sea, Yellow Sea or the Taiwan Strait."[44]

Last, but not least, the PLAN has a substantial and diverse submarine force. Even though many of the known subs in the fleet are old Romeo and Ming class—which are slow, noisy, and easy targets for modern antisubmarine warfare (ASW)—the PLAN has embarked on a substantial buying and building program in recent years. It has bought twelve Kilo-class diesel-electric attack submarines from Russia since the mid-1990s. Although the PLAN has experienced some maintenance problems with these, the Kilos are quiet, relatively fast, well armed, and can stay submerged for significant periods. Perhaps as important have been the very capable, adequately quiet, domestically developed Song-Yuan-Shang-and Jin-class submarines. The most noteworthy of these are the Type 093 and 094 programs (dubbed the Shang- and Jin-class respectively). The nuclear-powered 093 was first launched in December 2002, with two currently in service.[45] It is expected to replace the five Han-class and one Xia-class nuclear powered and nuclear armed strategic submarines (SSBNs). The 094 is now in production, with two having entered service and five more under construction. It will likely carry twelve 12,000-kilometer-range JL-2 submarine-launched ballistic missiles (SLBMs)—capable of striking the East Coast of the continental United States—once these missiles go into production (they are behind schedule). The 093 carries a similar complement of SLBMs, but with shorter 7,000 kilometer strike range (capable of striking the west coast of the United States). A follow-on type 095 SSBN is thought to be under development, with perhaps five to be put to sea in the coming years.[46] Clearly the Chinese are prioritizing submarine production, and this too is contributing to the altered balance of military power in the western Pacific. They also present a significant danger to both military and commercial vessels in time of conflict.

All in all, the PLAN is making some significant advances and China's shipbuilding industry has demonstrated the capacity to build at a rapid rate in recent years. Construction and deployments at this pace will give the PLAN expanded reach and presence in the western Pacific and beyond over the decades to come. To the extent that China's military "goes global" in the future, it will be the navy that does so. But to do so requires not only a full blue water capable oceangoing fleet, but a number of other key factors: access to neutral ports and airfields, perhaps naval bases on foreign soil, prepositioned equipment, long logistics supply chains and communications, underway replenishment, extended deployments, access to medical facilities and care, satellite communications, supply ships, and long-range air replenishment supply.[47]

This list of necessary capabilities for any navy operating out-of-area (away from immediate littoral) is daunting, and a good reminder of just how much would be required of China and the PLAN if it truly wanted to establish a global projection capability. Nonetheless, China is likely to incrementally pursue a broader area of operation for its navy in the years to come, particularly into the western Pacific and to Hawaii in the east and through the Indian Ocean to the east coast of Africa to the west. As one Chinese analyst noted, "Access rights for China around the Indian Ocean is [*sic*] a *must*, but we will not build a series of naval bases."[48]

Although the PLAN may have such aspirations, at present it is only the missile, space, and cyber forces that are capable of projecting power globally.

The Missile Forces

China's missile forces (known as the Second Artillery) have been the shining success story in the Chinese military. This was necessitated both by circumstance (Nikita Khrushchev's 1959 decision to discontinue support for China's atomic weapons development and delivery programs) and by skill (the knowledge of Chinese scientists). It is also the story of what sustained resources and political protection will do for the development of a high-priority military objective.[49] For six decades, beginning in the late 1950s, China's military-industrial complex has been producing a range of ballistic missiles, as well as the conventional and nuclear warheads deployed on them. Today China possesses a full range of short-range (SRBM), intermediate-range (IRBM), intercontinental-range (ICBM), and submarine-launched ballistic missiles (SLBM).

China now has a large and diversified inventory of deployed ballistic missiles, totaling approximately 1,370: 66 ICBMs, 118 IRBMs, 1,150 SRBMs, and 36 SLBMs.[50] The intercontinental- and intermediate-range missiles are deployed around the country, while the bulk of SRBMs are deployed on the eastern seaboard within range of Taiwan. The rail and road mobility of all of these missiles makes it very difficult to monitor their locations. In recent years, a priority has been placed on making the land-based missile forces more survivable, more mobile (and therefore harder to detect and thus more survivable), solid-fueled (and therefore much quicker to launch), and possessing smaller, more accurate, and more potent warheads. For example, the road-mobile DF-31 and DF-31A ICBMs have entered service; they possess a range of 11,200 kilometers and can thus reach most locations within the continental

United States. It is likely, but unclear, that these also are fitted with multiple independently targeted reentry vehicle (MIRV) warheads. It is important to note that only the SLBMs and ICBMs carry nuclear warheads (and some SLBMs may be fitted with conventional munitions). It is not known for sure, but China likely has a stockpile of 400–600 nuclear warheads—but when the aforementioned DF-31, DF-41, and JL-2 intercontinental missiles are deployed with multiple warheads, this number could double or triple.[51]

Taken together, the Second Artillery (China's missile force command) possesses the full spectrum of offensive missile forces as well as a bona fide second-strike nuclear deterrent. Numerically it remains the third-largest missile force in the world, after the United States and Russia, but both its quantity and quality made significant strides in recent years. The total number of deployed missiles has roughly doubled since 2005.

The PLA recently supplemented its strengths in ballistic missiles by adding a cruise missile capability to its inventory. Even though air- and sea-launched cruise missiles have been in the PLA's arsenal for a number of years, and more advanced versions have been transferred from Russia in recent years, China is now building and deploying its own land attack cruise missiles (LACMs). Several hundred LACMs are deployed, mainly opposite Taiwan. Longer-range LACMs are under development.

China's ballistic missile capability certainly qualifies it as a global power. This is also true of space and cyber capabilities, to which we turn next.

Space-Based Capabilities

China is becoming a major space power. In 2003, it became the third nation to send a human into space, as Taikonaut Yang Liwei orbited the earth fourteen times aboard the *Shenzhou V* spacecraft. This was followed in 2005 with the *Shenzhou VI* mission, when two taikonauts circumnavigated the earth for five days in low orbit. In September 2008, *Shenzhou VII* was launched with three aboard, and they successfully completed their three-day mission in a slightly higher orbit (including a first spacewalk). In 2011 China's first orbiting space station, the

Tiangong I, was launched. It was equipped with a docking port, to which the unmanned *Shenzhou VIII* successfully rendezvoused.[52] In June 2012 *Shenzhou IX* successfully ferried three taikonauts (including one female, for the first time) to dock with the *Tiangong I* space station. This was a significant achievement for China's space program.

China has a broad-gauged space program. In 2006, the China National Space Administration White Paper listed its short-term goals: to build a long-term earth observation system; to set up an independent satellite telecommunications network; to establish an independent satellite navigation and positioning system; to provide commercial launch services; to set up a remote sensing system; to study space science such as microgravity, space materials, life sciences, and astronomy; and to plan for exploration of the moon.[53] Among the longer-term goals were to establish a crewed space station, send crewed missions to the moon, and to establish a crewed lunar base.

This makes clear that China has serious and systematic ambitions in manned and unmanned space exploration. It clearly has a goal to put men on the moon, perhaps staying for weeks, sometime around 2020. It will launch its first lunar probe in 2013 with a rover to explore the lunar surface. Similar exploratory plans exist for Mars and Venus.

In addition to the manned space program, China is developing a significant military satellite program. China sent its first satellite into orbit in 1970 and since that time has launched nearly 130 satellites, currently with 69 in orbit.[54] China also has an active antisatellite weapons program,[55] as demonstrated in 2007 when it shot a meteorological satellite out of low earth orbit with a ballistic missile. As the U.S. Department of Defense 2010 report on the Chinese military noted, "China is developing the ability to attack an adversary's space assets, accelerating the militarization of space."[56] The United States is very concerned about this growing Chinese antisatellite capacity, given the heavy reliance of the U.S. military and intelligence community on such space-based assets.

Cyber Forces

The other domain in which China possesses global reach is its cyber capabilities. China has the capacity to strike anywhere on the planet, and it has done so with increasing frequency in recent years. In November 2011, the Office of the National Counterintelligence Executive, which reports to the U.S. government's Director of National Intelligence, issued a stinging public report to Congress accusing China and Russia of being the major perpetrators of cyber attacks on U.S. private sector companies (corporate espionage) and U.S. government agencies.[57] The U.S.-China Economic and Security Review Commission, a congressional body, noted in its 2009 Annual Report to Congress: "Malicious cyber activity has the potential to destroy critical infrastructure, disrupt commerce and banking systems, and compromise sensitive defense and military data. Malicious cyber incidents are on the rise, and attacks against U.S. Government computer systems illustrate the severity of the problem."[58] The report went on to note that the Department of Defense reported nearly 90,000 attempted attacks on DOD computer systems during 2009 alone.

There are a variety of Chinese cyber operations. These include offensive information warfare (IW) aimed at attacking other nations' critical military, intelligence, government, infrastructural, and commercial infrastructure; defensive IW, aimed at protecting China's own military and governmental computer systems, as well as critical infrastructure like the State Grid; commercial espionage, in which foreign companies' computer systems are penetrated and technologies and other trade secrets stolen; computer hacking to penetrate, without disabling, other nations' critical computer systems; "integrated network electronic warfare," which integrates electronic and computer network warfare; and penetration of private individual computers and financial accounts. Chinese cyber operations are active in all of these areas and others. In fact, China is widely known to be the most aggressive cyber state in the world today. An important Canadian study described Chinese cyber espionage as a "major global concern."[59] Cyber intrusions are but one element of China's increasingly sophisticated global espionage operation.[60] Many foreign government organs have reported attempted or successful cyber attacks originating from China.[61] Many foreign corporations have also been targeted, not the least of which was Google. In 2010 Google announced that its Gmail accounts had been hacked, it was no longer going to put up with censorship of the China portal Google.cn, and was going to cease operations in mainland China and operate only from Hong Kong. Subsequently a compromise was worked out whereby Google continued limited operations in mainland China. In addition to Google's Gmail accounts, those of many international China experts have been hacked in recent years, along with human rights and Tibet activists.

To be sure, China's international cyber hacking and espionage does not all originate with the PLA, but some of it does. The PLA General Staff Department's Third and Fourth Department are primarily responsible.[62] The PLA has organized a number of "cyber militias," such as the Nanhao Group, that are both sophisticated and aggressive in their operations.[63] The Ministry of State Security (MSS) and other intelligence-gathering organs are also involved.

In today's globalized world computers are ubiquitous and synonymous with globalization. There are few countries that have put as much effort and resources into simultaneously controlling cyber activities domestically and mastering intrusive techniques abroad as has China. In this regard, China's cyber warriors have certainly "gone global."

Peacekeeping Operations

Another dimension of China's global security impact is its contributions to UNPKO.[64] The origins of China's involvement date to the 1989–1992 period, when it first dispatched military observers to Africa and the Middle East, and military engineering corps to Cambodia. Since that time, China's contributions of personnel (but not budget, where it is the seventh-largest assessed financial contributor) to UNPKO operations has grown dramatically and positively. By 2010, China had contributed a total of 17,390 military personnel to nineteen UNPKO missions.[65] By the end of 2011, China had 1,845 military personnel and 91 police participating in ongoing missions.[66] China's deployments today are primarily in Africa (Liberia, Democratic Republic of the Congo, Côte d'Ivoire, southern Sudan and Darfur region), and in Lebanon. China now ranks as the 16th largest national contributor of personnel (out of 119 contributing countries), but first among permanent members of the UN Security Council. These are mainly in the form of logistical, engineering, transport, or medical personnel, although China has also contributed paramilitary

People's Armed Police, military observers, civilian police, and land-mine-clearing personnel.[67] China has yet to contribute combat forces. Although not a UNPKO mission, as discussed above, China is a contributor to the antipiracy and escort operations in the Gulf of Aden and waters off Somalia.[68]

China has received very high marks and positive evaluations for the quality and the integrity of its personnel and contributions to PKO operations (although their general inability to speak languages other than Chinese is seen as a detriment). They are increasingly involved in mission leadership and decision making. In a limited fashion, China has also contributed to the delivery (mainly by sea) of equipment and personnel of other contributing nations' PKO forces.

All in all, China's contributions to UNPKO have been a definite "net plus" for the UN, China, and the recipient countries. It is a tangible—perhaps *the* most tangible—indication of China's contribution to global governance. China's overseas disaster relief is also a significant contribution. Since the 2004 Asian tsunami, China has also contributed personnel and resources to disaster relief in Asia and other parts of the world.

Military Exchanges, Exercises, and Assistance

China is also stepping up its global military diplomacy, strategic dialogues, joint exercises, training programs, and arms transfers.

China places a great deal of importance on bilateral military-to-military exchanges, or what it calls "military diplomacy" (军事外交).[69] The PLA participates in military exchanges with more than 150 nations, having some 400 or more "contacts" annually.[70] China's biannual defense White Papers show that the PLA sent out official delegations to visit sixty countries every year from 2001 to 2007 (then it dipped to forty in 2007–08) while receiving 60–90 foreign military delegations per year. Since then they have been averaging about a hundred per year in both directions. Many of these visits are fairly routine: for consultations, visiting military academies, occasionally observing an exercise, and exchanging views on regional and global strategic issues. There are various types of military exchanges: high-level exchanges; operations, logistics, and training exchanges;

military medicine; ship visits; international conferences; defense and security dialogues; educational exchanges and training courses; service exchanges (army, navy, air force); joint exercises; and exchanges from specific departments and units in the PLA.[71] In addition, China posts more than 300 military attachés in 109 countries, while hosting 102 foreign military attaché offices in China.[72]

In recent years China has begun to increase its joint bilateral and multilateral military exercises, abandoning a previous self-imposed ban. These are primarily naval search-and-rescue and ground-based counterterrorism operations, although some maritime exercises are for patrolling and surveillance. China and Russia have held two large-scale multiservice exercises in recent years. Altogether, between 2005 and 2011, China's Defense Minister Liang Guanglie reported that China had participated in more than "forty joint military training and exercises in the land, sea, and air domains with more than twenty countries."[73]

China also maintains "defense dialogues" or "strategic dialogues" with twenty-six countries,[74] including the United States, Russia, Japan, India, Great Britain, France, Germany, Australia, Brazil, Egypt, European Union, Indonesia, Israel, Jordan, African Union, Gulf Cooperation Council, Mexico, Nigeria, Pakistan, Peru, Portugal, South Africa, South Korea, Syria, Turkey, and the United Arab Emirates. These began in 2005 and are now viewed by China as important venues for confidence building.[75] They usually (but not always) include PLA personnel. Their content varies by partner country, but they are generally surveys of regional and global security and foreign policy trends.

A less formal means of defense communication are telephonic "hotlines" established between the PLA Ministry of Defense and their counterparts in foreign countries (the United States and Russia are most noteworthy). In the case of South Korea, there are further secure telephone links with China's military regions and the navy and air force.[76]

The PLA is also "going global" by training an increasing number of foreign officers in Chinese military academies and institutions, and it is stepping up the number of PLA officers it sends to study in foreign institutions as well.[77] From 2006 to 2008, the PLA dispatched more than 900 military students abroad. Since the 1990s the majority have gone to Russia for training, often linked with training for specific arms transfer programs.[78] Altogether, official sources indicate that a total of about 4000 military personnel have been trained in China,[79] although China's defense minister provides a much loftier figure, claiming, "Over the years, we trained over 50,000 military personnel for over 130 countries."[80] Official figures reveal that China has trained about 10,000 foreign personnel from 2003 to 2010.[81] The PLA has 67 military academies today, about half of which are open to train foreign military officers.[82] The branch campus of the PLA National Defense University (NDU) at Changping, outside Beijing, is largely devoted to this purpose. It is here that the annual International Security Symposium is convened, drawing officers from nearly eighty nations.[83] The PLA University of Foreign Languages in Luoyang, a primary training facility for PLA intelligence personnel, has opened its doors to foreign officers in recent years.[84] The PLA Air Force Command College in Beijing trains not only pilots but also engineers, while the PLA Navy Command College in Nanjing offers courses for commanding officers, in radar and sonar. Other staff colleges offer training in telecommunications, artillery, armor, military medicine, foreign languages, demining, and engineering.[85] Commanding officers normally study for one year, although the technical training courses can vary from three months to two or three years. Language differences can be an obstacle, admitted Admiral Guan Youfei of the Ministry of Defense in an interview, but the PLA offers training in English, French, and Spanish. As a result, many officers from Africa take courses in French, those from Latin America in Spanish, and those from elsewhere in English. Most students come from developing countries. For these nations, China offers a useful option in terms of cost and effectiveness. Sometimes this training accompanies China's arms transfers to developing countries.

Arms Transfers

China is becoming a major seller of weapons abroad, ranking fourth internationally in 2010 according to the Stockholm International Peace Research Institute (SIPRI), selling approximately $1.4 billion worth of weapons and equipment during 2009.[86] China's sales began to pick up in 2008, when it ranked ninth and sold roughly half of its 2010 totals. Another source, the U.S. Congressional Research Service,

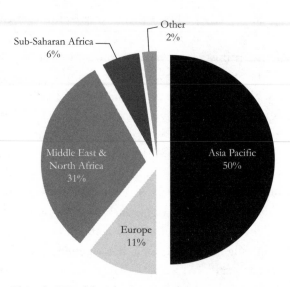

FIGURE 7.2 China's Worldwide Arms Sales, 2005–2010
Source: U.S. Department of Defense, *Annual Report to Congress: Military and Security Developments Involving the People's Republic of China,* 2011, p. 68.

has a similar estimate of Chinese arms transfers of $7.5 billion during the period 2006–2009.[87] The U.S. Department of Defense claims that China sold $11 billion in weapons from 2005 to 2010, as described in Figure 7.2.[88]

To be sure, China still lags far behind the world's two leading arms traders—the United States and Russia—but Beijing has now overtaken the United Kingdom and France. This trend is likely to continue in the coming years, with China likely surpassing Germany for third place. Yet once China does so, it may remain there indefinitely. The reason is that the United States and Russia have long-developed and carefully cultivated markets in the Middle East, South and East Asia, Latin America, and other newly industrializing country markets; but China can be expected to garner a larger and larger share of developing country markets over time.

Since the 1998 State Council and Central Military Commission divestiture directive, which was intended to divest the PLA of its commercial activities, it is no longer directly involved in arms sales and transfers; these are now largely administered by the State Administration for Science, Technology, and Industry for National

Defense (国家国防科技工业局). "During these twelve years [1998–2010], the PLA has not received a penny from such sales," claimed Rear Admiral Guan Youfei, deputy director of the Foreign Affairs Office of the Ministry of National Defense, in my interview with him.[89] Admiral Guan further indicated that there are ten corporate conglomerates under this bureau that are involved with arms production, transfer, and posttransfer assistance, and that cover all costs and derive any profit. But because these companies typically offer arms at reduced "friendship" prices, "China's position in the international market is low," opined Admiral Guan.

For the most part, China no longer engages in export of large platforms of conventional weapons, and it has curtailed its assistance to missile and nuclear weapons programs, so as to comply with its obligations under the Non-Proliferation Treaty (NPT) and its de facto adherence to the Missile Technology Control Regime (MTCR). In 1997 China also promulgated the official document *Export Controls for Military Goods*, which controls exports of certain types of equipment. Most of its exports are light weapons and mortars, ammunition, trucks and transport equipment, radar, and ship-to-ship and surface-to-air missiles. On occasion China sells armored personnel carriers and light tanks, and it is trying to market the export version of the J-10 fighter and light training aircraft.

Chinese arms are relatively cheap, so they appeal to developing countries in Africa and South Asia. Pakistan remains China's largest arms client, but the rest of China's client base is diversified. During 2006–2010 China exported conventional military weapons to Algeria, Argentina, Bangladesh, Benin, Bolivia, Cambodia, Chad, Colombia, Congo, Ecuador, Egypt, Gabon, Ghana, Indonesia, Iran, Kenya, Laos, Malaysia, Mexico, Myanmar, Namibia, Nepal, Niger, Nigeria, Pakistan, Peru, Rwanda, Saudi Arabia, Sierra Leone, Sri Lanka, Sudan, Tanzania, Thailand, Timor Leste, Turkey, Uganda, Venezuela, Zambia, and Zimbabwe.[90]

What does China have to offer and sell?[91] In terms of aircraft, the JF-17 "Thunder" fighter (which is currently co-produced with Pakistan) is becoming the mainstay of the Pakistani Air Force and is appealing to countries such as Egypt and Azerbaijan as well. At $15 million per plane, and for countries that do not need advanced fighters, the single-engine

JF-17 (also known as the FC-1) is a lightweight multirole fighter that has good versatility for both high-altitude and ground-attack modes. For countries that need a more advanced fighter capacity, China is developing the J-11B (a Chinese clone of the Russian Su-27SK) and export version of Chinese-made J-10. The F-7MG is adapted from the Soviet MiG-21 but with a larger wing; China has sold more than a hundred of the F-7 to Bangladesh, Namibia, Nigeria, Pakistan, and Sri Lanka. The K-8 trainer jet has been a very popular export over the past decade, with customers including Pakistan, Ghana, Namibia, Sri Lanka, Sudan, Zambia, Zimbabwe, and Venezuela. China has also sold MA-60 and Y-12 transport aircraft to Ghana, Nepal, and Uganda. Other than aircraft, China's market niche includes helicopter-carrying frigates, patrol boats, antiship missiles, surface-to-air missiles, antitank missiles, multiple rocket launchers, helicopters, tanks, armored personnel carriers, radars, small arms, and ammunition.[92]

Occasionally Chinese weapons wind up in the hands of regimes under international embargo or sanction—such as Iran, Libya, Myanmar, or Zimbabwe. In the case of Zimbabwe, in mid-2008 there was an internationally reported case of South African port authorities intercepting a shipment of Chinese arms (77 tons of AK-47 ammunition, rocket-propelled grenades, and mortar rounds worth $1.245 million) bound for the landlocked country. After holding the ship and crew in port for a week, South Africa finally had to return them to China with the arms still on board.[93] Today, the United Nations enforces arms embargoes against thirteen countries or groups (including the Taliban, al-Qaeda, and seven African countries). Generally speaking, once a nation is banned *by the United Nations* from receiving arms from abroad, China complies with the ban. Such was the case with Iran, a country with which China had been the principal external source of supply.[94] Since 2010, though, China has seemed to comply with UN Security Council resolutions and desisted from its previous arms exports and broader assistance to Iran's military-industrial complex. But even the case of Iran is murky. The case of Libya is also cloudy. During the moribund days of Col. Muammar Qaddafi's regime in the summer of 2011, Qaddafi's representatives went to Beijing in search of weapons. They met with unnamed Chinese arms-trading companies, allegedly without the knowledge of the government (according to government spokeswoman Jiang Yu), and negotiated a $200 million arms package. The rebel forces that overthrew the Qaddafi regime reported finding evidence that some of the arms were delivered, despite UN sanctions, although the Chinese government denied it.[95] In the case of China's arms transfers in sub-Saharan Africa (and sanctioned nations) the record is clearer: China has not only violated UN sanctions but sought to cover it up. United Nations investigators have uncovered Chinese light arms in conflict zones in the Democratic Republic of Congo, Ivory Coast, Somalia, and Sudan. Worse still, a review of Chinese compliance by SIPRI and reported in the *Washington Post* uncovered evidence that Chinese diplomats have repeatedly sought to intimate UN arms experts and attempted to block required annual reports to the Security Council.[96]

But for countries in which there is no UN sanction in place—only sanctions from individual nations—China feels no compulsion to comply. Such is the case with Myanmar. Beijing's supplies of military equipment to the junta in Yangon seem to have dissipated considerably since the 1980s and 1990s,[97] although it reportedly still continues in the form of anti-riot equipment, trucks, armored vehicles, and light weapons.[98] Harder to track, but of growing importance, is China's military-industrial and dual-use technology assistance to these countries, which helps recipients modernize their own indigenous defense industrial capacities. Again, this has particularly been the case with Iran. Tracking these transfers abroad is not easy. Since 2008 China has begun to comply with and contribute some (incomplete) data to the UN Arms Register.

We can expect arms sales and defense technology transfers to expand in the next few years, as China looks for more export markets while their generally low cost appeals to developing countries. One sign of China's growing interest in expanding its arms sales has been its marketing practices. Previously Chinese companies exhibited their weapons only at China's own Zhuhai Air Show, but beginning in 2010 they began to market their fighters at the Dubai and Farnborough (UK) International Air Shows.[99] With $88.7 billion in orders at stake at the 2009 Farnborough Show, Chinese defense contractors wanted to get a piece of the action. They also maintain a regular presence at African, Asian, and Middle Eastern arms sales conventions.

China's Future Global Security Role

China's future global security footprint will continue to evolve in all of these areas. Above all, we can expect continued and deepened modernization of China's military forces and capabilities. By 2020 it is quite conceivable that China will advance to possess the second most comprehensively capable military in the world after the United States. Although it will remain *far* behind the capabilities of the United States, it will likely pull ahead of Russia, the UK, Japan, Germany, and France—all roughly clustered together in terms of military spending and capabilities. In some areas, China's capacities have already pulled ahead, but over the next decade it will comprehensively do so (unless Russia undertakes a large-scale modernization program). Its nuclear weapons arsenal will, in particular, increase in number and improve in quality.

In the end, however, *all* of China's involvement in global security will be shaped by its own calculations of national interests (no matter what the inducements and pressure from the international community). Here, Beijing's continuing ambivalence over international involvements and self-preoccupation with domestic development and protecting its irredentist interests (Taiwan, Tibet, maritime claims) will continue to have a limiting effect on China's global security role.

8

Coping with a Globalized China

China has become a major player in the global system, highly interdependent with the rest of the world. China's growing weight means that its every action is scrutinized internationally, and its foreign and domestic policies invariably affect other countries. Hence, it is in China's own interests to take into account the impact of its policies on other countries.

—SINGAPORE PRIME MINISTER LEE HSIEN LOONG, 2012[1]

China's position is far behind the United States. We are not a peer of the United States. We have been elevated [in the eyes of others] against our will. We have no intention to compete for global leadership.

—VICE FOREIGN MINISTER CUI TIANKAI, 2012[2]

China is rising, but we are a lonely rising power.

—PROFESSOR ZHU FENG, Peking University, 2011[3]

NOW THAT CHINA IS going global in all the ways described in previous chapters, the pertinent questions are: What does it mean for the world, and how should the world respond? This final chapter considers these questions.

To look forward, it is instructive to first look backward. China's relationship with the international community during the modern era has always displayed a certain ambivalence and has revealed a repetitive set of choices for China's rulers: To what extent should China integrate into the world order, on what terms, and what is the likely impact on China's own domestic order? These questions have endured over time.

The Past Shapes the Future

Historically, China's traditional sense of centrality and greatness, as well as its insularity and self-preoccupation, preordained how the "Middle Kingdom" (中国) should interact with the outside world. The imperial Chinese state traditionally managed its relations with peripheral peoples through a series of elaborate ritual practices.[4] It dealt with those to the north and northwest (Mongols, Zunghars, Turkics, and Russians) through the Office of Border Affairs (*Lifan Yuan*), which was established in 1638. Contact with European missionaries and traders, arriving from the west in the eighteenth century, were handled mainly by the imperial household staff of the Qing emperor. Interactions with Koreans and those on the southern periphery were managed by the Ministry of Rituals of the imperial government, which managed the "tribute missions" to the imperial court. In 1861, the Qing consolidated these various mechanisms into a single Office for the Management of the Business of All Foreign Countries, or the *Zongli Yamen* (总理衙门).

What all of these methods to manage foreigners had in common was that they were to be integrated into Chinese rituals and practices, not vice versa. This was based on the idea of Chinese centrality and superiority. Invariably the foreigners played along and conceded to these practices. When they did not, such as Lord Macartney's infamous embassy of 1793, the Chinese proved uninterested in accommodating foreign preferences. This disjuncture triggered the subsequent 150 years of "shame and humiliation," as Chinese communist lore describes it. The Western world, and then Japan, entered China, forcefully "opening" the country to international commerce and religion. The moribund Qing state tried different methods during the Self-Strengthening Movement (1861–1895) to stave off foreign encroachment and modernize itself. All failed. The Qing gradually disintegrated and imploded in 1911. The imperial system that had endured in one form or another since 221 B.C. was replaced by a republican constitutional government in 1912. But this did not end China's brutish encounter with foreign imperialism.

This prolonged period of China's subjugation—which lasted until 1945 and Mao Zedong described as "semicolonialism"—gave rise to the birth of modern Chinese nationalism in the aftermath of the May Fourth Movement (1919) and eventually the victory of the CCP in 1949.

Thereafter, the world turned its back on China and China turned its back on the world during the Cold War, slipping the nation back into its more comfortable state of insularity and autarky. It was not until the 1978 "reform and opening" policies of Deng Xiaoping that China seriously began the process of integrating itself, really for the first time, into the international system.

Now, more than three decades later, on many levels and in many spheres, China has dramatically opened itself to the world and become integrated with the various structures and processes of the global order. The preceding chapters detail the manifest ways in which this integration has proceeded—but, at the same time, it shows clearly that this remains a *limited integration*. It is the central argument of this book that China remains highly ambivalent about its relations with the world and has only partially integrated into the international system. China is particularly ambivalent about the international rules and norms largely set by the West after 1945. Beijing is not comfortable with this "liberal international order"—despite having benefited greatly from it—and increasingly seeks to either amend or ignore it.

What Kind of Global Power Is China?

In the previous chapters we have carefully examined aspects of China's global presence and have concluded that, in each aspect, China is only a *partial power*.

Although Chinese diplomacy is active, I conclude that it is *not influential* in many parts of the world or on major international issues. China is not shaping events and actively contributing to solving problems. Rather, it is quite risk-averse and narrowly self-interested. Chinese officials are often more interested in the symbols than the substance of diplomacy, which is designed primarily to serve domestic economic development and protect the image and longevity of the ruling Communist Party. For all these reasons, I conclude that China "punches way below its weight" in international diplomacy. Beijing is not doing enough to shoulder its appropriate share of international responsibility and to be a world leader.

China is certainly more than a partial power in the economic realm—in terms of its global trade profile and energy and raw material imports—but the global impact of outbound investment and multi-national corporations has been fairly minimal to date (albeit growing). Similarly, China's aid programs are helpful in some regions, but at the same time they have undercut international donor standards and rank well below the ODA contributions of many other nations. So the economic picture is also mixed.

Consistent with the partial power thesis, we also found various aspects of China's global cultural footprint to be expanding: in tourism, education, art sales and exchanges, literature and film, fashion and design, and sports. But in all of these categories (save, perhaps, tourism and art purchasing), the global impact has been relatively minimal. This is an important finding for China's (lack of) soft power. China is *not* a magnet that attracts others. No nation seeks to emulate the political or social systems, the culture is *sui generis*, and the economic experience—though admirable—is not transferable. But this has not deterred the Chinese government from pouring huge resources into a multidimensional and multinational effort to boost the country's international image; yet, to date, these efforts have demonstrated little payoff.

Despite a rapidly modernizing military, we saw that China still has no conventional global power-projection capacities. Within the Asia-Pacific region, though, China's growing military (particularly naval) capabilities are expanding its footprint—which, in turn, is affecting the strategic balance of power in the region.

Along all of these dimensions, I therefore conclude that China is a *partial power*. It is nowhere near being in the league of the United States, either in individual categories or collectively—and therefore may better be thought as a "middle power" and regional power like Australia, Brazil, Britain, France, India, Japan, or Russia.

I further conclude from this study that China is, in essence, a very narrow-minded, self-interested, realist state, seeking only to maximize its own national interests and power. It cares little for global governance and enforcing global standards of behavior (except its much-vaunted doctrine of noninterference in the internal affairs of countries). Its economic policies are mercantilist and its diplomacy is passive. China is also a lonely strategic power, with *no allies* and experiencing distrust and strained relations with much of the world. At the same time, China displays periodic evidence of being a dissatisfied, frustrated, aggrieved, and angry nation that seeks redress against those that have wronged it in the past or with which it has disagreements at present. China carries a heavy burden of aggrievement and revaunchist nationalism from history that does not serve it well, currently or in the future. Further, its domestic political regime, led by the Chinese Communist Party, is insecure and deeply worried about its own longevity. After several years of adaptive policies, the party-state has reverted to atrophy.[5] Domestic social instabilities abound, threatening the ruling CCP from many directions.[6] China's occasionally assertive and truculent external posture is rooted in its domestic insecurities, rising nationalism, and historic experiences.

For all of these reasons, I argue that China is not ready for global leadership. Even if it were so inclined philosophically (and it is not), the evidence presented in this study has shown that the nation is far from possessing the tools to be a global great power. If these conclusions are correct, they should cause some reconsideration of common assumptions and predictions about China's rise and potential impact on the world.

Rethinking the Rise of China

This view of China's limited international impact has implications for the world and the United States. China is certainly not about to "rule the world," in the estimate of Martin Jacques's recent popular book.[7] To the contrary, as Joseph Nye has observed: "The greatest danger we have is overestimating China and China overestimating itself. China is nowhere near close to the United States. So this magnification of China, which creates fear in the U.S. and hubris in China, is the biggest danger we face."[8] I could not agree more with Professor Nye.

What this suggests is a different kind of "rising" China than is usually discussed in the academic literature and media. Considerable ink has been spilled and considerable speculation spent over the prospects and implications of China's rise. International relations scholars are generally of three theoretical views on the question, paralleling the three principal schools of IR theory: realism, liberalism, and constructivism.

Realists view China through a structural lens that emphasizes system polarity and asymmetrical relations between the principal established and rising power. In various ways, realists argue that China's rise inevitably and unacceptably challenges the United States and that the two are locked in a zero-sum contest for regional and global hegemony. In the words of Princeton professor Aaron Friedberg, it is a "contest for supremacy" and a "struggle for mastery in Asia."[9] What realists differ over are the modalities and timing of the challenge and the policy prescriptions for sustaining American primacy and countering the destabilizing effects of a rising China. As such, they see China as the "expanding" and "revisionist" power, while the United States is assumed to be the "status quo" power that must "respond" to this rise and occasional provocations. The counseled response by most realists is to sustain American primacy through "balancing" and "strategic hedging" tactics by the United States together with its Asian allies and partners.[10] Some realists, though, advocate a more accommodating posture,[11] while others believe that the strategic competition can be managed.[12] Realists tend to focus almost exclusively on the security and military variable while neglecting the economic and cultural variables that enmesh China in webs of interdependence with other nations. Many realists further argue that *transitions* from one leading power to another are likely to be unstable periods in which miscalculations frequently occur, tensions are aggravated, and conflicts often erupt. This is known in neorealist thinking as "power transition theory," which holds that the period when a rising power approaches parity with the established power is *the most* unstable and prone to conflict.[13] In this transitional period, either the predominant power is likely to launch a preemptive war to stave off the challenge of the rising power or, more commonly, the challenger may strike first.

In contrast to the pessimistic prognoses of realists, liberal IR theorists are more optimistic. They also view China through the prism of the international system but place much faith in the postwar system's ability to "regulate" and constrain China's rise through a dense web of intractable institutions, rules, laws, and procedures. Liberal theorists make a very strong case that China's evolution over the past three decades of reform, at present, and well into the future is profoundly conditioned by the international liberal order. In the words of Princeton University professor G. John Ikenberry:

> The existing international order is deeply entrenched. It is a layered system of Westphalian and liberal rules and institutions. It is an order that is wide and deep. It is not simply a political formation tied to American power. The constraints and obstacles on China's ability to overturn and reorganize international order are multiple: the Chinese "model" is unsustainable as a global system, Chinese revisionism will generate self-encirclement, and, in the background, the grand mechanism for overturning old international orders—great power war—has disappeared.[14]

Thus, liberals put their faith in constraining China's rise through enmeshing it—just as the Lilliputians ensnared Gulliver—through a web of institutions and procedures.

If liberals seek to constrain China, constructivists seek to condition it. Constructivist IR theory emphasizes the realm of ideas and norms—and, particularly, how they are "socially constructed" in societies and become socialized as behavior within and between societies. The formation, socialization, and transmission of individual and national identities are important processes for constructivists. As such, constructivists seek not only to enmesh China in a broad range of international institutions but to inculcate the norms of international behavior into Chinese society and individuals. Constructivists believe that if one does not accept the underlying norms, people (and nations) will not abide by the rules set by institutions. To be certain, many of these norms are rooted in liberalism.

All three of these mainstream international relations theories seek to condition and shape China's rise. It is not just a matter of theory but conscious government policy as well. It is no secret that Western and Asian governments have consciously sought to shape China's rise for several decades. After trying to shape it through containing it (1950s and 1960s), President Richard Nixon observed in a prophetic article in 1967: "We simply cannot afford to leave China forever outside the family of nations, there to nurture its fantasies, cherish its hates, and threaten its neighbors. There is no place on this small planet for a billion of its potentially most able people to live in angry isolation."[15] This recognition (plus the geopolitical realities of the Soviet Union) spurred Nixon to open America's relations with Beijing. Western and Asian governments that had not previously recognized the People's Republic (the vast majority) soon followed suit and thereafter began a three-decade-long effort to shape China's rise through its integration into the existing international order. The only major hiccup in this prolonged effort came with the 1989 massacre in Beijing. The West punished China for several years through condemnation, sanctions, and ostracism, before returning to the integrationist strategy (dubbed "engagement") by the mid-1990s. Much of Asia, led by senior Singaporean statesman Lee Kuan Yew, decided that punishment could be counterproductive and could return China to its "angry isolation." These Asian leaders thus opted to reach out to China and to continue the process of regional integration.

What about the future? Is the world still dealing with the same China—and does it still warrant the same integrationist strategy? China has changed, and the strategy for dealing with it should be adjusted as well. No strategy or policy should last forever, particularly when dealing with a nation that has undergone such dramatic change as has China in recent decades. At the same time, one should not throw the baby out with the bathwater. Adjustments of strategy and policy are called for—*not* jettisoning them.

The integrationist approach has not lost its efficacy. There literally is *no alternative* but to continue to engage China and integrate it into the institutions, rules, laws, and norms of the international community. It is the best hope for conditioning China's "peaceful rise." But the integration strategy is not sufficient in and of itself. We have seen (particularly in Chapter 4) that China is now formally in the international institutional infrastructure (except the OECD, the Missile Technology Control Regime, and some more minor agencies). This institutional integration does have a strong binding and socializing effect on all member states, including China. Beijing has willingly joined this club and benefited enormously from it. And, by and large, it has observed and upheld the rules of the system—although often selectively, partially, and minimally. As President Richard Nixon observed almost a half-century ago, it remains far better to have China in the international system than outside it. Even partial compliance is better than noncompliance. Although it is true that China remains a selective and partial participant in global governance and continues to exhibit deep ambivalence and dissatisfaction about elements of the existing international order, the efficacy of the logic and strategy of integrating China remains.

Now that China is "at the table" and a formal "member of the club," the adjustment that needs to be made in strategy is to focus more on the normative dimension of China's integration. Recognizing that it will always have differences and difficulties in accepting some international norms and rules, efforts need to be stepped up with respect to training and capacity-enhancement programs. This is where constructivism comes in, with its focus on the individual's worldview and orientation. Several nations and international organizations—notably the United Kingdom, Australia, Canada, United States, the European Union, the United Nations, and the Asian Development Bank—operate a variety of excellent training schemes for Chinese professionals across a range of professions. These should be continued, but perhaps more carefully focused on the key areas of civil society, media, rule of law, government transparency, human rights, and global governance. Although many developed nations are (appropriately) phasing out their aid programs to China, these kinds of capacity-building programs (in China and abroad) should be continued.

Just as integration remains the leitmotif of Grand Strategy for dealing with China's rise, so too is "containment" an equally absurd alternative. It is a complete nonstarter. Those who advocate it are detached from reality. China literally could *not* be contained even if it were decided that this was a wise course of action—precisely because of China's *existing integration* in the global system. The genie cannot be put back into the bottle. To "contain" a country—especially the size of China—requires the full agreement and compliance of other nations in the effort. Not a single nation on earth would go along with a containment strategy should the United States (or others) seek to pursue it. The interdependence and benefits of interaction and commerce with China are irreversible. I thus find the policy recommendations (and underlying arguments) of "preemptive containment" of China put forth by some scholars to be both folly and dangerous.[16]

Even though containment is untenable, it is clear that the world is now dealing with a different China. Various voices in China call for a more assertive foreign policy and defense posture, and the world saw evidence of Beijing's assertiveness during 2009–10. Whether China is assertive or not, this book offers ample evidence of an increasing international presence. China has definitely gone global, and this qualitatively changes the way it views and deals with the world, and vice versa. China's global strategy remains heavily influenced by its domestic development needs. Thus its preoccupation with securing steady and secure supplies of energy and raw materials results in a largely resource- and commerce-driven foreign policy. This is a foreign policy primarily driven by narrow national (economic) interests, not a foreign policy motivated by loftier international goals. China is surely not (yet) the "responsible stakeholder" Robert Zoellick envisioned.[17] As Elizabeth Economy of the Council on Foreign Relations aptly observes: "China needs a foreign policy 'reset.' It neither meets its own challenges nor successfully addresses the growing demands of the international community. Instead it is trapped by outdated foreign policy principles, ambition without accountability, and, above all, by a political model that undermines the country's potential for real leadership. The gap between oft-stated Chinese principles and the country's actions on the ground undermines, rather than reinforces, trust within the international community."[18]

Underlying China's inconsistent international behavior are an odd combination of contradictory attitudes toward the world: confident (sometimes overly so) but insecure, assertive but hesitant, occasionally arrogant but usually modest, a sense of entitlement growing out of historical victimization, risk-averse but increasingly engaged, a cautious internationalism combined with strong nationalism and deeply embedded parochialism, truculence combined with pragmatism, a regional power with a global sense of itself, a China that wishes to be left alone but finds itself dependent on the world, and an increasingly modern and industrialized but still poor and developing country. In short, China is a confused and conflicted rising power undergoing an identity crisis of significant proportions. We should expect these multiple international identities to play out simultaneously on the world stage.

This suggests to me that it is not so much an aggressive or threatening China with which the world should be concerned, but rather an insecure, confused, frustrated, angry, dissatisfied, selfish, truculent, and lonely power. More than anything, China wants to be prosperous, secure, respected, and left alone in its own geocultural orbit. This has been the core national mission since the 1870s. But as the country has become prosperous, national security and international respect have not naturally followed. Nor has its national confidence; China remains a hypersensitive, hypernationalist, and defensive power. As commentator Fareed Zakaria observes: "China's rise will reinforce Chinese nationalism and a sense of uniqueness, and actually make the country *less likely* to easily integrate into the global system."[19] Nor has a sense of international responsibility come with China's rise. "China wants to make the deals but not shoulder responsibilities. We are far from ready, psychologically, to make ourselves a dependable power," observes Peking University international relations professor Zhu Feng.[20] Vice Foreign Minister Fu Ying has a different take on the issue: "We don't view ourselves as a superpower. You are not going to see a USA or Soviet Union in China. You are going to see a culturally nourished country with a big population, being more content, being happy, being purposeful—and it will be a friend to the world. There is no reason to worry about China," Madame Fu told *Der Speigel*.[21]

This diversity of views about the implications of China's rise and globalization is testimony to the uncertainty associated with it. But one thing is certain: China's going global will undoubtedly be the most significant development in international relations in the years ahead. Since China's opening to the world in 1978, the world has changed China—and now China is beginning to change the world.

NOTES

———

Preface and Acknowledgments

1. For further consideration of the state of the China field, see Robert F. Ash, David Shambaugh, and Seiichiro Takagi (eds.), *China Watching: Perspectives from Europe, Japan, and the United States* (London: Routledge, 2007), particularly the Epilogue ("International China Watching in the 21st Century: Coping with a Changing Profession").

2. For a survey of the state of the field and what I learned about it during 2009–10, see David Shambaugh, "International Relations Studies in China: History, Trends, and Prospects," *International Relations of the Asia-Pacific* (September 2011).

Chapter 1

1. Lee Kuan Yew, "China's Growing Might and the Consequences," *Forbes*, March 9, 2011.

2. Henry Kissinger, *On China*, 2nd ed. (New York: Penguin, 2012), p. 546.

3. Xinhua News Agency, "Full Text of White Paper on China's Peaceful Development," September 6, 2011.

4. President Barack Obama, "Remarks at Welcoming Ceremony for President Hu Jintao," January 19, 2011, http://www.whitehouse.gov/photos-and-video/video/2011/01/19/china-state-visit-arrival-ceremony.

5. In 2012 the government allocated a larger budget for internal security ($111 billion) than for the military ($107 billion).

6. I wrote a newspaper article at the time expressing this hope. See David Shambaugh, "China's Competing Nationalisms," *International Herald Tribune*, May 5, 2008.

7. David Shambaugh, "The Chinese Tiger Shows Its Claws," *Financial Times*, February 17, 2010.

8. Notable examples include James Kynge, *China Shakes the World: The Rise of a Hungry Nation* (London: Weidenfeld & Nicolson, 2006); David M. Lampton, *The Three Faces of Chinese Power: Might, Money, and Minds* (Berkeley: University of California Press, 2008); Phillip C. Saunders, *China's Global Activism: Strategy, Drivers, and Tools* (Washington, DC: National Defense University Institute for National Security Studies, 2006); Robert Sutter, *Chinese Foreign Relations: Power and Policy Since the Cold War* (Lanham, MD: Rowman & Littlefield, 2009); Yong Deng and Fei-ling Wang (eds.), *China Rising: Power and Motivation in Chinese Foreign Policy* (Lanham, MD: Rowman & Littlefield, 2005); Avery Goldstein, *Rising to the Challenge: China's Grand Strategy and International Security* (Stanford: Stanford University Press, 2005); Evan S. Medeiros, *China's International Behavior: Activism, Opportunism, Diversification* (Santa Monica, CA: Rand, 2009); David C. Kang, *China Rising: Peace, Power, and Order in East Asia* (New York: Columbia University Press, 2007); Yong Deng, *China's Struggle for Status: The Realignment of International Relations* (Cambridge: Cambridge University Press, 2008); Michel E. Brown et al. (eds.), *The Rise of China* (Cambridge, MA: MIT Press, 2000); Robert S. Ross and Zhu Feng (eds.), *China's Ascent: Power, Security, and the Future of International Politics* (Ithaca, NY: Cornell University Press, 2008); Zhiqun Zhu, *China's New Diplomacy: Rationale, Strategies, and Significance* (Burlington, VT: Ashgate, 2010); C. Fred Bergsten et al., *China's Rise: Challenges and Opportunities* (Washington, DC: Peterson Institute for International Economics and Center for Strategic and International Studies, 2008).

9. See, for example, Robert S. Ross and Zhu Feng (eds.), *China's Ascent: Power, Security, and the Future of International Relations* (Ithaca, NY: Cornell University Press, 2008); John Mearsheimer, *The Tragedy of Great Power Politics* (New York: Norton, 2001); Aaron L. Friedberg, *A Contest for Supremacy: China, America, and the Struggle for Mastery in Asia* (New York: Norton, 2011).

10. See, for example, Herbert Yee and Ian Storey, *The China Threat: Perceptions, Myths, and Realities* (London: Routledge, 2002); Richard Bernstein and Ross Munro, *The Coming Conflict with China* (New York: Knopf, 1997); Ross Terrill, *The New Chinese Empire* (New York: Basic Books, 2003); Steven Mosher, *Hegemon: China's Plan to Dominate Asia and the World* (San Francisco: Encounter Books, 2000); Ted Galen Carpenter, *America's Coming War with China* (London: Palgrave Macmillan, 2006).

11. Martin Jacques, *When China Rules the World* (London: Allen Lane, 2009).

12. Pew Global Attitudes Project, "China Seen as Overtaking U.S. as Global Superpower," http://www.pewglobal.org/2011/07/13/china-seen-overtaking-us-as-global-superpower/.

13. Joseph Nye, *The Future of Power* (New York: Public Affairs, 2011). See, in particular, the definitions and discussion in his chap. 1.

14. Robert Dahl, *Who Governs? Democracy and Power in an American City* (New Haven, CT: Yale University Press, 1961).

15. Nye, *The Future of Power*, op. cit., p. 8.

16. Freedom House, "Freedom of Press 2009," http://www.freedomhouse.org/uploads/fop/2009/FreedomofthePresss2009_tables.pdf.

17. World Bank, *Country Data Report for China, 2006–2010* (Washington, DC: World Bank Institute, 2011).

18. World Economic Forum, *Global Competitiveness Report 2011*, http://www3.weforum.org/docs/WEF_GCR_CountryProfileHighlights_2011–12.pdf.

19. See http://www.transparency.org/policy_research/surveys_indices/cpi/2010.

20. See, for example, Joshua Kurlantzick, *Charm Offensive: How China's Soft Power Is Transforming the World* (New Haven: Yale University Press, 2008).

21. Wang Qian, "Info Official: Nation Needs to Extend Soft Power," *China Daily*, September 15, 2010.

22. http://www.pewglobal.org/2012/06/13/chapter-4-rating-countries-and-institutions/.

23. http://www.worldpublicopinion.org/.

Chapter 2

* Abbreviated versions of this chapter have appeared in Henry Nau and Deepa Ollapally (eds.), *Worldviews of Aspiring Powers* (Oxford University Press, 2012); and *Washington Quarterly*, Vol. 34, No. 1 (Winter 2011), pp. 7–271

1. Quoted in Tania Branigan, "China's Foreign Policy Is Playing Catch-Up with Its New Status," *Guardian*, March 22, 2012.

2. Wang Jisi, "Zhongguo de guoji dingwei wenti yu 'taoguang yanghui, yousuo zuowei' de zhanlue sixiang" [The Issue of China's International Position and 'Hide Brightness, Modest Demeanor, Do Some Things' in Strategic Thought], *Guoji Wenti Yanjiu*, No. 2 (2011), p. 9.

3. Presentation by Jin Canrong at the New Zealand Institute of International Affairs, June 28, 2010.

4. Presentation by Shen Dingli at "Roundtable with China Foreign Policy Experts," Wellington, New Zealand, June 29, 2010.

5. For recent assessments of China's future, see David Shambaugh (ed.), *Charting China's Future: Domestic and International Challenges* (London: Routledge, 2011).

6. Also see Mark Leonard, *What Does China Think?* (New York: Public Affairs, 2008); Zhu Liqun, *China's Foreign Policy Debates* (Paris: European Union Institute for Security Studies, 2010).

7. Despite the critical importance of the linkage between domestic perceptions and foreign policy, surprisingly few foreign scholars or analysts of Chinese foreign policy have focused on ideational variables and this linkage. Over the years, Bonnie Glaser, Banning Garrett, Alastair Iain Johnston, Evan Medeiros, Gilbert Rozman, Philip Saunders, and David Shambaugh have pioneered work on Chinese international perceptions. For a more recent assessment, see Daniel Lynch, "Chinese

Thinking on the Future of International Relations: Realism as the *Ti*,
Rationalism as the *Yong*?" *China Quarterly*, No. 197 (March 2009),
pp. 87–107.

8. See the excellent recent study by Linda Jakobson and Dean Knox, *New
    Foreign Policy Actors in China* (Stockholm: SIPRI, 2010).

9. The only recent published public opinion survey I am aware of appeared
    in December 2009, by the China Academy of Social Sciences. See Li
    Shenming and Zhou Hong (eds.), *Zhongguo minzhong de guojiguan* [The
    Chinese Public's View of the World], Vol. 1 (Beijing: Shehui kexue
    wenzhai chubanshe, 2009). Professor Alastair Iain Johnston of Harvard
    University has also collected and published some data on Beijing residents'
    perceptions of international issues. See Johnston, "Chinese Middle Class
    Attitudes Towards International Affairs: Nascent Liberalization," *China
    Quarterly*, No. 179 (September 2004), pp. 603–628.

10. See David Shambaugh, "International Relations Studies in China:
    History, Trends, and Prospects," *International Relations of the Asia-Pacific*
    (September 2011), pp. 339–372.

11. Interview with Shi Yinhong of Renmin University, April 30, 2010,
    Beijing.

12. Interview with Xue Fukang, China Reform Forum, April 30, 2010,
    Beijing.

13. Interview with Wang Jisi, Beijing University, January 22, 2010.

14. See Wu Wencong, Jiang Xueqing, and Li Jing, "Where 'Top Student'
    Has a New Meaning," *China Daily*, November 29, 2011.

15. Deng Xiaoping, "Gaige kaifang zhengce wending, Zhongguo da you
    xiwang" [The Stable Policy of Reform and Opening Up, China's Great
    Desire], *Selected Works of Deng Xiaoping, Vol. 3* (Beijing: Renmin
    chubanshe, 1993), p. 321.

16. For an elaboration of the etymology of this terminology, see the
    discussion in M. Taylor Fravel, *Strong Borders, Secure Nation* (Princeton:
    Princeton University Press, 2008), pp. 135–136.

17. This was Deng's first known reference to *taoguang yanghui*. See Leng
    Rong and Wang Zuoling (eds.), *Deng Xiaoping Nianpu* [Chronicle of
    Deng Xiaoping] (Beijing: Zhongyang wenxian chubanshe, 2004), p. 1346.

18. Jiang Zemin, *Selected Works of Jiang Zemin, Volume 2* (Beijing: Renmin
    chubanshe, 2003), p. 202.

19. For an excellent survey of this discourse see Dingding Chen and Jianwei
    Wang, "Lying Low No More? China's New Thinking on the *Tao Guang
    Yang Hui* Strategy," *China: An International Journal*, Vol. 9, No. 2 (2011),
    pp. 195–216.

20. Interview with Jin Canrong, People's University, January 29, 2010,
    Beijing.

21. Yan Xuetong, "China's Foreign Diplomacy Should Reflect Its World
    Number 2 Status," *Guoji Luntan Bao* [International Herald Leader],

December 6, 2010, http://news.xinhuanet.com/
herald/2010–12/06/c_13636783.htm.

22. "Zhongguo Guoji Guanxi Xuehui 2010 nian nianhui zai Lanzhou
zhaokai" [China's International Relations Society 2010 Annual Meeting
in Lanzhou Review], *Waijiao Pinglun*, No. 4 (2010), p. 157.

23. See Zheng Bijian, *China's Peaceful Rise: Speeches of Zheng Bijian, 1997–
2005* (Washington, DC: Brookings Institution Press, 2006).

24. See Bonnie Glaser and Evan Medeiros, "The Changing Ecology of
Foreign Policy Making in China: The Ascension and Demise of the
Theory of China's 'Peaceful Rise,'" *China Quarterly* (July 2007).

25. See Yu Xingtian et al., *Guoji Tixi zhong de Zhongguo Jiaose* [China's
Position in the International System] (Beijing: Zhongguo dabaike
quanshu chubanshe, 2008); Yang Chengxu, *Guoji Da Geju* [The Global
Grand Structure] (Beijing: Shijie zhishi chubanshe, 2006); Xia Liping,
Dangdai Guoji Tixi yu Daguo Zhanlue Guanxi [The Contemporary
International System and Major Power Strategic Relations] (Beijing:
Shishi chubanshe, 2008); Yang Jiemian (ed.), *Guoji Tixi Zhuanbian he
Duobian Zuzhi Fazhan* [The Transforming International System and
Development of Multilateral Organizations] (Beijing: Shishi
chubanshe, 2007); Qin Yaqing, *Guoji Tixi yu Zhongguo Waijiao* [The
International System and China's Diplomacy] (Beijing: Shijie zhishi
chubanshe, 2009); Zhu Liqun, *Guoji Tixi yu Zhong Ou Guanxi* [The
International System and China-Europe Relations] (Beijing: Shijie
zhishi chubanshe, 2008).

26. See Shang Shu, *Guoji Duoji Geju Zouxiang* [The Trajectory of Global
Multipolarity] (Beijing: Shishi chubanshe, 2010).

27. Interview with Guo Zhenyuan, March 9, 2010, Beijing.

28. Zhang Ruizhuang's statement at conference, Zhongshan University, May
8, 2010, Guangzhou.

29. Interview with Yang Jiemian, November 9, 2010, Shanghai.

30. See, for example, Yu Zhengliang, "Global Power Structure Has Shifted
and Transitional Multipolarity Has Emerged," *Global Review* (July–
August 2010), pp. 1–12.

31. Ibid., pp. 2–3.

32. Interview with scholar, Shanghai Academy of Social Sciences, January 28,
2010, Shanghai.

33. See Wang Yusheng, "The BRICs: Rhythm of the Era," *Foreign Affairs
Journal*, No. 96 (Summer 2010), pp. 32–37.

34. See, for example, Xu Jian, "Rise of the Intermediate Forces and Structural
Changes in the World Pattern," *China International Studies* (Spring
2008), pp. 4–19.

35. See Li Jie, "The Transition of the International System: From the
Perspective of the Theory of Responsibility," *China International Studies*
(Winter 2007), pp. 138–158.

36. Shanghai Academy of Social Sciences World Economics and Politics Research Academy (eds.), *Fuzeren Daguo de Lujing Xuanze* [Responsible Major Powers' Choices of Routes] (Beijing: Shishi chubanshe, 2007).

37. See Ma Zhengang, "China's Responsibility and the 'China Responsibility' Theory," *China International Studies* (Summer 2007), pp. 5–12.

38. For an excellent assessment of this literature (albeit somewhat dated), see Hongying Wang and James N. Rosenau, "China and Global Governance," *Asian Perspective*, Vol. 33, No. 3 (2009), pp. 5–39.

39. Interview, CCP International Department, July 14, 2010, Beijing.

40. No author, "Be on Guard Against the West's Insistence on 'China's Responsibility,'" *International Herald Leader*, August 12, 2011, http://news.xinhuanet.com/herald/2011–08/12/c_131043110.htm.

41. Shanghai Academy of Social Sciences World Economics and Politics Research Academy (eds.), *Duobian Jizhi yu Zhongguo de Dingwei* [The Multilateral System and China's Position] (Beijing: Shishi chubanshe, 2007); Shanghai Academy of Social Sciences World Economics and Politics Research Academy (eds.), *Duobian Hezuo yu Zhongguo Waijiao* [Multilateral Cooperation and China's Foreign Policy] (Beijing: Shishi chubanshe, 2010).

42. Interview with Song Xinning, May 3, 2010, Beijing.

43. Statement by Chen Hanxi of Guangdong Foreign Studies University at conference at Zhongshan University, May 8, 2010, Guangzhou.

44. For one review of the concept and discourse, see Zhang Yuquan and Michael Chang, "'Harmonious World': China's New Strategy of Cultural Diplomacy," *Ya-Tai Pinglun* [Asia-Pacific Review], Nos. 1–2 (2009), pp. 239–256.

45. Interview with IR scholar, April 30, 2010, Beijing.

46. Hu Jintao, "Build Towards a Harmonious World of Lasting Peace and Common Prosperity," speech at the United Nations Summit, September 15, 2005, http://www.fmprc.gov.cn/ce/ceun/eng/zt/shnh60/t212915.htm.

47. See, for example, the findings of a recent survey of Asian countries, in which large majorities in surveyed countries had never heard of the concept of "harmonious world." See Chicago Council of Global Affairs, *Soft Power in Asia: Results of a 2008 Multinational Survey of Public Opinion* (Chicago: CCGA, 2009).

48. Interview with scholar, May 9, 2010, Guangzhou.

49. It is better to think of these cohorts as "tendencies of analysis" than rigid schools of thought. The pioneering work on "tendency analysis" is H. Gordon Skilling and William Griffiths, *Interest Groups in Soviet Politics* (Princeton: Princeton University Press, 1971).

50. Song Xiaojun et al., *Zhongguo bu Gaoxing* (Jiangsu renmin chubanshe, 2009); He Xiongfei, *Zhongguo Weishenme bu Gaoxing?* (Beijing: Shijie zhishi chubanshe, 2009); Ye Dinghua et al., *Shei zai Zhongguo bu Gaoxing?* (Guangzhou: Huacheng chubanshe, 2009).

51. Song Xiaojun et al., *Zhongguo bu Gaoxing*, ibid.
52. For a good summary of *China Can Say No!* see Jing Li, *China's America: The Chinese View the United States, 1900–2000* (Albany: SUNY Press, 2011), pp. 211–214.
53. Song Xiaojun et al., *Zhongguo bu Gaoxing*, p. 77.
54. Ibid., p. 164.
55. Ibid., p. 99.
56. Ibid.
57. Ibid., p. 77.
58. Ibid., p. 102.
59. Zhang Wenmu, "Shijie lishi zhong de qiangguo zhilu yu Zhongguo de xuanze" [The Road of Great Powers in World History and China's Choice], in Guo Shuyong (ed.), *Zhanlue yu Tansuo* [Strategy and Exploration] (Beijing: Shijie zhishi chubanshe, 2008), pp. 33, 54.
60. Fang Ning, "Xin diguozhuyi yu Zongguo de zhanlue xuanze" [The New Imperialism and China's Strategic Choice] in Guo Shuying (ed.), *Zhanlue yanjianglu* [Lectures on Strategy] (Beijing: Peking University Press, 2006), pp. 132–133.
61. Illustrative is Wang Jinsong, *Diguozhuyi Lishi de Zhongjie: Dangdai Diguozhuyi de Xingcheng he Fazhan Qushi* [Imperialism Is the Final Stage of History: Contemporary Imperialism's Formation and Development Trends] (Beijing: Shehui kexue wenzhai chubanshe, 2008).
62. Ibid.
63. Zhang Wenmu, *The Road of the Great Powers*, op. cit., pp. 42–43.
64. Interview with Ding Kuisong, China Reform Forum, January 20, 2010, Beijing.
65. Interview with Yan Xuetong, July 14, 2010, Beijing.
66. Presentation by Shen Dingli at the New Zealand Institute of International Affairs, June 28, 2010.
67. Yan Xuetong, "An Analysis of the Advantages and Disadvantages of Containing Legal Taiwan Independence by Force," *Strategy and Management*, No. 3 (2004), pp. 1–5.
68. Yan Xuetong, *Zhongguo Jueqi* (Tianjin: Tianjin renmin chubanshe, 1997).
69. Interview, January 20, 2010, Beijing.
70. Statement by Zhang Ruizhuang at conference at Zhongshan University, May 7, 2010, Guangzhou.
71. Zhang Ruizhuang, "Chonggu Zhongguo waijiao suochu zhi guoji huanjing—heping yu fazhan bingfei dangdai shijie zhuti" [Reassessing the International Environment of China's Foreign Affairs—Peace and Development Are Not the Main Theme of Today's World], *Strategy and Management*, No. 1 (2001), pp. 20–30.
72. See Pan Wei, "Yetan heping jueqi" [Again Discussing Peaceful Rise], http://www.360doc.com/content/07/0831/17/41440_708164.shtml. Also see Pan Wei, "Diqiushang conglai mei fasheng guo 'heping jueqi' zhezhongshi" (There Was Never Such a Thing as "Peaceful Rise" in the

World's Past), http://www.360doc.com/content/09/1102/17/346405_82815 7.shtml.

73. Interview with Feng Yujun, China Institutes of Contemporary International Relations, May 18, 2010, Beijing.

74. See Wang Yizhou, *Zhongguo Waijiao Xin Gaodi* [High Land over China's Foreign Affairs] (Beijing: China Academy of Social Sciences Press, 2008), p. 7.

75. One official argues that although this was the case when Hu first came to office, over time he too has come to realize the primary importance of the United States and has accordingly reoriented China's priorities to Washington. Interview, Ministry of Foreign Affairs, April 30, 2010, Beijing.

76. Interview with Zhu Feng, March 25, 2010, Beijing.

77. Statement by Rong Xing at conference, China Institute of International Studies, June 1, 2011, Beijing.

78. See David Shambaugh, "China Engages Asia: Reshaping the Regional Order," *International Security*, Vol. 29, No. 3 (Winter 2004/2005), pp. 64–99.

79. Yu Xintian, "Zhongguo ying Zhuanbian dui dui fazhanzhong guojia de zhanlue" [China Should Change Its Strategy Toward Developing Countries], *Strategy and Management*, No. 3 (2003), pp. 40–45.

80. *Huanqiu* [Globe] (ed.), *Baiwen Zhongguo Weilai: Zhongguo Jingying Duihua Quanqiu* [A Hundred Questions on China's Future: Dialogues with Chinese Elites] (Beijing: Xinhua Press, 2009), p. 12.

81. See, for example, Men Honghua, "Daguo jueqi yu guoji zhixu" [The Rise of Great Powers and International Order], *Guoji Zhengzhi Yanjiu*, No. 2 (2004), pp. 133–142; Zhang Wenwu, "Jianli guoji zhixu de xin linian" [New Concepts of Establishing International Order], *Xueshu Tansuo*, No. 6 (2005), pp. 73–80.

82. See Wang Yusheng, "The BRICs: Rhythm of the Era," *Foreign Affairs Journal*, No. 96 (Summer 2010); He Hongyuan, "The Strategic Value and the Development Trends of the BRICs," *Foreign Affairs Journal*, No. 99 (Spring 2011); Du Youkang, "Cooperation Cements BRICs," *China Daily*, March 29, 2012.

83. Chang Gong, *Zhongguo Bu Zheteng* [China Is Not Disruptive] (Beijing: Zhongguo youyi chuban gongsi, 2010), p. 89.

84. Cited in David Pilling, "Keeping a Distance," *Financial Times*, February 11, 2010.

85. Ibid.

86. Jin Canrong, presentation to the forty-fifth Otago Foreign Policy School, University of Otago, New Zealand, June 26, 2010.

87. For a Chinese view, which stresses Chinese recognition of "international responsibility" and embrace of liberal IR, see Zhu Liqun, *China's Foreign Policy Debates*, Chaillot Papers No. 121 (Paris: European Institute of Security Studies, 2010).

88. Yang Jiechi, "A Changing China in a Changing World," Address to the Munich Security Conference, February 5, 2010.

89. Interview with Men Honghua of Institute of Strategic Studies, Central Party School, May 2, 2010, Beijing.

Chapter 3

1. Lucian W. Pye, "China: Erratic State, Frustrated Society," *Foreign Affairs*, Vol. 69, No. 1 (1990), p. 58.

2. No author, "Xi Jinping in Los Angeles," *Huffington Post*, February 17, 2012, http://www.huffingtonpost.com/2012/02/17/xi-jinping-in-los-angeles_n_1284514.html. Xi made these remarks in his capacity as vice president during a visit to the United States in February 2012.

3. "The Rapid Development of China's Diplomacy in a Volatile World," address by Assistant Foreign Minister Le Yucheng at a "Seminar on China's Diplomacy in 2011 and Its Prospects," China Foreign Affairs University, December 27, 2011, http://www.fmprc.gov.cn/eng/zxxx/t890675.htm.

4. These moves are all documented in Ezra Vogel, *Deng Xiaoping and the Transformation of China* (Cambridge, MA: Belknap Press of Harvard University Press, 2011), chaps. 7–11.

5. See David Shambaugh, *China's Communist Party: Atrophy and Adaptation* (Washington, DC, and Berkeley: Woodrow Wilson Center Press and University of California Press, 2008).

6. See David Finkelstein, *China Reconsiders Its National Security: The Great Peace and Development Debate of 1999* (Alexandria, VA: CNA Corporation, 1999).

7. See David Shambaugh, "China Engages Asia: Reshaping the Regional Order," *International Security*, Vol. 29, No. 3 (Winter 2004/2005), pp. 64–99.

8. See Michael D. Swaine, "Perceptions of an Assertive China," *China Leadership Monitor*, No. 32 (Spring 2010), http://media.hoover.org/sites/default/files/documents/CLM32MS.pdf; David Shambaugh, "The Chinese Tiger Shows Its Claws," *Financial Times*, February 17, 2010.

9. W. J. F. Jenner, *The Tyranny of History: The Roots of China's Crisis* (London: Penguin, 1995).

10. See, for example, Mark Mancall, *China at the Center* (New York: Free Press, 1984); John King Fairbank (ed.), *The Chinese World Order: Traditional China's Foreign Relations* (Cambridge, MA: Harvard University Press, 1968); John K. Fairbank, "China Foreign Policy in Historical Perspective," *Foreign Affairs* (April 1969); Morris Rossabi (ed.), *China Among Equals: The Middle Kingdom and Its Neighbors* (Berkeley: University of California Press, 1984); Warren Cohen, *East Asia at the Center: Four Thousand Years of Engagement with the World* (New York: Columbia University Press, 2000).

11. See David C. Kang, *China Rising: Peace, Power, and Order in East Asia* (New York: Columbia University Press, 2007); *East Asia Before the West* (New York: Columbia University Press, 2010); "Getting Asia Wrong: The Need for New Analytical Frameworks," *International Security*, Vol. 27, No. 4 (Spring 2003), pp. 57–85.

12. These are masterfully surveyed by John E. Wills, Jr., in "How Many Asymmetries? Continuities, Transformations, and Puzzles in the Study of Chinese Foreign Relations," in John E. Wills, Jr. (ed.), *Past and Present in China's Foreign Policy: From "Tribute System" to "Peaceful Rise"* (Portland, ME: MerwinAsia, 2010).

13. Ibid.

14. See Peter Hays Gries, *China's New Nationalism: Pride, Politics, and Diplomacy* (Berkeley: University of California Press, 2004).

15. Both figures were announced at the March 2012 National People's Congress. Moreover, the internal security budget figure only included funds for the Public Security forces nationwide and *does not* include monies for the People's Armed Police, Ministry of State Security, or People's Armed Militia. These budgets are not known publicly, but it is not unreasonable to assume that the PAP budget (for an estimated force of 1.2 million) is in the neighborhood of $40 billion; the MSS (with unknown numbers but one of the most powerful ministries in China) may be around an additional $20 billion; and the militia (with more than 20 million that can be mobilized) could be around $20 billion. In addition, there are other funds for local security forces. If thus added together, China's total internal security budget could plausibly be in the neighborhood of $200 billion!

16. Susan L. Shirk, *China: Fragile Superpower* (Oxford and New York: Oxford University Press, 2007), p. 53.

17. See M. Taylor Fravel, *Strong Borders, Secure Nation: Cooperation and Conflict in China's Territorial Disputes* (Princeton: Princeton University Press, 2008).

18. The Foreign Ministry and other agencies do declassify selected documents after thirty or more years.

19. Qiao Jianhua, *Yingxiang Zhongguo Waijiao Juece de Wu Da Yinsu* [Five Big Factors Influencing China's Foreign Policy Decision Making Process] (Beijing: Zhongyang bianyi chubanshe, 2010).

20. This is a large literature. Among the more important studies, see A. Doak Barnett, *The Making of Foreign Policy in China: Structure and Process* (Boulder: Westview Press, 1985); Michael D. Swaine, *The Role of the Military in National Security Policymaking* (Santa Monica, CA: Rand, 1996); David M. Lampton (ed.), *The Making of Chinese Foreign and Security Policy in the Era of Reform* (Stanford: Stanford University Press, 2001); Lu Ning, *The Dynamics of Foreign-Policy Decision Making in China* (Boulder: Westview Press, 2000); Hongyi Lai, *The Domestic Sources of China's Foreign Policy: Regimes, Leadership, Priorities, and*

Process (London: Routledge, 2010); Yufan Hao and Lin Su (eds.), *China's Foreign Policy Making: Societal Force and Chinese American Policy* (Burlington, VT: Ashgate, 2005); Richard Bush, *The Perils of Proximity: China-Japan Security Relations* (Washington, DC: Brookings Institution Press, 2010), chap. 8; Jakobson and Knox, *New Foreign Policy Actors in China*; John Wilson Lewis and Xue Litai, *Imagined Enemies: China Prepares for Uncertain War* (Stanford: Stanford University Press, 2006); Susan V. Lawrence, *Perspectives on Chinese Foreign Policy* (Washington, DC: Congressional Research Service, 2011); Bonnie S. Glaser and Phillip C. Saunders, "Chinese Civilian Foreign Policy Research Institutes: Evolving Roles and Increasing Influence," *China Quarterly* No. 171 (September 2002); David Shambaugh, "China's International Relations Think Tanks: Evolving Structure and Process," ibid.; David Shambaugh, "China's Quiet Diplomacy: The International Department of the Chinese Communist Party," *China: An International Journal*, No. 5 (2007); Wei Li, *The Chinese Staff System: A Mechanism for Bureaucratic Control and Integration* (Berkeley, CA: Institute for East Asian Studies, 1994); Alice Lyman Miller, "The Central Committee Departments under Hu Jintao," *China Leadership Monitor*, No. 27 (Winter 2009), http://media.hoover.org/sites/default/files/documents/CLM27AM.pdf; Alice Lyman Miller, "The CCP Central Committee's Leading Small Groups," *China Leadership Monitor*, No. 26 (Fall 2008), http://media.hoover.org/sites/default/files/documents/CLM26AM.pdf; Michael D. Swaine, "China's Assertive Behavior, Part III: The Role of the Military in Foreign Policy," *China Leadership Monitor*, No. 36 (2012), http://media.hoover.org/sites/default/files/documents/CLM36MS.pdf.

21. Interview with Central Committee member, June 25, 2011, Beijing.

22. Ibid. The frequency of these meetings has varied considerably over the years, but during the Jiang Zemin–Hu Jintao eras they have tended to meet at these general intervals.

23. See Lu Ning, "The Central Leadership, Supraministry Coordinating Bodies, State Council Ministries, and Party Departments," in Lampton (ed.), *The Making of Chinese Foreign and Security Policy*, op. cit., p. 42. Also see Lu Ning, *The Dynamics of Foreign-Policy Decision Making in China*, op. cit., chaps. 4–6.

24. For a description of the internal organization and functions of the Central Committee Policy Research Office, see Li Jianjun and Cui Shuyi (eds.), *Shijie Geguo Zhiku Yanjiu* [Global Nations Think Tank Research] (Beijing: Renmin chubanshe, 2010), p. 109.

25. Qiao Jianhua, *Yingxiang Zhongguo Waijiao Juece de Wu Da Yinsu*, op. cit., p. 205.

26. Wang Fuchun, *Waishi Guanlixue Gailun* [Introduction to Foreign Affairs Administration] (Beijing: Beijing Daxue chubanshe, 2003), p. 98.

27. Interview with Vice Foreign Minister Cui Tiankai, July 6, 2010, Beijing.

28. Interview with Du Qiwen, deputy director of the Central Committee Foreign Affairs Office, May 22, 2005, Beijing. For further description of the National Security Leading Small Group, see Yun Sun, "Chinese National Security Decision-Making: Processes and Challenges," unpublished paper prepared for Brookings Institution Center for Northeast Asian Policy Studies, 2012.

29. See Miller, "The CCP Central Committee's Leading Small Groups," op. cit.

30. In this instance, a State Council Leading Group was set up with Vice Premier Zhang Dejiang as head and State Councilor Dai Bingguo as deputy. Interview with Assistant Foreign Minister Ye Lucheng, June 2, 2010, Beijing.

31. Interview with State Councilor Dai Bingguo, June 26, 2007, Beijing.

32. Interviews with Qiu Yuanping, June 12, 2008, and Du Qiwen, May 22, 2005, Beijing. See, in particular, Wang Fuchun, *Waishi Guanlixue*, op. cit.; and Zhang Shishi, *Waijiao Juece* [Foreign Policy Decision Making] (Beijing: Shijie zhishi chubanshe, 2007); Wang Xiaodong, *Guojia Anquan Lingdao Zhidu de Gaige* [Reform of the National Security Leadership System] (Beijing: Shijie zhishi chubanshe, 2009).

33. If the FAO still has responsibility for this function, it is unclear what the division of labor is with the External Propaganda Leading Group (对外宣传领导小组) and the State Council Information Office. It is most likely that responsibility in this area has totally been transferred to the latter.

34. Wang Fuchun, *Waishi Guanlixue Gailun*, op. cit., p. 99.

35. Du Qiwen interview, ibid.

36. Interview with a knowledgeable governmental international affairs expert, June 1, 2011, Beijing.

37. Interview with Vice Foreign Minister Cui Tiankai, July 6, 2010, Beijing.

38. This estimate comes from a senior member of the MFA Information Department. Email correspondence, April 20, 2012. By contrast, the U.S. Foreign Service has approximately 11,500 officers.

39. Ng Tze-Wei, "LSE's Role in Guiding China's Budding Diplomats," *South China Morning Post*, December 14, 2010.

40. See http://www.fmprc.gov.cn/eng/wjb/zzjg/.

41. See http://www.fmprc.gov.cn/eng/wjb/zyzz/t558670.htm.

42. See David Shambaugh, "China's 'Quiet Diplomacy': The International Department of the Chinese Communist Party," *China: An International Journal*, No. 5 (2007), pp. 27–54.

43. "External Relations of the Communist Party of China" (September 25, 2003), printed description given to the author by the CCP/ID in October 2003.

44. For an evaluation of international relations studies at these universities, see David Shambaugh, "International Relations Studies in China: History, Trends, and Prospects," *International Relations of the Asia-Pacific* (September 2011), pp. 339–372.

45. For further discussion of China's international relations "think tanks," see Shambaugh, "China's International Relations Think Tanks: Evolving Structure and Process," ibid.; and Glaser and Saunders, "Chinese Civilian Foreign Policy Research Institutes," op. cit. For a Chinese assessment, see Song Xufeng, *Zhongguo Sixiang Ku: Zhengce Guochengzhong de Yingxiangli Yanjiu* [Chinese Think Tanks: Research on Their Influence in the Policy Process] (Beijing: Qinghua University Press, 2009).

46. Interview with Assistant Foreign Minister Ye Lucheng (then director of the MFA Policy Planning Department), June 2, 2010, Beijing.

47. Also see Joseph Fewsmith and Stanley Rosen, "The Domestic Context of Chinese Foreign Policy: Does 'Public Opinion' Matter?" in Lampton (ed.), *The Making of Chinese Foreign and Security Policy*, op. cit.

48. Interview with Ye Lucheng, June 2, 2010, Beijing.

49. Interview with Yang Jiemian, November 9, 2010, Shanghai.

50. See, for example, Jakobson and Knox, *New Foreign Policy Actors in China*, op. cit.

51. See David M. Lampton, "China's Foreign and National Security Policy-Making Process: Is It Changing and Does It Matter?" in Lampton (ed.), *The Making of Chinese Foreign and Security Policy*, op. cit.

52. Yan Sun, "Chinese National Security Decision-Making: Processes and Challenges," op. cit.

53. See Shambaugh, "China's International Relations Think Tanks"; and Glaser and Saunders, "Chinese Civilian Foreign Policy Research Institutes," op. cit.

54. Interview with Vice Foreign Minister Cui Tiankai, July 6, 2010, Beijing.

55. Alastair I. Johnston, "Is China a Status-Quo Power?" *International Security*, Vol. 27, No. 4 (2003), pp. 5–56.

56. Some of this section is adapted from my introductory chapter in David Shambaugh (ed.), *Tangled Titans: The United States and China* (Lanham, MD: Rowman & Littlefield, 2012).

57. For elaboration, see ibid.

58. For an excellent discussion of the issue of "strategic trust" see Kenneth Lieberthal and Wang Jisi, *Addressing U.S.-China Strategic Distrust* (Washington, DC, and Beijing: John L. Thornton China Center and Peking University Center for International and Strategic Studies, 2012). Also see David M. Lampton, *Power Constrained: Sources of Mutual Strategic Suspicion in U.S.-China Relations* (Seattle: National Bureau of Asian Research, 2010).

59. Such was the case, for example, with Vice President Biden's remarks in welcoming Vice President Xi Jinping in February 2012. See http://www.whitehouse.gov/the-press-office/2012/02/14/remarks-vice-president-biden-and-chinese-vice-president-xi-state-departm.

60. See G. John Ikenberry, "The Rise of China, the United States, and the Future of the Liberal International Order," in Shambaugh (ed.), *Tangled Titans*, op. cit.

61. See Lieberthal and Wang, *Addressing U.S.-China Strategic Distrust*, op. cit.

62. See Kenneth Lieberthal, "The China-U.S. Relationship Goes Global," *Current History* (September 2009), pp. 243–249; Evan Medeiros, "Beijing: The Ambivalent Power" *Current History* (September 2009), pp. 250–256; David Shambaugh, "A New China Requires a New U.S. Strategy," *Current History* (September 2010), pp. 219–226.

63. Also see Elizabeth C. Economy and Adam Segal, "The G-2 Mirage: Why the United States and China Are Not Ready to Upgrade Ties," *Foreign Affairs* (May/June 2009), pp. 14–23.

64. See http://www.whitehouse.gov/the-press-office/2011/01/19/ us-china-joint-statement; http://www.whitehouse.gov/the-press-office/ us-china-joint-statement; http://www.state.gov/r/pa/prs/ ps/2011/05/162967.htm.

65. See U.S. Census Bureau, "Trade in Goods with China: 2011," http:// www.census.gov/foreign-trade/balance/c5700.html#2011.

66. See David Shambaugh, *China's Communist Party: Atrophy and Adaptation* (Berkeley: University of California Press; Washington, DC: Woodrow Wilson Center Press, 2008), particularly chap. 4.

67. Ibid., pp. 124–127.

68. For a useful survey of the Sino-Russian relationship in the immediate post-Soviet era, see Jeanne L. Wilson, *Strategic Partners: Russian-Chinese Relations in the Post-Soviet Era* (Armonk, NY: M.E. Sharpe, 2004).

69. This period is well documented in Elizabeth Wishnick, *Mending Fences: The Evolution of Moscow's China Policy from Brezhnev to Yeltsin* (Seattle: University of Washington Press, 2001), chap. 8.

70. The text of the treaty is available at http://www.fmprc.gov.cn/eng/ wjdt/2649/t15771.htm.

71. See Bobo Lo, *Axis of Convenience: Moscow, Beijing, and the New Geopolitics* (London and Washington, DC: Chatham House and Brookings Institution Press, 2008); James Bellacqua (ed.), *The Future of China-Russia Relations* (Lexington: University of Kentucky Press, 2010).

72. "Medvedev: Sino-Russian Ties at 'Highest Point,'" *People's Daily Online*, September 28, 2010, http://english.people.com. cn/90001/90776/90883/7153214.html.

73. Ministry of Foreign Affairs, Department of Policy Planning, *China's Foreign Affairs 2010* (Beijing: Shijie zhishi chubanshe, 2010), p. 256.

74. "China, Russia Mark Completion of China-Russia Crude Oil Pipeline," *People's Daily Online*, http://english.cpc.people.com.cn/66102/7152702. html.

75. For a survey of the strategic dimension of the relationship, see Richard Weitz, *China-Russia Security Relations: Strategic Parallelism without Partnership or Passion?* (Carlisle Barracks, PA: U.S. Army War College Strategic Studies Institute, 2008).

76. Interview with Vassily Mikheev, deputy director of the Institute of World Economics and Politics, June 10, 2009, Moscow.

77. See Steven Blank, "Turning a New Leaf: Russia's Renewed Arms Sales to China," Jamestown Foundation *China Brief*, Vol. 11, No. 2, http://www.jamestown.org/programs/chinabrief/single/?tx_ttnews[tt_news]=37427&tx_ttnews[backPid]=25&cHash=c2050b9af5.

78. Statement by Song Xinning at Stockholm China Forum, December 6, 2008.

79. Interview with Feng Yujun, China Institutes of Contemporary International Relations, May 18, 2010, Beijing.

80. Interview with Shi Zhe at Chinese Embassy, December 4, 2010, Moscow.

81. Interview with Konstantin Vnoukov, Ministry of Foreign Affairs, June 9, 2009, Moscow.

82. Presentation by Sasha Lukin, Center for Strategic and International Studies (CSIS), September 20, 2010, Washington, DC.

83. Interview with Mikhail Titarenko, Institute of the Far East of the Russian Academy of Sciences, June 8, 2009, Moscow.

84. Interview with Vassily Mikheev, Institute of World Economics and Politics, June 10, 2009, Moscow.

85. Interview with Konstantin Vnoukov, op. cit.

86. Interview with Alexey Voskresensky, Moscow State Institute of International Relations, June 9, 2009, Moscow.

87. Interview with Dmitri Streltsov, Moscow State Institute of International Relations, June 9, 2009, Moscow.

88. Interview with Mikhail Troitskiy, Moscow State Institute of International Relations, June 9, 2009, Moscow.

89. Interview with Sergey Rogov, Institute of the USA and Canada, June 10, 2009, Moscow.

90. For a useful summary of Russian debates on China, see Andrey Tsygankov, *What Is China to Us? Westernizers and Sinophiles in Russian Foreign Policy* (Paris: IFRI Russia/NIS Center, 2009).

91. Bobo Lo, "A Partnership of Convenience," *International Herald Tribune*, June 8, 2012.

92. See http://ec.europa.eu/trade/creating-opportunities/bilateral-relations/countries/china/.

93. Zhao Junjie, "An Uneasy Balance," *Beijing Review*, Vol. 50, No. 2 (January 11, 2007), p. 10.

94. See Dan Levin, "Chinese Wrestle with Europe in Space," *International Herald Tribune*, March 23, 2009.

95. See David Shambaugh, "China's Quiet Diplomacy: The International Department of the Chinese Communist Party," *China: An International Journal*, Vol. 5, No. 1 (March 2007), pp. 26–54.

96. For a list of these dialogues, see http://ec.europa.eu/comm/external_relations/china/intro/sect.htm.

97. Speech by H.E. Wen Jiabao, premier of the State Council of the People's Republic of China, http://www.chinamission.be/eng/zt/t101949.htm.

98. These monies were expended in three program areas: economic and social reform (50 percent), sustainable development (30 percent), and good governance (20 percent). See http://eeas.europa.eu/delegations/china/index_en.htm.

99. "China and EU Begin Renegotiating Commercial Treaty," *International Herald Tribune*, January 18, 2007. This is also known as the "Framework Agreement."

100. European Commission, *A Long-Term Policy for China-Europe Relations*, COM (95), 279, Brussels, July 1995.

101. For surveys of the growth in relations during this period, see Katinka Barysch with Charles Grant and Mark Leonard, *Embracing the Dragon: The EU's Partnership with China* (London: Center for European Reform, 2005).

102. See Charles Grant with Katinka Barysch, *Can Europe and China Shape a New World Order?* (London: Center for European Reform, 2008).

103. See Hans Kundnani and Jonas Parello-Plesner, *China and Germany: Why the Emerging Special Relationship Matters for Europe* (London: European Council on Foreign Relations, 2012).

104. European Commission, *China-Europe: Closer Partners, Growing Responsibilities*; and European Commission, *Competition and Partnership: A Policy for EU-China Trade and Investment*. See respectively http://ec.europa.eu/comm/external_relations/china/docs/06-10-24_final_com.pdf and http://ec.europa.eu/trade/issues/bilateral/countries/china/pr241006_en.htm.

105. These are all selected direct quotations from *China-Europe: Closer Partners, Growing Responsibilities*, ibid.

106. "EU-China Strategic Partnership: Council Conclusions," 2771st Council Meeting, December 11–12, 2006, 16291/06 (Press 353), http://register.consilium.europa.eu/pdf/en/06/st16/st16291.en06.pdf.

107. François Godement and John Fox, *A Power Audit of EU-China Relations* (London: European Council on Foreign Relations, 2009), http://ecfr.eu/page/-/documents/A_Power_Audit_of_EU_China_Relations.pdf.

108. Interview with Ambassador Serge Abou, Delegation of the European Union, February 4, 2010, Beijing.

109. Interview with Madame Fu Ying, Ministry of Foreign Affairs, April 2, 2010, Beijing.

110. Interview with Executive Vice Foreign Minister Zhang Zhijun, Ministry of Foreign Affairs, April 21, 2010, Beijing.

111. See "Forum on China-EU Strategic Partnership," *Foreign Affairs Journal* (November 2009).

112. See http://ec.europa.eu/eu-china-intercultural-dialogue-2012.

113. For a comprehensive and overall assessment of China-Europe relations, see David Shambaugh, Eberhard Sandschneider, and Zhou Hong (eds.), *China-Europe Relations: Perceptions, Policies, and Prospects* (London: Routledge, 2008).

114. See John K. Fairbank, *The Chinese World Order* (Cambridge, MA: Harvard University Press, 1968); Mark Mancall, *China at the Center* (New York: Free Press, 1984); David C. Kang, *China Rising: Peace, Power, and Order in East Asia* (New York: Columbia University Press, 2007).

115. Discussion with a Chinese think tank analyst, October 19, 2003, Beijing.

116. For a survey of the period and different regional reactions, see Seiichiro Takagi, "The Asia-Pacific Nations: Searching for Leverage," in Ramon H. Myers, Michel C. Oksenberg, and David Shambaugh (eds.), *Making China Policy* (Lanham, MD: Rowman & Littlefield, 2001), pp. 241–268.

117. Ibid.; and Seiichiro Takagi, "Human Rights in Japanese Foreign Policy: Japan's Policy Toward China after Tiananmen," in James T. H. Tang (ed.), *Human Rights and International Relations in the Asia-Pacific Region* (London: Pinter, 1995).

118. This is well chronicled in Alastair Iain Johnston and Robert S. Ross (eds.), *Engaging China: The Management of an Emerging Power* (London: Routledge, 1999).

119. See Lee Kuan Yew, *From Third World to First: The Singapore Story, 1965–2000* (Singapore: Straits Times Press, 2000), chaps. 39–40.

120. Interviews with Foreign Ministry officials and policy analysts, June 2004, Beijing.

121. For analyses of Chinese thinking about such organizations, see Alastair I. Johnston and Paul Evans, "China's Engagement with Multilateral Security Institutions," in Johnston and Ross, *Engaging China*, chap. 10; and Jing-dong Yuan, "Regional Institutions and Cooperative Security: Chinese Approaches and Policies," *Korean Journal of Defense Analysis*, Vol. 13, No. 1 (Autumn 2001), pp. 263–294.

122. Discussion with Chinese Foreign Ministry official deeply involved in the ARF and CSCAP processes, November 6, 2003, Beijing.

123. See Wu Baiyi, "The Chinese Security Concept and Its Historical Evolution," *Journal of Contemporary China*, Vol. 10, No. 27 (May 2001), pp. 275–283; and "Chinese President Calls for New Security Concept," speech before the United Nations Conference on Disarmament, http://www.china-embassy.org.

124. Information Office of the State Council, *China's National Defense, 2000* (Beijing: Information Office of the State Council, 2000), p. 8.

125. Interview with Ministry of Foreign Affairs Director General for Asian Affairs Cui Tiankai, June 11, 2004, Beijing.

126. This was conveyed at high official levels as well as other regional forums. For example, at the 1999 meeting of the East Asia Vision Group, ASEAN representatives informed their Chinese counterparts that relations between China and ASEAN could develop successfully if Beijing met two conditions: (1) China did not push ASEAN governments to break their alliances or security arrangements with the United States; and (2) China did not mobilize overseas Chinese politically. Interview with Chinese representative, October 18, 2003, Beijing.

127. For an analysis of this debate, see David Finkelstein, *China Reconsiders Its National Security: The Great Peace and Development Debate of 1999* (Alexandria, VA: CNA Corporation, 2000).

128. For an elaboration, see David Shambaugh, "China Engages Asia: Reshaping the Regional Order," *International Security*, Vol. 29, No. 3 (Winter 2004/2005), pp. 64–99.

129. See Swaine, "Perceptions of an Assertive China," op. cit.

130. See Bruce Klinger, "China Shock for South Korea," *Asia Times Online*, September 11, 2004.

131. See David Shambaugh, "China and the Korean Peninsula: Playing for the Long Term," *Washington Quarterly* (Spring 2003); Scott Snyder, *China's Rise and the Two Koreas* (Boulder: Lynne Reinner, 2009); Jae Ho Chung, *Between Ally and Partner: Korea-China Relations and the United States* (New York: Columbia University Press, 2007).

132. Quoted in Jane Perlez, "North Korea Tests the Patience of Its Close Ally," *New York Times*, June 25, 2012.

133. The China Council for the Promotion of International Trade anticipates that ASEAN will become China's largest trading partner by 2015, growing from $362.3 billion in 2011 to more than $500 billion by 2015. See Bao Chang, "ASEAN to Be Top Trade Partner," *China Daily Asia Weekly*, April 27–May 3, 2012.

134. On Australian public perceptions, see Fergus Hanson, *Australia and the World: Public Opinion and Foreign Policy* (Sydney: Lowy Institute, 2010), http://www.lowyinstitute.org/Publication.asp?pid=1305; Rowan Callick, "Our Cool Customer," *The Australian*, May 16, 2012; and Australian Center on China in the World and China Institutes of Contemporary International Relations, *Australia and China: A Joint Report on the Bilateral Relationship* (Canberra: Australian National University, 2012); Carlyle A. Thayer, "China's Rise and the Passing of U.S. Primacy: Australia Debates Its Future," *Asia Policy*, No. 12 (July 2011); Hugh White, "Power Shift: Australia's Future Between Washington and Beijing," *Quarterly Essay*, No. 39 (September 2010); Hugh White, *The China Choice: Why America Should Share Power* (Collingwood, Australia: Black, 2012).

135. Interview at Australian Department of Foreign Affairs and Trade, May 11, 2012.

136. These are detailed in the joint report from the China Institutes of Contemporary International Relations (CICIR) and the Australian National University China in the World Institute (CIW), *Australia and China* (Canberra and Beijing: CICIR and CIW, 2012), op. cit.

137. For an excellent surveys of the relationship, see Mohan Malik, *China and India: Great Power Rivals* (Boulder and London: First Forum Press, 2011); George J. Gilboy and Eric Heginbotham, *Chinese and Indian Strategic*

Behavior: Growing Power and Alarm (Cambridge: Cambridge University Press, 2012); Waheguru Pal Singh Sidhu and Jing-dong Yuan, *China and India: Cooperation or Conflict?* (Boulder: Lynne Reinner, 2003).

138. These are described in David Shambaugh, "China's Military Views the World," *International Security* (Winter 1999/2000), p. 72.

139. See Wu Jiao, Zhou Wa, and Cui Haipei, "SCO Will Be Fortress of Security and Stability," *China Daily*, June 8, 2012.

140. See Mark Burles, *Chinese Policy Toward Russia and the Central Asian Republics* (Santa Monica, CA: Rand, 1999); Charles Hawkins and Robert R. Love, *Chinese Views on Central Asia* (Fort Leavenworth, KS: Foreign Military Studies Office, 2006); Paul Stares et al., *Managing Instability on China's Periphery* (New York: Council on Foreign Relations, 2011).

141. Also see Robert Sutter, *China's Rise in Asia: Promises and Perils* (Lanham, MD: Rowman & Littlefield, 2005); William W. Keller and Thomas G. Rawski (eds.), *China's Rise and the Balance of Influence in Asia* (Pittsburgh: University of Pittsburgh Press, 2007); Avery Goldstein, "U.S.-China Interactions in Asia," in Shambaugh (ed.), *Tangled Titans*, op. cit.

142. Geoffrey Kemp, *The East Moves West* (Washington, DC: Brookings Institution Press, 2010), p. 64.

143. Mohamed Bin Huwaidin, *China's Relations with Arabia and the Gulf, 1949–1999* (London: Routledge, 2002), p. 116.

144. John W. Garver, *China and Iran: Ancient Partners in a Post-Imperial World* (Seattle: University of Washington Press, 2007).

145. For a more extended assessment see Willem van Kemenade, *Iran's Relations with China and the West: Cooperation and Confrontation in Asia* (The Hague: Clingendael Diplomacy Papers No. 24, 2009).

146. The best single source of analysis on CASCF is Dawn Murphy, *Rising Revisionist: China's Relations with the Middle East and Africa* (George Washington University, Department of Political Science, Ph.D. Dissertation, 2012).

147. Dawn Murphy's discussion of China's Middle East Envoy is also the best available. See ibid.

148. For recent assessments of China's relations with the region, see Jon B. Alterman and John W. Garver, *The Vital Triangle: China, the United States, and the Middle East* (Washington, DC: CSIS, 2008); Ben Simpfendorfer, *The New Silk Road* (New York: Palgrave Macmillan, 2009); Geoffrey Kemp, *The East Moves West*, op. cit.; Bryce Wakefield and Susan L. Levenstein (eds.), *China and the Persian Gulf* (Washington, DC: Woodrow Wilson International Center for Scholars, 2011); Mao Yufeng, "China's Interests and Strategy in the Middle East and the Arab World," in Joshua Eisenman, Eric Heginbotham, and Derek Mitchell (eds.), *China and the Developing World: Beijing's Strategy for the Twenty-first Century* (Armonk, NY: M.E. Sharpe, 2007); Yitzhak Shichor, "China's Middle East Strategy: In Search of Wells and Power,"

in Lowell Dittmer and George T. Yu (eds.), *China, the Developing World, and the New Global Dynamic* (Boulder: Lynne Reinner, 2010).

149. A large and excellent literature has emerged on China-Africa relations in recent years. See David H. Shinn and Joshua Eisenman, *China and Africa: A Century of Engagement* (Philadelphia: University of Pennsylvania Press, 2012); Deborah Brautigam, *The Dragon's Gift: The Real Story of China in Africa* (New York: Oxford University Press, 2009); Robert I. Rotberg (ed.), *China Into Africa: Trade, Aid, and Influence* (Washington, DC: Brookings Institution Press, 2008); Sarah Raine, *China's African Challenges* (London: International Institute of Strategic Studies, 2009); Chris Alden, *China in Africa* (London: Zed Books, 2007); Harry G. Broadman, *Africa's Silk Road: China and India's New Economic Frontier* (Washington, DC: World Bank, 2007); Arthur Waldron (ed.), *China in Africa* (Washington, DC: Jamestown Foundation, 2008); Serge Michel and Michel Beuret, *China Safari: On the Trail of Beijing's Expansion in Africa* (New York: Nation Books, 2008); Chris Alden, Daniel Large, and Ricardo Soares De Oliveira (eds.), *China Returns to Africa: A Rising Power and a Continent Embrace* (London: Hurst, 2008); Meine Pieter van Dijk (ed.), *The New Presence of China in Africa* (Amsterdam: Amsterdam University Press, 2009); Kweku Ampiah and Sanusha Naidu (eds.), *Crouching Tiger, Hidden Dragon: Africa and China* (Scottsville, South Africa: University of KwaZulu-Natal Press, 2008); Marcel Kitissou (ed.), *Africa in China's Global Strategy* (London: Adonis and Abbey Publishers, 2007); *China Quarterly* Special Issue "China and Africa: Emerging Patterns in Globalization and Devleopment," No. 199 (2009); Linda Jakobson, "China's Diplomacy Toward Africa: Drivers and Constraints," *International Relations of the Asia-Pacific*, Vol. 9, No. 3 (2009).

150. Deborah Brautigam, *The Dragon's Gift*, ibid.

151. Interview with Song Aiguo, director general for West Asian and North African Affairs, Ministry of Foreign Affairs, June 29, 2007, Beijing.

152. For studies of China–Latin America relations, see "Latin America's Response to China's Rise," special issue of the *Journal of Current Chinese Affairs (China Aktuell)*, Vol. 41, No. 1 (2012); Adrian Hearn and José Luis León-Manríquez (eds.), *China Engages Latin America: Tracing the Trajectory* (Boulder: Lynne Reinner, 2011); Riordan Roett and Guadalupe Paz (eds.), *China's Expansion into the Western Hemisphere* (Washington, DC: Brookings Institution Press, 2008); R. Evan Ellis, *China in Latin America: The Whats and Wherefores* (Boulder: Lynne Reinner, 2009); Javier Santiso (ed.), *The Visible Hand of China in Latin America* (Paris: OECD, 2007); Kevin P. Gallagher and Roberto Porzecanski, *The Dragon in the Room: China and the Future of Latin American Industrialization* (Stanford: Stanford University Press, 2010); Robert Devlin et al. (eds.), *The Emergence of China: Opportunities and Challenges for Latin America and the Caribbean* (Washington, DC: Inter-American Development Bank, 2006); Alex E. Fernández Jilberto and Barbara Hogenboom (eds.), *Latin*

America Facing China: South-South Relations Beyond the Washington Consensus (New York and Oxford: Berghan Books, 2010); R. Evan Ellis, *The Expanding Chinese Footprint in Latin America* (Paris: IFRI Center for Asian Studies, 2012).

153. Much of this section also appears in David Shambaugh and Dawn Murphy, "U.S.-China Interactions in the Middle East, Africa, Europe, and Latin America," in Shambaugh (ed.), *Tangled Titans*, op. cit.

154. Interview with Wu Baiyi, Institute of Latin American Studies, April 29, 2010, Beijing.

155. Interview with Regina Dunlop, Brazil Ministry of Foreign Affairs, July 2, 2008, Brasilia.

156. Interview with Roberto Abdeneur, Brazil Center for International Relations, July 3, 2008, Rio de Janeiro.

157. Xinhua, "China, Brazil Pledge to Promote Strategic Partnership, Promote Cooperation," April 16, 2010, http://news.xinhuanet.com/english2010/china/2010–04/16/c_13253390.htm.

158. Statement by Yang Wanming, director general, Latin American and Caribbean Affairs Department, Ministry of Foreign Affairs, Inter-American Dialogue, Washington, DC, March 9, 2012. Also see Wu Hongying, "China and the U.S. in Latin America: Cooperation or Competition?" paper presented to the Fifth Dialogue on U.S.-China Relations in Global Context, June 2, 2011, Beijing.

159. For further discussion, see David Shambaugh, "Forward," in Adrian H. Hearn and José Luis León-Manríquez (eds.), *China Engages Latin America: Tracing the Trajectory* (Boulder: Lynne Reinner, 2011), pp. ix-xviii.

160. See Cynthia Watson, "China's Arms Sales to Latin America: Another Arrow in the Quiver," *China Brief*, Vol. 10, No. 4 (2010), http://www.jamestown.org/single/?no_cache=1&tx_ttnews[tt_news]=36053.

161. See R. Evan Ellis, *China-Latin America Military Engagement: Good Will, Good Business, and Strategic Position* (Carlisle Barracks, PA: U.S. Army War College Strategic Studies Institute, 2011).

162. See *2009 Statistical Bulletin of China's Outward Foreign Direct Investment* (Beijing: China Ministry of Commerce, 2009), http://chinainvests.files.wordpress.com/2010/12/2009-mofcom-investment-report1.pdf.

163. Ibid.

164. See Economic Commission for Latin America and the Caribbean, *Foreign Direct Investment in Latin America and the Caribbean* (Santiago, Chile: 2011).

165. For more on China's foreign direct investment into Latin America, see R. Evan Ellis, "China Comes Calling: Chinese Investment in Latin America Is on the Rise," *AFP Exchange* (September 2011), pp. 42–47.

166. See Jörn Dosch and David S. G. Goodman, "China and Latin America: Complementarity, Competition, and Globalization," *Journal of Current Chinese Affairs*, Vol. 41, No. 1 (2012), p. 12.

167. Yang Wanming, statement at Inter-American Dialogue, March 9, 2012, Washington, DC.
168. Ibid.; and Randal C. Archibold, "China Buys Inroads in the Caribbean, Catching U.S. Notice," *New York Times*, April 7, 2012.
169. See BBC World Service Poll: Attitudes Toward Countries, 2011, http://www.globescan.com/news_archives/bbc2011_countries/.
170. See Eric Farnsworth, "The New Mercantilism: China's Emerging Role in the Americas," *Current History* (February 2011), pp. 56–61.

Chapter 4

1. Interview with analyst, China Institutes of Contemporary International Relations, April 19, 2010, Beijing.
2. Statement by Chinese scholar at Zhongshan University conference, May 8, 2010.
3. Xinhua, "Full Text of White Paper on China's Peaceful Development," September 6, 2011.
4. To be sure, the issue is larger than just China—insofar as the role of other rising powers in global governance is also being questioned. See the excellent study by Alan S. Alexandroff and Andrew F. Cooper (eds.), *Rising States, Rising Institutions: Challenges for Global Governance* (Washington, DC: Brookings Institution Press, 2010).
5. Robert B. Zoellick, "Whither China: From Membership to Responsibility," Remarks to National Committee on U.S.-China Relations, September 21, 2005. Also see Evan S. Medeiros, "Is Beijing Ready for Global Leadership?" *Current History* (September 2009); Charles Grant, *Russia, China, and Global Governance* (London: Center for European Reform, 2012); Bates Gill and Michael Schiffer, "A Rising China's Rising Responsibilities," in Michael Schiffer and David Shorr (eds.), *Power and Principles: International Leadership in a Shrinking World* (Lanham: Lexington Books, 2009), pp. 99–123; Bates Gill, "China's Evolving Approach to Multilateralism and Global Governance: Implications for the European Union," in Bart Gaens, Juha Jokela, and Eiija Limnell (eds.), *The European Union's Role in Asia: China and India as Strategic Partners* (Surrey, UK: Ashgate, 2009); Hongying Wang and James Rosenau, "China and Global Governance," *Asian Perspective* Vol. 33, No. 3 (2009), pp. 5–39.
6. See Alastair I. Johnston, "Is China a Status Quo Power?" *International Security*, Vol. 27, No. 4 (Spring 2003), pp. 5–56.
7. National Intelligence Council and European Union Institute for Security Studies, *Global Governance 2025: At a Critical Juncture* (Washington, DC: National Intelligence Council, 2011), iii.
8. James N. Rosenau and Ernst Otto Czempiel (eds.), *Governance Without Governments: Order and Change in World Politics* (Cambridge: Cambridge University Press, 1992).

9. Commission on Global Governance, *Our Global Neighborhood: Report from the Commission on Global Governance* (Oxford: Oxford University Press, 1995), cited in Margaret P. Karns and Karen A. Mignst, *International Organizations: The Politics and Processes of Global Governance* (Boulder: Lynne Reinner, 2010), pp. 3–4.

10. Karns and Mignst, *International Organizations*, ibid., p. 66. Discussion of The Hague conferences draws on this work.

11. See Thomas G. Weiss and Ramesh Thakur, *Global Governance and the UN: An Unfinished Journey* (Bloomington: Indiana University Press, 2010).

12. Thomas Friedman, *The Lexus and the Olive Tree* (New York: Anchor Books, 2000); *The World Is Flat 3.0* (New York: Picador Books, 2007).

13. I am grateful to Rosemary Foot for clarifying this evolution and the roles played by the United States and China.

14. G. John Ikenberry, "The Three Faces of Liberal Internationalism," in Alexandroff and Cooper (eds.), *Rising States, Rising Institutions*, op. cit., p. 19.

15. See Mahathir bin Mohammed, *Reflections on Asia* (Kuala Lumpur: Pelanduk, 2002).

16. Kishore Mahbubani, *Can Asians Think? Reflections on the Divide Between East and West* (Singapore: Marshall Cavendish, 2004).

17. Gregory Chin, "China's Rising International Influence," in Alexandroff and Cooper (eds.), *Rising States, Rising Institutions*, op. cit., p. 100.

18. Ren Xiao, "A Reform Minded Status Quo Power? China, the G-20, and Changes in the International Monetary System," draft paper presented at a conference at Indiana University Research Center for Chinese Politics and Business, 2012.

19. James Politi, "World Bank Sees End to Dollar Hegemony," *Financial Times*, May 17, 2011.

20. No Author, "U.S. Dollar Is Still Top Choice," *New York Times*, August 11, 2011.

21. Interview, Ministry of Foreign Affairs, March 21, 2009, Singapore.

22. Interview, Ministry of Foreign Affairs, March 13, 2010, Singapore.

23. For an overview of Chinese research on global governance, see Chen Chengxin, "Guonei 'Quanqiu Zhili' Yanjiu Shuping" [A Review of Domestic Research on "Global Governance"], *Zhengzhixue Yanjiu*, No. 1 (2009), pp. 118–128.

24. Interview with Ye Jiang, Shanghai Institutes of International Studies, September 19, 2011.

25. See Wang Jisi, "Fuze Daguo de Quanqiu Jiaose" [Global Roles as a Responsible Power], *Zhongguo Waijiao*, No. 4 (2009), pp. 9–11; Wang Jisi, "Dangdai Shijie Zhengzhi Fazhan Qushi yu Zhongguo de Quanqiu Jiaose" [The Contemporary Trends in World Politics and the Global Role of China], ibid., pp. 3–6; Shi Yinhong, "Quanqiuxing Tiaozhan yu Zhongguo" [Globalizing Conditions and China], *Xiandai Guoji Guanxi*, No. 3 (2009), pp. 1–4.

26. Li Jie, "The Transition of the International System," *China International Studies* (Winter 2007), pp. 152–153.

27. Ma Zhengang, "China's Responsibility and the 'China Responsibility' Theory," *China International Studies* (Summer 2007), pp. 8–9.

28. Cao Yang, "Guoji zhixu zhong 'daguo zeren' de kunjing yu Zhongguo" ["Great Power Responsibility" in the International Order and China] *Dangdai Shijie* (November 2011), pp. 48–49.

29. Interview with Vice Foreign Minister Cui Tiankai, June 8, 2012, Beijing.

30. See John Ikenberry, "The Rise of China and Future of the West: Can the Liberal System Survive?" *Foreign Affairs* (January/February 2008).

31. Interview with Ye Jiang, "Shanghai Institutes of International Studies," op. cit.

32. Xinhua, "Full Text of White Paper on China's Peaceful Development," September 6, 2011.

33. Ann Kent, *Beyond Compliance: China, International Organizations, and Global Security* (Stanford: Stanford University Press, 2007).

34. See Jeffrey Checkel, "International Institutions and Socialization in Europe," *International Organization*, Vol. 59, No. 4 (2005), pp. 801–826.

35. See Martha Finnemore, *National Interest and International Society* (Ithaca, NY: Cornell University Press, 1996).

36. Kent, *Beyond Compliance*, op. cit., p. 56.

37. Yan Xuetong, "China Views China's Role in Global Governance," lecture at The Sigur Center for Asian Studies, Elliott School of International Affairs, George Washington University, November 8, 2011.

38. Ibid.

39. Katherine Morton, *China and the Future of International Norms* (Canberra: Australia Strategic Policy Institute, 2011), http://www.aspi.org.au/research/spf_article.aspx?aid=95.

40. See Harold K. Jacobson and Michel C. Oksenberg, *China's Participation in the IMF, World Bank, and GATT: Toward a Global Economic Order* (Ann Arbor: University of Michigan Press, 1990).

41. Ministry of Foreign Affairs, *China's Foreign Affairs 2010*, op. cit., p. 338.

42. Tsinghua University Department of International Relations and Economic Diplomacy Research Center, *Zhongguo Jingji Waijiao 2009* [China's Economic Diplomacy in 2009] (Beijing: Shijie zhishi chubanshe, 2009), p. 33.

43. See Kent, *Beyond Compliance*, op. cit.; Alastair I. Johnston, *Social States, Social States: China and International Institutions, 1980–2000* (Princeton: Princeton University Press, 2008); Evan S. Medeiros, *Reluctant Restraint: The Evolution of China's Nonproliferation Policies and Practices, 1980–2004* (Stanford: Stanford University Press, 2007).

44. See Samuel Kim, "China and the United Nations," in Michel Oksenberg and Elizabeth Economy (eds.), *China Joins the World*, op. cit., Table 2–2.

45. For an excellent study of this, see Xiaojun Li, "Learning and Socialization in International Institutions: China's Experience with the WTO Dispute

Settlement System," paper delivered to the conference on "China's Role in Global and Regional Governance," at the S. Rajaratnam School of International Studies, Nanyang Technological University, March 10–11, 2011.

46. No author, "Guoji Diwei" [International Position], *Renmin Ribao*, September 23, 2009.

47. Stephen Olson and Clyde Prestowitz, "The Evolving Role of China in International Institutions," paper prepared for the U.S. Economic and Security Review Commission (January 2011), p. 11, http://www.uscc.gov/researchpapers/2011/TheEvolvingRoleofChinainInternationalInstitutions.pdf.

48. In 1997 China vetoed sending cease-fire observers to Guatemala, as the government had diplomatic relations with Taiwan. In 1999 Beijing did the same with Macedonia for the same reason. In 2007 it vetoed (along with Russia) a resolution that was critical of Myanmar's human rights record. In 2008 it vetoed sanctions against Zimbabwe (again with Russia). In 2012 it vetoed (along with Russia) two resolutions on Syria.

49. See the discussion in Harry Harding, "China's Views of International Norms and Institutions," in Gudrun Wacker and David Shambaugh (eds.), *American and European Relations with China: Advancing Common Agendas* (Berlin: Stiftung Wissenschaft und Politik, 2008).

50. See Michael Fullilove, "China and the United Nations: The Stakeholder Spectrum," *Washington Quarterly* (Summer 2011), p. 71.

51. See Amitai Etzioni and G. John Ikenberry, "Point of Order: Is China More Westfalian than the West?" *Foreign Affairs* (November/December 2011), pp. 172–176.

52. Ministry of Foreign Affairs, *China's Foreign Affairs 2010*, op. cit., p. 323.

53. I am grateful to Ed Elmendorf for this observation.

54. Olson and Prestowitz, "The Evolving Role of China in International Institutions," op. cit., p. 47.

55. See Michael Wines, "Secret Bid to Arm Qaddafi Sheds Light on Tensions in China Government," *New York Times*, September 12, 2011; Jessica Silver-Greenberg, "Prosecutors Link Money from China to Iran," *New York Times*, August 30, 2012; Stephanie Kleine-Ahlbrandt and Andrew Small, "China's New Dictatorship Diplomacy," *Foreign Affairs*, Vol. 87, No. 1 (January/February 2008).

56. Fullilove, "China and the United Nations," op. cit., p. 78.

57. United Nations, "Image and Reality about the UN," http://www.un.org/geninfo/ir/index.asp?id=150.

58. I am grateful to Dawn Murphy for her research assistance and George Shambaugh IV for helping to interpret the data.

59. Another database measured the longer time period of 1974–2008 (3384) and found similar, but slightly different, patterns. See Erik Voeten and Adis Merdzanovic, United Nations General Assembly Voting Data, http://hdl:1901.1/12379UNF:3:Hpf6qOkDdzzvXF9m66yLTg=.html.

During this period, China voted 77.83 percent identically with Brazil; 77.36 percent identically with India; 78.58 identically with Mexico; 65.99 percent identically with Russia; 80.38 percent identically with South Africa (1994–2008); 36.26 percent identically with France; 33.42 percent identically with the United Kingdom; and 13.21 percent identically with the United States. I am grateful to Peter Ferdinand for bringing this data to my attention. See his "China and the Developing World," in David Shambaugh (ed.), *Charting China's Future: Domestic and International Challenges* (London: Routledge, 2010), p. 91.

60. Interview with Ambassador Wang Guangya, March 20, 2008, New York.

61. For a useful survey of this literature see Li Mingjiang, "Rising from Within: China's Search for a Multilateral World and Its Implications for Sino-U.S. Relations," *Global Governance*, No. 17 (2011), pp. 331–351.

62. See "A Chinese View of NPT Conference," http://www.cfr.org/publication/22032/chinese_view_of_npt_conference.html.

63. Kenneth Ward, "The BWC Protocol: Mandate for Failure?" *The Nonproliferation Review*, Vol. 11, Issue 2 (Summer 2004), p. 6. I am grateful to Matthew Hallex and his research, "A Responsible Stakeholder? Assessing Chinese Behavior in Nonproliferation Regimes," seminar paper, George Washington University, 2010.

64. This section draws on Craig Riley, "China and INTERPOL Participation," seminar paper, George Washington University, 2008.

65. Xinhua, "Jiang Zemin Speaks at 64th INTERPOL Assembly," April 10, 1995.

66. "Minister Explains China's Participation in Interpol," *Renmin Gong'an*, October 25, 1995, in FBIS-CHI-96–035.

67. Yan Liang, "China Cooperates with Other Countries to Pursue Corrupt Officials Abroad," Xinhua, April 25, 2008.

68. Xie Chuanjiao, "Beijing Seeks More Extradition Treaties," *China Daily*, May 28, 2007, http://www.chinadaily.com.cn/cndy/2007–05/28/content_881140.htm.

69. Yang Liang, "China Cooperates with Other Countries to Pursue Corrupt Officials Abroad," op. cit.

70. He Na, Zhang Yan, and Li Jing, "Long Arm of the Law Grabs Its Man," *China Daily*, July 26, 2011.

71. Ibid.

72. Interview with senior Canadian official, June 24, 2011, Beijing.

73. Andrew Jacobs, "Chinese Tycoon Gets Life for Bribes and Smuggling," *New York Times*, May 19, 2012.

74. This section has particularly benefited from Lai-Ha Chan, *China Engages Global Health Governance* (New York: Palgrave Macmillan, 2011).

75. See Bates Gill and Michael Schiffer, "A Rising China's Rising Responsibilities," in Michael Schiffer and David Shorr (eds.), *Power and Principles: International Leadership in a Shrinking World* (Lanham: Lexington Books, 2009), p. 107.

76. "HIV/AIDS in China," http://www.chinadaily.com.cn/cndy/2007–05/28/content_881140.htm.

77. Lai-Ha Chan, *China Engages Global Health Governance*, op. cit., pp. 61–62.

78. Permanent Mission of the People's Republic of China to the United Nations Office at Geneva, "China's Relationship with the World Health Organization (WHO)," http://www.china-un.ch/eng/zmjg/jgjblc/t85563.htm.

79. This section has benefited much from Katherine Morton, *China and the Global Environment: Learning from the Past and Anticipating the Future* (Sydney: Lowy Institute for International Policy, 2009). Statistics are drawn from this and other studies.

80. "The G2: The Key to CO_2," *Financial Times*, December 9, 2009.

81. "The World's Most Polluted Places," *Time*, September 12, 2007.

82. "Raising a Stink," *Economist*, August 5, 2010.

83. Morton, *China and the Global Environment*, op. cit., p. 4.

84. The World Bank, *Addressing China's Water Scarcity: Recommendations for Selected Water Resource Management Issues* (Washington, DC: World Bank, 2009).

85. Asia Water Project, *In Deep Water: Ecological Destruction of China's Water Resources* (2007), as cited in Reuters, "China Says Water Supplies Exhausted by 2030," December 14, 2007.

86. Xinhua, "Half of China's Ground Water Contaminated," October 9, 2006, http://www.china.org.cn/english/environment/183230.htm.

87. Morton, *China and the Global Environment*, op. cit., p. 4.

88. See Katherine Morton, "Climate Change and Security at the Third Pole," *Survival*, Vol. 53, No. 1 (February–March 2011).

89. Katherine Morton, *China and the Global Environment*, p. 39; Ministry of Environmental Protection of the People's Republic of China, "Laws, Statues, and Regulations," http://english.sepa.gov.cn/Policies_Regulations/.

90. Xinhua, "Chinese Environmental NGOs Called to Play a Bigger Role," October 30, 2006, http://www.china.org.cn/english/environment/186754.htm.

91. See Peter Ho and Richard Louis Edmonds, *China's Embedded Activism: Opportunities and Constraints of a Social Movement* (London: Routledge, 2007); and Andrew Mertha, *China's Water Warriors: Citizen Action and Policy Change* (Ithaca, NY: Cornell University Press, 2008).

92. Stephen Mufson, "China Steps Up, Slowly But Surely," *Washington Post*, October 24, 2009.

93. Hu Jintao, "Statement at the Opening Plenary Session of the United Nations Summit on Climate Change," *Beijing Review*, No. 44, November 5, 2009, p. 3.

94. See Keith Bradsher, "China Benefits as U.S. Solar Industry Withers," *New York Times*, September 2, 2011.

95. No author, "A New Energy Era Begins," *Magazin-Deutschland*, No. 2 (2011), p. 10.

96. For a full listing see Lester Ross, "China and Environmental Protection," in Oksenberg and Economy (eds.), *China Joins the World*, op. cit., Table 9–1.

97. See, for example, Ed Miliband, "How Do I Know China Wrecked the Copenhagen Deal? I Was in the Room," *Guardian*, December 22, 2009, http://www.guardian.co.uk/environment/2009/dec/22/copenhagen-clima te-change-mark-lynas.

98. For a fuller evaluation, see Rosemary Foot and Andrew Walter, *China, the United States, and Global Order* (Oxford: Oxford University Press, 2011), chap. 5.

99. The best study of Chinese political culture remains Lucien W. Pye, *The Mandarin and the Cadre* (Ann Arbor: Michigan Monographs in Chinese Studies, 1988).

100. In the context of China's approach to international organizations, this is consistent with the earlier findings of Stephen Krasner, Robert Keohane, and Ernest Haas. See Stephen D. Krasner, *Structural Conflict: The Third World Against Global Socialism* (Berkeley: University of California Press, 1985); Robert Keohane, "The Demand for International Regimes," *International Organization*, Vol. 36, No. 2 (Spring 1982); Ernst Haas, "Why Collaborate? Issue-Linkage and International Regimes," *World Politics*, Vol. 32, No. 3 (April 1980).

101. See David Shambaugh, "The Evolving and Eclectic Chinese State," and Lyman H. Miller, "The Late Imperial Chinese State," in David Shambaugh (ed.), *The Modern Chinese State* (Cambridge: Cambridge University Press, 2000).

Chapter 5

1. Wen Jiabao, "Full Text: Report on the Work of the Government," http://www.chinadaily.com.cn/china/2012–03/16/content_14847640_5. htm.

2. Quoted in Wang Bo, "CIC Getting Decent Returns, Chief Says," *China Daily*, October 29, 2009.

3. Fuels and mining products accounted for 2.9 percent, with agricultural products accounting for 3.4 percent. World Trade Organization, "China," http://stat.wto.org/CountryProfile/WSDBCountryPFView. aspx?Language=E&Country=CN.

4. In 2010 China's surplus with the United States was a record $273.1 billion, while with the EU it was €108.175 billion. Sources: U.S.-China Business Council, "China's Trade with the United States, 2001–2010" (Table 1), https://www.uschina.org/statistics/tradetable.html; European Commission (DG Trade), "China, Trade with the European Union," TRADE A2-CG/MP, June 8, 2011.

5. EUROSTAT, June 2011. The IMF *Direction of Trade Statistics* (2011) places the total at €363.224 billion.

6. Information on FTAs derives from MOFCOM website, http://fta. mofcom.gov.cn/english/fta_qianshu.shtml.

7. Xinhua, "Full Text of China's White Paper on Peaceful Development," September 6, 2011.

8. Wang Chao, "China Investments Meet Bottleneck Overseas," *China Daily*, December 21, 2010.

9. Xinhua, "China Still Struggling for Market Economy Status from EU," May 21, 2009, http://news.xinhuanet.com/english/2009–05/21/ content_11415493.htm.

10. Lingling Wei, "China Shows Its Growing Might—New Move to Make Yuan a Global Currency," *Wall Street Journal*, January 12, 2011.

11. See, for example, Meredith Woo-Cumings, *The Developmental State* (Ithaca, NY: Cornell University Press, 1999).

12. See Ashlee Vance, "China Takes Top Spot for Fastest Computer," *International Herald Tribune*, October 29, 2010.

13. Jamil Anderlini, "Autocratic Directives Fail to Spark Creativity," *Financial Times*, October 26, 2011.

14. David Barboza and John Markoff, "Power in Numbers: China Aims for High-Tech Primacy," *New York Times*, December 6, 2011.

15. International Crisis Group, *China's Thirst for Oil* (Seoul and Brussels: International Crisis Group, 2008), p. 3.

16. Zhou Yan, "Shale Gas, Emission Cuts Urged to Reduce China's Oil Imports," *China Daily*, August 4, 2011.

17. International Energy Agency, *World Energy Outlook 2008* (Paris: OECD/ IEA, 2008), pp. 93, 102.

18. Also see Henry Lee and Dan A. Shalmon, "Searching for Oil: China's Initiatives in the Middle East," *Environment*, Vol. 49, No. 5 (2007), pp. 10–21.

19. "China's Crude Oil Imports by Source," FACTS Global Energy (2009), http://www.fgenergy.com.

20. Julie Jiang and Jonathan Sinton, *Overseas Investments by Chinese National Oil Companies: Assessing the Drivers and Impacts* (Paris: OECD International Energy Agency, 2011), p. 8.

21. Jeremy Page, "Daqing-Skovorodino Oil Pipeline to Pump 300,000 Barrels a Day for 20 Years," *Wall Street Journal*, September 27, 2010.

22. "Country Comparison: Oil Exports," *CIA World Factbook 2010*, http:// www.cia.gov.library/publications/the-world-factbook.html.

23. Some Chinese analysts argue that Russia should be China's favored supplier of choice. See Wang Yong, *Zhongguo Duiwai Shiyou Zhanlue Yanjiu* [Research on China's Overseas Oil Strategy] (Hangzhou: Zhejiang University Press, 2009), p. 179.

24. Hal Foster, "China Will Be Involved in 50 Percent of Kazakhstan's 2010 Oil Output," *Central Asia Newswire*, August 20, 2010. This point and paragraph have benefited from research done by Russell Sticklor, "China's Quest for Energy Security," seminar paper, George Washington University, December 2010.

25. Erica Downs, "Who's Afraid of China's Oil Companies?" http://www.brookings.edu/research/papers/2010/07/china-oil-downs.

26. "Global 500," http://money.cnn.com/magazines/fortune/global500/2011/full_list/.

27. Sinopec website, "About the Sinopec Group," http://www.sinopecgroup.com/english/Pages/guanyu_gsjs.aspx.

28. The Sinopec Group's listed arm is Sinopec Corporation, which raised $3.5 billion in its initial public offering; CNPC's is PetroChina Ltd., which raised $2.9 billion; while CNOOC established CNOOC Ltd., and raised $1.3 billion in its IPO. See Trevor Houser, "The Roots of Chinese Oil Investment Abroad," *Asia Policy*, No. 5 (2008), p. 146.

29. I am grateful to Erica Downs on this point.

30. Chih-Shian Liou, "Bureaucratic Politics and Overseas Investment by Chinese State-Owned Oil Companies: Illusory Champions," *Asian Survey*, Vol. 49, No. 4 (2009), p. 677.

31. This description is drawn from Jill Shankleman, *Going Global: Chinese Oil and Mining Companies and the Governance of Resource Wealth* (Washington, DC: Woodrow Wilson International Center for Scholars, no date), p. 21.

32. Data drawn from IEA, *World Energy Outlook*, op. cit.

33. "Global 500," op. cit.

34. Philip Andrews-Speed and Roland Dannreuther, *China, Oil, and Global Politics* (Routledge: London, 2011), p. 79.

35. Guy Chazan and Shai Oster, "Sinopec Pact for Addax Boosts China's Buying Binge," *Wall Street Journal*, June 25, 2009; Chris Nicholson, "Sinopec Makes Offer for Addax," *International Herald Tribune*, June 29, 2009.

36. Andrew Higgins, "A Booze Blowout for China's Oil Giant," *Washington Post*, May 7, 2011.

37. Zhou Yan, "CNOOC Agrees to Acquire Distressed Oil Sands Firm," *China Daily*, July 21, 2011.

38. Jiang and Sinton, *Overseas Investments by Chinese National Oil Companies*, op. cit., p. 43.

39. Shankelman, *Going Global*, op. cit., p. 22.

40. Leslie Hook, "An Unlikely Visionary: CNOOC's Fu Chengyu," *Financial Times*, April 5, 2011.

41. "Sinochem: Corporate Profile," http://www.sinochem.com/english/tabid/615/Default.aspx.

42. Jiang and Sinton, *Overseas Investments by Chinese Oil Companies*, op. cit., p. 37.

43. Wan Zhihong, "PetroChina Lines Up $60 b to Boost Overseas Oil, Gas," *China Daily*, May 21, 2010.

44. Data from EIA, op. cit.

45. Jiang and Sinton, *Overseas Investments by Chinese Oil Companies*, op. cit., p. 37.

46. Sylvia Pfeifer and Leslie Hook, "Chinese Demand for Energy Pumps Up M&A Share," *Financial Times*, November 8, 2010.

47. Ibid.

48. Andrews-Speed and Dannreuther, *China, Oil, and Global Politics*, op. cit., p. 78.

49. Zhu Feng, a Peking University scholar, is quoted in Richard McGregor, "China's Diplomacy 'Hijacked' by Companies," *Financial Times*, March 16, 2008. Zhu was specifically referring to the case of Sudan.

50. These are noted in Julie Jiang and Jonathan Sinton, *Overseas Investments by China's National Oil Companies*, op. cit., p. 13.

51. Ibid.; Theodore H. Moran, *China's Strategy to Secure Natural Resources: Risks, Dangers, and Opportunities* (Washington, DC: Peterson Institute for International Economics, 2010), pp. 45–48; and International Crisis Group, *China's Thirst for Oil*, op. cit., p. 11.

52. Downs, "Who's Afraid of China's Oil Companies?" op. cit., pp. 88–89.

53. Keith Bradsher, "China's Buying Spree Elevates Commodities," *International Herald Tribune*, June 11, 2009.

54. Jack Farchy and Javier Blas, "Chinese Buying Drives Copper to Record with More Rises Expected," *Financial Times*, November 12, 2010.

55. No author, "Copper Imports May Drop 50%: Demand Last Year Driven by Stockpiling, Government Spending," *China Daily*, February 10, 2010.

56. Karen Maley, "China's Gold Tsunami," *Business Spectator*, February 8, 2011.

57. "China Remains Hungry for Commodities," *Miner's Choice*, n.d., http://www.minerschoice.co.za/commodity_news1.html.

58. No author, "Iron Rations," *Economist*, March 15, 2008, pp. 7–8.

59. Of these imports, Australian suppliers accounted for 41.8 percent, Brazil for 22.6 percent, India for 17.1 percent, South Africa for 5.44 percent, and other suppliers 13.06 percent. Wang Chao, "China Investments Meet Bottleneck Overseas," op. cit.

60. Bradsher, "China's Buying Spree Elevates Commodities," op. cit.

61. The Minmetals website is http://www.minmetals.com/english/introduction.jsp.

62. Ibid.

63. No author, "China Invests About 24% Outbound FDI in Mining," *People's Daily Online*, November 2, 2010, http://www.chinamining.org/News/2010–11–02?1288660641d40323.html.

64. Leslie Hook, "China's Miners Set to Make Tracks Overseas," *Financial Times*, April 4, 2011.

65. Tuo Yannan and Zhang Qi, "Rare Earth Prices 'Reflect Market,'" *China Daily*, July 22–24, 2011.

66. Zhou Yan and Zhang Qi, "Rare Earth Output to Be Halted," *China Daily*, August 3, 2011.

67. See Stephen Castle, "WTO Faults China over Raw Materials," *International Herald Tribune*, July 6, 2011; Keith Bradsher, "Supplies

Squeezed, Rare Earth Prices Surge," *New York Times*, May 2, 2011; No author, "China Dangles Rare-Earth Resources to Lure Investment," *Wall Street Journal*, August 16, 2010.

68. Tuo Yannan and Zhang Qi, "Rare Earth Prices 'Reflect Market,'" op. cit.

69. Keith Bradsher, "In Victory for the West, WTO Orders China to Stop Export Taxes on Minerals," *New York Times*, January 31, 2012; Joshua Chaffin and Alan Beattle, "China Chastised on Rare Earths," *Financial Times*, January 31, 2012.

70. Xinhua, "Full Text of White Paper on China's Peaceful Development," September 6, 2011.

71. References to these speeches and Jiang's role in developing the "going out" policy are traced in some detail in Chen Yangyong, "Jiang Zemin 'zou chuqu' zhanlue de xingcheng jiqi zhongyao yiyi" [Jiang Zemin's 'Going Out' Strategic Influence and Important Formulation], http://theory.people.com.cn/GB/40557/138172/138202/8311431.html. I am grateful to Kristin Burke for drawing my attention to this speech. See Kristin Burke, "China's Outbound Foreign Direct Investment: Tools and Impact," seminar paper, George Washington University, December 2010.

72. "Full Text of Jiang Zemin's Report to the 14th Party Congress," available at http://www.bjreview.com.cn/document/txt/2011–03/29/content_363504.htm.

73. "Full Text of Jiang Zemin's Report to the 15th Party Congress," available at http://english.people.com.cn/200211/18/eng20021118_106984.shtml.

74. Ibid.

75. Chen Yangyong, "Jiang Zemin 'zou chuqu' zhanlue de xingcheng jiqi zhongyao yiyi," op. cit.

76. Ibid.

77. Duncan Freeman, "China's Outward Investment: A Policy Overview," (Brussels: BICCS Policy Paper, 2008), p. 8.

78. OECD, *Investment Policy Reviews: China 2008* (Paris: OECD, 2008), p. 85. The relevant MOFCOM and NDRC guidelines and regulations are well discussed in this source.

79. Shangwubu, Guojia he Gaige Weiyuanhui, Waijiaobu Guanyu Xuanbu *Duiwai touzi guobie chanye zhiying (2011) de zhidao* [Ministry of Commerce, National Reform Development Commission, and Foreign Ministry Announce Directive on Overseas Investment for Certain Industries], http://hzs.mofcom.gov.cn/aarticle/zcfb/b/201109/20110907731140.html.

80. Zhang Yansheng, "'Shi Er Wu' Qijian Zhongguo Shishi 'Zou Chuqu' de Zhanlue Yuanze" [China's Strategic Choice of 'Going Global' During the Twelfth Five-Year Plan], *Dangdai Shijie* (June 2011), pp. 4–9.

81. UNCTAD, "Total of Bilateral Investment Treaties Concluded, June 1, 2011: China," http://www.unctad.org/sections/dite_pcbb/docs/bits_china.pdf.

82. These periods roughly parallel those identified in Nargiza Salidjanova, *Going Out: An Overview of China's Outward Foreign Direct Investment*, USCC Staff Research Report (March 30, 2011) pp. 4–5.

83. John Wong and Sarah Chan, "China's Outward Direct Investment: Expanding Worldwide," *China: An International Journal*, Vol. 1, No. 2 (September 2003), p. 280. Data for phase 2 and 3, ibid.

84. Frederick Wu, "Corporate China Goes Global," in Henry Wai-Chung Yeung (ed.), *Handbook of Research on Asian Business* (Cheltenham: Edward Elgar, 2007), pp. 445–465. I am indebted to Dawn Murphy for this source.

85. Of this total amount, financial ODI outflows (in banks, insurance, and other financial institutions) were $8.63 billion in 2010 with an accumulated stock of $55.25 billion, while nonfinancial outflows for 2010 were $60.18 billion with an accumulated total stock of $261.96 billion. MOFCOM, *2010 Statistical Bulletin of China's Outward Foreign Direct Investment* (Beijing: Ministry of Commerce, State Statistical Bureau, State Foreign Exchange Administration, 2011), p. 79.

86. Wen Jiabao, *Report on the Work of the Government*, National People's Congress, March 5, 2012, p. 7.

87. MOFCOM, *2010 Statistical Bulletin of China's Outward Foreign Direct Investment*, op. cit., p. 96.

88. Daniel H. Rosen and Thilo Hanemann, *An American Open Door* (New York: Asia Society, 2011), p. 18.

89. Peter Nolan, *Is China Buying the World?* (Cambridge: Polity Press, 2012), pp. 96–97.

90. Rosen and Hanemann, *An American Open Door*, op. cit., p. 22; Jamil Anderlini, "China Investment in Europe Triples," *Financial Times*, June 6, 2012.

91. Cited in Anderlini, ibid.; Neil Gough, "Companies from China Snapping Up Deals Abroad," *International Herald Tribune*, June 8, 2012.

92. Ding Qingfen, Li Jiabao, and Oswald Chen, "Ministry Predicts New Surge in ODI," *China Daily*, January 5, 2012.

93. No Author, "Cheapness Alone Won't Cut It for China's Overseas Workers: Interview with Diao Chunhe," *Global Times*, November 20, 2009.

94. Ibid.; also see Ed Wong, "China's Export of Labor Faces Scorn," *New York Times*, December 20, 2009.

95. Ibid.

96. Simon Rabinovitch, "Chinese Builders Target Contracts in EU and US," *Financial Times*, September 14, 2011.

97. Wang Xinyuan, "M&A Deals Balloon to $200 Billion," *Global Times*, January 18, 2011, citing PricewaterhouseCoopers data.

98. As cited in Wang Ying, "Taste for Outbound M&A's Strong in First Half, May Double in Second," *China Daily*, September 11, 2011.

99. Wang Chao, "China Investments Meet Bottleneck Overseas," op. cit.

100.   OECD, *Investment Policy Reviews: China 2008*, op. cit., pp. 74–75.

101.   For two extensive studies of China's M&A activity, see Economist Intelligence Unit, *A Brave New World: The Climate for Chinese M&A Abroad*, op. cit.; and Deloitte, *Emerging from the Twilight: The Next Chapter of Chinese Outbound M&A*, op. cit.

102.   Ding Qingfen, "More Chinese Firms Opt for M&As," *China Daily*, July 10, 2012. Source of data: MOFCOM.

103.   See, for example, China-Brazil Trade Council, *Chinese Investments in Brazil: A New Phase in the China-Brazil Relationship* (Rio de Janeiro: Conselho Empresarial Brasil-China, 2011).

104.   See Liz Alderman, "Beijing Seen as Striving for Influence in Europe," *New York Times*, November 2, 2010; Mark Blyth, "China's European Shopping Spree," *Foreign Affairs*, July 25, 2011; François Godement and Jonas Parello-Plesner with Alice Richard, *The Scramble for Europe* (Paris: European Council on Foreign Relations, 2011); David Wroe, "How China Is Taking Over Europe," *Global Post*, July 1, 2011; No author, "FDI into UK Hits Record High," *Global Times*, July 16, 2010; Nora Burghart and Vanessa Rossi, *China's Overseas Investment in the UK* (London: Chatham House, 2009).

105.   "China's Investments in Europe Doubled in 2010," *People's Daily Overseas Edition*, September 17, 2011, http://news.sohu.com/20110917/n319690526.shtml.

106.   Ding Qingfen and Li Jiabao, "Euro Debit Crisis Creates Opportunities," op. cit.

107.   See Paul Geithner, "China, Amid Uncertainty at Home and in Europe, Looks to Germany," *New York Times*, April 22, 2012.

108.   The former perspective is represented by François Godement et al., while the latter is expressed in Nin-hai Tseng, "Can China Save Europe?" *Fortune*, July 1, 2011.

109.   Godement et al., *The Scramble for Europe*, op. cit.

110.   See Jade Le Van, "A Road Accident: The Inside Story of the Polish Highway That Wasn't Built by Chinese Firms," European Council of Foreign Relations, *China Analysis* (January 2012), http://www.ecfr.eu/page/-/China_Analysis_Facing_the_Risks_of_the_Going_Out_Strategy_January2012.pdf.

111.   Rosen and Hanemann, *An American Open Door?*, op. cit.

112.   See Rocky Barker, "As Economic Power Shifts to Asia, Idaho's Location Makes It a Prime Site for an Industrial Foothold," *Idaho Statesman*, December 31, 2010, http://www.idahostatesman.com/2010/12/31/1472023/chinese-company-eyes-boise.html.

113.   See Rocky Barker, "Bloggers Fear a Chinese Takeover of Idaho: State Officials Say the Investments Will Be a Boon and Pose No Danger," *Idaho Statesman*, June 26, 2011; William F. Jaspar, "'China' The New Investment Savior?" *New American*, May 12, 2011.

114. See, for example, Xinhua, "China's Investment in U.S. to Expand in Future: Geithner," May 11, 2011; Chen Weihua, "U.S. Calms Concerns Over Chinese Investments," *China Daily*, September 20, 2011.

115. See Kathrin Hille, "China and the U.S.: Access Denied," *Financial Times*, April 8, 2011.

116. Eric Engleman and Jonathan D. Salant, "Chinese Firm Beefs Up Its Lobbying Amid National Security Probe on Hill," *Washington Post*, August 27, 2012.

117. On CIC origins and evolution, see Yu Xiaodong, "China Investment Corporation: Charting a Voyage Through Troubled Waters," *News China*, Vol. 110, June 5, 2009, pp. 18–21; Michael H. Cognato, "China Investment Corporation: Threat or Opportunity?" *NBR Analysis*, Vol. 19, No. 1 (July 2008), pp. 9–20.

118. Interview with Jin Liqun, May 22, 2009, Beijing.

119. Cited in Chen Yang, "Sovereign Wealth Fund Speeds Up Overseas Investment," *Global Times*, December 7, 2009.

120. Li Luxiang, "The Talent Chase Doesn't Add Up," *Global Times*, July 19, 2010.

121. Wang Bo, "CIC Reaps Gains from Rosy Overseas Investments," *China Daily*, July 30, 2010; Wei Tian and Liu Baijia, "CIC Reports $51.5 bn. Net Profit in 2010," *People's Daily Online*, July 27, 2011, http://english.peopledaily.com.cn/90001/90778/90860/7452544.html.

122. Wei Tian and Diao Ying, "CIC Hit by Global Conditions," *China Daily*, July 26, 2012.

123. No author, "Chinese Wealth Fund Urges West to Spend More on Infrastructure," *China Daily*, November 30, 2011.

124. Ding Qingfen, "More Chinese Firms Opt for M&As," op. cit.

125. Li Xiang, "More Chinese Companies Make Fortune 500 List," July 9, 2011.

126. Arthur Yeung et al., *The Globalization of Chinese Companies* (Singapore: Wiley, 2011), p. 39.

127. Dianna Farrel and Andrew J. Grant, "China's Looming Talent Shortage," *McKinsey Quarterly*, No. 4 (2005).

128. Agence France Presse (AFP), "'Go East': China Inc. Recruiting in London, New York," November 6, 2008.

129. Diao Ying, Li Xiang, and Lan Lan, "Investing Overseas Delivers Dividends," *China Daily*, November 9, 2011.

130. See http://www.interbrand.com/en/best-global-brands/best-global-brands-2008/best-global-brands-2010.aspx.

131. See, for example, Liang Limin, "'Made in China' Ad Sends Wrong Message," *Global Times*, December 9, 2009.

132. Carl E. Walter and Fraser J. T. Howie, *Red Capitalism* (Singapore: Wiley, 2011), p. 167. Walter and Howie cite unpublished research by Danish expert Kjeld Erik Brødsgaard. For a more extensive examination of the linkages between the Chinese Communist Party and China's SOEs, see

Richard McGregor, *The Party: The Secret World of China's Communist Rulers* (New York: HarperCollins, 2010).

133. See "Overseas Expansion of the Party," *Xuexi Shibao* [Study Times], December 27, 2010, http://www.studytimes.com.cn:9999/epaper/xxsb/html/2010/12/27/08/08_13.htm.

134. This is one of the principal findings in Yeung et al., *The Globalization of Chinese Companies*, op. cit.

135. See David Shambaugh, "Training China's Political Elite: The Party School System," *China Quarterly*, Vol. 196 (January 2009), pp. 827–844; Gregory T. Chin, "Innovation and Preservation: Remaking China's National Leadership Training System," *China Quarterly*, Vol. 205 (April 2011), pp. 18–39; Frank N. Pieke, *The Good Communist: Elite Training and State Building in Today's China* (Cambridge: Cambridge University Press, 2009).

136. See, for example, David Barboza and Azam Ahmed, "Muddy Waters Is a Thorn to Some Chinese Companies," *New York Times*, June 9, 2011; Lynn Cowan, "Chinese IPOs No Longer Sizzling," *Wall Street Journal*, May 17, 2011.

137. David Barboza and Azam Ahmed, "China to Wall Street: The Side-Door Shuffle," *New York Times*, July 23, 2011.

138. Ajay Makan and Kara Scannell, "Accounts Probe Dents Chinese Stocks in U.S.," *Financial Times*, September 30, 2011.

139. "More Chinese Companies Delist Their Overseas Stock," *International Herald Leader*, March 6, 2012, as reported on Xinhuanet, March 6, 2012, http://news.xinhuanet.com/herald/2012–03/06/c_131442157.htm.

140. Ding Qingfen, "Green Norms for Overseas Investment Soon," *China Daily*, July 9, 2010.

141. See Alan Wheatley, "Big Obstacles to China's Ambitions: Companies May Lack Skills Needed for Overseas Operations," *International Herald Tribune*, January 21, 2010.

142. The TCL case is detailed, and this description draws on Yeung et al., *The Globalization of Chinese Companies*, op. cit., pp. 2–3, 8, 103–106; Xiaofei Li, *China's Outward Foreign Investment*, op. cit., pp. 202–216.

143. Zhang Chunyan and Yui-tak Wan, "TCL Makes Overseas Headway," *China Daily*, September 9–15, 2011.

144. Information on Huawei in this section comes from the following sources: Huawei's website (http://www.huawei.com/en/); Ariel Tung, "Huawei Longs for Breakthrough in U.S.," *China Daily*, September 9–15, 2011; John Boudreau, "China's Huawei Pushes to Become Major Global Company," *Mercury News*, October 1, 2011; Shen Jingting, "Huawei Makes First Cloud-Computing Phone," *China Daily*, August 1, 2011; Matthew Morgan, "Huawei Tunes Strategy to Stay Ahead in Europe," *China Daily*, July 22–24, 2011; Chen Limin, "China Propels Huawei's Sales," *China Daily*, September 28, 2011; Christopher Williams, "Huawei: China's Best-Kept Secret," *Telegraph*, June 18, 2011; Owen Fletcher,

"Huawei Fares Well Overseas," *Wall Street Journal*, April 18, 2011; John Bussy, "In Huawei's Bid to Crack Market, U.S. Sees a Threat from China, Inc.," *Wall Street Journal*, February 28, 2011; Tuo Yannan, "Huawei Sales Revenue up 24%," *China Daily*, February 1, 2011; Xu Donghuan, "Australia Accuses Huawei of Espionage: Report," *Global Times*, September 7, 2009; Kevin O'Brien, "From China, a Global Player in Technology," *International Herald Tribune*, November 30, 2009; Stephanie Kirchgaessner, "U.S. Panel Deals Blow to Huawei Growth Plans," *Financial Times*, February 14, 2011.

145. Shen Jingting, "Huawei Becomes Top Telecom Gear Maker," *China Daily*, July 26, 2012.

146. On Ren Zhengfei's background, see Lee Chyen Yee, "At Huawei, an Eccentric Force Drives the Company Forward," Reuters, April 24, 2012.

147. Quoted in Huawei's 2010 *Annual Report*, http://www.huawei.com/en/about-huawei/corporate-info/annual-report/annual-report-2010/corporate-governance-report/index.htm.

148. Kathrin Hille and Neil Hume, "Huawei Tries to Allay Australian Fears," *Financial Times*, March 27, 2012.

149. Author's interview with João Pedro Flecha de Lima, Huawei senior vice president, June 30, 2009, Sao Paulo, Brazil.

150. Engleman and Salant, "Chinese Firm Beefs Up Its Lobbying Amid National Security Probe on Hill," op. cit.

151. Tung, "Huawei Longs for Breakthrough in U.S.," op. cit.

152. Ibid.

153. Morgan, "Huawei Tunes Strategy to Stay Ahead in Europe," op. cit.

154. Geely, Chery, Shanghai Auto (SAIC), Beijing Auto, Guangzhou Auto, Changchun Auto, the Lifan Group (Chongqing), the FAW Group, Dongfeng Motor, BYD Company, Pang Da Auto, Zhejiang Longmen Lotus Auto, Chang'an Auto Group, Brilliance China Automotive Holdings, Sichuan Tengzhong Heavy Industrial Group, Hawtai Motor, Great Wall Motor, and others.

155. Xinhua, "Chinese Automakers Seek Global Growth," *China Daily*, July 25, 2011, http://www.chinadaily.com.cn/bizchina/2011–07/25/content_12977898.htm.

156. See Fang Yan and Edmund Klamann, "Challenges for Chinese Automakers," *International Herald Tribune*, January 5, 2010.

157. AFP, "China Carmakers Chart Path to Global Stage," http://motoring.asiaone.com/Motoring/News/Story/A1Story20110427–275884.html.

158. Li Fangfang, "Chinese Automakers Build Overseas Plants," *China Daily*, August 15, 2012.

159. Wang Chao, "Stalled Chery Looks for Some Cheer," *China Daily*, August 1, 2011.

160. Li Fangfang and Ding Qingfen, "Chinese Car Makers Pushed to Build Abroad," *China Daily*, September 20, 2011.

161. See Li Fangfang, "Geely Buys Volvo in Biggest Overseas Foray," *China Daily*, March 29, 2010; Keith Bradsher, "Ford Sells Volvo Brand to Chinese Conglomerate," *International Herald Tribune*, March 29, 2010; Matthew Dolan and Norihiko Shirouza, "New Life Under Chinese: Geely Hopes to Boost Volvo Globally," *Wall Street Journal*, March 29, 2010.

162. Gong Zhengzheng and Han Tianyang, "Volvo: Solid First Year Under Geely," *China Daily*, August 29, 2011.

163. Hu Yinan and Cui Haipei, "Volvo Agreement Connects China and Sweden," *China Daily Asia Weekly*, April 27–May 3, 2012.

164. AFP, "China Carmakers Chart Path to Global Stage," op. cit.

165. IBM Institute for Business Value, *"Going Global": Prospects and Challenges for Chinese Companies on the World Stage* (Somers, NY: 2006), http://www-31.ibm.com/cn/services/bcs/iibv/pdf/company_world_0529_en.pdf.

166. See the company's website: http://www.haieramerica.com/.

167. Marie Jones, "Haier Tops World Appliances Rankings Again," *Channel News*, December 13, 2010, http://www.channelnews.com.au/Appliances/Kitchen/W7A8M4N9.

168. Data from Haier official website: http://www.haieramerica.com/media/cms/about/2011-haier-corporate-brochure.pdf#zoom=50.

169. He Wei, "Lenovo Seeks to Become the Apple of the World's Eye," *China Daily*, June 20, 2011.

170. Ibid.

171. See, for example, Michael Wines, "Australia, Nourishing China's Economic Engine, Questions Ties," *New York Times*, June 3, 2009.

172. Andrew Ward, Jamil Anderlini, and Leslie Hook, "China and the World: A Chilly Reception," *Financial Times*, September 2, 2011.

173. Mei Jia, "Land Deal in Iceland Rejected, Huang Says," *China Daily*, November 28, 2011.

174. See Godement et al., *The Scramble for Europe*, op. cit.

175. See Ian Bremmer, "As China Rises, So Does Its Risk," *Fortune*, June 8, 2006.

176. Andrew Higgins, "As China Finds Bigger Place in World Affairs, Its Wealth Breeds Hostility," *Washington Post*, September 8, 2010.

177. No author, "China Earns Distrust," *Economist*, April 24, 2011; Barry Bearak, "Zambia Uneasily Balances Chinese Investment and Workers' Resentment," *New York Times*, November 20, 2010; Simon Mundy, "Chinese Accused of Zambian Labor Abuses," *Financial Times*, January 20, 2011.

178. Simon Romero, "As China Expands in Latin America, Tensions Fester at a Mining Venture," *New York Times*, August 15, 2010.

179. See, for example, Tang Hao, "Guanyu Zhongguo haiwai liyi de zhanlue sikao" [Strategic Thinking on the Protection of China's Overseas Interests], *Xiandai Guoji Guanxi*, No. 6 (2011); Zhang Shuguang, "Guojia haiwai liyi fengjin de waijiao guanli" [Foreign Affairs Management of

Expanding Overseas National Interests], *Shijie Jingji yu Zhengzhi*, No. 8 (2009); Su Changhe, "Lun Zhongguo haiwai liyi" [On China's Overseas' Interests], ibid.; Chen Weishu, "Zhongguo haiwai liyi yanjiu de zongti shiye" [A Comprehensive Research Approach to China's Overseas Interest], *Zhongguo Waijiao*, No. 7 (2009); Zhang Jinjie, "Guojia fengjin xingcheng, ping'gu ji Zhongguo duice" [Country Risk: Formation, Evaluations, and Countermeasures for China], *Shijie Jingji yu Zhengzhi*, No. 3 (2008).

180. Tao Jian, "Ways to Advance China's 'Going Out' Policy," *Contemporary International Relations*, Vol. 21, No. 5 (September/October 2011), pp. 101–102.

181. Jiang Yong, "Problems Facing China's 'Going Out'," ibid., pp. 107–108.

182. Cited in David Pilling, "The Trials of a Reluctant Superpower," *Financial Times*, February 2, 2012.

183. According the OECD's defining criteria, overseas development assistance (ODA) includes "Grants or loans to countries and territories on the DAC List of ODA Recipients (developing countries) and to multilateral agencies which are: (a) undertaken by the official sector; (b) with promotion of economic development and welfare as the main objective; (c) at concessional financial terms (if a loan, having a grant element of at least 25 percent). In addition to financial flows, technical co-operation is included in aid. Grants, loans and credits for military purposes are excluded. Transfer payments to private individuals (e.g., pensions, reparations, or insurance payouts) are in general not counted." Source: http://www.oecd.org/document/32/0,3343 ,en_2649_33721_42632800_1_1_1_1,00.html#ODA.

184. Information Office of the State Council, *China's Foreign Aid* (April 2011), http://news.xinhuanet.com/english2010/china/2011–04/21/c_13839683. htm.

185. On China's infrastructure assistance see Vivien Foster et al., *Building Bridges: China's Growing Role as Infrastructure Financier for Sub-Saharan Africa* (Washington, DC: International Bank for Reconstruction and Development/World Bank, 2008).

186. Information Office of the State Council, *China's Foreign Aid*, op. cit.

187. Also see Deborah Brautigam, *The Dragon's Gift: The Real Story of China in Africa* (New York: Oxford University Press, 2009).

188. As cited in Thomas Lum et al., *China's Foreign Aid Activities in Africa, Latin America, and Southeast Asia* (Washington, DC: Congressional Research Service, 2009), p. 3.

189. Information Office of the State Council, *China's Foreign Aid*, op. cit.

190. Deborah Brautigam's study remains the most detailed assessment available. See *The Dragon's Gift*, op. cit., chap. 4. Also see Zhou Hong, "Zhongguo duiwai yuanzhu yu gaige kaifang 30 nian," [China's Overseas Aid Program and 30 Years of Reform], *Shijie Jingji yu Zhengzhi* (November 2008), pp. 33–43.

191. See Stefan Stähle, "Towards China's Integration into the Aid Donor Architecture: Learning from Chinese Participation in International Regimes," *China Aktüell*, No. 3 (2008).

192. On issues related to China's aid transparency, see Sven Grimm et al., *Transparency of Chinese Aid* (Stellenbosch, South Africa: Stellenbosch University, 2011).

Chapter 6

1. Hu Jintao, "Speech at Meeting Commemorating the 90th Anniversary of the Founding of the Communist Party of China," July 1, 2011.

2. Yang Jiechi, "Promoting Public Diplomacy," *China Daily*, September 2, 2011.

3. Author's interview with Lee Kuan Yew, March 15, 2011, Singapore.

4. See, for example, Li Jinzhang, "Guojia xianxiang de jianshe yu Zhongguo gonggong waijiao" [International Image Construction and China's Public Diplomacy], *Guoji Wenti Yanjiu*, No. 2 (2011), pp. 1–3; Yu Xintian, "Ruan shili jianshe yu Zhongguo duiwai zhanlue" [Soft Power and China's Foreign Strategy], *Guoji Wenti Yanjiu*, No. 2 (2008), pp. 15–20.

5. Xinhua Domestic Service, "Communiqué of the Sixth Plenary Session of the 17th CPC Central Committee," October 18, 2011, as translated by the Open Source Center CPP20111018136003.

6. Hu's speech was reprinted in the January 2012 issue of *Qiushi* (Seeking Truth), the CCP's ideological journal, and translated by the Open Source Center (CPP20120103704003). Also see Edward Wong, "China Must Raise Cultural Influence, Leader Says," *New York Times*, January 4, 2012.

7. See Zhang Jianying, *Wenhua Anquan Zhanlue Yanjiu* (Beijing: Guofang Daxue chubanshe, 2011).

8. Quoted in "State Council Information Chief: Improve External Communication to Develop Cultural Soft Power," Xinhua, October 28, 2011, http://news.xinhuanet.com/2011–10/28/c_111131045.htm.

9. Xinhua News Agency, "Premier: China to Continue Cultural System Reform," *China Daily*, March 5, 2010, http://www.chinadaily.com.cn/china/2010npc/2010–03/05/content_9544382.htm.

10. Ibid.

11. Quoted in Wang Yan, "Chinese Media and Culture Heading Abroad," *China Daily*, April 29, 2010.

12. State Council of the People's Republic of China Notice, *Outline of the National Plan for Cultural Development During the Period of the Eleventh Five-Year Plan*, www.gov.cn/gongbao/content/2006/content_431834.htm.

13. Liu Wei, "Culture to Be Pillar Industry," *China Daily*, February 16, 2012.

14. See Sheng Ding, *The Dragon's Hidden Wings: How China Rises with Its Soft Power* (Lanham, MD: Lexington Books, 2008); William A. Callahan and Elena Barabantseva (eds.), *China Orders the World: Normative Soft Power and Foreign Policy* (Washington, DC, and Baltimore: Woodrow Wilson Center Press and Johns Hopkins University Press, 2012); Jian

Wang (ed.), *Soft Power in China: Public Diplomacy Through Communication* (New York: Palgrave Macmillan, 2011); Joshua Kurlantzick, *Charm Offensive: How China's Soft Power Is Transforming the World* (New Haven: Yale University Press, 2007); Li Mingjiang (ed.), *Soft Power: China's Emerging Strategy in International Politics* (Lanham, MD: Lexington Books, 2009); Hongyi Lai and Yiyi Lu (eds.), *China's Soft Power in International Relations* (London: Routledge, 2011); Carola McGiffert (ed.), *Chinese Soft Power and Its Implications for the United States* (Washington, DC: Center for Strategic and International Studies, 2009); Congressional Research Service of the Library of Congress, *China's Foreign Policy and Soft Power in South America, Asia, and Africa* (Washington, DC: U.S. Government Printing Office, 2008); U.S. Senate Committee on Foreign Relations, *Another U.S. Deficit—China and America—Public Diplomacy in the Age of the Internet* (Washington, DC: U.S. Government Printing Office, 2011); Joshua Kurlantzick, *China's Charm: Implications of Chinese Soft Power* (Washington, DC: Carnegie Endowment for International Peace Policy Brief No. 47, 2006); Ingrid d'Hooghe, *The Limits of China's Soft Power in Europe: Beijing's Public Diplomacy Puzzle* (The Hague: Clingendael Diplomacy Papers No. 25, 2010); Joseph S. Nye, Jr., et al., *The Rise of China's Soft Power* (Cambridge, MA: Harvard University John F. Kennedy School of Government Institute of Politics, 2006); Bates Gill and Yanzhong Huang, "Sources and Limits of Chinese Soft Power," *Survival*, Vol. 48, No. 2 (Summer 2006), pp. 17–36; Young Nam Cho and Jong Ho Jeong, "China's Soft Power: Discussions, Resources, and Prospects," *Asian Survey*, Vol. 48, No. 3 (2008), pp. 453–472; Li Mingjiang, "China Debates Soft Power," *Chinese Journal of International Politics*, Vol. 2 (2008), pp. 287–308; Ingrid d'Hooghe, "Into High Gear: China's Public Diplomacy," *The Hague Journal of Diplomacy*, No. 3 (2008), pp. 37–61; Joseph S. Nye and Wang Jisi, "The Rise of China's Soft Power and Its Implications for the United States," in Richard Rosecrance and Gu Guoliang (eds.), *Power and Restraint: A Shared Vision for the U.S.-China Relationship* (New York: Public Affairs, 2009); Sheng Ding, "To Build a 'Harmonious World': China's Soft Power Wielding in the Global South," *Journal of Chinese Political Science*, Vol. 13, No. 2 (2008), pp. 193–213; Yiwei Wang, "Public Diplomacy and the Rise of Chinese Soft Power," *The Annals of the American Academy of Political and Social Science*, Vol. 616 (March 2008), pp. 257–273; Gregory Holyk, "Paper Tiger? Chinese Soft Power in Asia," *Political Science Quarterly*, Vol. 126, No. 2 (2011), pp. 223–254.

15.   Joseph S. Nye, Jr., *Soft Power: The Means to Success in World Politics* (New York: Public Affairs, 2004), p. 5.

16.   Joseph S. Nye and Wang Jisi, "The Rise of China's Soft Power and Its Implications for the United States," op. cit., p. 25; also see Nye, "The Rise of China's Soft Power," op. cit., p. 7.

17. Sometimes the term *ruan quanli* (软权力), *ruan liliang* (软力量), or *ruan guoli* (软国力) is used.

18. Wang Huning, "Zuowei guojia shili de wenhua: Ruan quanli" [Culture as National Power: Soft Power], *Fudan Daxue Xuebao*, No. 3 (1993). At the time of writing, Wang was a member of the CCP Secretariat and director of the Central Committee's Policy Research Office and possibly due to be vaulted onto the Politburo at the Eighteenth Party Congress in November 2012.

19. "Full Text of Hu Jintao's Report to the 17th Party Congress," http://www.xinhuanet.com/english/2007–10/24/content_6938749_6.html.

20. For one prominent article by the deputy director of the Central Committee's Foreign Affairs Office, see Qiu Yuanping, "Zhongguo de heping fazhan yu gonggong waijiao" [China's Peaceful Development and Public Diplomacy], *Guoji Wenti Yanjiu*, No. 6 (2010), pp. 1–3.

21. For a fine previous assessment of this subject, see Hongying Wang, "National Image Building and Chinese Foreign Policy," *China: An International Journal*, Vol. 1, No. 1 (March 2003), pp. 46–72.

22. See, for example, Li Zhengguo, *Guojia Xingxiang Goujian* [National Image Building] (Beijing: Chuanmei Daxue chubanshe, 2006); Liu Ming (ed.), *Xin Zhuanmei Huanjing Zhong Guojia Xingxiang de Goujian yu Zhuanbo* [National Image Building and Broadcasting in the New Media Environment] (Beijing: Waiwen chubanshe, 2008).

23. Zhou Mingwei (ed.), *Guojia Xingxiang Zhuanbo Yanjiu Luncong* [National Image Broadcasting Research Series] (Beijing: Waiwen chubanshe, 2008), pp. 53–69.

24. See Zheng Biao, *Zhongguo Ruan Shili* [China's Soft Power] (Beijing: Zhongyang bianyi chubanshe, 2010); Chen Zhengliang, *Zhongguo "Ruan Shili": Fazhan Zhanlue Yanjiu* [China's Soft Power: Development Strategy Research] (Beijing: Renmin chubanshe, 2008); Tu Chenglin et al., *Guojia Ruan Shili yu Wenhua Anquan Yanjiu* [Research on National Soft Power and Cultural Security] (Beijing: Zhongyang bianyi chubanshe, 2009); Yi Heng, *Wenhua Zhuquan yu Guojia Wenhua Ruan Shili* [Cultural Sovereignty and National Cultural Soft Power] (Beijing: Shehui kexue wenzhai chubanshe, 2009); Han Bo, *Ruan Shili: Zhongguo Shijiao* [Soft Power: China's Perspective] (Beijing: Renmin chubanshe, 2009); Men Honghua (ed.), *Zhongguo: Ruan Shili Fanglue* [China's Soft Power Strategy] (Hangzhou: Zhejiang chubanshe, 2007); Tang Daixing, *Wenhua Ruan Shili Zhanlue Yanjiu* [A Strategic Study of Cultural Soft Power] (Beijing: Renmin chubanshe, 2008); Shu Mingwu, *Zhongguo Ruan Shili* [China's Soft Power] (Shanghai: Shanghai Daxue chubanshe, 2010).

25. Men Honghua, "Zhongguo Ruan Shili Ping'gu Baogao" [An Assessment Report on China's Soft Power] *Guoji Guancha*, No. 2 (2007), pp. 15–26.

26. For an assessment of Chinese use of traditional culture as the basis for contemporary soft power, see Callahan and Barabantseva (eds.), *China Orders the World*, op. cit.

27. See Men Honghua (ed.), *Zhongguo Ruan Shili Fanglue,* op. cit., pp. 92–93.
28. Interview with Men Honghua, May 2, 2010, Beijing.
29. Interview with Men Honghua, October 5, 2011, Washington, DC.
30. See Yu Xintian, "Ruan shili jianshe yu Zhongguo duiwai zhanlue" [Soft Power and China's Foreign Strategy], *Guoji Wenti Yanjiu,* No. 2 (2008), pp. 15–20; "China's National Interests from the Cultural Perspective," *International Studies* (Spring 2006), pp. 102–115.
31. Yu Xintian, "Ruan shili jianshe yu Zhongguo duiwai zhanlue," ibid., p. 17.
32. Xu Xintian, "Soft Power Enhancement and China's External Strategy," *International Studies* (Fall 2008), p. 23.
33. Interview with Madame Yu Xintian, September 18, 2011, Shanghai. Professor Yu's views on soft power and China's foreign policy are elaborated in her book *Zhangwo Guoji Guanxi Miyue: Wenhua, Ruan Shili yu Zhongguo Duiwai Zhanlue* [The Secret Key to Mastering International Relations: Culture, Soft Power, and China's Foreign Strategy] (Shanghai: Renmin chubanshe, 2010).
34. Interview with Ambassador Wu Jianmin, January 18, 2010, Beijing.
35. Ibid.
36. Yan Xuetong, "Ruan shili de hexin shi zhengzhi shili" [The Core of China's Soft Power Is Political Power], in Wang Wen (ed.), *Zhengbian Zhongguo* [China's Debates] (Shanghai: Renmin chubanshe, 2010), pp. 199–203; Yan Xuetong and Xu Jin, "Zhong-Mei ruan shili bijiao" [A Soft Power Comparison Between China and the United States], *Xiandai Guoji Guanxi,* No. 1 (2008), pp. 24–29.
37. Interview with Yan Xuetong, January 22, 2010, Beijing.
38. Yan Xuetong and Xu Jin, "Zhong-Mei ruan shili bijiao," op. cit.
39. Interview with Yan Xuetong, July 14, 2010, Beijing.
40. Joshua Cooper Ramo, *The Beijing Consensus* (London: Foreign Policy Center, 2004).
41. Interview with Men Honghua, October 5, 2011, Washington, DC.
42. Interview with Yan Xuetong, January 22, 2010, Beijing.
43. Interview with Ding Gang, November 2, 2009, Beijing.
44. Pan Zhongying, "Lun Zhongguo de ruan liliang he fazhan zhanlue," op. cit., p. 270.
45. Huang Renwei and Hu Jian, "Ruan shili yu Zhongguo heping fazhan daolu," in Li Zhong and Xiao Huanrong (eds.), *Guoji Xingshi yu Zhongguo Waijiao* [The International System and China's Foreign Policy] (Beijing: Zhongguo zhuanmei chubanshe, 2009), pp. 133–134. A similar version of Huang and Hu's article is published in Wang Ronghua (ed.), *SASS Papers, Volume 1* (Shanghai: Shanghai Academy of Social Sciences Press, 2008), pp. 8–25.
46. Pan Zhongqi and Huang Renwei, "Zhongguo de diyuan wenhua zhanlue" [China's Geocultural Strategy] *Xiandai Guoji Guanxi,* No. 1 (2008), pp. 44–49.

47. Interview with Fu Ying, Ministry of Foreign Affairs, April 2, 2010, Beijing

48. For more on China's propaganda system, see David Shambaugh, "China's Propaganda System: Institutions, Process & Efficacy," *China Journal*, No. 57 (January 2007); Anne-Marie Brady, *Marketing Dictatorship* (Lanham, MD: Rowman & Littlefield, 2009); Anne-Marie Brady (ed.), *China's Thought Management* (London: Routledge, 2012); Daniel Lynch, *After the Propaganda State* (Stanford: Stanford University Press, 1999); He Qinglian, *The Fog of Censorship: Media Control in China* (New York: Human Rights in China, 2008).

49. Anne-Marie Brady, *Making Foreign Things Serve China: Managing Foreigners in the People's Republic* (Boulder: Lynne Reinner, 2003).

50. Beijing Foreign Languages Institute, *A Chinese-English Dictionary* (Beijing: Shangwu Yinshuguan, 1985), p. 41.

51. This is a central argument in Lucian Pye, *The Mandarin and the Cadre: China's Political Cultures* (Ann Arbor: Center for Chinese Studies of the University of Michigan, 1988).

52. The FPPC are mutual respect for each other's territorial integrity and sovereignty (互相尊重主权和领土完整), mutual nonaggression (互不侵犯), mutual noninterference in each other's internal affairs (互不干涉内政), equality and mutual benefit (平等互利), and peaceful coexistence (和平共处).

53. See http://www.china.org.cn/english/features/dengxiaoping/103340.htm.

54. See http://www.mfa.gov.cn/eng/wjb/zzjg/gjs/gjzzyhy/2612/2614/t15319.htm.

55. See http://www.china.org.cn/english/features/book/152684.htm.

56. See Zheng Bijian, "China's Peaceful Rise to Great Power Status," *Foreign Affairs* (September–October 2005).

57. Deng Xiaoping, "Heping he fazhan shi dangdai shijie de liang da wenti," [Peace and Development Are the Contemporary World's Two Biggest Issues] in *Deng Xiaoping Wenxuan* [Selected Works of Deng Xiaoping, Vol. 3] (Beijing: Renmin chubanshe, 1993), pp. 104–106.

58. For good analyses of the "peaceful rise" saga, see Ren Xiao, "A Rising China Sees Itself in Asia's Mirror" (Seattle: National Bureau of Asian Research, 2009); Bonnie S. Glaser and Evan S. Medeiros, "The Changing Ecology of Foreign Policy Making in China: The Ascension and Demise of the Theory of 'Peaceful Rise,'" *China Quarterly*, Vol. 190 (June 2007), pp. 291–310; Robert L. Suettinger, "The Rise and Descent of 'Peaceful Rise,'" in *China Leadership Monitor*, No. 12 (Fall 2004), www.hoover.org/publications/clm/issues/2903986.html.

59. Hu Jintao, "Build Toward a Harmonious World of Lasting Peace and Common Prosperity," speech at the United Nations Summit, September 15, 2005, http://www.fmprc.gov.cn/ce/ceun/eng/zt/shnh60/t212915.htm.

60. *Soft Power in Asia: Results of a Multinational Survey of Public Opinion* (Chicago: Chicago Council on Global Affairs, 2009), http://www.

thechicagocouncil.org/UserFiles/File/POS_Topline%20Reports/Asia%20
Soft%20Power%202008/Soft%20Power%202008_full%20report.pdf.

61. Keynote speech by SCIO Minister Wang Chen to Fourth World Forum of China Studies, November 6, 2010, Shanghai, author's verbatim notes.

62. Interview with SCIO Vice Minister Qian Xiaoqian, op. cit.; Interview with former SCIO Minister Zhao Qizheng, ibid. Also see Wang Jingsong, *Zhonghua Renmin Gongheguo Zhengfu yu Zhengzhi*, p. 401.

63. This bureaucratic fact was officially confirmed in the author's interview with CCP Publicity Department head and Politburo member Liu Yunshan. Liu further indicated that he serves simultaneously as vice chair of both the Central Propaganda Leading Group *and* the External Propaganda Leading Group. Interview with Liu Yunshan, June 7, 2011, Beijing.

64. SCIO Vice Director Qian Xiaoqian succinctly summarized the SCIO's twin missions: "to present China's image to the world and be in charge of China's media." Interview with Qian Xiaoqian, SCIO vice director, May 21, 2009, Beijing.

65. George Orwell, *1984* (New York: Harcourt Brace, 1949).

66. In 2008 the SCIO convened more than eighty press conferences. Interview with Qian Xiaoqian, ibid.

67. See Maura Elizabeth Cunningham and Jeffrey N. Wasserstrom, "Authoritarianism: There's an App for That," *Chinese Journal of Communication*, Vol. 5, No. 1 (March 2012), pp. 43–48.

68. These are drawn from Zhang Jingyuan (ed.), *Dangwu Gongzuo Zhishi Shouce* (Beijing: Zhongguo renshi chubanshe, 1994), p. 130.

69. Ibid., p. 244.

70. Interview with SCIO Vice Director Qian Xiaoqian, op. cit.

71. Interview with SCIO Vice Minister Jiang Weiqiang, November 27, 2009, Beijing.

72. Ibid.

73. See Chinese Academy of Social Sciences Institute of Journalism and Broadcasting (ed.), *Zhongguo Xinwen Nianjian* [China Media Yearbook] (Beijing: Zhongguo Shehui kexue wenzhai chubanshe, 2009), pp. 63–67; ibid. (2008), pp. 64–66; ibid. (2007), pp. 62–64.

74. "Quanguo duiwai xuanchuan gongzuo huiyi zhaokai tuidong waixuan gongzuo fazhan" [National Foreign Propaganda Work Meeting Held to Promote Foreign Propaganda Development], January 6, 2011, http://news.sina.com.cn/c/2011–01–06/180921772084.shtml.

75. Quotation from Lu Suo and Jin Jun, "Zhongguo xiandai zhuanbo tixi de quanqiu jiangou" [The Global Building of China's Modern Broadcasting System], *Zhongguo Shehui Kexue Xuebao* [China Social Science Review], February 2, 2010, p. 1.

76. For an interesting history of the MFA spokesmen, see Qiu Jianhua, *Waijiaobu Fayanren* (Beijing: Shijie zhishi chubanshe, 2005).

77. Interview with Ma Zhaoxu, May 18, 2010, Beijing.

78. Interview with Ma Zhaoxu, October 23, 2009, Beijing.

79. Based on communication from Shao Zheng, director of MFA Spokesman's Office, March 18, 2010, Beijing.

80. This list was compiled by the author from discussions with a range of foreign journalists in China.

81. Sharon LaFraniere and Edward Wong, "Even with Protests Averted, China Turns to Intimidation of Foreign Journalists," *New York Times*, March 7, 2011.

82. Interview with MFA Spokesman Ma Zhaoxu, October 8, 2009, Beijing.

83. Yang Jiechi, "Promoting Public Diplomacy," op. cit.

84. Interview with Wei Xin, director of the Office of Public Diplomacy in the Ministry of Foreign Affairs, February 8, 2010, Beijing.

85. Interview with Vice Minister of Foreign Affairs Zhang Zhijun, April 21, 2010, Beijing.

86. Interview with Foreign Minister Yang Jiechi, June 2, 2011, Beijing.

87. For a review of China's public diplomacy, see Yu Xintian, "Gojian Zhongguo gonggong waijiao lilun de sikao" [Theory and Thoughts on Building China's Public Diplomacy], *Guoji Wenti Yanjiu*, No. 6 (2010), pp. 10–17.

88. Interview with Qiao Mu, Director of Center for International Communication Studies, Beijing Foreign Studies University, April 21, 2010, Beijing. Also see Zhang Xiaoling, *Chinese State Media Going Global* (Singapore: East Asia Institute Background Brief No. 488, 2009).

89. Interview with Tian Jin, Vice Minister of the State Administration of Film, Radio, and Television (SAFRT), June 26, 2007, Beijing.

90. *2008 China Statistical Yearbook* (Beijing: Zhongguo tongji chubanshe, 2009), pp. 849–850. The website figure comes from an interview with Xinhua News Agency Executive Deputy Editor-in-Chief Zhou Xisheng, May 20, 2009, Beijing.

91. David Barboza, "China Yearns to Form Its Own Media Empires," *New York Times*, October 5, 2009.

92. Guo Qiang and Du Guodong, "Media Summit Brings Together World's Voices," *Global Times*, October 9, 2009.

93. Conversation with Western journalist, October 26, 2010, Beijing.

94. Interview with Qian Wenrong, former Xinhua correspondent, November 5, 2009, Beijing.

95. Information from interviews at Xinhua, November 5, 2009, Beijing; and James F. Scotton and William A. Hachten (eds.), *New Media for a New China* (West Sussex, UK: Wiley-Blackwell, 2010), p. 115.

96. Anton Troianovski, "China Agency Nears Times Square," *Wall Street Journal*, July 1, 2010.

97. See Isaac Stone Fish, "All the Propaganda That's Fit to Print," *Newsweek*, September 3, 2010.

98. See David Barboza, "With New TV Channel, China to Air Its Perspectives Globally," *International Herald Tribune*, July 3–4, 2010.

99. Jason Dean, "China's Xinhua to Launch English Language Channel," *Wall Street Journal*, May 1, 2010.

100. "Xinhua TV Services to Cover Europe, the Middle East, and North Africa," http://news.xinhuanset.com/2010–12/09/c_13642442.htm.

101. David Bandurski, "Xinhua News Agency Steps Out into the World," Hong Kong University China Media Project, http://cmp.hku. hk/2009/10/22/2390.html.

102. Interview with Ma Guihua, November 5, 2009, Beijing.

103. Interview with Qian Wenrong, op. cit.

104. Interview with Zhou Qisheng, May 20, 2009, Beijing.

105. Ibid.

106. Much of this information derives from "About CCTV 9," http://english. cctv.com/english/about/index.shtml.

107. CCTV-4: 15 million viewers in 95 countries; CCTV News (formerly CCTV-9): 100+ million viewers in 120 countries and territories; CCTV-F (French): 10.16 million in 36 countries and regions; CCTV-E (Espanōl): 15.82 million in 13 countries; CCTV-Arabic: 6 million in 2 countries; CCTV-Russian: 1.1 million in 8 countries, but with a goal to increase to 300 million. See http://blog.cctv.com/?uid-806173-action-spacelist-typ e-blog-itemtypeid-72; Tania Branigan, "Chinese State TV Targets 300 Million Russian Viewers," *Guardian*, September 11, 2009.

108. See Xiaoling Zhang, "China's International Broadcasting: A Case Study of CCTV International," in Jian Wang (ed.), *Soft Power in China*, op. cit.

109. See Andrew Jacobs, "Live From Nairobi, China Puts Its Stamp on News in Africa," *New York Times*, August 17, 2012.

110. See Paul Farhi, "In DC, China Builds a News Hub to Help Polish Its Global Image," *Washington Post*, January 16, 2012.

111. Text message from Yang Rui, October 27, 2009.

112. See http://blogs.wsj.com/chinarealtime/2012/05/18/state-tv-host-offers-advice-on-how-to-throw-out-foreign-trash/.

113. Matthew Garrahan and Kathrin Hille, "China Looks to Boost Image with Global English Language Drive," *Financial Times*, November 8, 2011.

114. CCTV America Fact Sheet, February 6, 2012, Washington, DC.

115. Ibid.

116. Information in this section derives largely from an interview at CRI with Director Xia Jixuan, November 6, 2009, Beijing; *China Radio International: The Multilingual International Media Group* (Beijing: no publisher, no date); CRI's website http://gb.cri.cn/; and http://en. wikipedia.org/wiki/China_Radio_International.

117. Erika Engle, "Chinese Music Replaces Country on AM," *Honolulu Star Bulletin*, July 5, 2009. Also see John Pomfret, "From China's Mouth to Texans' Ears," *Washington Post*, April 25, 2010.

118. Pomfret, ibid.

119. Interview with CRI Director Xia Jixuan, November 6, 2009, Beijing.

120. Ibid.
121. Both the *Global Times* English and Chinese editions (环球时报) are wholly owned by the *People's Daily* (人民日报), and their editorial offices are in the *Renmin Ribao* compound.
122. Interview with *China Daily* Deputy Editor-in-Chief Qu Yingpu, February 3, 2010, Beijing.
123. Interview with Senior Editor Ding Gang, November 2, 2009, Beijing.
124. Ibid.
125. Interview with Qu Yingpu, op. cit.
126. Ibid.
127. Qiu Bo, "Investment in Media to Present True Picture of China," *China Daily*, January 4, 2011.
128. China Academy of Social Sciences Institute of Journalism and Broadcasting (ed.), *China Media Yearbook*, op. cit., p. 66.
129. Mu Qian, "Publishers Enjoy Roaring Trade at German Book Festival," *China Daily*, October 19, 2009.
130. Quoted in Kathrin Hille, "China to Loosen Control over Books," *Financial Times*, March 8, 2010.
131. Interview with CIPG Director Zhou Mingwei, November 6, 2009, Beijing.
132. Ibid.
133. See David Shambaugh, "China's Quiet Diplomacy: The International Department of the Chinese Communist Party," *China: An International Journal*, Vol. 5, No. 1 (2007), pp. 26–54.
134. For further on China's international relations think tanks, see David Shambaugh, "China's International Relations Think Tanks: Evolving Structure and Process," op. cit.; Glaser and Saunders, "Chinese Civilian Foreign Policy Research Institutes: Evolving Roles and Increasing Influence," op. cit.; Bates Gill and James C. Mulvenon, "Chinese Military-Related Think Tanks and Research Institutes," *China Quarterly*, Vol. 171 (September 2002).
135. See http://www.chahar.org/.
136. See Shambaugh, "China's Propaganda System," op. cit.
137. For a list of China's inventions, see Simon Winchester's masterful study of Dr. Joseph Needham, *The Man Who Loved China* (New York: Harper, 2008), Appendix I.
138. See Chen Yuan, "Zhongguo wenhua: Da guimo zouxing shijie" [Chinese Culture: The Big Effort to Go Global], *Renmin Ribao* [People's Daily], November 20, 2009.
139. Xinhua, "Europalia China Arts Festival Opens in Brussels," October 9, 2009, http://news.xinhuanet.com/english/2009–10/09/content_12196326.html; "Europalia Arts Festivals," *Beijing This Month* (January 2010), pp. 13–16.
140. Interview with Minister of Culture Cai Wu, May 23, 2009, Beijing.

141. "China Arts and Entertainment Group," http://www.ccnt.gov.cn/English/jgsz/Central_Affiliated/200808/t20080807_62394.html.

142. China Academy of Social Sciences Institute of Journalism and Broadcasting (ed.), *Zhongguo Xinwen Nianjian* [China Media Yearbook] (Beijing: Shehui kexue wenzhai chubanshe, 2009), p. 66.

143. Quoted in Wang Yan, "Chinese Media and Culture Heading Abroad," *China Daily*, April 29, 2010.

144. See Song Chao (ed.), *The World Exposition Reader* (Shanghai: Shanghai Scientific and Technological Literature Publishing House, 2008).

145. Geoffrey Fowler and Stacey Meichtry, "China Counts the Cost of Hosting the Olympics," *Wall Street Journal*, July 16, 2008.

146. Shirong Chen, "Chinese Overseas Students Hit Record High," *BBC News*, April 18, 2011.

147. See World Education Information, "The Number of Chinese Students Studying Abroad Has Increased for 30 Years," http://www.wei.moe.edu.cn/article.asp?articleid=2693; and Kathrin Hille, "China's Overseas Students Set Stage for Shift in Values," *Financial Times*, April 4, 2012.

148. All figures derived from "Table of Overseas Students Accepted by China from Countries Having Diplomatic Ties with China," *China's Foreign Affairs 2010* (Beijing: Ministry of Foreign Affairs, 2010), pp. 662–666; and Li Xing and Tan Yingzi, "China Offers Scholarships," *China Daily*, July 22–24, 2011.

149. Edward Wong, "China: Effort to Attract Foreign Students," *New York Times*, September 30, 2010.

150. "Foreign Student Quota to Expand," *China Daily*, July 29, 2008; Chen Jia, "Class Act Promotes Global 'Soft Power,'" *China Daily*, November 11, 2010.

151. Interview with China Scholarship Council, November 5, 2009, Beijing. This figure contradicts the figure of 11,185 foreign student scholarships given in the White Paper *China's Foreign Aid*, op. cit.

152. Chen Jia, "Class Act Promotes Global 'Soft Power,'" op. cit.

153. Interview with China Scholarship Council, op. cit., indicated the balance was 5 percent/95 percent.

154. See Liu Dong, "Universities to Rival West's in 25 Years," *Global Times*, February 4, 2010.

155. "World University Rankings 2010," http://www.timeshighereducation.co.uk/world-university-rankings/2010–2011/top-200.html.

156. Wang Wei, "China's Ivy League May Lift Higher Education," *China Daily*, November 24, 2009.

157. Michael Wines, "China Premier Details Economic Plan," *New York Times*, March 5, 2010; "Highlights of Wen's Government Work Report," *Xinhua News Agency*, March 5, 2010.

158. Zhao Gang, "On Course for Science Supremacy," *China Daily*, July 2, 2012.

159. "Poor Quality Scientific Research Fetters China's Strength," *Global Times*, March 9, 2010.

160. Ibid.

161. See Daniel Kwok, *Scientism in Chinese Thought, 1900–1950* (New Haven: Yale University Press, 1965); James Reardon-Anderson, *A Study of Change: Chemistry in China, 1840–1949* (Cambridge: Cambridge University Press, 1992).

162. Also see Jamil Anderlini, "Autocratic Directives Fail to Spark Creativity," *Financial Times*, October 26, 2011.

163. Interview with *Hanban* Director Xu Lin, February 4, 2010, Beijing.

164. "Cultural Exports Can Reshape Chinese Image," *Global Times*, April 8, 2010.

165. Chen Jia, "Making a World of Difference," *China Daily*, December 14, 2011.

166. Kelly Chung Dawson, "Confucius Institutes Enhance China's International Image," *China Daily*, April 23, 2010.

167. Chen Jia, "Making a World of Difference," op. cit.

168. Data comes from a comparative study done by Ye Juan of the China Academy of Social Sciences Institute of Foreign Literature. See Ye Juan, "Kongzi xueyuan de qishi: wenhua waijiao yao you 'rouli qiangshi' de lixiang" [The Inspiration of Confucius Institutes: Cultural Diplomacy Should Have 'Soft Power' Ideals], *Zhongguo Shehui Kexue Bao* [China Social Science Daily], January 7, 2010.

169. Information in this section derives from *Han Ban* printed materials, and an interview with Chief Executive of Confucius Institute Headquarters Madame Xu Lin, op. cit.

170. "Confucius Institutes," *Beijing Review*, July 29, 2010, op. cit.

171. Interview with Xu Lin, op. cit.

172. Interviews with CI directors in Europe and the United States, 2009, 2011, 2012.

173. Chen Jia, "Making a World of Difference," op. cit.

174. *Hanban, Annual Report 2010* (Beijing: Hanban, 2010). This amount does not include any matching funds from partner institutions.

175. Interview with Xi Lin, op. cit.

176. See Guo Ying, "Chinese Books Eye Global Market," *Global Times*, September 8, 2009; Chitralekha Basu, "The Slim Years," *China Daily*, July 15–17, 2011.

177. "Forum: Language Barrier Still Blocks Chinese Li Overseas," *Global Times*, October 26, 2009.

178. Chitralekha Basu, "The Slim Years," op. cit.

179. References for this section on the 2009 Frankfurt Book Fair include Jonathan Fenby, "Seeking Soft Power, But Not by the Book," *YaleGlobal Online*, October 26, 2009; Sonia Kolesnikov-Jessop, "Sold in Translation," *Newsweek International*, January 11, 2010; Ming Wong, "China on Show at Frankfurt Fair," *Global Times*, October 13, 2009; Mu

Qian, "Frankfurt Opens a New Chapter," *China Daily*, October 14, 2009; Steven Erlanger, "Officer Fired over Book Fair Missteps," *International Herald Tribune*, October 23, 2009; Steven Erlanger and Jonathan Ansfield, "China Shares Culture at Book Fair, Without Controlling It," *International Herald Tribune*, October 20, 2009; Mu Qian, "Publishers Enjoy Roaring Trade at German Book Festival," *China Daily*, October 19, 2009; Duan Congcong, "German Book Fair Invites Chinese Dissidents," *Global Times*, September 14, 2009; Duan Congcong, "German Media Rips China for Flexing Muscles in Book Fair," *Global Times*, September 11, 2009; notes from Foreign Correspondent Club of China (FCCC) Forum on the Frankfurt Book Fair, December 4, 2009, Beijing.

180. Xi Jinping, "Jiaqiang Wenhua Jiaoliu, Sujin Shijie Heping" [Increase Cultural Exchange, Push Forward World Peace], *Renmin Ribao*, October 14, 2009.

181. Steven Erlanger and Jonathan Ansfield, "China Shares Culture at Book Fair, Without Controlling It," op. cit.

182. Chen Xuegen, "Cultural Diplomacy Will Complement China's Power," *Global Times*, October 16, 2009.

183. Julie Zeveloff, "Meet the Average Chinese Millionaire: 39, Plays Gold, Owns an iPad," *Business Insider*, August 1, 2012; Karen Yip, "Investors Develop New Appreciation for Art, Fine Wine," *China Daily*, August 12–14, 2011.

184. Kevin Lim, "Tread Carefully in Chinese Art Market, Experts Say," *Thomson-Reuters*, January 16, 2012.

185. Sotheby's 2011 Catalogue, *Leading Asia: The US $1 Billion Milestone* (Hong Kong: Sotheby's, 2012), p. 3.

186. Andrew Moody, "Art Makes a Valuable Contribution," *China Daily*, May 24, 2010.

187. Georgina Adam, "Record Breakers and Fakers," *Financial Times*, December 31, 2011.

188. Moody, "Chinese Take the Art Market by Storm," op. cit.

189. Robin Pogrebin, "China's New Cultural Revolution: A Surge in Art Collecting," *New York Times*, September 7, 2009.

190. Lin Qi, "Calligraphy Masterpiece Sets Record," *China Daily*, June 5–6, 2010.

191. Pogrebin, "China's New Cultural Revolution," op. cit.

192. Moody, "Chinese Take the Art Market by Storm" op. cit.

193. Ibid.

194. Souren Melikian, "A Shifting Balance of Power," *New Tork Times*, September 24, 2010.

195. "The Art Market Becomes Truly Global, Reveals New TEFAF Report," *Art Daily*, March 8, 2010, http://www.artdaily.org/index.asp?int_sec=11&int_new=29061. For an interesting assessment of the Chinese domestic art market, and its development from 2000–2008, see Lin Ercai,

"2008 nian Zhongguo wenwu yishipin shichang fazhan baogao" [2008 Report on China's Cultural Celics and Art Market Development], in *2009 Nian Zhongguo Wenhua Chanye Fazhan Baogao* [2009 Annual Report on Development of China's Cultural Industries] (Beijing: Shehui kexue wenzhai chubanshe, 2009).

196. As cited in Pogrebin, "China's New Cultural Revolution," op. cit.

197. Yip, "Investors Develop New Appreciation of Art, Fine Wine," op. cit.

198. Data from Artprice.com, as cited in David Barboza, "China's Art Market: Cold or Maybe Hibernating?" *New York Times*, March 10, 2010.

199. Ibid.

200. For a history of the Palace collection and previous Chinese attempts to retrieve its art, see Jeannette Shambaugh Elliott with David Shambaugh, *The Odyssey of China's Imperial Art Treasures* (Seattle: University of Washington Press, 2007).

201. Lin Shujuan, "Experts Track Relics from Old Palace," *China Daily*, January 19, 2010.

202. In addition to sources in previous two footnotes, also see Qin Zhongwei, "Bringing China's Treasures Home" and "Documenting the Past Key to Repatriation," in *China Daily*, March 11, 2010; Andrew Jacobs, "Uneasy Engagement: China Hunts for Art Treasures in U.S. Museums," *New York Times*, December 16, 2009.

203. Xu Shenglan, "China Introduces Cash Rewards for Cultural Relics Lost Overseas," *Global Times*, November 25, 2009.

204. Ian Johnson, "At China's New Museum, History Toes the Party Line," *New York Times*, April 3, 2001.

205. Jonathan Van Meter, "Go East!" *Vogue* (September 2011), pp. 614–659.

206. Robin Pogrebin, "For First Time, Architect in China Wins Top Prize," *New York Times*, February 27, 2012.

207. Zan Jifang, "Cultural Industries Bloom," *Beijing Review*, June 3, 2010.

208. As cited in Fu Mengzi, "China's International Influence," *Contemporary International Relations*, Vol. 21, No. 2 (2011), p. 19. The 2011 figure comes from Matthew Garrahan and Kathrin Hille, "DWA Set for Chinese Tie-Up," *Financial Times*, February 16, 2012.

209. Garrahan and Hille, ibid.

210. Discussion with Chinese professor, October 24, 2011, Washington, DC.

211. Edward Wong, "Eagerly Balancing Art with the Demands of State," *International Herald Tribune*, January 7–8, 2012.

212. Kathrin Hille and Matthew Garrahan, "Chinese Eye Hollywood Deals," *Financial Times*, January 23, 2012.

213. Michael White and Alan Ohnsman, "DreamWorks Animation Announces China Venture During Xi Visit," *BusinessWeek*, February 17, 2012.

214. Xin Dingding, Zheng Yangpeng, and Shi Yingying, "More Efficient Visa Procedures Are Passport to Success," *China Daily*, February 8, 2012.

215. Wang Zhenghua, "UK Hopes to Welcome More Chinese Visitors," *China Daily*, April 12, 2012.

216. Jamil Anderlini and Patti Waldmeir, "Chinese Doubt the Road Ahead," *Financial Times*, November 5–6, 2011.

217. "China Ranked Fourth in Travel Money Spent," *China Daily*, April 30, 2010.

218. Cited in Evan Osnos, "The Grand Tour: Europe on Fifteen Hundred Yuan a Day," *New Yorker*, April 18, 2011.

219. Xin Dingding et al., "More Efficient Visa Procedures are Passport to Success," op. cit.

220. Elizabeth Holmes, "Stores Push for Chinese Tourists," *Wall Street Journal*, June 10, 2011.

221. Stephen Clifford, "Luxury Stores Pull Out Mandarin Phrase Books to Make the Sale," *New York Times*, April 15, 2012.

222. Liz Alderman, "China Looms Large in Luxury Industry's Vision," Nov. 9, 2010.

223. Yu Tianyu, "Number of Outbound Tourists Soaring," op. cit.

224. Data in this paragraph is drawn from Steven Erlanger, "From China to Paris, to Shop," *International Herald Tribune*, September 15, 2011.

225. Ed Cody, "In France, Chinese Swoop in to Buy Stake in Savoir-Faire," *Washington Post*, July 26, 2009.

226. Patti Waldmeir, "Chinese Acquire Taste for French Wine," *Financial Times*, September 27, 2010.

227. No author, "A New Grand Tour," *Economist*, December 18, 2010.

228. Fiona Walsh, "China's Bordeaux Lovers Heat up France's Wine Industry," *Guardian*, June 13, 2011.

229. Jancis Robinson, "Has It Been a Vintage Year?" *Financial Times*, December 31, 2011.

230. Rahul Jacob, "Wealthy Chinese Feast on HK Luxury Goods," *Financial Times*, January 3, 2011.

231. Zhang Zhao, "Bavarian Heartland Lures Tourists," *China Daily*, February 2, 2012.

232. Mei Jia, "Tuscany Beckons Chinese Tourists," *China Daily*, June 28, 2011.

232. Xi Dingding, "Chinese Tourists Spend Lots of Money Abroad," *China Daily*, February 25, 2010.

234. Melissa Pang et al., "Big Spenders from China," *Straits Times*, May 10, 2010.

235. Mure Dickie, "Wealthy Chinese Fill Gap Left by Tourist Shortfall in Japan," *Financial Times*, January 28–29, 2012.

236. As quoted in Shino Yuasa, "Chinese Export Comes to Japan's Rescue: Swarms of Big-Spending Tourists," *International Herald Tribune*, July 1, 2010.

237. Pang et al., "Big Spenders from China," op. cit.

238. Melanie Lee, "Redefining a Sense of Prestige in China," *International Herald Tribune*, June 8, 2012.

239. Karl Wilson, "In Love with Luxury," *China Daily*, January 16, 2012.

240. Hu Yuanyuan, "Overseas Realty Proves Safe Bet," *China Daily*, March 20–21, 2010.

241. Julia Werdigier and Bettina Wassener, "Chinese Bet on London Real Estate," *International Herald Tribune*, September 18–19, 2010.

242. Ibid.

243. Hiroko Tabuchi, "Chinese Buyers Worry Japan," *International Herald Tribune*, September 30, 2010.

244. Chris Vellacott, "London Still Beckons to the World's Restless Rich," *International Herald Tribune*, December 9, 2009; and ibid.

245. Kirk Semple, "In Surge with Little Fanfare, Chinese Are Pouring Their Money into New York City," *New York Times*, August 11, 2011.

246. Ibid.

247. Wei Ling, "The Chinese Wave," op. cit.

248. See, for example, Guo Lufang and Zhang Su, "Zhongguo gongmin chujing luyou wenming yu ruan shili tisheng yanjiu" [Promote Research on Chinese Citizens Outbound Tourism Civilized Behavior and Soft Power], *Luyou Xuekan* [Tourism Tribune], No. 12 (2008), pp. 18–22.

249. "Fifteen Guidelines for Chinese Tourists Abroad," *Shanghai Daily*, October 3, 2006, http://www.chinasnippets.com/2006/10/03/15-guidelines/.

250. Rachel Donadio, "Stitched in Italy, by Chinese: Newcomers Redefine a Label," *New York Times*, September 13, 2010.

251. See Jim Yardley, *Brave Dragons: A Chinese Basketball Team, An American Coach, and Two Cultures Clashing* (New York: Knopf, 2012); No author, "Little Red Card: Why China Fails at Soccer," *Economist*, December 17, 2011.

252. Tang Yue and Craig McIntosh, "Gold Standard," *China Daily*, March 1, 2010.

253. Kathrin Hille and Alan Rappeport, "China Tackles Image Problem in West," *Financial Times*, January 19, 2011.

254. Interview with Liu Yunshan, June 7, 2011, Beijing.

255. Wu Jiao and Ai Yang, "Yang Sketches Out Country's Global Vision," *China Daily*, March 8, 2010.

256. Yang Jiechi, "Promoting Public Diplomacy," op. cit.

257. Interview with CPPCC Spokesman Zhao Qizheng, February 8, 2010, Beijing.

258. Interview with SCIO Director Wang Chen, March 23, 2010, Beijing.

259. Interview with SCIO Vice Director Qian Xiaoqian, May 21, 2009, Beijing.

260. Verbatim quotation taken by European correspondent present, March 2, 2010, Beijing.

261. Interview with Vice Foreign Minister Fu Ying, April 2, 2010, Beijing.

262. Quoted in Robert Lawrence Kuhn, *How China's Leaders Think* (Singapore: Wiley (Asia), 2010), p. 407.

263. Interview with China Radio International Director Xia Jixuan, November 6, 2009.

264. Liu Mingfu, *Zhongguo Meng: Hou Meiguo Shidai de Daguo Sichao yu Zhanlue Dingwei* [The China Dream: The Position of Big Power Thinking and Strategy in the Post-American Era] (Beijing: Zhongguo youhao chubanshe, 2010).

265. Interview with SCIO Director Wang Chen, March 23, 2010, Beijing.

266. Joseph Nye, "Why China Is Weak on Soft Power," *International Herald Tribune*, January 18, 2012.

Chapter 7

1. Liang Guanglie, "A Better Future Through Security Cooperation," address to the 2011 Shangri-la Dialogue, Singapore, June 5, 2011.

2. U.S. Department of Defense, *Annual Report to Congress: Military and Security Developments Involving the People's Republic of China, 2011,* http://www.defense.gov/pubs/pdfs/2011_cmpr_final.pdf.

3. See, for example, Philip Sunders et al. (eds.), *The Chinese Navy: Expanding Capabilities, Evolving Roles* (Washington, DC: National Defense University, Institute for National Strategic Studies, Center for the Study of Chinese Military Affairs, 2001); Thomas J. Bickford et al., *Uncertain Waters: Thinking About China's Emergence as a Maritime Power* (Alexandria, VA: CNA Corporation, 2011); Ryan Clarke, *Chinese Energy Security: The Myth of the PLAN's Frontline Status* (Carlisle Barracks, PA: U.S. Army War College Strategic Studies Institute, 2010); Robert E. Ebel, *China's Energy Future: The Middle Kingdom Seeks Its Place in the Sun* (Washington, DC: Center for Strategic and International Studies, 2005); Theodore H. Moran, *China's Strategy to Secure Natural Resources: Risks, Dangers, and Opportunities* (Washington, DC: Peterson Institute for International Economics, 2010).

4. For an excellent assessment, see Christopher D. Yung and Ross Rustici with Isaac Kardon and Joshua Wiseman, *China's Out of Area Naval Operations: Case Studies, Trajectories, Obstacles, and Potential Solutions* (Washington, DC: National Defense University Institute for National Strategic Studies, 2010).

5. See speech by Lt. General Liu Chengjun, "Deepening Practical Cooperation in Non-Traditional Security and Vigorously Preserving Common Security of Mankind," address at the Second Xiangshan Forum, October 24, 2008, Beijing; Katherine Morton, "China and Non-Traditional Security: Toward What End?" lecture at Nanyang Technological University, http://www.rsis.edu.sg/nts/article.asp?id=180&prev=Event.

6. See Thomas Christensen, "The Advantages of an Assertive China," *Foreign Affairs* (March/April 2011). Also see Alan Wachman's thoughtful testimony before the U.S.-China Economic and Security Review

Commission, April 13, 2011, http://www.uscc.gov/hearings/2011hearings/written_testimonies/11_04_13_wrt/11_04_13_wachman_testimony.pdf.

7. See David Shambaugh, *China's Communist Party: Atrophy and Adaptation* (Washington, DC, and Berkeley: Woodrow Wilson Center Press and University of California Press, 2008), chap. 4.

8. See Jane Perlez, "Continuing Buildup, China Increases Military Spending More Than 11 Percent," *New York Times*, March 5, 2012.

9. See David Shambaugh, "Calculating China's Military Expenditure," paper prepared for the Council on Foreign Relations Task Force on Chinese Military Power, June 25, 2002. External estimates of China off-budget defense expenditure vary widely, from two to twelve times the official budget, but I argue that since the establishment of a zero-based budgeting (ZBB) system and a stricter auditing system around 2000, the extra expenditures have continually shrunk—to the point where I would now estimate them to be in the range of 10–15 percent of the official budget. For the most thorough discussion of China's military expenditures, see Keith Crane et al., *Modernizing China's Military: Opportunities and Constraints* (Santa Monica, CA: Rand, 2005), chaps. 3, 4, 7, 8.

10. By far the best study of this war is Ed O'Dowd's *Chinese Military Strategy in the Third Indochina War: The Last Maoist War* (London: Routledge 2007). Also see King Chen, *China's War with Vietnam* (Stanford: Hoover Institution Press, 1987).

11. "Military Must Be Self-Reliant: Minister," *People's Daily Online*, December 29, 2010, http://English.peopledaily.com.cn/90001/90776/90786/7245014.html.

12. See Tai Ming Cheung, *Fortifying China: The Struggle to Build a Modern Defense Economy* (Ithaca, NY: Cornell University Press, 2008); James Mulvenon, *New Directions for China's Defense Industry* (Santa Monica, CA: Rand, 2005).

13. Xinhua, "Full Text of White Paper on China's Peaceful Development," September 6, 2011.

14. Department of Defense, *Annual Report to Congress: Military and Security Developments Involving the People's Republic of China 2011*, http://www.defense.gov/pubs/pdfs/2011_cmpr_final.pdf.

15. See Hu Jintao, "Understand the New Historic Missions of Our Military in the New Period of the New Century," http://gfjy.jianxi.gov.cn/yl.asp?did+11349.htm.

16. See David Shambaugh, "A Matter of Time: Taiwan's Eroding Military Advantage," *Washington Quarterly* (Spring 2000), pp. 119–133.

17. Department of Defense, *Annual Report to Congress: Military and Security Developments Involving the People's Republic of China, 2010*, p. i, http://www.defense.gov/pubs/pdfs/2010_CMPR_Final.pdf.

18. See Roy Kamphausen, David Lai, and Andrew Scobell (eds.), *Beyond the Strait: PLA Missions Other Than Taiwan* (Carlisle Barracks, PA: U.S. Army War College Strategic Studies Institute, 2009).

19. Defense Minister Liang Guanglie, "A Better Future Through Security Cooperation," op. cit.

20. State Council Information Office, *China's National Defense 2010*, http://news.xinhuanet.com/english2010/china/2011–03/31/c_13806851_4.htm.

21. There are a number of excellent book-length assessments of the PLA. See, for example, Dennis Blasko, *The Chinese Army Today* (London: Routledge, revised edition 2011); Anthony H. Cordesman and Martin Kleiber, *Chinese Military Modernization: Force Development and Strategic Capabilities* (Washington, DC: CSIS Press, 2007); Richard D. Fisher, *China's Military Modernization: Building for Regional and Global Reach* (Stanford: Stanford University Press, 2011); Crane et al., *Modernizing China's Military*, op. cit.; Kim Nodskov, *The Long March to Power: The New Historic Mission of the People's Liberation Army* (Copenhagen: Royal Danish Defense College, 2009); David Shambaugh, *Modernizing China's Military: Progress, Problems, and Prospects* (Berkeley: University of California Press, 2003); Council on Foreign Relations, *Chinese Military Power* (New York: Council on Foreign Relations, 2003).

22. The following survey of the PLA force structure draws on my "China's Military Modernization: Making Surprising and Steady Progress," in Ashley J. Tellis and Michael Wills (eds.), *Strategic Asia, 2005–06* (Seattle: National Bureau of Asian Research, 2006).

23. This is one of the central arguments of my *Modernizing China's Military: Progress, Problems, and Prospects*, op. cit.

24. Quoted in Reuben F. Johnson, "China Gets Military Helping Hand from Russia," *Washington Times*, August 29, 2011.

25. The estimate of 1.6 million derives from the International Institute of Strategic Studies, *The Military Balance 2011* (London: Routledge, 2001), p. 234. The U.S. Department of Defense 2010 annual report on the Chinese military provides a lower figure of 1.25 million.

26. Zhao Shengnan, "Chinese Delegation in Libya to Discuss Post-War Business," *China Daily*, February 6, 2012.

27. PLA Daily, "PLA NCOs Grow to Vital Force in Modernization Drive," November 12, 2008, as cited in Nodskov, *The Long March to Power*, op. cit., p. 81.

28. All estimated numbers derive from IISS, *The Military Balance 2011*, op. cit., p. 231.

29. See Austin Ramzy, "China Flexes Its Muscles with Stealth Fighter Test," *Time*, January 11, 2011, http://www.time.com/time/world/article/0,8599,2041755,00.html.

30. "Chinese Air Force Successfully Performs Aerial Refueling over Sea," *Zhongguo Wang*, April 25, 2005, as cited in Kenneth Allen, "Reforms in the PLA Air Force," Jamestown Foundation *China Brief*, Vol. 5, No. 15 (July 5, 2005), http://www.jamestown.org/publications_details.php?volume_id=408&issue_id=3390&article.id=2369972.

31. See "Hong-6 Bomber," http://www.sinodefence.com/airforce/groundattack/h6.asp.

32. Nodskov, *The Long March to Power*, op. cit., p. 142.

33. No author, "Ten Percent of GDP Now Comes from the Sea, Says Report," *China Daily,* April 10, 2007.

34. See Crane et al., *Modernizing China's Military*, op. cit., pp. 180–183.

35. Philip Andrews-Speed and Roland Dannreuther, *China, Oil, and Global Politics* (London: Routledge, 2011), p. 82.

36. Among other reports, see Bill Gertz, "China Has Carrier-Killer Missile, Admiral Says," *Washington Times*, December 27, 2010, http://www.washingtontimes.com/news/2010/dec/27/china-deploying-carrier-sinking-ballistic-missile/.

37. Department of Defense, *Military and Security Developments Involving the People's Republic of China 2011*, op. cit., p. 2.

38. See Andrew S. Erickson, "Chinese Sea Power in Action: The Counter-Piracy Mission in the Gulf of Aden and Beyond," in Roy Kamphausen et al., *The PLA at Home and Abroad: Assessing the Operational Capabilities of China's Military* (Carlisle Barracks, PA: U.S. Army War College Strategic Studies Institute, 2010), pp. 296–297.

39. See James R. Holmes and Toshi Yoshihara, *Chinese Naval Strategy in the 21st Century: The Turn to Mahan* (London: Routledge, 2007), and *Red Star over the Pacific: China's Rise and the Challenge to U.S. Maritime Strategy* (Annapolis, MD: Naval Institute Press, 2010). For an interesting review of the latter and a rejoinder from the authors, see "Book Review Roundtable" in *Asia Policy*, No. 12 (July 2011), pp. 142–168.

40. Perhaps the most well-known of such studies is Robert D. Kaplan, *Monsoon: The Indian Ocean and the Future of American Power* (New York: Random House, 2010).

41. All figures come from IISS, *The Military Balance 2011*, op. cit., pp. 231–233.

42. A good account of the history of the ship can be found in Michael Wines, "China Begins Sea Trails of Its First Aircraft Carrier," *New York Times*, August 11, 2011.

43. Damion Bristow, "Chinese Aircraft Carrier Confirmed by General," *BBC News*, June 8, 2011, http://www.bbc.co.uk/news/world-asia-pacific-13692558.

44. Ibid.

45. *Military and Security Developments Involving the People's Republic of China 2010*, op. cit., p. 3.

46. Ibid.

47. These elements of extended out-of-area naval missions are provided in Christopher D. Yung et al., *China's Out of Area Naval Operations*, op. cit., pp. 40–46.

48. Statement by Zheng Ruixiang at Fifth Symposium on U.S.-China Relations in Global Context, June 1, 2011, Beijing.

49. See Evan A. Feigenbaum, *China's Techno-Warriors: National Security and Strategic Competition from the Nuclear to the Information Age* (Stanford: Stanford University Press, 2003); John Wilson Lewis and Xue Litai, *China Builds the Bomb* (Stanford: Stanford University Press, 1991).

50. Numbers for ICBM, IRBM, and SRBM from IISS, *The Military Balance 2011*, op. cit.; numbers for SRBMs from Department of Defense, *Military and Security Developments Involving the People's Republic of China 2010*, op. cit.

51. See Keith Bradsher, "China Said to Bolster Missile Capabilities," *New York Times*, August 25, 2012.

52. See Andrew Jacobs, "China's Space Program Bolstered by First Docking," *New York Times*, November 4, 2011.

53. Information Office of the State Council, *China's Space Activities* (Beijing: State Council Information Office, 2006), http://www.china.org. cn/e-white/8/index.htm.

54. See Union of Concerned Scientists, "Satellite Database," http://www. ucsusa.org/nuclear_weapons_and_global_security/space_weapons/ technical_issues/ucs-satellite-database.html.

55. See Dean Cheng, "Prospects for China's Military Space Efforts," in Kamphausen et al. (eds.), *Beyond the Strait*, pp. 211–252.

56. Department of Defense, *Military and Security Developments Involving the People's Republic of China 2010*, op. cit., p. 25.

57. See Geoff Dyer and Joseph Menn, "Chinese and Russian Cyberspies Threaten U.S., Say Intelligence Chiefs," *Financial Times*, November 4, 2011; Thom Shanker, "In Blunt Report to Congress, U.S. Accuses China and Russia of Internet Spying," *New York Times*, November 4, 2011; Ellen Nakashima, "U.S. Cyber-Spying Report Points to China, Russia," *Washington Post*, November 4, 2011.

58. U.S.-China Economic and Security Review Commission, *2009 Report to Congress of the U.S.-China Economic and Security Review Commission* (Washington, DC: U.S. Government Printing Office, 2009), pp. 167–181, http://www.uscc.gov/annual_report/2009/chapter2_section_4.pdf.

59. Information Warfare Monitor, *Tracking "GhostNet": Investigating a Cyber Espionage Network* (Toronto: University of Toronto Munk Center for International Studies, 2009), http://www.nartv.org/mirror/ghostnet.pdf.

60. See David Wise, *America's Secret Spy War with China* (Boston: Houghton, Mifflin, Harcourt, 2011).

61. The German Federal Chancellery and several German government ministries; the Foreign and Commonwealth Office (FCO) and MI5 in Britain; New Zealand and Australian intelligence agencies; the Australian Prime Minister's Office and Department of Foreign Affairs and Trade; the South Korean Ministry of Finance; several Indian government ministries; the Philippines Ministry of Foreign Affairs; virtually all Taiwan government and military organs; in the United States, the White House, Department of State, Defense, Homeland Security, NASA,

Kennedy Space Center, Naval War College, the Oak Ridge, Sandia, and Livermore national laboratories, and several members of Congress. These are all openly reported in the media. The list derives from pages 68–74 of the U.S.-China Economic and Security Review Commission, *Capability of the People's Republic of China to Conduct Cyber Warfare and Computer Network Exploitation*, http://www.uscc.gov/researchpapers/2009/ NorthropGrumman_PRC_Cyber_Paper_FINAL_Approved%20 Report_16Oct2009.pdf.

62. For an excellent overview of PLA cyber capabilities, see James Mulvenon, "PLA Computer Network Operations: Scenarios, Doctrine, Organizations, and Capability," in Kamphausen et al. (eds.), *Beyond the Strait*, op. cit., pp. 253–285.

63. Kathrin Hille, "Chinese Military Mobilizes Cyber Militias," *Financial Times*, October 12, 2011.

64. Three excellent studies of China's PKO involvement are Bates Gill and Chin-Hao Huang, *China's Expanding Role in Peacekeeping: Prospects and Policy Implications* (Stockholm: SIPRI Policy Paper No. 25, 2009); Yin He, *China's Changing Policy on UN Peacekeeping Operations* (Stockholm: Institute for Security & Development Policy, 2007); International Crisis Group, *China's Growing Role in UN Peacekeeping* (Beijing, Brussels, New York: Asia Report No. 166, 2009). Much of the data cited above is drawn from these reports.

65. State Council Information Office, *China's National Defense in 2010*, op. cit., p. 18. There is a slight discrepancy in figures provided by the Ministry of Foreign Affairs, which claims 2,143 personnel deployed in ten peacekeeping missions at the end of 2010. See Ministry of Foreign Affairs Department of Policy Planning, *China's Foreign Affairs 2010* (Beijing: World Affairs Press, 2010), p. 323.

66. United Nations, "Troop and Police Contributors," http://www.un.org/ en/peacekeeping/resources/statistics/contributors.shtml.

67. In 2009 the Chinese Foreign Ministry claimed to have trained three hundred demining specialists from fifteen countries over the previous decade, including personnel from Afghanistan, Angola, Ethiopia, Iran, Iraq, and Sudan. Mark McDonald, "China Ties Mine-Clearing to Its Quest for Foreign Oil," *International Herald Tribune*, September 16, 2009.

68. See No author, "Sailing into the Storm," *Beijing Review*, April 22, 2010.

69. See Zhao Jingfang and Zhu Tao, "Xin Zhongguo junshi waijiao 60 nian: licheng, tedian, yu jingyan" [Sixty Years of New China's Military Diplomacy: Process, Characteristics, and Experiences], *Shijie Jingji yu Zhengzhi*, No. 9 (2009), pp. 33–43; Chen Zhiyong, "Xin Zhongguo junshi waijiao huigu sikao" [Retrospect and Reflections on Sixty Years of New China's Military Diplomacy], *Zhongguo Junshi Kexue*, No. 5 (2009), pp. 34–39; Wang Hongwei, "Zhongguo junshi waijiao ji guoji xianxiang" [China's Military Diplomacy and Its International Image], *Dangdai Shijie*, No. 4 (2009), pp. 50–52.

70. Liang Guanglie, "A Better Future Through Security Cooperation," op. cit., p. 5.

71. These distinctions are based on Kenneth W. Allen and Eric A. McVadon, *China's Foreign Military Relations* (Washington, DC: Henry L. Stimson Center, 1999); and Heidi Holz and Kenneth W. Allen, "Military Exchanges with Chinese Characteristics," in Kamphausen et al. (eds.), *The PLA at Home and Abroad*, op. cit. The Holz and Allen study is a particularly comprehensive, up-to-date, and excellent study.

72. Qian Lihua, "New China's Remarkable Achievements in Military Diplomacy," *Foreign Affairs Journal*, No. 93 (2009), p. 45. The author is the director of the Foreign Affairs Office of the Ministry of National Defense. Also see Department of Defense, *Annual Report to Congress: Military and Security Developments Involving the People's Republic of China 2011*, op. cit., p. 65.

73. Liang Guanglie, "A Better Future Through Security Cooperation," op. cit.

74. Ibid.

75. See Chen Xulong, "Understanding China's Strategic Dialogues," *China International Studies* (November/December 2010), pp. 16–36.

76. Interview with Admiral Guan Youfei, Ministry of National Defense, July 14, 2010, Beijing.

77. Unless otherwise noted, figures derive from *China's National Defense in 2004, 2006, 2008, and 2010*.

78. For a description of these programs, see Pavel Kamennov, "China: Military Diplomacy Today," *Far Eastern Affairs*, No. 1 (2010), pp. 7–8.

79. State Council Information Office, *China's National Defense in 2008* (Beijing: State Council Information Office, 2009, p. 74).

80. Liang Guanglie, "A Better Future Through Security Cooperation," op. cit.

81. Figures all drawn from *China's National Defense*, annual 2003–2008. No figure was given in the 2010 report, but Admiral Guan Youfei gave an approximation of 2000 from 110 countries. Admiral Guan Youfei interview, op. cit.

82. Admiral Guan Youfei, interview, ibid.

83. Information provided when the author lectured at the symposium in 2007.

84. Shi Libin and Men Qiang, "The PLA University of Foreign Languages," *China Armed Forces* (September 2010), pp. 83–85.

85. Interview with Admiral Guan Youfei, op. cit.

86. Stockholm International Peace Research Institute (SIPRI), Arms Transfer Database, http://www.sipri.org/contents/armstrad/output_types_TIV.html.

87. Congressional Research Service, *Conventional Arms Transfers to Developing Nations, 2002–2009* (Washington, DC: Congressional Research Service, 2010), Table IX, http://www.fas.org/sgp/crs/weapons/R41403.pdf.

88. U.S. Department of Defense, *Annual Report to Congress: Military and Security Developments Involving the People's Republic of China 2011*, p. 68.

89. Interview with Admiral Guan Youfei, op. cit.

90. For a full description of all military weapons transferred, see SIPRI, "Global Transfers of Major Conventional Weapons Sorted by Supplier (Exporter), 2006–2010," http://www.sipri.org/databases/armstransfers/recent_trends/Exporter-2006–2010.pdf.

91. See Richard Bitzinger, "China's Reemergence as an Arms Dealer: The Return of the King?" Jamestown Foundation *China Brief*, Vol. 9, No. 14 (July 2009).

92. See Stockholm International Peace Research Institute (SIPRI) database, http://www.sipri.org/contents/armstrad/output_types_TIV.html; U.S. Department of Defense, *Annual Report to Congress: Military and Security Developments Involving the People's Republic of China 2011*, p. 68.

93. See Russell Hsiao, "Chinese Soldiers and Arms Exports Embroiled in Zimbabwe's Electoral Impasse," Jamestown Foundation *China Brief*, Vol. 8, No. 9 (August 2008).

94. System designations, types, amounts, and years derived from SIPRI arms transfer database, http://armstrade.sipri.org/armstrade/page/trade_register.php. Also see Arms Control Association, "The UN Sanctions' Impact on Iran's Military," *Issue Brief*, Vol. 1, No. 7 (2010), http://www.armscontrol.org/issuebriefs/iransanctionseffectonmilitary.

95. Michael Wines, "China Says It Will Tighten Procedures on Arms Sales," *New York Times*, September 7, 2011.

96. Colum Lynch, "China's Arms Exports Flooding Sub-Saharan Africa," *Washington Post*, August 25, 2012; "China's Guns," *Washington Post*, September 4, 2012.

97. See Daniel L. Byman and Roger Cliff, *China's Arms Sales: Motivations and Implications* (Santa Monica, CA: Rand, 1999).

98. Chinese arms transfers to Myanmar are very difficult to track. Indeed, the SIPRI database does not contain any data. Nonetheless, reports continue to emerge from the region (with India as a principal source).

99. Interview with Admiral Guan Youfei, op. cit., and Zhang Haizhou, "China's Fighters Shine at International Show" and "China-Made Planes Set to Soar into World Market," *China Daily*, July 21, 2010.

Chapter 8

1. "Speech by Prime Minister Lee Hsien Loong at Central Party School," September 6, 2012.

2. Interview with Vice Foreign Minister Cui Tiankai, June 8, 2012, Beijing.

3. Zhu Feng quoted in Peter Ford, "The Rise of an Economic Superpower: What Does China Want?" *Christian Science Monitor*, November 5, 2011.

4. An excellent description of these practices can be found in Jonathan Spence, *The Search for Modern China* (New York: Norton, 1990), chap. 6.

5. See David Shambaugh, *China's Communist Party: Atrophy and Adaptation* (Berkeley and Washington, DC: University of California Press and Woodrow Wilson Center Press, 2008).

6. See David Shambaugh, "International Perspectives on the Communist Party of China," *China: An International Journal,* Vol. 10, No. 2 (2012).

7. Martin Jacques, *When China Rules the World: The Rise of the Middle Kingdom and End of the Western World* (London: Allen Lane, 2009).

8. "Dialogue: Crisis of Confidence," *Aspen Idea* (Winter 2011/2012), p. 45; also see Joseph S. Nye, Jr., "The Premature Superpower," *Aspenia,* No. 49/50 (2010).

9. Aaron L. Friedberg, *A Contest for Supremacy: China, America, and the Struggle for Mastery in Asia* (New York: Norton, 2011).

10. See, for example, Evan Medeiros, "Strategic Hedging and the Future of the Asia-Pacific Region," *Washington Quarterly,* Vol. 29, No. 1 (2005), pp. 145–167.

11. See, for example, Hugh White, *The China Choice: Why America Should Share Power* (Collingwood, Australia: Black, 2012).

12. See Shambaugh (ed.), *Tangled Titans*; Michael D. Swaine, *America's Challenge: Engaging a Rising China in the Twenty-first Century* (Washington, DC: Carnegie Endowment for International Peace, 2011).

13. A. F. K. Organski and Jacek Kugler, *The War Ledger* (Chicago: University of Chicago Press, 1980).

14. G. John Ikenberry, "The Rise of China, the United States, and the Future of Liberal International Order," in Shambaugh (ed.), *Tangled Titans*, op. cit.; and "The Rise of China and Future of the West," *Foreign Affairs* (January/February 2008).

15. Richard Nixon, "Asia After Vietnam," *Foreign Affairs*, Vol. 46, No. 1 (October 1967), pp. 111–125.

16. John Mearsheimer, *The Tragedy of Great Power Politics* (New York: Norton, 2001); "Clash of the Titans: A Debate with Zbigniew Brzezinski," *Foreign Policy*, No. 146 (January/February 2005).

17. Robert B. Zoellick, "Whither China: From Membership to Responsibility," Remarks to National Committee on U.S.-China Relations, September 21, 2005; also see Amitai Etzioni, "Is China a Responsible Stakeholder?" *International Affairs*, Vol. 87, No. 3 (2011).

18. Elizabeth Economy, "Time for a Strategic Reset," *Americas Quarterly* (Winter 2012), pp. 54, 58.

19. Fareed Zakaria, "Clash of the Titans," *Newsweek International*, January 25, 2010.

20. Zhu Feng quoted in Peter Ford, "The Rise of an Economic Superpower: What Does China Want?" *Christian Science Monitor*, op. cit.

21. "Interview with China's Vice Foreign Minister of Foreign Affairs," *Spiegel Online*, August 22, 2011, http://www.spiegel.de/international/world/0,1518,781597,00.html.

INDEX

Abdeneur, Roberto, 114
Abou, Serge, 93
academic corruption, 244
Academy of Military Sciences,
    PLA, 68–69
Acer, 199
acid rain, 149
ADB. *See* Asian Development
    Bank
ad campaigns, 187
Addax Petroleum, 167
Aden. *See* Gulf of Aden
ADS. *See* approved destination
    status
AD/SD. *See* area denial and
    sea denial
Afghanistan, 40, 46, 48, 75,
    378n67
Africa, 10. *See also* South
    Africa; *specific countries
    in Africa*
    China as viewed by, 12
    China's diplomacy with,
        51–52, 55, 108–11
    CIC and, 184
    FOCAC, 108–10
    indentured Chinese labor
        in, 108–9
    Maoist ideology in, 109
    oil in, 110, 163

overseas aid in, 204
slave trade, 108
trade with, 110
Afro-Asian People's Solidarity
    Conference, 97
Agreement on Mutual Non-
    Aggression, 80
agricultural projects, 203
agriculture. *See* Ministry of
    Agriculture
Ahmed, Azam, 354n136
aid, humanitarian, 203. *See also*
    overseas aid
AIDS/HIV, 147–48
Air China, 187
air force. *See* PLA Air Force
Air Force Command College,
    PLA, 301
air pollution, 149
Ai Weiwei, 248, 250–51, 266
Alcatel, 192–93
Algeria, 166, 303
Alliance Française, 245
aluminum, 117, 171
AMC Entertainment, 254
ancient China, as international
    image, 211–12
Angola, 163, 164f, 166,
    378n67
animals, 239, 250

anquan (complete tranquility),
    59. *See also* security
anti-Chinese sentiments,
    200–201
anti-dumping, 76, 160
anti-hegemony, 26. *See also*
    hegemony
antisatellite capacity, 296
antisubmarine warfare (ASW),
    292–93
anti-Western sentiments
    books with, 28–29
    by CCTV, 232
    against EU, 28–29, 141,
        155, 232
    global governance and, 40,
        131–32, 155
    Nativists with xenophobia
        and, 27–31
    Realists with, 33–34
    UN votes and, 141
    against U.S., 28–29, 31,
        33–34, 40, 85, 141, 155,
        232
AOL Time Warner, 231
APEC. *See* Asia-Pacific
    Economic Cooperation
    organization
Apple, 199
appliances, 197–98

approved destination status
(ADS), 255
Arab League, 108
Arab Spring, 225
architects, 252–53
area denial and sea denial
(AD/SD), 280
ARF. *See* ASEAN Regional
Forum
Argentina, 111, 113, 114, 117, 120
arms
artillery, 286–88, 291
chemical warfare, 144
Chinese sales to Latin
America, 116
control and
nonproliferation,
142–44, 303
disarmament conference, 97
embargo, 90, 283, 304
General Armaments
Department, 283
Iran-Iraq war and sales
of, 106
long-range stealth bombs,
276
missiles, 142, 276, 279–80,
294–95, 303
Russia sales to China, 283
transfers, 301–5
U.S. sales to Taiwan, 77
weapons systems, 277–78
worldwide sales of, 302f
art, 10, 248. *See also* culture
global appetite for
contemporary Chinese,
250
Gugong, 249, 251, 370n200
with harassment of artists,
251
Hong Kong auctions,
249–50
with inventory teams sent
abroad, 251
looted, 250–51
market for domestic,
369n195
National Museum, 251–52
Picasso's, 249
sales of high-priced,
249–50, 259
artillery, 286–88, 291. *See also*
arms; weapons

Artprice.com, 250
ASEAN. *See* Association of
Southeast Asian Nations
ASEAN-China Free Trade
Area (CAFTA), 102
ASEAN Regional Forum
(ARF), 61, 97, 335n122
Asia. *See also* Southeast Asia;
specific countries in Asia
China's diplomacy with, 51,
55, 95–105
financial crisis in, 96
tribute system and, 95
U.S. and pivot to, 77, 100
Asia First, 36, 37, 38
Asian Development Bank
(ADB), 134
Asia-Pacific Economic
Cooperation (APEC)
organization, 115
The Asia Foundation, 67
assertiveness, year of, 4, 77, 316
Association of International
Relations, 20
Association of Southeast Asian
Nations (ASEAN), 22,
37, 51, 77, 96, 127, 159
CAFTA, 102
Regional Forum, 61, 97,
335n122
ASW. *See* antisubmarine
warfare
Australia, 4, 77, 167, 200
China as viewed by, 12,
102–3
trade with, 158t, 159f
wine in, 158
Australian National
University, 135
auto companies, 181–82,
195–97
Avian influenza (H_5N_1),
147–48
Azerbaijan, 166, 170, 303

backlash, energy, 199–202
Bahrain, 106
Bain & Company, 258
Baltic states, 90
Bandung Interregnum phase,
47, 95
Bangladesh, 303–4
Bank of China, 255

banks, 114–15, 124, 138, 157, 315.
See also specific banks
ADB, 134
with overseas aid, 203
World Bank, 10, 124,
126–27, 134, 150, 204
Baosteel, 172
al-Bashir, Omar, 111
BBC. *See* British Broadcasting
Service
Beijing Auto, 195–96, 355n154
Beijing Foreign Studies
University, 67, 69
The Beijing Consensus (Ramo),
214
Beijing University, 210
Belarus, 118
Belgium, 240
benevolence, 43, 212
Benin, 303
Bergdorf Goodman, 256
BHP Billiton, 173
biaotai (to declare where one
stands), 217–18
Biden, Joe, 74, 331n59
biding-time debate, 18–20, 219
"big fish swallowing the small,"
media and, 227–28, 236
billionaires, 157
biofuels, 151
Biological Weapons
Convention (BWC),
142, 144
Blackstone Group, 184
bloggers, 15, 70, 187, 365n112
Bloomberg, 227
Bloomingdale's, 256
Blossom Press, 236
Bolivia, 114, 303
bombings
car, 200
of Chinese embassy, 98
long-range stealth, 276
Bonaparte, Napoleon, x
books
with anti-Western
sentiments, 28–29
literature and, 10, 247–48
as messengers of global
culture, 209, 235–37
monitoring of foreign, 235
State Press and Publishing
Administration and, 222

border dispute
  India, 103
  Palestinian, 108
  South China Sea, 102
borders
  Office of Border Affairs, 308
  security, 53, 60, 84
boycotts, Tibet and Olympic,
  93
BP, 165, 170
brand recognition
  for China as country,
    211–12
  Chinese tourists and, 258
  corporations and, 187,
    191–92
  in fashion, 252
  global, 187, 191–92, 199,
    353n130
Brautigam, Deborah, 110
Brazil, 21, 38, 111, 112, 116
  BRICS, 22, 23, 39, 114
  China as viewed by, 113–14
  imports from, 349n59
  oil in, 117, 164f
  strategic partnership with,
    114
  trade with, 158t, 159f
  with UN voting history,
    141, 343n59
Brazil, Russia, India, China,
  South Africa (BRICS),
  22, 23, 39, 114
Bretton Woods, 123, 130, 134
Brezhnev Doctrine, 48
bribery
  academic, 215
  financial, 146, 147, 167
BRICS. See Brazil, Russia,
  India, China, South
  Africa
Brilliance China Automotive
  Holdings, 355n154
British Broadcasting Service
  (BBC), 12, 119, 230–32,
  253, 264
British Council, 245
British Telecom, 195
British Virgin Islands, 118,
  180, 181t
brochures, 209
Brookings Institution, 71, 170
Brown, Gordon, 93

budgets
  annual defense, 274f, 379n77
  internal security and
    military, 319n5, 328n15,
    374n9
  PAP, 328n15
  propaganda and
    decentralized, 238
  security, 59, 319n5, 328n15,
    374n9
  for three program areas,
    334n98
  UN, 140
  ZBB system of, 275, 374n9
bullying, 72
Burke, Kristin, 350n71
Bush, George W., 22–23
business culture, 187–89, 215
BWC. See Biological Weapons
  Convention
BYD Company, 355n154

CAFTA. See ASEAN-China
  Free Trade Area
Cai Jinyong, 128
Caijung, 236
Cai Wu, 209, 240, 265
Cambodia, 48–49, 298, 303
Cameron, David, 89
Canada
  China as viewed by, 12
  China's diplomacy with,
    146–47
  CRI broadcasting in, 233
  oil in, 168
  with UN operating budget
    contributions, 140
canola, 171
Capital Steel. See Shougang
  Group
Caribbean, 111, 113, 118,
  339n158. See also specific
  countries in Caribbean
Carrefour, 93
cars. See also auto companies
  bombings, 200
  luxury, 259
CASCF. See China-Arab States
  Cooperation Forum
CASS. See China Academy of
  Social Sciences
catalysts, for military
  modernization, 275–78

cautious power, 120
CCP. See Chinese Communist
  Party
CCTV. See China Central
  Television
censorship, 221, 224–25, 254
Census Bureau, U.S., 332n65
Center for Strategic and
  International Studies
  (CSIS), 333n82
Central Committee. See Chinese
  Communist Party
Central Foreign Affairs Office
  (CFAO), 211. See also
  Foreign Affairs Office
Central Military Commission,
  63, 69, 116, 275, 279, 302
Central Party School, xiii, 21,
  43, 188, 210, 212
  CRF and, 237
  Institute of Strategic
    Studies, 69, 327n89
  peaceful rise and, 218–19
  on soft power, 215
Central Propaganda Leading
  Group, 363n63
CFAO. See Central Foreign
  Affairs Office
CFISS. See China Foundation
  for International
  Strategic Studies
CFIUS. See Committee on
  Foreign Investment in
  the United States
Chad, 167, 303
Chang'an Auto Group,
  355n154
Changchun Auto, 355n154
Chang Gong, 40
charm offensive, 26, 57. See
  also soft power
Charnuis, Betty, 252
Chavez, Hugo, 117, 119, 163
chemicals. See Ministry of
  Chemical Industry
chemical warfare, 144
Chemical Weapons
  Conventions (CWC),
  142, 144
Chen Jian, 181
Chen Kaige, 253
Chen Shuibian, 277
Chen Tonghai, 167

Chen Xuegen, 248
Chery, 196, 355n154
Chicago Council on Global
    Affairs, 25, 220, 324n47
Chile, 111, 113, 114, 117, 120
    China as viewed by, 12
    trade with, 118
Chin, Gregory, 126
China, 332n75
    Africa and diplomacy with,
        51–52, 55, 108–11
    Asia and diplomacy with,
        51, 55, 95–105
    Australia's opinion of, 12,
        102–3
    as brand, 211–12
    BRICS, 22, 23, 39, 114
    Canada and diplomacy
        with, 146–47
    China-EU Think
        Tank Roundtable
        Mechanism, 87
    coping with globalized,
        307–17
    EU and diplomacy with,
        50, 51, 86–94, 334n113
    EU as viewed by, 36, 93–94
    EU-China Project on
        the Protection of
        Intellectual Property, 88
    Europe-China Business
        Management Training
        Project, 88
    EU's opinion of, 93
    GDP of, 151, 156, 206, 289
    global impact of, 4–10
    global perceptions of, 11–12,
        209, 262–66
    India's opinion of, 12, 103
    intercultural dialogues with
        EU and, 334n112
    as international actors with
        diplomacy, 45–47
    Ivy League of, 243
    Japan as viewed by, 56
    Japan's diplomacy with,
        101–2
    Japan's opinion of, 11, 12
    Latin America and
        diplomacy with, 51–52,
        55, 111–20
    Latin America's opinion of,
        113–14, 119–20

    as lonely power, 7, 310
    Middle East and diplomacy
        with, 52, 55, 105–8
    myths about, 265
    as nuclear threat, 48, 143
    ODI of, 10, 156–57
    as partial power, x, 7–8, 10,
        45, 157, 270, 309–11
    PCA, 88, 92
    population, 132
    as returning world power,
        1–4
    rule of law in, 10
    Russia and diplomacy with,
        49, 78–86, 347n23
    Russia as viewed by, 35–36
    Russia's opinion of, 11,
        84–85
    Russia with arms sales to, 283
    sentiments against,
        200–201
    Singapore's opinion of, 307
    South Korea and diplomacy
        with, 100–101
    South Korea's opinion of,
        12, 100–101
    as status quo or revisionist
        power, 72, 121, 134
    three international images
        of, 211–12
    in UN, 24–25, 133, 137–42
    with UN operating budget
        contributions, 140
    with UN voting history, 141
    U.S. and diplomacy with,
        51–52, 73–78
    U.S. as largest source of
        FDI in, 73
    U.S. as viewed by, 26,
        129–30
    U.S. opinion of, 12
    World Bank loans to, 134
China: Fragile Superpower
    (Shirk), 60
China Academy of Social
    Sciences (CASS), 37,
    238, 322n9
    Contemporary China
        Institute, 29
    Institute of European
        Studies, 36
    Institute of Foreign
        Literature, 368n168

    Institute of Political
        Science, 30
    Marxism Academy of, 29
China Aluminum Corporation.
    See Chinalco
China-Andean Community
    Consultation Forum, 115
China and Iran: Ancient
    Partners in a Post-
    Imperial World
    (Garver), 106
China-Arab States
    Cooperation Forum
    (CASCF), 108, 337n146
China Arts and Entertainment
    Group, 240
China Association for
    International Friendly
    Contact, 237
China Can Say No!, 27, 28
China-Caribbean Economic
    and Trade Cooperation
    Forum, 115
China Center for International
    Economic Exchanges,
    69
China Central Television
    (CCTV)
    as messenger of global
        culture, 227, 229, 230–33
    "Rising Powers," 17–18
    viewers in other countries,
        365n107
China Collapse theory, 219
China Council for the
    Promotion of
    International Trade,
    336n133
China Daily, 146, 187, 227,
    233–35, 263, 346n1
China Doesn't Express Its
    Dissatisfaction, 27
China-EU Partnership and
    Cooperation Agreement
    (PCA), 88, 92
China-Europe: Closer Partners,
    Growing Responsibilities,
    334n105
China-EU Think Tank
    Roundtable
    Mechanism, 87
China Firsters, 31. See also
    Realists

China Foreign Affairs University, xiii, xv, 37, 67, 69

China Foundation for International Strategic Studies (CFISS), 68, 237–38

China Import Company, 169

China Institute for International Strategic Studies (CIISS), xiii, 22, 68–69, 129, 237–38

China Institute of International Studies (CIIS), 22, 68

China Institutes of Contemporary International Relations (CICIR), xiii, 35–36, 68–69, 83, 202, 210, 238

China International Contractors Association, 179

China International Exhibition Agency, 240

China International Publishing Group (CIPG), 236–37

China International Travel Service, 258

China Investment Corporation (CIC), 156, 183–84, 201, 353n117

China Is Not Disruptive (Chang Gong), 40

China Is Unhappy (Song Xiaojun et al), 28–29

China-Latin America Common Market Dialogue, 115

China-Latin America Forum, 115

China-Latin American Business Summit, 115

Chinalco (China Aluminum Corporation), 172–73

China Media Capital, 254

China Media Yearbook, 222

China Metallurgical Construction Corporation, 172

China Minmetals Corporation, 172, 200, 349n61

China Model, 214

China National Blue Star, 182

China National Offshore Oil Corporation (CNOOC), 165–66, 168, 182, 186, 200, 348n28

China National Petroleum Corporation (CNPC), 164–69, 186

China National Publications Import and Export Corporation, 235

China National Tourism Administration (CNTA), 255–56, 260

China Network Corporation (CNC), 229

China Nine, 243

China Non-Ferrous Metals Mining Corporation, 172

China Ocean Shipping Company (COSCO), 182

China Performing Arts Agency, 240

China Petrochemical Corporation (Sinopec), 165–70, 186, 348n27, 348n28

China Pictorial Publishing House, 236

China Publishing Group (CPG), 236

China Radio International (CRI), 227–28, 233, 265, 365n116

China Reform Forum (CRF), 21, 33, 69, 219, 237

China Scholarship Council, 242, 367n151

China's Communist Party: Atrophy and Adaptation (Shambaugh), x, 79

"China's Competing Nationalisms" (Shambaugh), 319n6

China's National Defense, 379n77, 379n81

China's Rise (Yan Xuetong), 33–34

China's Soft Power Strategy (Men Honghua), 212

China Statistical Yearbook, 204, 364n90

The China Dream (Liu Mingfu), 265

China Threat theory, 21, 219

Chinese Academy of Art, 253

Chinese Academy of International Trade and Economic Cooperation, 68–69

Chinese Academy of Sciences Institute of Computing Technology, 199

Chinese Academy of Social Sciences, xii, 21, 68, 111, 113

Chinese Communist Party (CCP), 2, 26, 49. See *also specific ministries*
with business culture, 188
Central Committee, 29, 43, 62–66, 69, 80, 207, 222, 228, 275, 329n21, 329n24
diplomacy in service of politics and, 56–59
EPLSG, 63, 221, 330n33, 363n63
ID, 64, 66–68, 87, 94, 115, 129, 237, 330n43
massacre of June 4, 1989, and, 3, 18, 50, 79, 88, 95–96
midcareer training and, 189
Nativists in, 29
newspapers, 188
peaceful evolution and, 60
Politburo, 18, 63–64, 208, 360n18
Propaganda Department, 2, 21, 208, 217, 220–21, 228
Xinhua News Agency with, 23–24, 66, 146, 227, 228–30

Chinese People's Association for Friendship with Foreign Countries, 237

Chinese People's Institute of Foreign Affairs (CPIFA), xiii, 94, 237, 255

Chinese People's Political Consultative Congress (CPPCC), 210, 264

Christie's, 249–50, 251
chromium ores, 171
CIC. *See* China Investment
    Corporation
CICIR. *See* China Institutes
    of Contemporary
    International Relations
CIIS. *See* China Institute of
    International Studies
CIISS. *See* China Institute for
    International Strategic
    Studies
CIPG. *See* China International
    Publishing Group
CIs. *See* Confucius Institutes
civilization, history and,
    239–41
climate change, 38, 51, 73,
    76, 151
Clinton, Bill, 50
CNC. *See* China Network
    Corporation
CNN, 2, 187, 230, 231–32, 264
CNOOC. *See* China
    National Offshore Oil
    Corporation
CNPC. *See* China National
    Petroleum Corporation
CNTA. *See* China National
    Tourism Administration
Cohen, Warren, 53, 327n10
Cold War, 9, 88–89
Colombia, 120, 167, 201, 303
commerce. *See* Ministry of
    Commerce
commercial espionage, 297
Commission on Global
    Governance, 122
Committee on Foreign
    Investment in the United
    States (CFIUS), 200
commodity markets, global, 8
companies, auto, 181–82,
    195–97, 355n154. *See also*
    corporations; *specific
    companies*
competitive coexistence, 74
compliance, feigned, 217
comprehensive power, 5–6
Comprehensive Test Ban
    Treaty, 142
computers, 161, 198–99, 225
Confucian values, 43

Confucius (film), 239
Confucius Institutes (CIs), 112,
    116, 245–47, 368n168
conglomerates (*jituan*), 165.
    See also national oil
    companies
Congo, 298, 303, 305
Constructivists, 131, 313
consumption, oil, 162–63,
    290–91
"containment" policies
    EU, 91–92
    as untenable, 315, 316
    U.S., 77, 97, 129, 315–16
contamination, water, 149–50
Contemporary China
    Institute, CASS, 29
cooperation
    APEC, 115
    assistance with EU, 88
    CASCF, 108, 337n146
    China-Caribbean
        Economic and Trade
        Cooperation Forum, 115
    CSCAP, 97, 335n122
    energy, 81
    FOCAC, 108–10
    forging, 74
    HR development, 203
    international, 42
    OECD, 124, 136, 180,
        202–4, 314, 357n183
    Russia and military pact of,
        80–83
    SCO, 22, 25, 61, 80, 84–85,
        104
    technical, 203
    Treaty of Neighborliness
        and Friendly, 80–81
copper ores, 110, 117, 171
corporate accountability, 10
corporate espionage, 297
corporations. *See also specific
    corporations*
    auto companies and,
        181–82, 195–97, 355n154
    with brand recognition,
        187, 191–92
    business culture in, 187–89
    Chinese characteristics
        built into multinational,
        184–93
    HR as Achilles' heel for, 186

localities and, 62, 69–70
    with midcareer training,
        189
    NOCs, 162, 164–71, 186,
        348n28
    reverse mergers and, 190
    taxes, 155
corruption, 10, 154, 187, 244.
    See also crime
COSCO. *See* China Ocean
    Shipping Company
Cosmopolitan, 236
Costa Rica, 118
Council on Security
    Cooperation in the
    Asia-Pacific (CSCAP),
    97, 335n122
counterterrorism, 41, 76
countries. *See also specific
    countries*
    China's overseas aid in
        comparison to other, 10
    developing, 38–39
    GDP of average
        developing, 38
    least-developed, 38
CPG. *See* China Publishing
    Group
CPIFA. *See* Chinese People's
    Institute of Foreign
    Affairs
CPPCC. *See* Chinese People's
    Political Consultative
    Congress
CRF. *See* China Reform
    Forum
CRI. *See* China Radio
    International
crime
    corruption and, 10, 154,
        187, 244
    Hong Kong, 145–46
    INTERPOL and
        international, 144–47
    kidnappings, 200–201, 202
    NCB, 145
    piracy, 40, 41, 46, 82, 144
CSCAP. *See* Council on
    Security Cooperation in
    the Asia-Pacific
CSIS. *See* Center for Strategic
    and International
    Studies

Cuba, 49, 114, 119
Cui Tiankai, 66, 71, 97–98,
    101, 129–30, 307
cultural footprint, global
    art, 248–52
    CIs, 245–47
    education and research,
        241–45
    expanding, 238–39
    fashion and design, 252–53
    film, 253–55
    history and civilization,
        239–41
    impact of, 262
    literature, 247–48
    as misunderstood or
        disrespected, 262–66
    sports, 261–62
    tourism, 255–61
cultural industries, GDP, 209
Cultural Industries
    Revitalization Plan, 208
cultural power, 210
cultural presence, global
    with expanding footprint,
        238–66
    with image, soft power
        and public diplomacy,
        210–16
    influence on, 10, 207–10
    messengers, 220–38
    public face with, 216–20
    soft power and, 266–68
Cultural Revolution, 64, 252
    core values destroyed
        during, 212
    Gang of Four, 109, 133, 134
    self-imposed isolation
        during, 95
    xenophobia of, 47–48
culture. See also art
    business, 187–89, 215
    clash, 260
    ministry of, 66, 68, 253
    political, 154–55, 217–19
    soft power and, 212–13
    soft power with traditional,
        360n26
currency
    controls, 96
    Euro, 126
    global finance and multi-,
        126–28

manipulation, 78
RMB, 126–27, 160
swapping, 160–61
U.S. dollar, 126
Curse of the Golden Flower
    (film), 254
CWC. See Chemical Weapons
    Conventions
cyber hacking, 41, 78,
        378n62
    China's influence in
        global, 8
    countries reporting, 297,
        377n61
cyber forces, espionage and,
        296–98
cyber militias, PLA, 298
cyber security, 279
Czechoslovakia, 48, 89

Dahl, Robert, 8
Dai Bingguo, 64, 65, 128
Dalai Lama, 58, 92–93, 103,
        263
Dalian Wanda Group, 254
danger, of peaceful rise, 33,
        316–17
da Silva, Lula, 114
The Days (film), 253
DEA. See Drug Enforcement
    Agency, U.S.
death sentences, 146, 167
debates, on China, 333n90
debt
    relief, 203
    U.S., 73, 157
decentralization, 71
decision-making, in foreign
    policy
    hierarchy of actors in, 61,
        62f, 63–72
    intelligence organs and, 62,
        68–69
    localities, corporations and,
        62, 69–70
    ministries and, 62, 66–68
    senior leaders and, 62–65
    society and, 62, 70
declassifying, of documents,
        328n18
decline
    myth of U.S., 22–23, 99
    Russia in, 35, 36

defense. See also military;
    Ministry of Defense;
    People's Armed Police;
    People's Liberation
    Army
    budgets, 274f, 379n77
    dialogues, 300
defense technologies
    embargo, 283
    piracy of, 82
defensive nationalism, 56, 58
defensive Realists, 32
deficit
    Nobel Prize, 267
    soft power, 212, 215
    values, 213
Deloitte & Touche, 180
demining specialists, 378n67
Deng Liqun, 27, 29. See also
    Nativists
Deng Xiaoping, 9, 35, 55, 79,
    106, 309
    biding time, hiding
        brightness, do more
        things and, 18–20, 219
    diplomacy by, 48–49, 95
    lying low strategy and, 75,
        322n17
    with peace and
        development, 21, 30,
        98–99, 218
    "Southern Sojourn" of, 19,
        30, 51
    with system studying
        phase, 134
    on trade, 157
    UN speech of, 133
Department of Defense, U.S.,
    269, 290, 375n25
Department of Policy
    Planning, MFA, 129
design, fashion and, 252–53
Deutsche Telekom, 195
Deutsche Welle, 230
developing countries, 38–39
development, peace and. See
    peace, development and
dialogues
    China-Latin America
        Common Market, 115
    defense, 300
    SAED, 74
    sectoral, 87, 333n96

diamonds, 110
Ding Gang, 215, 234
Ding Kuisong, 33
diplomacy
    with Africa, 51–52, 55,
        108–11
    with Asia, 51, 55, 95–105
    biding-time, hiding-
        brightness and do-more-
        things, 18–20, 219
    cautious power with, 120
    charm offensive with
        public, 26, 57
    by Deng Xiaoping, 48–49,
        95
    economic development
        and, 54–56
    with EU, 50, 51, 86–94,
        334n113
    face, 57
    Five Principles of Peaceful
        Coexistence, 53, 97, 218
    foreign policy decision-
        making and, 61–72
    global presence with, 45–47
    with historical imperatives,
        53–54
    with Latin America, 51, 55,
        111–20
    with Middle East, 52, 55,
        105–8
    military, 299–301
    Office of Public, 210–11,
        223–27
    omnidirectional, 51
    outputs, 72–73
    passive, 8–9, 83, 100–101
    policy recommendations
        for, 20
    politics served by, 56–59
    preemptive, 58
    with regional groupings,
        41–42
    with Russia, 49, 78–86,
        347n23
    security served by, 59–61
    slogan, 217
    smile, 57
    soft-power, 4–5, 20, 25–26,
        210–16
    with soft power, culture,
        image and public,
        210–16

    soft power distinct from
        public, 209–10
    strategic maneuvering and
        ten phases of, 47–53
    with Syria, 8, 83
    with U.S., 51–52, 73–78
    yin and yang of, 58–59
Diplomatic Service Personnel
    Bureau, 225
directors, film, 253
disarmament conference, 97
disaster relief, 40, 299
Disneyland, in Hong Kong,
    260
Dittmer, Lowell, 337n148
dollar, hegemony of U.S., 126
Dolphin Books, 236
do more things, 18–20, 40
Dongfeng Motor, 355n154
Dosch, Jörn, 339n166
Downs, Erica, 170, 348n29
The Dragon's Gift (Brautigam),
    110
DreamWorks Animation, 254
Drug Enforcement Agency
    (DEA), U.S., 146
drug trafficking, 144–47
dumping, anti-, 76, 160
Dunlop, Regina, 113–14
Du Qiwen, 65, 71
dynasties
    Qing, 31, 54, 108, 308
    Song, 108

Earth Summit, 152
East Asia Vision Group,
    335n126
East China Normal
    University, 69
East Turkestan Independence
    Movement (ETIM), 145
ECLAC. See Economic
    Commission for Latin
    America and the
    Caribbean
eclecticism, in thinking, 27
Economic Commission for
    Latin America and the
    Caribbean (ECLAC),
    118
economic presence, global
    energy needs, 162–202
    overseas aid, 202–5

    as powerhouse, 156–57
    prospects, 205–6
    as trading superstate, 157–61
economy
    diplomacy and
        development of, 54–56
    security of, 41
    soft power and
        development of, 214–15
    "Southern Sojourn" with,
        19, 30, 51
Economy, Elizabeth, 316
Ecuador, 114, 167, 303
education
    academic bribery in, 215
    CIs, 112, 116, 245–47,
        368n168
    EU exchange, 87
    global rankings for, 242–43
    of ground force officers, 285
    Japan exchange, 102, 242
    of MFA personnel, 67
    overseas aid with, 204
    research and, 241–45
    Russia exchange, 242
    scholarships, 242
    South Korea exchange, 100,
        102, 241
    Thailand exchange, 242
    U.S. exchange, 73, 241–42
    Vietnam exchange, 242
Egypt, 48, 105, 196, 198, 201,
    300, 303
Elliott, Jeannette Shambaugh,
    370n200
Ellis, R. Evan, 338n152,
    339n161, 339n165
Elmendorf, Ed, 343n53
embargo
    arms, 90, 283, 304
    defense technology, 283
    EU and military arms, 90
    on Libya, 137–38
emigration, Chinese, 261
energy
    appliances, 197–98
    auto companies, 195–97
    backlash and risk, 199–202
    China's influence in global,
        8, 156
    clean, 151
    computers, 198–99
    consumption, 73

cooperation, 81
crude oil imports by
    source, 164f
global mining operations,
    171–74, 201
"going out" and "going
    global" policy with,
    174–83, 350n71
multinational corporations
    with Chinese
    characteristics, 184–93
natural gas, 107, 164–65,
    167–68
needs, 162–64
NOCs, 162, 164–71, 186,
    348n28
nuclear, 151
ODI, 174
ODI flows for 1982–2010,
    178f
ODI in 2010, top ten
    destinations, 181t
overseas aid with, 202–5
solar, 151–52
sovereign wealth fund,
    183–84
supplies as imports, 117
telecoms, 191, 193–95
Enterovirus (EV-71), 147
environment
    acid rain and air pollution,
        149
    climate change, 38, 51, 73,
        76, 151
    global, 148–53
    greenhouse gasses, 73, 149
    policy criticisms, 11
    water contamination,
        149–50
environmental protection.
    See Ministry of
    Environmental
    Protection
environmental protection
    laws, 150
EPLSG. See External
    Propaganda Leading
    Small Group
Ericsson, 193
espionage
    commercial, 297
    corporate, 297
    cyber, 296–98

by foreign countries, 232
    industrial, 78, 89
Ethiopia, 123, 378n67
ethnic minorities. See Xinjiang
    Autonomous Region
ETIM. See East Turkestan
    Independence
    Movement
etiquette, 43, 212
EU. See European Union
EU-China Project on
    the Protection of
    Intellectual Property, 88
Euro, 126
European Council on Foreign
    Relations, 182
Europeanists, 36
European Union (EU), 4, 22
    with absence of military
        presence, 89
    anti-Western sentiments
        against, 28–29, 141,
        155, 232
    China as viewed by, 93
    China's diplomacy with,
        50, 51, 86–94, 334n113
    China's opinion of, 36,
        93–94
    Chinese tourists in, 255
    CIC and, 184
    "containment" policies,
        91–92
    cooperation assistance with,
        88, 92
    education exchange with,
        87
    EU-China Project on
        the Protection of
        Intellectual Property, 88
    Europe-China Business
        Management Training
        Project, 88
    intercultural dialogues with
        China and, 334n112
    as largest source of
        technology, 86–87
    Major Powers School and,
        34, 36
    military arms embargo, 90
    overseas aid of, 10
    PCA, 88, 92
    sanctions dropped by, 88
    sectoral dialogues with, 87

strategic partnerships with,
    87–89, 90, 94
    with Taiwan issue, 89, 91
    tourism, 87
    trade with, 86–87, 92, 159,
        346n4
European Union Institute for
    Security Studies, 340n7
Europe-China Business
    Management Training
    Project, 88
EV-71. See Enterovirus
Evans, Paul, 335n121
example, China, 214
exchange organizations
    with education, 73, 87, 100,
        102, 241–42
    as messengers of global
        culture, 237–38
exhibitions, traveling
    historical, 240
experience, China, 214
exports
    autos, 196
    global, 158, 160
    of labor, 179
    military weapons, 303–4
external propaganda, 65,
    216–17, 220–22, 226,
    267
External Propaganda Leading
    Group, 363n63
External Propaganda Leading
    Small Group (EPLSG),
    63, 221, 330n33, 363n63.
    See also State Council
    Information Office
extradition treaties, 146–47
Exxon Mobil, 165, 170

face
    culture and presenting
        global, 216–20
    diplomacy, 57
    saving, 54, 56–57
Fairbank, John King, 53,
    327n10
FALSG. See Foreign Affairs
    Leading Small Group
Falun Gong, 58
Fang Ning, 30
FAO. See Foreign Affairs
    Office

Farewell My Concubine (film), 253

Farnsworth, Eric, 340n170

fashion, design and, 252–53

FAW Group, 355n154

FBI. *See* Federal Bureau of Investigation

FCCC. *See* Foreign Correspondents Club of China

FCO. *See* Foreign and Commonwealth Office

FDI. *See* foreign direct investment

Federal Bureau of Investigation (FBI), 246

feigned compliance, 217

Femme Lisant (*Deux Personnages*), 249

Feng Shanshan, 262

Feng Yujun, 35, 83

Ferrero-Waldner, Benita, 88

Fewsmith, Joseph, 331n47

fighter jets, 287–88

films, 10
  censorship, 254
  Confucius, 239
  Curse of the Golden Flower, 254
  The Days, 253
  directors, 253–54
  domestic box office, 253, 254
  famous Chinese, 253
  foreign market for, 254–55
  Kung-fu Panda and *Transformers 3*, 254
  State Press and Publishing Administration with, 222

finance
  global, 126–28
  ministry of, 66, 246, 275

financial bribery, 146, 147, 167

financial crisis
  Asian, 96
  global, 22, 23, 30–31, 33, 214

Fissile Material Cutoff Treaty (FMCT), 143

Five Principles of Peaceful Coexistence, 53, 97, 218

FLP. *See* Foreign Languages Press

FMCT. *See* Fissile Material Cutoff Treaty

FOCAC. *See* Forum on China-Africa Cooperation

Foot, Rosemary, 341n13, 346n98

Ford Foundation, 67

Ford Motor Company, 196

foreign affairs. *See* Ministry of Foreign Affairs

Foreign Affairs, 219

Foreign Affairs Leading Small Group (FALSG), 63–65, 221

Foreign Affairs Office (FAO), 63, 64–65, 69, 133, 330n33
  Central, 211

foreign aid. *See* overseas aid

Foreign and Commonwealth Office (FCO), 377n61

Foreign Correspondents Club of China (FCCC), 225

foreign direct investment (FDI), 50, 55, 73, 100, 102, 156, 174, 177

foreign film market, 254–55

foreign labor, 187

Foreign Languages Press (FLP), 211, 236

foreign news journalists, 224–26, 364n80

foreign policy, 62f
  conflicting, 14
  decision-making in, 61–72
  economic development, diplomacy and, 54–56
  historical imperatives and, 53–54
  kouhao or slogans, 218
  politics, diplomacy and, 56–59
  security, diplomacy and, 59–61

Foreign Service, U.S., 330n38

Fortune Global 500 list, 165, 169, 184–85

Forum on China-Africa Cooperation (FOCAC), 108–10

FPPC, 362n52

France, 89, 93, 240

Chinese tourists in, 256–57
  with UN operating budget contributions, 140
  with UN voting history, 141, 343n59

France Télécom, 195

Frankfurt Book Fair (Frankfurter Buchmesse), 247–48, 368n179

freedom, of press, 10

Freedom House, 10

free trade agreements (FTAs), 159

Friedberg, Aaron, 312

Friedman, Thomas, 124

Frigidaire, 198

FTAs. *See* free trade agreements

Fu Chengyu, 168

Fudan University, 13, 33, 67, 69, 210, 216

Fullilove, Michael, 140

The Future of Power (Nye), 8

Fu Ying, 93, 94, 216, 264–65, 317, 334n109, 362n47

G-2, 75

G-20, 45, 127

Gabon, 163, 303

gambling, 144, 259

Gang of Four, 109, 133, 134

Gao Xingjian, 247

Garver, John, 106

GAs. *See* Group Armies

gasses, 346n3
  greenhouse, 73, 149
  natural, 107, 164–65, 167–68

Gates, Robert, 287

GATT. *See* General Agreement on Tariffs and Trade

GDP. *See* Gross Domestic Product

GE, 198

Geely, 182, 187, 195, 196–97, 355n154

General Agreement on Tariffs and Trade (GATT), 134

General Armaments Department, 283

General Motors (GM), 195

General Office of the Central
    Committee, 63
Genghis Khan, 85
genocide, 124
geography, military and, 277
Georgetown University, 67
George Washington
    University, 67, 186
German Federal Chancellery,
    377n61
Germany, 89, 90, 123, 240
    China as viewed by, 11
    Chinese tourists in, 257
    takeovers in, 182
    trade with, 158t, 159f
    with UN operating budget
        contributions, 140
Ghana, 12, 163, 303, 304
gift-giving, in business, 215
glasnost (openness), 79
Global Competitiveness
    Index, 10
Globalists
    with regional diplomatic
        groupings, 42
    with soft power and
        humanitarianism, 41, 43
globalization
    of China, 307–17
    as new imperialism with
        Nativists, 30
    origins, 124
    with past shaping future,
        308–9
    policy process changing
        with, 71
Global Refund, 255
Global South School, 38–39, 43
global superpower. See
    superpower, global
Global Times, 215, 228, 233–35,
    248, 366n121
GM. See General Motors
Godement, François, 352n108
Goethe Institute, 245
"going out" and "going global"
    policy
    criticism of, 213
    ODI and, 174–83, 350n71
gold, 171, 258
gold medals, 261
goods and materials, 203
Google, 297–98

Google.cn, 297
Gorbachev, Mikhail, 49, 79
governance, global
    attitudes and questions
        about, 121–22, 340n4
    Chinese research on, 341n23
    definition, 122
    with global environment,
        148–53
    INTERPOL and
        international crime,
        144–47
    multilateralism and
        responsible-power
        theory with, 23–25
    nonproliferation and arms
        control, 142–44, 303
    origins, 122–25, 128
    in perspective, 153–55
    public health and, 147–48
    record in, 125–28
    as responsible major power,
        128–32
    road to, 132–42
    system challenger phase, 133
    system studying phase, 134
    system exploitation phase,
        134–35
    system altering phase, 136
    as trap, 40, 131–32, 155
    with UN, 123–24, 137–42
GQ, 236
Grand Cayman Islands, 180,
    181t
Great Hall of the People, 57,
    228
Great Leap Forward, 79, 105,
    252
Great Wall Motor, 182,
    355n154
greenhouse gasses, 73, 149
Gries, Peter Hays, 57
Gross Domestic Product
    (GDP), 202
    of average developing
        countries, 38
    of China, 151, 156, 206, 289
    cultural industries, 209
    defense and military
        spending, 274f
ground forces, military,
    284–86
Group Armies (GAs), 284

Guangdong Foreign Studies
    University, 324n43
Guangzhou Auto, 355n154
guanxi (reciprocal obligations),
    154, 242
Guan Youfei, 303
Guatemala, 343n48
Gugong (Palace Museum),
    249, 251, 370n200
Gu Guoliang, 358n14
Guinea, 163, 168
Gulf of Aden, 40, 46, 271, 299
Gulf War, 276
Guo Xin Ban/Wai Xuan Ban,
    221. See also State
    Council Information
    Office
Guo Zhenyuan, 22

H_5N_1. See Avian influenza
Haas, Ernest, 346n100
hacking, computer, 225
The Hague, 122–23
Haier Corporation, 186, 187,
    197–98, 356n166, 356n168
Ha Jin, 247
Hallex, Matthew, 344n63
Han Ban. See Office of
    International Language
    Council
Han Han, 247
Harding, Harry, 343n49
hard power, 4
    definition, 209
    Realists, 32
harmonious world theory, 25,
    219–20, 324n47
harmony, peace and, 43, 212
Harper, Steven, 147
Harvard University, 8, 72, 135,
    209, 322n9
Havel, Vaclav, 93
havens, tax, 180
Hawaiian Islands, 256
Hawtai Motor, 355n154
health, public, 41, 147–48, 203
Hebei Lingyun, 182
hegemony
    U.S., 23, 26
    with U.S. dollar, 126
Henan International Mining
    Company, 172
Hero (film), 253

Hewlett Packard (HP), 199
hiding-brightness debate,
    18–20
Hilton, 256
Hirshhorn Museum, 248
Hisense, 187
history
    civilization and, 239–41
    diplomacy with imperatives
        of, 53–54
    traveling exhibits, 240
    UN voting, 141, 343n59
HIV/AIDS, 147–48
Hobbes, Thomas, 154
Hollywood, 253
Hong Kong, 67, 184, 192, 200,
    222, 234, 243, 292
    acid rain in, 149
    art auctions in, 249–50
    with China's ODI, 181t
    crime and, 145–46
    Disneyland, 260
    Google in, 298
    as tax haven, 180
    tourism, 255–60
    trade with, 158t, 159f
hotels, luxury, 255–56
household products, 158
House of the Flying Daggers
    (film), 253
HP. See Hewlett Packard
HR. See human resources
Huang Jisu, 28
Huang Nubo, 200
Huang Renwei, 215–16
Huawei, 182, 183, 186, 187,
    193–95, 200, 354n144,
    355n146
Hu Jintao, 2, 18, 35, 36, 51,
    63, 219, 291, 326n75,
    328n20, 329n22, 358n6
    with body language and
        political rituals, 57
    in Brazil, 112
    on climate change, 151
    on global cultural presence,
        207, 208
    harmonious world and, 25,
        219–20
    on military, 279
    on oil dependency, 163
    on soft and cultural power,
        210

soft power and, 26, 210
humanitarian aid, emergency,
    203
humanitarianism, Globalists
    with soft power and,
    41, 43
human resources (HR)
    as Achilles' heel, 186
    development cooperation,
        203
human rights, 39, 46, 76, 124,
    204
    China's stance on, 9, 11
    Myanmar's, 343n48
human smuggling, 144
Hunan Non-Ferrous Metals
    Holding Group, 172
Huntsman, Jon, 3
Hurun Report, 255

IBM, 180, 199
ICBMs. See intercontinental
    range ballistic missiles
ICJ. See International Court
    of Justice
ID. See International
    Department
identities, global, 13–14
    Asia First and, 36–38
    with biding-time, hiding-
        brightness and do-more-
        things debate, 18–20, 219
    with global governance,
        multilateralism and
        responsible power
        theory, 23–25
    globalists and, 41–43
    Global South School and,
        38–39, 43
    harmonious world theory
        and, 25, 219–20, 324n47
    hegemony debate and, 26
    with issues of contention,
        18–26
    Major Powers School and,
        34–36, 43
    Nativists and, 27–31
    with open discourse
        in constrained
        environment, 15–18
    peaceful-rise debate and, 21
    perspectives in conflict
        with, 43–44

Realists and, 31–34
Selective Multilateralists
    and, 39–41
soft power debate and,
    25–26, 210–16
spectrum of Chinese, 27f
with spectrum of discourse,
    26–43
with structure of
    international order
    debate, 21–23
IFIs. See international financial
    institutions
Ikenberry, G. John, 75, 125,
    313, 331n60
image, international. See also
    cultural footprint,
    global
    as ancient, modern and
        peaceful China, 211–12
    with intentionally
        transmitted messages,
        217–20
    as marketed via media, 211
    with soft power, culture
        and public diplomacy,
        210–16
    soft power and, 5, 208
IMEMO. See Institute of World
    Economics and Politics
IMF. See International
    Monetary Fund
immigrants
    Latin America and
        Chinese, 115
    Russia and Chinese, 85
impact, global
    China's, 4–10
    public perception of
        China's, 7–8, 10–12
imperialism, Nativists on
    globalization as new, 30
imports
    gold, 171
    minerals and energy
        supplies, 117
    oil, 73, 107, 146, 156,
        162–63, 164f, 289,
        290–91
    from other countries,
        349n59
    wine, 117, 257
India, 21, 37, 47, 51, 77, 377n61

BRICS, 22, 23, 39, 114
  China as viewed by, 12, 103
  Dalai Lama in exile in, 103
  imports from, 349n59
  relations deteriorating with,
    95, 100
  trade with, 158t, 159f
  with UN voting history,
    141, 343n59
Indiana University Research
  Center for Chinese
  Politics and Business,
  341n18
Indonesia, 11, 77, 95, 97
  arms deals with, 303
  auto factories in, 197
  with currency swap lines,
    161
  with harmonious world, 220
  natural gas in, 168
  oil in, 167
  with PLAN, 289
  with South China Sea
    claims, 102
  strategic dialogues with, 300
  trade with, 118
industrial espionage, 78, 89
industry, ministry of
  information technology
  and, 221–22
Ineos, 182
Information Department,
  MFA, 221–24, 330n38
  Office of Public
  Diplomacy, 225–26
information technology,
  ministry of industry
  and, 221–22
information warfare (IW), 297
INSEAD, 189
Institute of European Studies,
  CASS, 36
Institute of Foreign Literature,
  CASS, 368n168
Institute of Political Science,
  CASS, 30
Institute of Strategic Studies,
  69, 327n89
Institute of the Far East, 84,
  333n83
Institute of World Economics
  and Politics (IMEMO),
  84–85, 333n76, 333n84

Instituto Cervantes, 245
integrity, territorial, 362n52
Intel, 161
intellectual property rights
  (IPR), 76, 78, 244
intelligence organs, 62, 68–69
intercontinental range ballistic
  missiles (ICBMs),
  294–95, 377n50
intermediate range ballistic
  missiles (IRBMs), 294,
  377n50
international affairs, 330n36
International Convention on
  Biological Diversity, 152
International Court of Justice
  (ICJ), 123
International Department
  (ID), xiii, 64, 66–68, 87,
  94, 115, 129, 237, 330n43
international financial
  institutions (IFIs), 50
International Herald Leader,
  24, 190, 324n40
International Institute of
  Strategic Studies, 375n25
International Monetary Fund
  (IMF), 96, 124, 126–28,
  134, 204
international order, structure
  of, 21–23
International Police. See
  INTERPOL
International Postal Union, 122
international relations (IR)
  with eclectic thinking of
    scholars, 27
  open discourse in, 15–18
  with structure of
    international order,
    21–23
  studies, 330n44
  with two stages of
    socialization, 131
international responsibility,
  326n87
International Telegraph
  Union, 122
INTERPOL (International
  Police), 144–47
inventions, 366n137
investment. See also overseas
  direct investment

CIC, 183–84
FDI, 50, 55, 73, 100, 102,
  156, 174, 177
  ODI, 10, 174, 178f, 181t
  treaties, 159
  in U.S., 182–83
IPR. See intellectual property
  rights
IR. See international relations
Iran, 21, 40, 46, 76, 105, 137, 140,
  163, 164f, 303, 378n67
  China's diplomatic
    passivity in, 8
  oil in, 138
  sanctions against, 107, 138
  Sextet on, 41
  trade with, 106–7
  with UN voting history, 141
Iraq, 40, 46, 75, 83, 163, 164f,
  378n67
IRBMs. See intermediate range
  ballistic missiles
iron ores, 110, 117, 171
Is China Buying the World?
  (Nolan), 178
Israel, 105, 107
issues, contentious
  biding-time, hiding-
    brightness and do-more
    things debate, 18–20, 219
  global governance,
    multilateralism and
    responsible-power
    theory, 23–25
  harmonious world theory,
    25, 219–20
  hegemony debate, 26
  peaceful-rise debate, 21
  soft-power debate, 25–26,
    210–16
  structure of international
    order debate, 21–23
Italy, 12, 123, 140, 257, 261
Ivy League, China's, 243
IW. See information warfare

Jacques, Martin, 311
Jakobson, Linda, 71, 322n8
Japan, 21, 37, 51, 54, 77, 99, 123
  China as viewed by, 11, 12
  China's diplomacy with,
    101–2
  China's opinion of, 56

Japan (*Cont.*)
  Chinese tourists in, 258
  education exchange with,
    102, 242
  espionage by, 232
  overseas aid of, 10
  shipbuilding industry, 290
  trade with, 102, 158*t*, 159*f*
  with UN operating budget
    contributions, 140
  yakuza in, 144
Al Jazeera, 230
Jenner, William F., 53
jets, fighter, 287–88
jewelry, 258
Jiang, Julie, 349n50
Jiang Jiemin, 169
Jiang Rong, 247
Jiang Weiqiang, 222
Jiangxi Metals and Minerals
    International Trade
    Corporation, 172
Jiang Zemin, 21, 35, 51, 80, 97,
    210, 329n22, 344n65
  in Africa, 109–10
  biding time, hiding
    brightness and, 19
  "going out" and "going
    global" policy and,
    174–75, 350n71
Jin Canrong, 13, 19, 41
Jinchuan Group, 172
Jing Li, 325n52
Jin Jun, 363n75
Jin Liqun, 183, 353n118
jituan (conglomerates), 165.
    See also national oil
    companies
Johns Hopkins University, 67
Johnston, Alastair Iain, 72, 135,
    321n7, 322n9, 335n121
journalists, foreign, 224–26,
    364n80
Joyson Investment Holdings,
    182
Ju Dou (film), 253
June 4, 1989
  massacre of, 3, 18, 50, 79,
    88, 95–96
  reaction in Asia, 96

Kang, David, 53
Kazakhstan, 80, 164*f*

Kennedy Space Center, 377n61
Kent, Ann, 131, 135
Kenya, 11, 168, 231, 303
Keohane, Robert, 346n100
Khmer Rouge, 49
Khomeini (Ayatollah), 106
kidnappings, 200–201, 202
Kiekert, 182
Kissinger, Henry, 1
Knox, Dean, 71, 322n8
Koguryo, 101. *See also* North
    Korea; South Korea
Korea. *See* North Korea; South
    Korea
Kosovo War, 30, 124
kouhao (slogans), 217–19
Koxinga (warrior), 108
Krasner, Stephen, 346n100
Kravchuk, Leonid, 80
Kung-fu Panda (film), 254
Kurile Islands, 289
Kuwait, 107, 163, 164*f*
Kyoto Protocol, 152

labor
  abuses, 201
  exports, 179
  foreign, 187
laboratories, U.S., 377n61
LACMs. *See* land attack cruise
    missiles
Lai Changxing, 146–47
Lampton, David M., 71
land. *See* Ministry of Land and
    Resources
land attack cruise missiles
    (LACMs), 295
Laos, 303
Lao Zi, 239
Latin America. *See also specific
    countries in Latin
    America*
  arms sales to, 116
  China as viewed by, 113–14,
    119–20
  China's diplomacy with,
    51–52, 55, 111–20
  Chinese immigrants in, 115
  Chinese military in, 116
  CIC and, 184
  ECLAC, 118
  leftists in, 114
  oil in, 117

  without strategies for
    China, 111–13
  tourism in, 115
  trade with, 112, 116–18
  trade with U.S., 117
Latin American and Caribbean
    Affairs Department,
    MFA, 339n158
Latin American Studies, 113
laws, environmental
    protection, 150
LDK Solar, 182
leaders, senior, 62, 63–65
League of Nations, 123
least-developed countries, 38
Lee Hsien Loong, 307
Lee Kuan Yew, 1, 96, 207, 314
Lee Teng-hui, 277
left. *See also* Nativists
  attacks against, 30
  in Latin America, 114
  new, 27
Lenin, Vladimir, 30, 72
Lenovo, 187, 198–99
Leonard, Mark, 334n101
Le Yucheng, 45, 327n3
Liang Guanglie, 269, 277, 300
Liberals, 39, 125, 313
Liberia, 163
Libya, 40, 46, 64, 76, 137–38,
    140, 163
  Chinese civilian personnel
    evacuated from, 285
  oil in, 164*f*
Li Congjun, 229
Lieberthal, Kenneth, 74,
    332n62
Lifan Group, 355n154
Li Meng, 258
Lin, Justin Yifu, 128
Li Na, 262
Lin Biao, 47
Li-Ning, 187
Li Songsong, 250
literature, 10, 247–48. *See also*
    books
Liu Mingfu, 265
Liu Shaoqi, 21
Liu Xiang, 262
Liu Xiaobo, 89, 266
Liu Yan, 28
Liu Yunshan, 208–9, 263,
    363n63

Livermore laboratory, 377n61
Lo, Bobo, 86
loans, 134, 203, 357n183
localities, corporations and,
    62, 69–70
Locke, John, 155
London Business School, 189
London School of Economics,
    67
*Long Live the Victory of People's
    War!* (Lin Biao), 47
Lou Jiwei, 156
Lowy Institute, 140
Lukin, Vladimir "Sasha," 84,
    333n82
Luxembourg, 180, 181t, 240
luxury goods
    China's influence in global
        sales of, 8
    tourism and sale of, 256–59
lying low (*taoguang yanghui*)
    strategies, 75, 322n17
Lynch, Daniel, 321n7

Macartney, George (Lord),
    308, 364n78
Macedonia, 343n48
Madagascar, 163
Major Powers School, 43
    EU and, 34, 36
    Europeanists in, 36
    Marxists and scholars in, 35
    Russia and, 34–36
    U.S. and, 34–36
Malacca Straits, 291
Malaysia, 96, 158t, 159f, 303
Malik, Mohan, 336n137
Mancall, Mark, 53, 327n10
manganese ores, 171
manners, guidelines for good,
    260
Mao Zedong, 1, 47, 48, 106,
    308
    administration, 52, 54–55
    death of, 134, 252
    ideology in Africa, 109
    with media instructions,
        229
    Stalin and, 79
    theory of three worlds, 133
marine corps. *See* People's
    Liberation Navy
maritime security, 279

maritime trade, 289
Market Economy Status
    (MES), 90, 117–18, 160
Mars, 296
Marxism Academy, CASS, 29
Marxists, 27, 31, 35. *See also*
    Nativists
massacres
    June 4, 1989, 3, 18, 50, 79,
        88, 95–96
    Nanjing, 254
materials, goods and, 203
Maytag, 198
Ma Zhaoxu, 223–24
Ma Zhengang, 129
McGregor, Richard, 353n132
McKinsey & Company, 186
McVadon, Eric A., 379n71
Medeiros, Evan, 135, 321n7
media. *See also specific media
    outlets*
    ad campaigns criticized
        by, 187
    "big fish swallowing the
        small" with, 227–28, 236
    CCP newspapers, 188
    CCTV, 17–18, 227, 229,
        230–33, 365n107
    censorship, 221
    China Daily, 146, 187, 227,
        233–35, 263, 346n1
    CRI, 227–28, 233, 265,
        365n116, 365n119,
        373n263
    foreign news journalists,
        224–26, 364n80
    freedom of press, 10
    Global Times, 215, 228,
        233–35, 248, 366n121
    International Herald Leader,
        24, 190, 324n40
    Mao's instructions for, 229
    as messengers of global
        culture, 227–28
    monitoring of, 224–25
    People's Daily, 136, 215, 221,
        234, 277, 366n121
    State Press and Publishing
        Administration with,
        222
    as tool for marketing
        international image, 211
    watchdog, 221

Xinhua News Agency,
    23–24, 66, 146, 227,
    228–30
Medvedev, Dmitry, 81
Mei Zhaorong, 248
Melikian, Souren, 249–50
Mencian values, 43
Men Honghua, 43, 212, 215
Men's Health, 236
MERCOSUR, 115
mergers, reverse, 190
Merkel, Angela, 89, 90, 92–93,
    248
MES. *See* Market Economy
    Status
messages, intentionally
    transmitted, 217–20
messengers, of global culture,
    220
    books and periodicals, 209,
        235–37
    CCTV, 17–18, 227, 229,
        230–33, 365n107
    CRI, 227–28, 233, 265,
        365n116, 365n119, 373n263
    exchange organizations,
        237–38
    media, 227–28
    MFA Information
        Department, 221–27,
        330n38
    newspapers, 209, 233–35
    Office of Public
        Diplomacy, 210–11,
        223–27
    oversight, 238
    SCIO, 221–23
Mexico, 38, 113, 114, 303
    China as viewed by, 11, 12
    trade with, 117–18
    with UN voting history,
        343n59
MFA. *See* Ministry of Foreign
    Affairs
MG Rover, 181, 196
MI$_6$, 377n61
midcareer training, 189
Middle East. *See also specific
    countries in Middle East*
    Arab Spring in, 224
    China's diplomacy with,
        52, 55, 105–8
Mikheev, Vassily, 84–85

military. *See also* People's
    Liberation Army
AD/SD, 280
air force, 285, 286–88, 301
annual defense budget,
    274f, 379n77
with antisubmarine
    warfare, 292–93
arms embargo by EU, 90
ASW, 292–93
budgets, 319n5, 328n15,
    374n9
capabilities, 282–84
catalysts for modernization
    of, 275–78
cooperation pact with
    Russia, 80–83
cyber forces, 296–98
cyber militias, 298
diplomacy, 299–301
EU and absence of, 89
with evolving missions,
    278–82
export of goods, 303
General Armaments
    Department, 283
geography and, 277
global prospects, 269–71
ground forces, 284–86
Latin American and
    presence of Chinese, 116
Ministry of Defense, xiii,
    66, 300, 303
missile forces, 294–95
modernization, 11, 273–98
navy, 270–71, 285, 288–94,
    376n47
NCOs, 285
North Korean, 101
parades, 1–3, 277–78
paradox of threat with,
    272–73
with partial-power
    capabilities, 270
peacekeeping operations,
    40, 46, 139, 271, 298–99
as purely defensive and
    without threat, 220
Red Guards, 48, 252
RRUs, 284–85
SOFs, 276
space-based capabilities,
    295–96

with strategic dialogues, 300
strength and pro-, 32–33
transparency, 76
U.S. arms sales to Taiwan, 77
weapon exports, 303–4
White Paper on defense,
    281–82
ZBB system, 275, 374n9
militias
    cyber, 298
    People's Armed, 328n15
Millennium Development
    Goals, UN, 38
Miller, Alice Lyman, 328n20
millionaires, 157, 249, 255
minerals. *See also specific*
    minerals
    as imports, 117
    ores, 110, 117, 171
    with rare earth elements,
        173–74
mining operations, global,
    171–74, 201, 346n3
ministries, 62, 66–68
Ministry of Agriculture, 151
Ministry of Chemical
    Industry, 165
Ministry of Commerce
    (MOFCOM), 66, 69,
    118, 172, 176–78, 181,
    187, 204–5, 223, 347n6,
    350n78
Ministry of Culture, 66, 68, 253
    China Arts and
        Entertainment
        Group, 240
Ministry of Defense, xiii, 66,
    300, 303
Ministry of Education, 241–42
Ministry of Environmental
    Protection, 151
Ministry of Finance, 66, 246,
    275
Ministry of Foreign Affairs
    (MFA), 62, 66, 70, 71
    CIIS, 238
    CPIFA, xiii, 94, 237, 255
    with demining specialists,
        378n67
    Department of Policy
        Planning, 129
    with documents
        declassified, 328n18

education of personnel
    from, 67
Information Department,
    221–27, 330n38
Latin American and
    Caribbean Affairs
    Department, 339n158
Office of Public Diplomacy,
    210–11, 223–27
Ministry of Land and
    Resources, 151
Ministry of Petroleum
    Industry, 165
Ministry of Public Security, 145
Ministry of Science and
    Technology, 66, 151, 243
Ministry of State Security
    (MSS), 66, 145, 225, 298
    budget for, 328n15
    CICIR, 35–36, 68–69, 83,
        202, 210, 238
Ministry of Water Resources,
    151
missiles
    ballistic, 294–95, 377n50
    LACMs, 295
    Taiwan crisis, 276, 279–80
Missile Technology Control
    Regime (MTCR), 142,
    303
modern China, as international
    image, 211–12
MOFCOM. *See* Ministry of
    Commerce
Mongolia, 100
Monroe Doctrine, 119
morality, 43, 212
Morgan Stanley, 184
Morton, Katherine, 132, 345n79
Moscow State Institute of
    International Affairs, 85,
    333n86
MSS. *See* Ministry of State
    Security
MTCR. *See* Missile
    Technology Control
    Regime
multicurrency, 126–28
multilateralism
    global governance,
        responsible power
        theory and, 23–25
    selective, 39–41

multilateral regionalism, 37
multipolarity, 22–23, 34, 107,
    135. *See also* polarities
Murphy, Dawn, 337n146,
    337n147, 339n153
mutual nonaggression, 362n52
mutual noninterference,
    362n52
Myanmar, 76, 100, 103, 137,
    140, 303, 343n48
myths
    about China, 265
    of U.S. decline, 22–23, 99

Namibia, 303
Nanjing Automobile
    Corporation, 182, 196
Nanjing massacre, 254
Nankai University, 22, 33, 67
narcotics, 22, 144–47
NASDAQ, 190
National Autonomous
    University, 113
National Basketball Association
    (NBA), 198, 261
National Center for
    Supercomputing, 161
National Crime Bureau of
    China (NCB), 145
National Day Parade, 1–3,
    277–78
National Defense University
    (NDU), 68, 265, 301
National Development and
    Reform Commission
    (NDRC), 66, 150–51,
    176, 350n78
National Football League
    (NFL), 262
National Foreign Investment
    Work Conference, 175
National Image (Zhou
    Mingwei), 211–12
National Intelligence Council,
    340n7
nationalism
    affirmative, 57
    assertive, 58
    defensive, 56, 58
    populist, 58
    retributive, 56, 58
nationalists, 27, 31, 79. *See also*
    Nativists; Realists

selective multi-, 40–41
National Museum, 251–52
national oil companies
    (NOCs), 162, 164–71,
    186, 348n28
National People's Congress,
    148, 175, 208, 225, 243,
    263, 328n15
national security, 61, 78, 95
National Security Leading
    Small Group, 63–64,
    330n28
Nativists, 43
    anti-Western sentiments
    and xenophobia of,
    27–31
    on globalization, 30
    international cooperation
    rejected by, 42
    organizations, 29
    as populists, nationalists
    and Marxists, 27
NATO. *See* North Atlantic
    Treaty Organization
natural gas, 107, 164–65,
    167–68
naval missions, out-of-area,
    376n47
Naval War College, 377n61
navy. *See* People's Liberation
    Navy
Nazarbayev, Nursultin, 80
Nazis, 123
NBA. *See* National Basketball
    Association
NCB. *See* National Crime
    Bureau of China
NCOs. *See* noncommissioned
    officers
NDRC. *See* National
    Development and
    Reform Commission
NDU. *See* National Defense
    University
Needham, Joseph, 366n137
Nepal, 100, 303–4
Netherlands, 178, 240
News Corp, 227, 230–31
New Security Concept (NSC),
    97–98, 218
newspapers. *See also specific
    newspapers*
    CCP, 188

China Daily, 146, 187, 227,
    233–35, 263, 346n1
Global Times, 215, 228,
    233–35, 248, 366n121
    as messengers of global
    culture, 209, 233–35
    numbers of, 228
People's Daily, 136, 215, 221,
    234, 277, 366n121
New Star Press, 236
Newsweek, 236
New World Press, 236
New York Stock Exchange,
    190
New York University, 186
New Zealand, xiv, 103, 289,
    377n61
New Zealand Institute of
    International Affairs,
    321n1, 325n66
Nexen, 168
Nextel Sprint, 183
NFL. *See* National Football
    League
NFU. *See* No First Use pledge
NGOs. *See* nongovernmental
    organizations
Nicaragua, 114
nickel, 117, 171
Nie Zhenning, 236
Niger, 303
Nigeria, 12, 22, 163, 303
Ningbo Contemporary Art
    Museum, 253
Ningbo Historical Museum,
    253
Nixon, Richard, 48, 313–15
Nobel Prize, 89, 247, 267
NOCs. *See* national oil
    companies
No First Use (NFU) pledge,
    142
Nolan, Peter, 178
nonaggression, mutual, 362n52
noncommissioned officers
    (NCOs), 285
nongovernmental
    organizations (NGOs),
    132, 151
noninterference, mutual,
    362n52
nonproliferation, arms control
    and, 142–44, 303

Non-Proliferation Treaty
    (NPT), 303
nontraditional security, 41
Noranda, 200
North Atlantic Treaty
    Organization (NATO),
    98, 137–38, 200, 273,
    276, 286
North Korea, 7, 40, 76, 83,
    137, 140
    China's diplomatic
        passivity with, 8,
        100–101
    military, 101
    as nuclear threat, 46, 101
    sanctions against, 138
    Six Party Talks on, 41, 45,
        46, 101, 142
no (political) strings attached
    policy, 38, 107, 110, 202,
    204, 246, 247
nouveau riche, 256–58
NPT. *See* Non-Proliferation
    Treaty
NSC. *See* New Security
    Concept
NSG. *See* Nuclear Suppliers
    Group
nuclear power, 151, 293
Nuclear Suppliers Group
    (NSG), 142
nuclear threat
    China as, 48, 143
    with nonproliferation and
        arms control, 142–44,
        303
    North Korea as, 46, 101
    Pakistan as, 143
Nude, Green Leaves, and Bust,
    249
NVIDIA, 161
Nye, Joseph, 8, 209, 210, 216,
    239, 266–67, 311

Oak Ridge laboratory, 377n61
OAS. *See* Organization of
    American States
Obama, Barack, 1, 22, 242,
    319n4
obligations. *See* reciprocal
    obligations
ODA. *See* overseas
    development assistance

ODI. *See* overseas direct
    investment
O'Dowd, Ed, 374n10
OECD. *See* Organization of
    Economic Cooperation
    and Development
offensive Realists, 32
Office of Border Affairs, 308
Office of International
    Language Council (Han
    Ban), 245–47, 368n169,
    368n174
Office of Public Diplomacy,
    MFA, 210–11, 223–27
Office of the National
    Counterintelligence
    Executive, U.S., 297
oil. *See also* Ministry of
    Petroleum Industry
    in Africa, 110, 163
    in Brazil, 117, 164f
    in Canada, 168
    consumption, 162–63,
        290–91
    as import, 73, 107, 146, 156,
        162–63, 164f, 289, 290–91
    in Indonesia, 167
    in Iran, 138
    kidnappings related to,
        200–201
    in Latin America, 117
    NOCs, 162, 164–71, 186,
        348n28
    pipeline, 81–82, 163–64
Old Summer Palace. *See*
    Yuanmingyuan
Olympics, Beijing, 3–4, 57,
    92–93, 145, 239, 241, 261
Oman, 107, 163, 164f
omnidirectional diplomacy, 51
Opel, 196
openness (*glasnost*), 79
Open Source Center, 358n6
opium, 22
Opti Canada, 168
ores, 110, 117, 171
Organization of American
    States (OAS), 115, 124
Organization of Economic
    Cooperation and
    Development (OECD),
    124, 136, 180, 202–4, 314,
    357n183

organizations, exchange. *See*
    exchange organizations
Orkla, 182
outlets, shopping, 258
*Outline of the National Plan for
    Cultural Development
    During the 11th Five
    Year Plan*, 209
overseas aid, 132
    in comparison to other
        countries, 10, 204
    with education, 204
    eight types of, 203
    with energy, 202–5
    transparency with, 358n192
    White Paper on, 203–4
overseas development
    assistance (ODA), 132,
    157, 357n183
overseas direct investment
    (ODI)
    China's, 10, 156–57
    energy, 174
    energy and top ten
        destinations in 2010, 181t
    energy flows for 1982–2010,
        178f
    financial outflows, 351n85
    "going out" and "going
        global" policy, 174–83,
        350n71
    sovereign wealth fund,
        183–84
    U.S., 10

Pakistan, 7, 103–4, 303
    China as viewed by, 11
    as nuclear threat, 143
Palace Museum. *See* Gugong
Palestine, 108
pandas, 239
Pang Da Auto, 355n154
Pan Wei, 35
Pan Zhongying, 215–16
PAP. *See* People's Armed
    Police
parades, National Day, 1–3,
    277–78
paradox, military, 272–73
Paraguay, 114
partnerships, strategic
    with Brazil, 114
    with EU, 87–89, 90, 94

passive diplomacy, 8–9, 83,
    100–101
patents
    applications, 73
    global, 161
path, China, 214
PCA. See China-EU
    Partnership and
    Cooperation Agreement
peace
    harmony and, 43, 212
    SCIO on, 220, 378n65
peace, development and, 34,
    37, 219
    Deng Xiaoping and, 30,
    98–99, 218
    White Paper on, 121, 130,
    218
peaceful China, as
    international image,
    211–12
peaceful evolution, CCP
    and, 60
peaceful rise, 362n57
    Central Party School and,
    218–19
    as dangerous, 33, 316–17
    debate, 21, 219
peacekeeping missions, SCIO,
    378n65
peacekeeping operations, UN,
    40, 46, 139, 271, 298–99
Pei, I. M., 253
Peking University, 13, 16, 20,
    35–36, 49, 67, 69, 186,
    307, 317
    ranking for, 243
PEN, 248
Pentagon, U.S., 281
People's Armed Militia, 328n15
People's Armed Police (PAP),
    145, 299, 328n15
People's Bank of China, 66
People's Daily, 136, 215, 221,
    234, 277, 366n121
People's Liberation Army
    (PLA), 5, 65–66, 237,
    375n21, 375n22
    Academy of Military
    Sciences, 68–69
    air force, 285, 286–88, 301
    Air Force Command
    College, 301

capabilities, 282–84
cyber militias, 298
future missions for, 280–82
Group Armies (Gas), 284
geography influencing, 277
ground forces, 284–86
Gulf War influencing, 276
with military exchanges,
    exercises and assistance,
    299–301
navy, 270–71, 285, 288–94,
    376n47
NDU, 68, 265, 301
operative doctrine of, 279
People's Armed Militia,
    328n15
Realists and, 43
Taiwan and, 279–80
University of Foreign
    Languages, 301
in Vietnam, 275–76, 279
People's Liberation Navy
    (PLAN), 270–71, 288–94
Marine Corps, 285
out-of-area missions,
    376n47
perestroika (restructuring), 79
periodicals
    as messengers of global
    culture, 209, 235–37
    numbers of, 228
    State Press and Publishing
    Administration and, 222
Permanent Court on
    Arbitration, 123
Persian Gulf, 76, 106, 291
Peru, 111, 114, 117, 120, 303
    China as viewed by, 12
    trade with, 118
Petrobras, 163
PetroChina, 169, 182
petroleum. See Ministry of
    Petroleum Industry
Pew Research Center Global
    Attitudes Project,
    320n12
    global perception of China,
    11–12
    pubic opinion on China as
    global power, 7
Ph.D.s, numbers of, 73, 243
Philippines, 12, 77, 377n61
Picasso, Pablo, 249

pipeline, oil, 81–82, 163–64
piracy, 40, 41, 46
    maritime, 144
    of Russian defense
    technologies, 82
PLA. See People's Liberation
    Army
PLA Air Force (PLAAF), 285,
    286–88, 301
PLAN. See People's Liberation
    Navy
pluralization, 71
Poland, 89
polarities, 21
    multi-, 22–23, 34, 107, 135
    uni-, 22, 31
police. See INTERPOL;
    People's Armed Police
policies
    "containment," 77, 91–92,
    97, 129, 315–16
    diplomacy and decision-
    making in foreign,
    61–72
    "going out" and "going
    global," 174–83, 350n71
    no (political) strings
    attached, 38, 107, 110,
    202, 204, 246, 247
    process changers, 71
    recommendations, 20
Policy Research Office of the
    Central Committee, 63,
    329n24
Politburo, CCP, 18, 64, 360n18
    Standing Committee, 63,
    208
political culture, 154–55
    with biaotai, 217–18
    with kouhao, 217–19
political dissent, 58
political rituals, 57
politics
    Cold War mentality and
    power, 9
    diplomacy in service of,
    56–59
    rhetoric, 223
    with slogans parroted back,
    217–18
    soft power and, 214
pollution, air, 149
Polo, Marco, 257

Pontifica Universidad Católica de Chile, 113
population, of China, 132
populists, 27. See also Nativists nationalism, 58
Portugal, 12, 17, 300
Porzecanski, Roberto, 338n152
power. See also superpower, global
    cautious diplomatic, 120
    China as global, 309–11
    China as lonely, 7, 310
    China as partial, x, 7–8, 10, 45, 157, 270, 309–11
    China's view as returning world, 1–4
    Cold War mentality and politics of, 9
    comprehensive, 5–6
    cultural, 210
    definition, 8
    global governance and responsible major, 128–32
    hard, 4, 32, 209
    military parade and show of hard, 1–3
    nuclear, 151, 293
    politics, 9
    "Rising Powers," 17–18
    Russia as declining, 35, 36
    school of Major, 34–36
    soft, 4–5, 20, 25–26, 32, 41, 208–16, 212–13, 266–68, 360n26
    status quo or revisionist, 72, 121, 134
    theory of responsible, 23–25, 40
    tourism and spending, 255–57
    transition theory, 312
    U.S. and myth of declining, 22–23, 99
    wind, 152
preemptive diplomacy, 58
Preh, 182
PricewaterhouseCoopers, 179–80
Princeton University, 313
Pritzker Architecture Prize, 253
propaganda, 228. See also cultural footprint, global; cultural

presence, global; image, international; soft power; State Council Information Office
    decentralized budgets and, 238
    EPLSG, 63, 221, 330n33, 363n63
    external, 65, 216–17, 220–22, 226, 267
Propaganda Department, CCP, 2, 21, 208, 217, 220–21, 228
proper conduct, ritual of, 43
prospects, for global economic presence, 205–6
protests
    Arab Spring, 225
    ethnic riots and, 224
    pro-Tibet, 92–93
    student, 3, 18, 49–50, 79, 88, 95–96
public, health, 41, 147–48
public diplomacy, 226–27. See also diplomacy; soft power
Public Diplomacy (CPPCC), 210
public perception, of China as global power, 7–8, 10–12
Public Security forces, 328n15
publishers, of books, 235–37
Putin, Vladimir, 81
Putzmeister, 182
Pye, Lucian, 45, 217, 346n99, 362n51

el-Qaddafi, Muammar, 137–38, 140, 304–5
al-Qaeda, 146
Qatar, 106, 167–68
Qian Qichen, 97
Qian Xiaoqian, 264, 363n64
Qiao Guanhua, 133
Qi Jianguo, 292
Qing dynasty, 31, 54, 108, 308
Qin Yaqing, 37
Qiushi (Seeking Truth), 358n6
Qiu Yuanping, 65, 360n20
Qu Yingpu, 235

R₂P principle. See Responsibility to Protect principle

radar, 291
radio, State Press and Publishing Administration with, 222
Radio Beijing, 233. See also China Radio International
rain, acid, 149

Raise the Red Lantern (film), 253
Ramo, Joshua Cooper, 214
Rand Corporation, 135
rapid reaction units (RRUs), 284–85
rare earth elements, 173–74
RCA, 192
R&D. See research and development
real estate
    buying binge, 259–60
    China's influence in global purchases of, 8
Realists, 16, 40, 42, 312
    anti-Western sentiments of, 33–34
    hard- and soft-power, 32
    as nationalists and China Firsters, 31
    offensive and defensive, 32
    PLA and, 43
    as pro-military strength, 32–33
    retaliatory mentality of, 33
    xenophobia of, 31
reciprocal obligations (guanxi), 154, 242
Red Guards, 48, 252
Red Sorghum (film), 253
religion, 58, 215, 239, 308
renminbi (RMB), 126–27, 160
Renmin Ribao, 366n121
Renmin University, 13, 15, 19, 24, 41, 67, 69, 83, 128, 215
Ren Xiao, 126
Ren Zhengfei, 193–94, 355n145
reporters, foreign, 224–26, 364n80
Report to Congress on Military and Security Developments Involving the People's Republic of China (U.S. Pentagon), 281

research
    education and, 241–45
    on global governance,
        341n23
    institutes, 238
research and development
    (R&D), 195
Research Triangle Park, 199
resources. *See* Ministry of Land
    and Resources; Ministry
    of Water Resources
responsibility, international,
    326n87
Responsibility to Protect (R$_2$P)
    principle, 124, 138–39
responsible-power theory,
    23–25, 40
restructuring (*perestroika*), 79
retributive nationalism, 56, 58
Reuters, 264
revisionist power, 72, 121, 134
rhetoric, political, 223
right, 39. *See also* Selective
    Multilateralists
rights
    human, 9, 11, 39, 46, 76,
        124, 204, 343n48
    IPR, 76, 78, 244
Rio Tinto, 173
rise
    horizontal and vertical, 6
    peaceful, 21, 33, 218–19,
        316–17
    as problematic term, 219
    rethinking China's, 311–17
    revival and, 21
    "Rising Powers," 17–18
    soft-power diplomacy
        obscuring drive to, 4
    in wealth and disposable
        income, 255
"Rising Powers," 17–18
risks, energy, 199–202
ritual of proper conduct, 43,
    212
rituals, body language and
    political, 57
RMB (*renminbi*), 126–27, 160
Robinson, Jancis, 257
Rodium Group, 183
Rogov, Sergey, 86, 333n89
Rosenau, James N., 122,
    324n38

Rossabi, Morris, 53
Rousseff, Dilma, 114
Royal Dutch Shell, 165, 170
Rozman, Gilbert, 321n7
RRUs. *See* rapid reaction units
ruan shili. See soft power
Russia, 7, 54, 332n75
    arms sales to China, 283
    BRICS, 22, 23, 39, 114
    China as viewed by, 11,
        84–86
    China's diplomacy with,
        49, 78–86, 347n23
    China's opinion of, 35–36
    Chinese immigrants in, 85
    Chinese tourists in, 256
    debates on China, 333n90
    as declining power, 35, 36
    education exchange with,
        242
    Major Powers School and,
        34–36
    military cooperation pact
        with China, 80–83
    military spending, 274f
    oil, 164f
    trade with, 81–82
    with UN voting history,
        141, 343n59
Rwanda, 124, 303

Saab, 196
SAED. *See* Strategic and
    Economic Dialogue
SAFE Capital, 184
SAFRT. *See* State
    Administration of Film,
    Radio and Television
Saint Laurent, Yves, 250
Saks Fifth Avenue, 256
Salvador University, 113
Samsung, 198
sanctions
    EU and dropped, 88
    against Iran, 107, 138
    for June 4 massacre, 96
    on Libya, 138
    against North Korea, 138
    Singapore with, 314
    against Zimbabwe, 343n48
Sandia laboratory, 377n61
Santiso, Javier, 338n152
Sany, 182

São Tomé, 163
Sarkozy, Nicolas, 89, 93
SARS. *See* Severe Acute
    Respiratory Syndrome
satellites, 296
Saudi Arabia, 107, 163, 164f,
    303
saving face, 54, 56–57
Scandinavia, 10
Schaeffer, Michael, 3
Schneider Electronics AG, 192
scholars
    based abroad, 244–45
    as eclectic thinkers, 27
    in Major Powers School, 35
scholarships, 242
schools
    Central Party, xiii, 21, 43,
        69, 188, 210, 212, 215,
        218–19, 237
    Global South, 38–39, 43
    Major Powers, 34–36, 43
Schroeder, Gerhard, 92
Schwing, 182
science, 302–3. *See also*
    Ministry of Science and
    Technology
SCIO. *See* State Council
    Information Office
SCO. *See* Shanghai
    Cooperation
    Organization
Sebed Arms Control Treaty,
    142
SEC. *See* Securities and
    Exchange Commission,
    U.S.
secessionist forces, 90, 108,
    145, 146
Secretariat of the Central
    Committee, 63
sectoral dialogues, 87, 333n96
secure sea lines of
    communication
    (SLOCs), 103, 291
Securities and Exchange
    Commission (SEC),
    U.S., 190
security
    arms transfers and, 301–5
    border, 53, 60, 84
    budgets, 59, 319n5, 328n15,
        374n9

security (*Cont.*)
    contradictions of China's
        global, 271–73
    CSCAP, 97, 335n122
    cultural, 208
    cyber, 279
    dilemma, 102–3, 273
    diplomacy in service of,
        59–61
    economic, 41
    forces, 202
    future role with global, 306
    global, 260–71
    INTERPOL, international
        crime and, 144–47
    maritime, 279
    with military exchanges,
        exercises and assistance,
        299–301
    with military modernization,
        273–98
    MSS, 35–36, 66, 68–69, 83,
        145, 202, 210, 225, 238,
        298, 328n15, 336n136
    national, 61, 78, 95
    nontraditional, 41
    peacekeeping operations
        and, 298–99
    Public Security forces,
        328n15
    space, 279
    threats, 104
    with worldwide arms sales,
        302f
Security Council, UN, 9, 41,
    45, 83, 133, 137
Selected Works (Deng
    Xiaoping), 19
Selective Multilateralists, 39
    factions within, 40
    as selective
        multinationalists, 40–41
    with UN, 40
Self-Strengthening Movement,
    31, 54, 308
Serbia, 124, 276
Severe Acute Respiratory
    Syndrome (SARS),
    147, 148
Sextet, on Iran, 41
sex trade networks, 144
SEZs. *See* Special Economic
    Zones

Shambaugh, David, , 319n2,
    319n6, 321n7, 362n48
    *China's Communist Party:
    Atrophy and Adaptation*,
    x, 79
Shanghai Academy of Social
    Sciences, 215, 238, 323n32
Shanghai Alliance Investment,
    254
Shanghai Auto, 182, 196,
    355n154
Shanghai Cooperation
    Organization (SCO),
    22, 25, 61, 80, 84–85, 104
Shanghai Foreign Studies
    University, 67
Shanghai Institutes of
    International Studies
    (SIIS), xiii, 22, 68,
    70–71, 213, 238
Shanghai International Studies
    University, 69
Shanghai Media Group
    (SMG), 228, 254
Shao Zheng, 364n79
Shen Dingli, 13, 33, 325n66
Shenhua Group, 172
Shen Xue, 261
shipbuilding industry, 289–90
Shirk, Susan, 60
Shi Yinhong, 15, 128
Shi Zhe, 83
shopping, luxury, 255–58
short range ballistic missiles
    (SRBMs), 294, 377n50
Shougang (Capital Steel)
    Group, 172
Sichuan Tengzhong Heavy
    Industrial Group,
    355n154
Sierra Leone, 163, 303
SIIS. *See* Shanghai Institutes of
    International Studies
Singapore, 50, 77, 96, 127,
    163, 166
    China as viewed by, 307
    with China's ODI, 181t
    with sanctions, 314
    tourism, 258, 259
Sinolingua, 236
Sinopec. *See* China
    Petrochemical
    Corporation

Sinosteel, 172
SIPRI. *See* Stockholm
    International Peace
    Research Institute
Six Party Talks, on North
    Korea, 41, 45, 46, 101, 142
Skoda, 182
slaves, 108
SLBMs. *See* submarine-
    launched ballistic
    missiles
SLOCs. *See* secure sea lines of
    communication
slogans (*kouhao*)
    diplomacy, 217
    parroting back, 217–18
    Zheng Bijian's "peaceful
        rise," 219
smile diplomacy, 57
Smithsonian Institution, 248
smuggling, human, 144
socialization, stages of, 131
society, decision-making and,
    62, 70
SOEs. *See* state-owned
    enterprises
SOFs. *See* special operations
    forces
Soft Power (Nye), 210
soft power (*ruan shili*)
    with cultural footprint,
        266–68
    culture and, 212–13
    debate, 25–26, 210–16
    deficit, 212, 215
    definition, 209–10
    diplomacy, 4–5, 20, 25–26,
        210–16
    economic development
        and, 214–15
    Globalists with
        humanitarianism and,
        41, 43
    international image and
        build-up of, 5, 208
    international image with
        culture and public
        diplomacy, 210–16
    policy recommendations,
        20
    politics and, 214
    public diplomacy and rise
        embedded in, 4

Realists, 32
with traditional culture,
360n26
Soft Power in Asia (Chicago
Council on Global
Affairs), 220
solar energy, 151–52
Somalia, 46, 201, 271, 289,
299, 305
sonar, 291
Song Aiguo, 111, 338n151
Song dynasty, 108
Song Qiang, 28
Song Xiaojun, 28–29
Song Xinning, 24, 83
Sony, 198
Sotheby's, 249, 250, 251, 257
South Africa, 38
BRICS, 22, 23, 39, 114
China as viewed by, 12
imports from, 349n59
with UN voting history,
343n59
South China Sea, 52, 60, 102,
288, 289, 292
Southeast Asia, 102. *See also*
specific countries in
Southeast Asia
"Southern Sojourn," 19, 30, 51
South Korea, 38, 51, 77, 377n61
China as viewed by, 12,
100–101
CIs in, 245
diplomacy with, 100–101
education exchange with,
100, 102, 241
espionage by, 232
shipbuilding industry, 290
trade, 100, 158*t*, 159*f*
sovereignty, territorial, 362n52
sovereign wealth fund, 183–84
soybeans, 117, 171
space-based capabilities, 295–96
space security, 279
Spain, 11, 140
Special Economic Zones
(SEZs), 157
special operations forces
(SOFs), 276
Spence, Jonathan, 380n4
sports, 261–62
Sprint Nextel, 183, 195
spying. *See* espionage

SRBMs. *See* short range
ballistic missiles
Sri Lanka, 303–4
Stalin, Joseph, 79
Standing Committee, CCP,
63, 208
Starwood, 256
State Administration for
Science, Technology
and Industry for
National Defense, 302–3
State Administration of
Cultural Heritage, 251
State Administration of Film,
Radio and Television
(SAFRT), 364n89
State Council Information
Office (SCIO), 63–64,
238, 264–65, 267,
330n33, 363n62, 363n64,
363n66
agenda, 11
with arms transfers, 302
CCP's Propaganda
Department and, 2, 21,
208, 217, 220–21, 228
China National
Publications Import and
Export Corporation, 235
Cultural Industries
Revitalization Plan of
2009, 208
EPLSG, 63, 221, 330n33,
363n63
exhibitions staged by, 240
inner workings and
departments, 221–23
leading group, 330n30
military and, 275
on peace, 220
peacekeeping missions,
378n65
State Press and Publishing
Administration and, 222
State Forestry Administration,
151
State Grid, 185
state-owned enterprises
(SOEs), 69, 160, 165–66,
171, 175, 177–78, 184
State Press and Publishing
Administration, 222
State Reserve Bureau, 171

state security. *See* Ministry of
State Security
state sovereignty, 32
status quo power, 72, 121, 134
Stockholm China Forum,
333n78
Stockholm International
Peace Research
Institute (SIPRI), 301,
305, 379n86, 380n90,
380n92, 380n94, 380n98
stocks, 156, 177–80, 190, 236,
351n85
The Story of Qiu Ju (film), 253
strategic
with China and Russia
relations, 332n75
diplomatic maneuvering
and, 47–53
EU partnership, 87–89,
90, 94
Latin America without
strategy for China,
111–13
lying low, 75, 322n17
military dialogues, 300
trust, 331n58
Strategic and Economic
Dialogue (SAED), 74
Streltsov, Dmitri, 85
students protests, 3, 18, 49–50,
79, 88, 95–96
submarine-launched ballistic
missiles (SLBMs),
294–95
submarines, 292–93
Sudan, 76, 378n67
crisis, 46, 83, 137, 140
oil, 163, 164*f*
relationships with, 111
Suntech Power, 152
Sunways, 182
supercomputers, 161
superpower, global, 10, 22
surplus, 346n4
surveys, global, 12
Su Shulin, 167
Su Yu, 278
Suzhou University, 253
Sweden, 181*t*, 196
Switzerland, 159
Syria, 8, 40, 46, 76, 83, 108,
138, 140, 343n48

system phases
  challenger, 133
  studying, 134
  exploitation, 134–35
  altering, 136

Tai Siju, 145
Taiwan, 38, 46, 51, 58, 262,
    343n48, 377n61
  China's stance on, 9, 95,
    109, 137
  EU on issue of, 89, 91
  missile crisis, 276, 279–80
  secessionist forces in, 90
  trade with, 158t, 159f
  U.S. arms sales to, 77
Taiwan Affairs Leading Small
    Group, 63
Taiwan Affairs Office of the
    State Council, 21
Tam, Vivienne, 252
Tangled Titans: The United
    States and China
    (Shambaugh), 331n56
Tang Yongming, 145
Tanzania, 303
taoguang yanghui (lying low)
    strategies, 75, 322n17
Tao Jian, 201–2
Taonghua Iron and Steel, 172
taxes
  corporate, 155
  foreign, 189
  havens, 180
  rebates, 255
TCL Group, 191–93, 354n142
tea chat, 225
teamwork, 189
technical cooperation, 203
technology, 302–3
  computers, 161, 198–99
  embargo on defense, 283
  EU as largest source of,
    86–87
  ministry of industry and
    information, 221–22
  ministry of science and, 66,
    151, 243
  piracy of Russian defense,
    82
telecoms, 191, 193–95
Telefónica, 195
television stations, 222, 228

temples, 239
tendencies of analysis, 26,
    324n49
Tengzhong Heavy, 195
territorial integrity, 362n52
territorial sovereignty, 362n52
terrorism, 104, 145–46
  counter-, 41, 76
Thailand, 49, 96, 167, 242, 303
theft, of intellectual property
    rights, 244
theories
  China Collapse, 219
  China Threat, 21, 219
  Constructivists, 131, 313
  harmonious world, 25,
    219–20, 324n47
  Liberals, 39, 125, 313
  power transition, 312
  Realists, 16, 31–34, 40,
    42–43, 312
  responsible-power, 23–25,
    40
  of three worlds, 133
thinking, eclecticism in, 27
think tanks, 69, 87, 200, 238,
    247, 331n45, 335n115,
    366n134
Thomson-CSF, 191, 193
3Com, 183, 195
3Leaf, 183, 195
Three Kingdoms era, 31
three worlds theory, 133
Tiananmen Square, 1, 57, 251
  Confucius statue in, 239
  June 4, massacre in, 3, 18,
    50, 79, 88, 95–96
  student protests in, 3, 18,
    49–50, 79, 88
Tianhe-1A computer, 161
Tian Wei, 231
Tibet, 39, 46
  China's stance on, 9, 58,
    92–93, 103, 137
  Dalai Lama and, 58, 92–93,
    103, 263
  India as supporter of, 103
  international support for,
    92–93, 103, 227
  restricted travel to, 224
  secessionist forces in, 90
Tiffany's, 256
timber, 110, 171

Times Square, New York
    City, 229
Time Warner, 227, 230, 231
Timor Leste, 303
tin, 171
Titarenko, Mikhail, 84
to declare where one stands
    (biaotai), 217–18
To Live (film), 253
tourism industry
  ADS with, 255
  art and, 259
  brand recognition and, 258
  with Chinese emigration,
    261
  with EU, 87
  fifteen guidelines for good
    manners, 260
  gambling and, 259
  global cultural footprint of,
    255–61
  with Hong Kong, 255–60
  influence in global, 8
  in Latin America, 115
  luxury sales and, 256–59
  with real estate buying
    binge, 259–60
  shopping habits of Chinese
    tourists, 258
  spending power of Chinese
    tourists, 255–57
  with U.S., 73
Tow, Theow, 249
trade
  Africa, 110
  ASEAN with, 336n133
  CAFTA, 102
  EU, 86–87, 92, 159, 346n4
  FTAs, 159
  GATT, 134
  global influence in, 8, 11
  Indonesia, 118
  Iran, 106–7
  Japan, 102, 158t, 159f
  Latin America, 112, 116–18
  maritime, 289
  regional partners in, 159f
  Russia, 81–82
  sex, 144
  slave, 108
  South Korea, 100, 158t, 159f
  as superstate for, 157–61
  top partners in, 158t

U.S., 73, 77, 117, 158t, 159f, 346n4
U.S. and Latin America, 117
WTO, 91, 124, 136, 157, 160, 174–75, 342n45, 346n3
trademarks, 161, 196, 199
training, midcareer, 189
tranquility, complete (anquan), 59
Transformers 3 (film), 254
transparency
military, 76
with overseas aid, 358n192
Transparency International, 10
traps, global governance as Western, 40, 131–32, 155
Treasuries, U.S., 183
treaties, 332n70
Agreement on Mutual Non-Aggression, 80
extradition, 146–47
investment, 159
NATO, 98, 137–38, 200, 273, 276, 286
nonproliferation and arms control, 142–44, 303
Treaty of Neighborliness and Friendly Cooperation, 80–81
triads, 145–46
tribute system, 95
Trina Solar, 152
Troitskiy, Mikhail, 85
trust, 154–55, 331n58
Tsinghua University, 13, 19, 33, 40, 67, 69, 88, 131, 210
Department of International Relations, 342n42
ranking for, 243
on soft power, 214–15
Tsingtao, 187
tsunami, 299
tuberculosis (XDR-TB), 147
Tufts University, 67
Tunisia, 170, 198
Turkey, 11, 38, 108, 303
Turkmenistan, 167

UAE. See United Arab Emirates
Uganda, 163, 303

Uighurs, 108, 146. See also Xinjiang Autonomous Region
UK. See United Kingdom
Ukraine, 80, 197, 292
UN. See United Nations
UNCLOS. See UN Law of the Sea Convention
unemployment, 201
UNESCO World Heritage Sites, 133, 239
Union of Concerned Scientists, 377n54
unipolarity, 22, 31. See also polarities
United Arab Emirates (UAE), 106–7
United Front Work Department, CCP, 222
United Kingdom (UK), 90
with UN operating budget contributions, 140
with UN voting history, 141, 343n59
United Nations (UN)
China in, 24–25, 133, 137–42
Conference on Disarmament, 97, 335n123
global governance and, 123–24, 137–42
Law of the Sea Convention, 102
Millennium Development Goals, 38
with operating budget contributions by country, 140
peacekeeping operations, 40, 46, 139, 271, 298–99
sanctions against Iran, 107
Security Council, 9, 41, 45, 83, 133, 137
Selective Multilateralists with, 40
specialized agencies, 133
UNCLOS, 102
voting history by country, 141, 343n59
United States (U.S.), 4, 47, 377n61
anti-Western sentiment against, 28–29, 31, 33–34,
40, 85, 131–32, 141, 155, 232
arms sales to Taiwan, 77
CFIUS, 200
China as viewed by, 12
China's diplomacy with, 51–52, 73–78
China's opinion of, 26, 129–30
Chinese investments in, 182–83
Chinese tourists in, 255, 258
Chinese tourists purchasing real estate in, 259–60
competitive coexistence with, 74
"containment" policies, 77, 97, 129, 315–16
CRI broadcasting in, 233
DEA, 146
debt to China, 73, 157
in decline as myth, 22–23, 99
dollar hegemony and, 126
education exchange with, 73, 241–42
energy consumption, 73
films and domestic box office in, 253
Foreign Service, 330n38
as global superpower, 10, 22
Gulf War and, 276
hegemony, 23, 26
laboratories, 377n61
Major Powers School and, 34–36
military spending, 274f
ODI of, 10
Office of the National Counterintelligence Executive, 297
oil consumption, 162
overseas aid of, 10, 204
pivot to Asia, 77, 100
Times Square, 229
tourism, 73
trade with, 73, 77, 158t, 159f, 346n4
trade with Latin America, 117
with UN operating budget contributions, 140
with UN voting history, 141, 343n59
Universidad de Bogotá, 113

Universidad del Desarrollo, 113
universities. *See specific universities*
University of Foreign Languages, PLA, 301
University of Hong Kong, 243
University of International Relations, 67, 69, 201
University of Otago, 326n86
UN Law of the Sea Convention (UNCLOS), 102
Unocal, 168, 182
U.S. *See* United States
Uzbekistan, 140

values
    Chinese style universal, 216
    Confucian and Mencian, 43
    Cultural Revolution and destruction of, 212
    four core cultural, 212
    lack of, 213
Venezuela, 114, 117, 119, 163, 167, 303
Venus, 296
vetoes, in UN Security Council, 9, 137
Viacom, 227, 230
Vietnam, 37, 47, 48, 49, 51, 54, 77
    China's attack on, 275–76, 279
    education exchanges with, 242
    war in, 95
Vnoukov, Konstantin, 84, 85
Vodafone, 195
Vogel, Ezra, 327n4
Vogue, 236, 252
Volkswagen, 182
volunteer programs, overseas, 203
Volvo, 182, 195, 196–97
Voskresensky, Alexey, 85

Wallace, Mike, 231
Wal-Mart, 165
Wang, Ed, 261–62
Wang, Sue, 252
Wang Chen, 208, 220–23, 264–65, 267, 363n62

Wang Guangya, 67, 141, 344n60
Wang Guoqing, 11
Wang Huning, 210, 360n18
Wang Jinsong, 325n61
Wang Jisi, 13, 16, 74, 128, 322n13
Wang Shu, 253
Wang Xiaodong, 28–29
Wang Xiaoshuai, 253
water contamination, 149–50
wealth
    billionaires, 157
    disposable income and rising, 255
    millionaires, 157, 249
    nouveau riche and, 256–58
    private, 249
    sovereign wealth fund, 183–84
weapons. *See also* arms; military; People's Armed Police; People's Liberation Army
    artillery, 286–88, 291
    BWC and CWC, 142, 144
    exports of military, 303–4
    systems, 277–78
Wei Xin, 226–27
Wen Jiabao, 87, 92, 93, 94, 104, 334n97
    on education, 243
    on global cultural presence, 208
    on global economic presence, 156
Whirlpool, 198
White Papers
    development and peace, 130, 218
    on military defense, 281–82
    overseas aid, 203–4
    SCIO and publication of, 222
    on space program, 296
WHO. *See* World Health Organization
Who in China Is Unhappy?, 27
Why Is China Unhappy?, 27
Willard, Robert, 290
Wills, John E., Jr., 328n12
wind power, 152
wine

China as world's largest producer by volume, 158
    as import, 117, 257
Wolf Totem (Jiang Rong), 247
world, harmonious, 25, 219–20, 324n47
World Bank, 124, 126–27, 150, 204
    loans to China, 134
    overseas aid of, 10
World Cup, 187
World Economic Forum, 10–11, 219
World Expo of 2010, 239, 240
World Health Organization (WHO), 148, 345n78
World Luxury Association, 258
World Media Summit, 228
World Trade Organization (WTO), 91, 124, 136, 157, 160, 174–75, 342n45, 346n3
Wu Baiyi, 111, 339n154
Wuhan Iron and Steel, 172
Wu Jianmin, 213

XDR-TB. *See* tuberculosis
xenophobia, 54
    in Cultural Revolution, 47–48
    Nativists with anti-Western sentiments and, 27–31
    Realists with, 31
Xia Jixuan, 233, 265, 365n116
Xi Jinping, 45, 74, 248, 254, 279, 331n59
Xinhua News Agency, 23–24, 66, 146, 227, 228–30. *See also* Chinese Communist Party
Xinjiang Autonomous Region
    China's stance on, 9, 108
    ethnic riots in, 224
    secessionist forces in, 90, 108, 145, 146
Xu Bing, 250
Xue Fukang, 322n12
Xu Lin, 245–46
Xuzhou Construction Machinery, 182

yakuza, in Japan, 144
yang, yin and, 58–59

Yang Jiechi, 42, 67, 207, 226, 263
Yang Jiemian, 22, 70–71
Yang Liwei, 295
Yang Rui, 231–32, 365n111
Yang Wanming, 339n158, 340n167
Yan Xuetong, 13, 19–20, 214, , 342n37,
    on global governance as trap, 40, 131–32
    as Realist, 33–34
Yao Ming, 261
Year of China festivals, 240
Yee, Herbert, 320n10
Ye Jiang, 278
Ye Juan, 368n168
Yellow Earth (film), 253
yellow peril, 85
Yeltsin, Boris, 80
Ye Lucheng, 69, 70, 330n30
Yemen, 105, 107, 201
Ye Zicheng, 20
yin and yang, of diplomacy, 58–59
Yingli Green Energy, 152
Yingli Solar, 187
Yuanhua, 146

Yuanmingyuan (Old Summer Palace), 250, 251
Yugoslavia, 98
Yun Sun, 71, 330n28
Yu Xintian, 38, 213, 361n33, 364n87
Yu Zhengliang, 323n30

Zakaria, Fareed, 317
Zambia, 201–2, 303, 304
Zangger Committee, 142, 144
Zao Wouki, 250
ZBB. *See* zero-based budgeting system
Zeng Fanzhi, 250
zero-based budgeting (ZBB) system, 275, 374n9
Zhang Dejiang, 330n30
Zhang Huan, 250
Zhang Ruimin, 197
Zhang Ruizhuang, 22, 33–34
Zhang Xiaogang, 250
Zhang Yesui, 67
Zhang Yimou, 253–54
Zhang Yunling, 37
Zhang Zhijun, 67, 94, 227
Zhao Hongbo, 261
Zhao Qizheng, 264

Zhao Zhiyun, 243–44
Zhao Ziyang, 157
Zhejian Longmen Lotus Auto, 355n154
Zheng Bijian, 21, 218–19
Zheng He, 105, 108
Zheng Jie, 262
Zhong Hua, 168
Zhongnanhai leadership compound, 57, 94
Zhongshan University, 323n28, 325n70, 340n2
Zhou Enlai, 97
Zhou Mingwei, 211–12, 236–37
Zhou Qisheng, 230
Zhou Wenzhong, 67
Zhou Xiaochuan, 126
Zhu Feng, 36–37, 307, 317
Zhu Min, 128
Zhu Muzhi, 245
Zhu Rongji, 109, 166, 175, 275
Zhu Yinghuang, 263
Zimbabwe, 137, 140, 303, 304, 343n48
zinc, 171
Zoellick, Robert, 23, 121, 130–31, 316